In Search of Respect
Second Edition

Philippe Bourgois's ethnographic study of social marginalization in inner-city America won critical acclaim when it was first published in 1995. For the first time, an anthropologist had managed to gain the trust and long-term friendship of street-level drug dealers in one of the nation's roughest ghetto neighborhoods – East Harlem. This new edition adds a prologue describing the major dynamics that have altered life on the streets of East Harlem in the years since the first edition. In a new epilogue, Bourgois brings up to date the stories of the people – Primo, Caesar, Luis, Tony, Candy – whom readers come to know in this remarkable window onto the world of the inner-city drug trade.

Philippe Bourgois is Professor and Chair of the Department of Anthropology, History and Social Medicine at the University of California, San Francisco. He has conducted fieldwork in Central America on ethnicity and social unrest and is the author of *Ethnicity at Work: Divided Labor on a Central American Banana Plantation* (Johns Hopkins University Press, 1989). With photographer Jeff Schonberg he is writing a book on homeless heroin addicts in San Francisco.
http://www.ucsf.edu/dahsm/pages/faculty/bourgois.html

of gang rape as an accepted rite of adolescent passage, seeing mothers casually pushing strollers into crack houses, and witnessing the calculated use of violence as an accepted business practice – does not hesitate to express his disgust. At the same time, Bourgois seeks to understand the sources of such behavior. . . . A fascinating account." — Michael Massing, *The New York Review of Books*

"*In Search of Respect* . . . brings the lives of these crack sellers into brilliant focus. Bourgois's raw and poignant book delivers a message about the economics of exclusion that should shake public perceptions of the inner-city drug trade. For anyone interested in the brutal truth about drug dealing in our inner cities, *In Search of Respect* is the place to look." — Greg Donaldson, *The Washington Post*

"Vigorous and often harrowing, this book is an eye-opener." — *Kirkus Review*

"The beauty of the book is in the author's sharing of his academic mind with the organic intellect of the people who are forced to live in ghettos for economic reasons. Philippe has put together between two covers the harsh reality of the streets. . . . *In Search of Respect: Selling Crack in El Barrio* is must reading for those who care to learn." — Piri Thomas, poet and author of *Down These Mean Streets*

"Bourgois spent hundreds of nights with a handful of small-time, mainly Nuyorican dealers and, as they got high and recovered from the daily grind, recorded their comments about work, politics, sexuality, substance abuse, and style. . . . The crack dealers' talk – ribald, morbid, and improvisatory – crackles with a brio that would be the envy of Quentin Tarantino." — Adam Shatz, *The Nation*

"Once in awhile, a new book will offer up a rich, deep, interesting, even exciting look at the entrenched, complex social problems that plague the country's most troubled urban neighborhoods. Philippe Bourgois's book does just that." — Marjorie Valbrun, *The Philadelphia Inquirer*

"An intimate, disturbing portrait of an alternate world in which the crack-dealing and -using minority dominates public space. . . . The author does not absolve his subjects of individual responsibility, but he compellingly concludes that drugs are more a symptom than the root of the problem: class and ethnic 'apartheid.'" — *Publishers Weekly*

"[The book] intercuts five years' worth of interviews with Puerto Rican crack dealers in New York's El Barrio district with popular press and scholarly research on informal economies and immigrant communities, as well as numerous informative yet unobtrusive statistics. . . . For Bourgois, the dealers' main problem is not lack of skills – they manage a complex system involving marketing, distribution of resources, and human relations – but rather their lack of 'cultural capital' – literacy, savvy in handling city agencies, or the ability to switch between the street and white-collar worlds." — Carolina Gonzalez, *The San Francisco Bay Guardian*

Structural Analysis in the Social Sciences

Mark Granovetter, editor

The series *Structural Analysis in the Social Sciences* presents approaches that explain social behavior and institutions by reference to *relations* among such concrete entities as persons and organizations. This contrasts with at least four other popular strategies: (a) reductionist attempts to explain by a focus on individuals alone; (b) explanations stressing the causal primacy of such abstract concepts as ideas, values, mental harmonies, and cognitive maps (thus, "structuralism" on the Continent should be distinguished from structural analysis in the present sense); (c) technological and material determinism; (d) explanations using "variables" as the main analytic concepts (as in the "structural equation" models that dominated much of the sociology of the 1970s), where structure is that connecting variables rather than actual social entities.

The social network approach is an important example of the strategy of structural analysis; the series also draws on social science theory and research that is not framed explicitly in network terms, but stresses the importance of relations rather than the atomization of reductionism or the determinism of ideas, technology, or material conditions. Though the structural perspective has become extremely popular and influential in all the social sciences, it does not have a coherent identity, and no series yet pulls together such work under a single rubric. By bringing the achievements of structurally oriented scholars to a wider public, the *Structural Analysis* series hopes to encourage the use of this very fruitful approach.

Mark Granovetter

Other books in the series:

Continued on page following the index

IN SEARCH OF RESPECT

Selling Crack in El Barrio

Second Edition

PHILIPPE BOURGOIS

University of California, San Francisco

CAMBRIDGE
UNIVERSITY PRESS

CAMBRIDGE UNIVERSITY PRESS
Cambridge, New York, Melbourne, Madrid, Cape Town, Singapore,
São Paulo, Delhi, Dubai, Tokyo

Cambridge University Press
32 Avenue of the Americas, New York, NY 10013-2473, USA

www.cambridge.org
Information on this title: www.cambridge.org/9780521017114

First published 2003
13th printing 2010

Printed in the United States of America

A catalog record for this publication is available from the British Library.

IISBN 978-0-521-81562-8 Hardback
ISBN 978-0-521-01711-4 Paperback

For Emiliano

Born Anew at Each A.M.

The street's got its kicks, man,
like a bargain shelf.
In fact, cool-breeze, it's got
love like anywhere else.

Vaya!

It's got lights that shine up the dark
like new.
It sells what you don't need
and never lets you forget
what you blew.

It's got high-powered
salesmen who push *mucho* junk,
and hustlers who can swallow you
up in a chunk.
Aha, check it out.

It's got out beautiful children
living in all kinds of hell,
hoping to survive and making it well,
swinging together in misty darkness
with all their love to share
smiling their Christ-like forgiveness
that only a ghetto cross can bear.
Oh, yeah, *vaya*, check it out!

Hey, the street's got life, man,
like a young tender sun,
and gentleness
like a long awaited dream to come.
Oye, vaya, check it out.

The children are roses,
with nary a thorn.
Forced to feel racist scorn.

Ha, ha, *vaya,* check it out!

Our children are beauty
with the right to be born.
Born anew at each A.M.
like a child out of twilight
flying towards sunlight
born anew at each A.M.

Punto!

Piri Thomas

CONTENTS

ACKNOWLEDGMENTS

This book could not have been written without my friends and neighbors in El Barrio who welcomed me so openly and generously. I changed everyone's name and camouflaged the street addresses to protect individual privacy. Above all, I thank my close friend whom I have called Primo in these pages. He followed my work since the beginning, and he guided much of it. His comments, corrections, and discussions on the half-dozen versions of the manuscript that he read and/or listened to were most helpful. The other major character, whom I have called Caesar, also provided me with analytical insights and critiques on various early drafts of this book. Similarly, Candy was extraordinarily helpful and supportive throughout the fieldwork process and in the early stages of writing. María provided me with comments and moral support right through the final phases of writing the book. More recently, Esperanza and Jasmine, who appear only in the epilogue to this second edition, greatly facilitated my follow-up visits to El Barrio by making me feel warmly welcome in their homes and among their extended families following the publication of the first edition.

I also want to thank the following institutions for their generous financial support: the Harry Frank Guggenheim Foundation, the Russell Sage Foundation, the Social Science Research Council, the Ford Foundation, the National Institute on Drug Abuse (grants RO1 DA10164 and RO3 DA06413), the Wenner-Gren Foundation for Anthropological Research, the United States Bureau of the Census, and at San Francisco State University Marilyn Boxer, Brian Murphy, and Joe Julian. I appreciated having institutional research affiliations with The Research Institute for the Study of Man, the Centro de Estudios Puertorriqueños of Hunter College, Columbia University's School of Architecture and Urban Planning, and San Francisco State University's Urban Institute and Anthropology

Department. Of course, I am most grateful for the faculty position I hold in the Department of Anthropology, History, and Social Medicine at the University of California, San Francisco, which provides me with the long-term financial and logistical security that permits me to write books on social suffering and injustice in the United States.

I am grateful to Marc Edelman, Robert Merton, and the late Eric Wolf, who gave generously of their time to provide me with detailed critiques of substantial portions of the manuscript. No one comes close, however, to the brilliance, precision, and inspired obsession of Loïc Wacquant when it comes to editing text and critiquing intellectual argument. The first half of this book was practically rewritten by him in a forty-eight-hour nonstop binge of editing that only he would have the energy, clarity of mind, and delicacy of plume to deliver just in time. Dozens of other friends, students, colleagues, and mentors also read drafts of this book – or at least heard portions of its central arguments. Many useful insights or points of information were conveyed to me in informal conversations after seminars, classes, and conferences, or even at parties. Some of the feedback was critical, and I did not always incorporate it in the text, but I am thankful for its constructive engagement. In this vein, I thank the late Pierre Bourdieu, who made possible the French translation of this book in his series, and who, more importantly, provided so much clarity and inspiration with his critique of the practice of symbolic power in reproducing hierarchy; Karen Colvard, John Devine, Amy Donovan, Eloise Dunlap, Angelo Falcon, Jerry Floersch, Charles Hale, Arthur Kleinman, Antonio Lauria-Petrocelli, Gloria Levitas, Roberto Lewis-Fernandez, Jeff Longhofer, Peter Lucas, Susan Meiselas, Jim Quesada, Clara Rodriguez, the late Ulysses Santamaria, Saskia Sassen, Nancy Scheper-Hughes, Carol Smith, Carl Taylor, Frank Vardi, Joel Wallman, Eric Wanner, Terry Williams, William Julius Wilson, and my grandmother, the late Peggy Regler.

I owe a great deal to Mark Granovetter, the series editor at Cambridge, who intervened on my behalf with comments and support at a crucial phase in the writing when I was despairing of ever finishing. My in-house editors at Cambridge – Emily Loose, Russell Hahn, and especially Elizabeth Neal, followed by Mary Child and Alia Winters – were also extremely helpful. The copy editors, Nancy Landau and Phyllis L. Berk, greatly improved the final quality of the text, catching several dozen embarrassing errors and cleaning up an untold number of awkward sentence constructions.

Acknowledgments

The original manuscript could not have been produced without the typing, emotional support, and ethical backbone of Harold Otto and Ann Magruder, who both became respected friends despite working side by side with me for so many anxiety-filled months. Others who provided crucial research and logistical support at the Russell Sage Foundation include Eileen Ferrer, James Gray, Clay Gustave, Pauline Rothstein, Madge Spitaleri, Camille Yezzi, and Adrienne Zicklin. At San Francisco State University, Thoreau Lovell kindly provided me with after-hours computer access and frequent technical advice. At the Research Institute for the Study of Man, Florence Rivera Tai was of great help and friendship.

Reading Piri Thomas's *Down These Mean Streets* when I was in high school planted the seed for this book. I owe him a great debt for making me confront poverty, racism, and drugs in the city where I grew up. It is a special honor and pleasure for me, consequently, to have his permission to publish in the front the fax he sent me after reading a manuscript version of this book.

Finally, I want to thank my family. I will always be grateful to Charo Chacón-Méndez for immigrating from Costa Rica directly to El Barrio, where we married at the very beginning of this research project. Her help was invaluable during our residence in the neighborhood. I apologize for imposing so much anxiety on her when I regularly stayed out all night on the street, and in crackhouses, for so many years. I hope that is not one of the reasons we are no longer together. If it is, I regret it profoundly. Our son, Emiliano (Nano), loved El Barrio. He was never intimidated by the street. His cerebral palsy was first diagnosed when we had no health insurance by a brusque, harried intern in a free clinic a few blocks from our tenement. I suspect that Nano's tremendous self-confidence, and his wonderful social skills, were partially forged by the success with which he carved respect for himself from even the toughest street hustlers on our block. He melted everyone's heart while proudly learning to use his walker over broken sidewalks littered with crack vials. Better yet, all through the often frustrating process, full of scrapes and tumbles, Nano exuded that magical joy-of-living that only two-and-something-year-olds know the secret to. He helped me appreciate some of the joys of life on the street. The bright flash in his eyes continues to guide me a dozen years later as he enters adolescence full of energy, appreciation, and empathy for most everyone around him.

My mother and father were also supportive throughout the research and writing of this book. I am sure I was deeply shaped by the fact that my mother violated apartheid almost every weekday during the 1980s through the 1990s while working with literacy programs in the South Bronx. In the same vein, my father provided me with the wonderful experience of growing up as a New Yorker in a bicultural household. His "typically French" trenchant criticisms of U.S. culture, and especially his abhorrence of the excesses of racism and class inequality in New York City, were a wonderful antidote to the stultifying ideological perspectives that bombarded those of us who grew up at the height of the Cold War in the United States. Perhaps the fact that he escaped on June 7, 1944, from I. G. Farben Community Camp Dwory at Auschwitz instilled in me a commitment to document institutionalized racism in my own lifetime, especially in my own hometown. He may also have first sensitized me to addication when I was a teenager by telling me, as we were sharing a cigarette, "I was one of the stupid ones in the camps who used to trade his bread for tobacco." More importantly, my father's ongoing humble outrage over the fact that so many of those living directly downwind from the Auschwitz gas chambers – himself included – managed to either ignore or joke about the smell of burning human flesh at the height of the Holocaust motivated me, I think, to write this book on the everyday violence of U.S. apartheid at the turn of the twenty-first century.

– *University of California, San Francisco*
August 2002

PREFACE TO THE 2003
SECOND EDITION

In the seven years since the first edition of this book went to press in the fall of 1995, four major dynamics altered the tenor of daily life on the streets of East Harlem and deeply affected the lives of the crack dealers and their families depicted in these pages: 1) The U.S. economy entered the most prolonged period of sustained growth in its recorded history; 2) the size of the Mexican immigrant population in New York City and especially in East Harlem increased dramatically; 3) the war on drugs escalated into a quasi-official public policy of criminalizing and incarcerating the poor and the socially marginal; and 4) drug fashion trends among inner-city youth rendered marijuana even more popular and crack and heroin even less popular among Latinos and African Americans.

In 2002, crack, cocaine, and heroin were still sold on the block where I lived, but they were sold less visibly by a smaller number of people. It was still easy to purchase narcotics throughout East Harlem, but much of the drug dealing had moved indoors, out of sight of the police. There were fewer small-time hawkers competing openly on street corners, shouting out the brand names of their drugs. Most importantly, heroin and crack continued to be spurned by Latino and African American youth who had witnessed as children the ravages that those drugs committed on the older generations in their community. Recovered crack addicts in New York City even developed a new genre of autobiographical literature (Stringer, 1998; S. and Bolnick, 2000). Nevertheless, in the U.S. inner city there remained an aging hard-core cohort of addicts. It is difficult to trust the accuracy of surveys on drugs that are conducted over the telephone by government-sponsored interviewers, but the National Household Survey on Drug Abuse, which has been conducted every year in the United States since 1994, did not report a decrease in "frequent crack use" during the 1990s (Substance

Abuse and Mental Health Services Administration, 2000). Hospital emergency room and arrest statistics, however, reported dramatically decreasing cocaine-positive blood tests among males during the late 1990s through the year 2000 (CESAR FAX, 2001).

In most large cities, crack was most visibly ensconced in predominantly African American neighborhoods on the poorest blocks. Crack sales spots often continued to be located in or near large public housing projects, vacant lots, and abandoned buildings. In New York City, Puerto Rican households also continued to be at the epicenter of the ongoing cyclone of crack consumption – even if it was more self-contained than it used to be.

In contrast to crack, heroin consumption increased in many cities during the latter half of the 1990s and early 2000s. Throughout most of the United States, heroin became cheaper and purer, belying any claims that the U.S. war on drugs was winnable. Heroin's new appeal, however, was primarily among younger whites outside the ghetto for whom crack was not a drug of choice. Heroin, especially in intravenous form, remained unpopular among Latino and African American youth in the inner city. In East Harlem, crack- and heroin-copping corners in the year 2001 appeared to be almost geriatric scenes, with the average age of addicted clients hovering in their late thirties through late forties and early fifties.

To summarize, in 2002 both heroin and crack continued to be multibillion-dollar businesses that ravaged inner-city families with special virulence. The younger generations of East Harlem residents, however, were more involved as sellers than as consumers. Those Latino and African American youth who did use crack or heroin generally tried to hide the fact from their friends. We understand poorly why drug fashions change so markedly, but at the opening of the twenty-first century, we were lucky in the United States that for more than a dozen years, marijuana and malt liquor beer had been the substances of choice for use and abuse by African American and Latino youth who participate in street culture (Golub and Johnson, 1999).

More important than changing drug-consumption fashions or the posturing of politicians over drug war campaigns was the effect of the dramatic long-term improvement in the U.S. economy, which resulted in record low rates of unemployment in the late 1990s. Somewhat to my surprise, some of the crack dealers and their families featured in this book benefited from this sustained economic growth spurt, at least up to its nosedive in 2001–02. Slightly less than half of the characters in this book managed to enter the lower echelons of the legal labor market prior to the 2001–02 economic downturn. I outline this with greater personal details in the new epilogue to this second edition, but to provide a brief overview during the 2001–02 recession: One dealer was a unionized doorman, another a home health-care attendant, another a plumber's assistant. Three others were construction workers for small-time unlicensed contractors. One was a cashier in a discount tourist souvenir store. Two of the sisters of the crack dealers depicted in this book were nurses aides and another was a secretary. One of the women companions of one of the crack dealers was a bank teller, another was a security guard, and a third sold Avon products. One of the sons of the dealers was a cashier in a fast food restaurant, while another sold drugs and yet another two were incarcerated for the sale of drugs and petty burglary, respectively. Three or four of the dealers were still selling drugs, but most of them were selling marijuana instead of crack or heroin. Another three of the dealers were in prison with long-term sentences and, ironically, were probably employed at well below minimum wage in the burgeoning prison-based manufacturing sector.

In short, the dramatic improvement in the U.S. economy in the late 1990s forced employers and unions to integrate increasing numbers of marginalized Puerto Ricans and African Americans into the labor market. This represented a structural contrast to the late 1980s and early 1990s when the research for this book was conducted and the economy was weaker. Nevertheless, even at the height of the surge in the U.S. economy in the summer of 2000, a large sector of street youth found themselves excluded. These marginals had become almost completely superfluous to the legal economy; they remained enmeshed in a still lucrative drug economy, a burgeoning prison system, and a quagmire of chronic substance abuse and everyday interpersonal violence. From a long-term political and economic perspective, the future did not bode well for the inner-city poor of New York, irrespective of the shorter-term fluctuations in the national and regional economy, as was evidenced by the economic downturn following the September 11, 2001, World Trade Center disaster. In the year 2000, the United States had the largest disparity between rich and poor of any industrialized nation in the world – and this gap was increasing rather than decreasing (*New York Times,* September 26, 2001:A12; see also U.S. Census Bureau, 2001). At a more local level, over the last three decades of the twentieth century, the state of New York suffered the largest growth in income inequality of all fifty states in the nation (*New York Times,* January 19, 2000:B5).

A side effect of New York's strong but poorly paid entry-level employment market was the accelerated immigration of undocumented Mexicans fleeing rural poverty, who were prepared to work hard for poverty wages. When I left the neighborhood in 1991, Mexican immigration was, of course, already extremely visible, and I discussed the rising violent tensions between young Puerto Ricans and new Mexican immigrants. In the original epilogue to the English edition written in late 1994 and included in this edition, I provide statistics on the rapid rise in the local Mexican population. This increase proceeded at an even faster pace during the second half of the 1990s and was palpably visible on the street where I lived. In 1991 on the blocks immediately surrounding me, there were at least three buildings entirely occupied by Mexican new immigrants (not to mention two by rural Senegalese new immigrants). On one of my recent return visits to prepare the preface for this second edition, I found that an entire block (next to the one where I lived) had "become Mexican." Throughout the rest of East Harlem, dozens of Mexican restaurants and specialty grocery stores were visible. In contrast, when I resided there, I knew of only one Mexican restaurant and it did not sport a sign, presumably because it was not licensed to sell food. In short, yet another new wave of ethnic succession was remaking East Harlem at the dawn of the twenty-first century on the fringes of the U.S. economy, but striving for the American Dream.

Throughout East Harlem, new small businesses in the year 2002 were visible on formerly boarded-up, abandoned blocks. On the block where I lived, for example, the revitalization that I described as incipient in 1994 had accelerated significantly. The garbage-strewn lot, which had stood vacant for well over a dozen years on one side of the apartment where I lived, was occupied by a row of newly constructed four-story tenements. The large, abandoned building on the other side of my tenement, which had been burned down ten years before I moved onto the block, was a renovated halfway house for mothers recovering from substance abuse. There were five new legal businesses on the block: two hairdressers, a video rental store, a Chinese takeout restaurant, and a pizzeria.

Only one of the two original grocery stores on the block still sold drugs and its sales were limited to marijuana. Heroin could still be obtained on the corner, purer than ever, but no longer from three competing brand-name companies. At night, the working class majority of the population still ceded much of their control of public space to drug dealers and addicts, just as they had in the late 1980s and early 1990s when I lived there.

Overall, however, the significantly strengthened economy, buttressed by the coincidences of evolving drug fashions and the logic of large-scale, low-wage labor migration streams, had reinvigorated working class culture on the street, decreasing the destructive magnetism of drugs, crime, and violence for those pursuing upward mobility.

In contrast to the invigorating effects on the neighborhood of private sector growth and of undocumented working class migration, the U.S. public sector continued its policy of malign neglect toward the inner city, especially toward Latino and African American neighborhoods. During the 1990s, the formerly underfunded and rachitic U.S. social welfare safety net was refurbished into an expensive, rigorous, criminal dragnet. The already enormous U.S. penal system grew vertiginously to become a bona fide criminal industrial complex larger in the year 2000 in relative per capita terms than that of any other nation in the world except Russia and Rwanda. The U.S. incarceration rate doubled during the 1990s; it was six to twelve times higher than that of any of the nations in the European Union (Wacquant, 1999:72). The sheer mass of people locked up assumed an aura of apartheid when one examines the racial disparities involved (Wacquant, 2000). According to objective statistical probability, one in three African American males could expect to be incarcerated in their lifetime, compared to one in twenty-five white males and one in six Latinos. The ethnic disparities in incarceration rates were driven in the 1990s and 2000s by the "War on Drugs." African Americans were twenty times more likely to be incarcerated on drug offenses than were whites. In New York State, where 89 percent of the prisoners are African American or Latino, this carceral segregation is even more dramatic (Macallair and Taqi-Eddin, 1999).

The mayor of New York City from 1993 to 2001, Rudolph Giuliani, became known worldwide for promoting a zero-tolerance approach to petty crime, implementing the notorious "fixing broken windows" policy (Kelling and Coles, 1996). He targeted "quality-of-life crimes," which meant aggressively arresting beggars, window washers, fare dodgers on the subway, and black and Latino youth dressed in hip hop style who loitered on the street. This policy came at a high cost in human rights violations due to a dramatic increase in racially targeted police brutality culminating in public scandals, such as the torture of a Haitian immigrant who was repeatedly sodomized with a broken broom stick by police interrogators in a precinct office, and the murder of an unarmed Guinean immigrant who was shot forty-one times in the foyer of his own apartment building.

New York's get-tough-on-crime policy was also extraordinarily expensive. The number of New York City police dramatically increased by more than 7,000 officers in the 1990s to 40,000, the largest in its history, even as the budgets for health, education, foster child care, public education, and so on were streamlined. During the 1990s, New York State spent more than $4.5 billion building new prisons. This figure does not include operating costs, which in 1998 ran $32,000 per inmate per year in the upstate prisons and more than $66,000 per capita per year on Riker's Island, New York City's municipal jail (Camp and Camp, 1998).

Proponents of repressive drug enforcement policy point to significantly reduced crime rates in New York City during the late 1990s. They fail to note, however, that New York did not lower its crime rate significantly more than those cities that did not criminalize street people or increase police arrest rates. In fact, statisticians have calculated that states that increased their prison populations the most in the 1990s benefited from a smaller reduction in crime rate than those states with below-average increases in incarceration (*New York Times*, September 28, 2000). Most importantly, crime in New York, as well as throughout the nation, had already begun dropping in the years before the New York City's mayor's get-tough-on-crime measures were instituted in 1994. Policy analysts who crunch numbers argue that the overall improvement of the economy and the demographic shifts that have reduced the number of eighteen- to twenty-year-olds have had a far larger effect on decreasing crime rates than have changes in crime-control strategies (Blumstein and Wallman, 2000). Academic and statistical policy critiques notwithstanding, New York City policing became a triumphant symbol for neoliberal solutions to urban plight: "locking up petty delinquents and especially addicts" and "criminalizing misery" (Wacquant, 1999:74, 151). The unsightliness of the poor living in crisis was removed from white, middle class public space in the city. With the festering signs of social suffering safely sanitized, property values soared and tourism reached record highs.

Almost surprisingly, most of the dealers I befriended, with the exception of the younger, inexperienced, and more violent ones, have managed to avoid incarceration. The immediate concrete effect of the escalation in the war on drugs in the late 1990s on the lives of the major characters in this book has been the strict enforcement of federal public housing one-strike-you're-out rulings by New York City officials. The presence of a felon in a household living in public housing in the mid-1990s became legal cause for all the members of that household to be evicted, no matter their age or level of social vulnerability. Many cities have not chosen to enforce this federal edict aggressively, but New York City did. Most of the dealers consequently were evicted from their homes, usually with their extended families; most – including the two main characters in this book – were forced to move out of Manhattan or even out of state. Throughout New York City, grandparents found themselves on the street for sheltering their grandson or granddaughter on their living room couch. It did not matter that a grandmother may have been senile and was unaware of the criminal activity of her grandchild or was perhaps intimidated by the child (cf. *New York Times*, March 27, 2002). Most dramatically, because of New York's unconditional enforcement of one-strike-you're-out, in three separate cases newborns whose mothers allowed dealers (who are major characters in this book) to live with them ended up taking refuge in homeless shelters or doubling up in the living rooms of relatives.

The most troubling trend is the ongoing pattern of destruction befalling most of the children of the crack dealers in this book. I have returned to New York at least once or twice a year since the publication of the first edition of this book. I seek out the characters from the book to say hello and catch up on the old days. On my follow-up visits I have had a chance to meet, as budding adolescents and subsequently as young adults, the former children of the crack dealers, many of whom appear only occasionally in these pages. Spending time with these children provided me with yet another glimpse of the chronic social suffering that continued to be generated in East Harlem despite any positive fluctuation in the economy, and despite the decrease in youthful hard-drug consumption. The most vulnerable inner-city residents are the children of children. They are chewed up and spit out by the American Dream, only to find themselves recycled a dozen or so years later at extraordinary financial and human cost into the prison industrial complex.

San Francisco, April 2002

INTRODUCTION

Man, I don't blame where I'm at right now on nobody else but myself.

Primo

I was forced into crack against my will. When I first moved to East Harlem — "El Barrio"[1] — as a newlywed in the spring of 1985, I was looking for an inexpensive New York City apartment from which I could write a book on the experience of poverty and ethnic segregation in the heart of one of the most expensive cities in the world. On the level of theory, I was interested in the political economy of inner-city street culture. From a personal, political perspective, I wanted to probe the Achilles heel of the richest industrialized nation in the world by documenting how it imposes racial segregation and economic marginalization on so many of its Latino/a and African-American citizens.

I thought the drug world was going to be only one of the many themes I would explore. My original subject was the entire underground (untaxed) economy, from curbside car repairing and baby-sitting, to unlicensed off-track betting and drug dealing. I had never even heard of crack when I first arrived in the neighborhood — no one knew about this particular substance yet, because this brittle compound of cocaine and baking soda processed into efficiently smokable pellets was not yet available as a mass-marketed product.[2] By the end of the year, however, most of my friends, neighbors, and acquaintances had been swept into the multibillion-dollar crack cyclone: selling it, smoking it, fretting over it.

I followed them, and I watched the murder rate in the projects opposite my crumbling tenement apartment spiral into one of the highest in Manhattan.[3] The sidewalk in front of the burned-out abandoned building and the rubbish-strewn vacant lot flanking each side of my tenement began to crunch with the sound of empty crack vials underfoot. Almost a decade later, as this book goes to press, despite the debates of the "drug experts" over whether or not the United States faces a severe "drug problem," this same sidewalk continues to be littered with drug paraphernalia. The only difference in the mid-1990s is that used hypodermic needles lie alongside spent crack vials in the gutter. Heroin has rejoined crack and cocaine as a primary drug of choice available in the inner city as international suppliers of heroin have regained their lost market share of substance abuse by lowering their prices and increasing the quality of their product.[4]

The Underground Economy

This book is not about crack, or drugs, per se. Substance abuse in the inner city is merely a symptom – and a vivid symbol – of deeper dynamics of social marginalization and alienation. Of course, on an immediately visible personal level, addiction and substance abuse are among the most immediate, brutal facts shaping daily life on the street. Most importantly, however, the two dozen street dealers and their families that I befriended were not interested in talking primarily about drugs. On the contrary, they wanted me to learn all about their daily struggles for subsistence and dignity at the poverty line.

According to the official statistics, my neighbors on the street should have been homeless, starving, and dressed in rags. Given the cost of living in Manhattan, it should have been impossible for most of them to afford rent and minimal groceries and still manage to pay their electricity and gas bills. According to the 1990 census, 39.8 percent of local residents in East Harlem lived below the federal poverty line (compared to 16.3 percent of all New Yorkers) with a total of 62.1 percent receiving less than twice official poverty-level incomes. The blocks immediately surrounding me were significantly poorer with half of all residents falling below the poverty line.[5] Given New York City prices for essential goods and services, this means that according to official economic measures, well over half the population of El Barrio should not be able to meet their subsistence needs.

In fact, however, people are not starving on a massive scale. Although many elderly residents and many young children do not have adequate diets and suffer from the cold in the winter, most local residents are adequately dressed and reasonably healthy. The enormous, uncensused, untaxed underground economy allows the hundreds of thousands of New Yorkers in neighborhoods like East Harlem to subsist with the minimal amenities that people living in the United States consider to be basic necessities. I was determined to study these alternative income-generating strategies that were consuming so much of the time and energy of the young men and women sitting on the stoops and parked cars in front of my tenement.

Through the 1980s and 1990s, slightly more than one in three families in El Barrio received public assistance.[6] The heads of these impoverished households have to supplement their meager checks in order to keep their children alive. Many are mothers who make extra money by baby-sitting their neighbors' children, or by housekeeping for a paying boarder. Others may bartend at one of the half-dozen social clubs and after-hours dancing spots scattered throughout the neighborhood. Some work "off the books" in their living rooms as seamstresses for garment contractors. Finally, many also find themselves obliged to establish amorous relationships with men who are willing to make cash contributions to their household expenses.

Male income-generating strategies in the underground economy are more publicly visible. Some men repair cars on the curb; others wait on stoops for unlicensed construction subcontractors to pick them up for fly-by-night demolition jobs or window renovation projects. Many sell "numbers" – the street's version of offtrack betting. The most visible cohorts hawk "nickels and dimes" of one illegal drug or another. They are part of the most robust, multibillion-dollar sector of the booming underground economy. Cocaine and crack, in particular during the mid-1980s and through the early 1990s, followed by heroin in the mid-1990s, have been the fastest growing – if not the only – equal opportunity employers of men in Harlem. Retail drug sales easily outcompete other income-generating opportunities, whether legal or illegal.[7]

The street in front of my tenement was not atypical, and within a two-block radius I could – and still can, as of this final draft – obtain heroin, crack, powder cocaine, hypodermic needles, methadone, Valium, angel dust,[8] marijuana, mescaline, bootleg alcohol, and tobacco. Within one hundred yards of my stoop there were three competing crackhouses selling vials at two, three, and five dollars. Just a few blocks farther down, in one of several local "pill mills," a doctor wrote $3.9 million worth of Medicaid prescriptions in only one year, receiving nearly $1 million for his services. Ninety-four percent of his "medicines" were on the Department of Social Services' list of frequently abused prescription drugs. Most of these pills were retailed on the corner or resold in bulk discounts to pharmacies. Right on my block, on the second floor above the crackhouse where I spent much of my free time at night, another filthy clinic dispensed sedatives and opiates to flocks of emaciated addicts who waited in decrepit huddles for the nurse to raise the clinic's unidentified metal gates and tape a handwritten cardboard DOCTOR IS IN sign to the linoleum-covered window. I never found out the volume of this clinic's business because it was never raided by the authorities. In the projects opposite this same pill mill, however, the New York City Housing Authority police arrested a fifty-five-year-old mother and her twenty-two- and sixteen-year-old daughters while they were "bagging" twenty-one pounds of cocaine into $10 quarter-gram "jumbo" vials of adulterated product worth over $1 million on the street. The police found $25,000 cash in small-denomination bills in this same apartment.

In other words, millions of dollars of business takes place within a stone's throw of the youths growing up in East Harlem tenements and housing projects. Why should these young men and women take the subway to work minimum wage jobs – or even double minimum wage jobs – in downtown offices when they can usually earn more, at least in the short run, by selling drugs on the street corner in front of their apartment or school yard? In fact, I am always surprised that so many inner-city men and women remain in the legal economy and work nine to five plus overtime, barely making ends meet. According to the 1990 Census of East Harlem, 48 percent of all males and 35 percent of females over sixteen were employed in officially reported jobs, compared to a citywide average of 64 percent for men and 49 percent for women.[9] In the census tracts surrounding my apartment, 53 percent of all men over sixteen years of age (1,923 out of 3,647) and 28 percent of all women over sixteen (1,307 out of 4,626) were working legally in officially censused jobs. An additional 17 percent of the civilian labor force was unemployed but actively looking for work compared to 16 percent for El Barrio as a whole, and 9 percent for all of New York City.[10]

The difficulty of making generalizations about inner-city neighborhoods on the basis of official U.S. Census Bureau statistics cannot be

Map of East Harlem

Washington Heights

Hudson River

South Bronx

Harlem River

135th Street

Central Harlem

Harlem River Dr.

Randall's Island

125th Street

Marcus Garvey Park

Columbia University

Morningside Park

116th Street

Fifth Ave.
Madison Ave.
Park Ave.
Lexington Ave.
Third Ave.
Second Ave.
First Ave.
Pleasant Ave.

Jefferson Park

FDR Drive

Riverside Park

Upper West Side

110th Street

East Harlem

Ward's Island

Manhattan Island

Hell Gate

Mt. Sinai Hospital

96th Street

Metropolitan Hospital

East Harlem

East River

Central Park

Fifth Ave.
Madison Ave.
Park Ave.
Lexington Ave.
Third Ave.
Second Ave.
First Ave.
York Ave.

86th Street

Metropolitan Museum of Art

Upper East Side

Housing Projects

Whitney Museum of Art

Sources: Housing Environments Research Group, City University of New York; Kevin Kearney, New York City Housing Authority; New York City Department of City Planning

overemphasized. Studies commissioned by the Census Bureau estimate that between 20 and 40 percent of African-American and Latino men in their late teens and early twenties are missed by the Census. Many of these individuals purposely hide their whereabouts, fearing reprisals for involvement in the underground economy.[11] A good example of the magnitude of concealment in the inner city is provided by a 1988 New York City Housing Authority (NYCHA) report, which calculates that 20 percent more people lived on their premises than were officially reported in the official rolls. The Housing Authority arrived at this "estimate of overcrowding" by cross-tabulating statistics from the Welfare Department and the Board of Education with the increase in expenditures of their maintenance departments.[12] On the blocks immediately surrounding my tenement a vague idea of how many men were missed by the Census is provided by the imbalance between males and females over sixteen years of age: 3,647 versus 4,626. In other words, if one assumes an equal ratio of males to females, 979 men, or 21 percent of the number counted, were missing. In New York City as a whole, 16 percent more men over sixteen years of age would have been needed for there to be a perfect balance between adult males and females. Using this same yardstick of men to women, in El Barrio as a whole 24 percent of all men were "missed."

The difficulty of estimating the size of the underground economy – let alone drug dealing – is even thornier.[13] By definition, no Census Bureau data exists on the subject. Because fewer households than individuals are missed by the Census in urban settings, one possible measure for the size of the underground economy is the figure for households that declare no "wage or salary income." This provides only the very roughest comparative measure for the size of the underground economy in different neighborhoods because some households survive exclusively on retirement income or on strictly legal self-employment revenues. Furthermore, this proxy figure measures drug dealing even more tenuously since many, perhaps most, of those households that rely on the untaxed economy for supplemental income, work at legal tasks and shun drugs. Conversely, many people involved in the underground economy also work at legally declared jobs. Nevertheless, one has to assume that a high proportion of households with no wage or salary income probably rely on some combination of untaxed, undeclared income in order to continue subsisting, and that drug dealing represents an important source of this supplemental

Table 1. *Comparative Social Indicators by Neighborhood from 1990 Census*

	Total population	% Puerto Rican	% African-American	% residents below poverty	% h-holds receiving public assistance	% h-holds with no wage or salary income	% females >16 employed	% males >16 employed	% males >16 missing to balance # of females >16
Crack House micro-neighborhood	11,599	56	33	49	42	46	28	53	21
East Harlem	110,599	52	39	40	34	40	35	48	24
New York City	7,322,564	12	25	19	13	26	49	64	16

Sources: New York City Department of City Planning, Population Division 1992 [August 26]; New York City Department of City Planning 1993 [March]; New York City Department of City Planning 1993 [December]; *1990 Census of Population and Housing Block Statistics.*

income. In any case, according to official Census Bureau statistics, 40 percent of all households in El Barrio as a whole received no legally declared wages or salary, compared to 26 percent for New York City as a whole. The blocks immediately surrounding my apartment were probably slightly more enmeshed in the underground economy, with only 46 percent of the 3,995 households reporting wage or salary income. The percentage of households receiving public assistance is another useful figure for gauging the relative size of the underground economy, since no household can survive on welfare alone and any legal income reported by a household receiving public assistance is deducted from its biweekly welfare check and its monthly food stamps allotment. On the blocks surrounding my tenement 42 percent of all households received public assistance compared to 34 percent in East Harlem as a whole and 13 percent for all households in New York City. [14]

Street Culture: Resistance and Self-Destruction

The anguish of growing up poor in the richest city in the world is compounded by the cultural assault that El Barrio youths often face when they venture out of their neighborhood. This has spawned what I call "inner-city street culture": a complex and conflictual web of beliefs, symbols, modes of interaction, values, and ideologies that have emerged in opposition to exclusion from mainstream society. Street culture offers an alternative forum for autonomous personal dignity. In the particular case of the United States, the concentration of socially marginalized populations into politically and ecologically isolated inner-city enclaves has fomented an especially explosive cultural creativity that is in defiance of racism and economic marginalization. This "street culture of resistance" is not a coherent, conscious universe of political opposition but, rather, a spontaneous set of rebellious practices that in the long term have emerged as an oppositional style. Ironically, mainstream society through fashion, music, film, and television eventually recuperates and commercializes many of these oppositional street styles, recycling them as pop culture. [15] In fact, some of the most basic linguistic expressions for self-esteem in middle-class America, such as being "cool," "square," or "hip," were coined on inner-city streets.

Purveying for substance use and abuse provides the material base for contemporary street culture, rendering it even more powerfully appealing

Repopulating El Barrio: The stuffed animals were arranged by the former superintendent of this abandoned building to protest the decay of his block, which had become a haven for drug dealing. Photo by Henry Chalfant.

than it has been in previous generations. Illegal enterprise, however, embroils most of its participants in lifestyles of violence, substance abuse, and internalized rage. Contradictorily, therefore, the street culture of resistance is predicated on the destruction of its participants and the community harboring them. In other words, although street culture emerges out of a personal search for dignity and a rejection of racism and subjugation, it ultimately becomes an active agent in personal degradation and community ruin.

As already noted, it is impossible to calculate with any accuracy what

Memorial to a youth murdered not far from the Game Room. He had aspired to be a professional boxer. Photo by Oscar Vargas.

proportion of the population is involved in the untaxed, underground economy. It is even harder to guess the number of people who use or sell drugs. Most of El Barrio's residents have nothing to do with drugs.[16] The problem, however, is that this law-abiding majority has lost control of public space. Regardless of their absolute numbers, or relative proportions, hardworking, drug-free Harlemites have been pushed onto the defensive. Most of them live in fear, or even in contempt, of their neighborhood. Worried mothers and fathers maintain their children locked inside their apartments in determined attempts to keep street culture out. They hope someday to be able to move out of the neighborhood.

The drug dealers in this book consequently represent only a small minority of East Harlem residents, but they have managed to set the tone for public life. They force local residents, especially women and the elderly, to fear being assaulted or mugged. The sight of emaciated addicts congregating visibly on street corners provokes pity, sadness, and anger among the majority of East Harlemites who do not use drugs. Most important, on a daily basis, the street-level drug dealers offer a persuasive, even if violent and self-destructive, alternative lifestyle to the youths growing up around them.

No matter how marginal they may be in absolute numbers, the people who are carving out hegemony on inner-city streets cannot be ignored; they need to be understood. For this reason, I chose addicts, thieves, and dealers to be my best friends and acquaintances during the years I lived in El Barrio. The pathos of the U.S. inner city is most clearly manifested within the street dealing world. To borrow the cliché, "in the extraordinary we can see the ordinary." The extreme — perhaps caricatural — responses to poverty and segregation that the dealers and addicts in this book represent, afford insight into processes that may be experienced in one form or another by major sectors of any vulnerable population experiencing rapid structural change in the context of political and ideological oppression. There is nothing exceptional about the Puerto Rican experience in New York, except that the human costs of immigration and poverty have been rendered more clearly visible by the extent and rapidity with which the United States colonized and disarticulated Puerto Rico's economy and polity. On the contrary, if anything is extraordinary about the Puerto Rican experience, it is that Puerto Rican cultural forms have continued to expand and reinvent themselves in the lives of second- and third-generation immigrants around a consistent theme of dignity and autonomy. Indeed, some Puerto Rican scholars refer to this as Puerto Rico's "oppositional mentality," forged in the face of long-term colonial domination.[17]

Ethnographic Methods and Negative Stereotyping

Any detailed examination of social marginalization encounters serious problems with the politics of representation, especially in the United States, where discussions of poverty tend to polarize immediately around race and individual self-worth. I worry, consequently, that the life stories and events presented in this book will be misread as negative stereotypes of Puerto Ricans, or as a hostile portrait of the poor. I have struggled over these issues for several years because I agree with those social scientists who criticize the inferiorizing narratives that have predominated in much of the academic and popular literature on poverty in the United States.[18] At the same time, however, countering traditional moralistic biases and middle-class hostility toward the poor should not come at the cost of sanitizing the suffering and destruction that exists on inner-city streets. Out of a righteous, or a "politically sensitive," fear of giving the poor a bad image, I refuse to ignore or minimize the social misery I witnessed, because that would make me complicitous with oppression.[19]

This book consequently confronts the contradictions of the politics of representation of social marginalization in the United States by presenting brutal events, uncensored as I experienced them, or as they were narrated to me, by the perpetrators themselves. In the process, I have tried to build an alternative, critical understanding of the U.S. inner city by organizing my central arguments, and by presenting the lives and conversations of the crack dealers, in a manner that emphasizes the interface between structural oppression and individual action. Building on the analytic framework of cultural production theory and drawing from feminism, I hope to restore the agency of culture, the autonomy of individuals, and the centrality of gender and the domestic sphere to a political economic understanding of the experience of persistent poverty and social marginalization in the urban United States.

As I have already noted, traditional social science research techniques that rely on Census Bureau statistics or random sample neighborhood surveys cannot access with any degree of accuracy the people who survive in the underground economy — and much less those who sell or take illegal drugs. By definition, individuals who have been marginalized socially, economically, and culturally have had negative long-term relationships with mainstream society. Most drug users and dealers distrust representatives of mainstream society and will not reveal their intimate experiences of substance abuse or criminal enterprise to a stranger on a survey instrument, no matter how sensitive or friendly the interviewer may be. Consequently, most of the criminologists and sociologists who painstakingly undertake epidemiological surveys on crime and substance abuse collect fabrications. In fact, one does not have to be a drug dealer or a drug addict to hide the details of one's illicit activities. Even "honest" citizens, for example, regularly engage in "underground economy" practices when they finesse their deductions on income tax returns. In short, how can we expect someone who specializes in mugging elderly persons to provide us with accurate data on his or her income-generating strategies?

The participant—observation ethnographic techniques developed primarily by cultural anthropologists since the 1920s are better suited than exclusively quantitative methodologies for documenting the lives of people who live on the margins of a society that is hostile to them. Only by establishing long-term relationships based on trust can one begin to ask provocative personal questions, and expect thoughtful, serious answers. Ethnographers usually live in the communities they study, and they establish long-term, organic relationships with the people they write about. In other words, in order to collect "accurate data," ethnographers violate the canons of positivist research; we become intimately involved with the people we study.

With this goal in mind, I spent hundreds of nights on the street and in crackhouses observing dealers and addicts. I regularly tape-recorded their conversations and life histories. Perhaps more important, I also visited their families, attending parties and intimate reunions – from Thanksgiving dinners to New Year's Eve celebrations. I interviewed, and in many cases befriended, the spouses, lovers, siblings, mothers, grandmothers, and – when possible – the fathers and stepfathers of the crack dealers featured in these pages. I also spent time in the larger community interviewing local politicians and attending institutional meetings.

The explosion of postmodernist theory in anthropology in the 1980s and 1990s has critiqued the myth of ethnographic authority, and has denounced the hierarchical politics of representation that is inherent to anthropological endeavors. The self-conscious reflexivity called for by postmodernists was especially necessary and useful in my case: I was an outsider from the larger society's dominant class, ethnicity, and gender categories who was attempting to study the experience of inner-city poverty among Puerto Ricans. Once again, my concerns over these complicated issues are conveyed in my contextualization and editing of the tape-recorded crackhouse conversations. In fact, they are reflected in the very structure of the book.

While editing thousands of pages of transcriptions I came to appreciate the deconstructionist cliché of "culture as text." I also became acutely aware of the contradictory collaborative nature of my research strategy. Although the literary quality and emotional force of this book depends entirely on the articulate words of the main characters, I have always had the final say in how – and if – they would be conveyed in the final product.[20]

Having raised the specter of poststructural theoretical critiques, I must now express my dismay at the profoundly elitist tendencies of many postmodernist approaches. Deconstructionist "politics" usually confine themselves to hermetically sealed academic discourses on the "poetics" of social interaction, or on clichés devoted to exploring the relationships between self and other. Although postmodern ethnographers often claim to be subversive, their contestation of authority focuses on hyperliterate critiques of form through evocative vocabularies, playful syntaxes, and polyphonous voices, rather than on engaging with tangible daily struggles. Postmodern debates titillate alienated, suburbanized intellectuals; they are completely out of touch with the urgent social crises of the inner-city unemployed. Scholarly self-reflection often degenerates into narcissistic celebrations of privilege. Most important, however, radical deconstructionism makes it impossible to categorize or prioritize experiences of injustice and oppression. This subtly denies the very real personal experience of pain and suffering that is imposed socially and structurally across race, class, gender, sexuality, and other power-ridden categories.

Irrespective of the petty theoretical infighting of academic intellectuals, the unique insights provided on the methodological level by the participant–observation techniques of cultural anthropology are further fraught with fundamental analytical and political tensions. Historically, ethnographers have avoided tackling taboo subjects such as personal violence, sexual abuse, addiction, alienation, and self-destruction. Part of the problem is rooted in anthropology's functionalist paradigm, which imposes order and community on its research subjects. Furthermore, the methodological logistics of participation–observation requires researchers to be physically present and personally involved. This encourages them to overlook negative dynamics because they need to be empathetically engaged with the people they study and must also have their permission to live with them. This leads to an unconscious self-censorship that shapes the research settings and subjects anthropologists choose to study. It is easier to obtain the "informed consent" of the individuals one is writing about if one is addressing relatively harmless, "quaint" subjects. Finally, on a more personal level, extreme settings full of human tragedy, such as the streets of East Harlem, are psychologically overwhelming and can be physically dangerous.

Anthropology's obsession with the "exotic other" has discouraged anthropologists from studying their own societies and puts them at risk of exoticizing what they find when they study close to home; hence, I guarded myself consciously in this work from a voyeuristic celebration of street dealers and inner-city street culture. The dearth of ethnographic research on devastating urban poverty, especially in the 1970s and 1980s, is also related to the fear – addressed earlier – of succumbing to a pornography of violence that reinforces popular racist stereotypes. Most ethnographers offer sympathetic readings of the culture or people they study. Indeed, this is enshrined in the fundamental anthropological tenet of cultural relativism: Cultures are never good or bad; they simply have an internal logic. In fact, however, suffering is usually hideous; it is a solvent of human integrity, and ethnographers never want to make the people they study look ugly. This imperative to sanitize the vulnerable is particularly strong in the United States, where survival-of-the-fittest, blame-the-victim theories of individual action constitute a popular "common sense." The result, as I have noted, is that ethnographic presentations of social marginalization are almost guaranteed to be misread by the general public through a conservative, unforgiving lens. This has seriously limited the ability of intellectuals to debate issues of poverty, ethnic discrimination, and immigration. They are traumatized by the general public's obsession with personal worth and racial determinism.

In the United States there are few nuances in the popular understanding of the relationships between social structural constraints and individual failure. As a result, intellectuals have retreated from the fray and have unreflexively latched on to positive representations of the oppressed that those who have been poor, or lived among the poor, know to be completely unrealistic. Indeed, I have noticed this when presenting the main arguments of this book in academic settings. Progressive and often cultural nationalist colleagues – who are almost always middle class – often seem to be incapable of hearing the arguments I am making. Instead, some react in outrage at superficial images taken out of context. It is as if they are so terrified of the potential for "negative connotations" that they feel compelled to suppress complex, unpleasant messages before even listening to them. Ironically, many of their criticisms in these public academic settings embody central dimensions of precisely what I am trying to convey in these pages about the individual experience of social structural oppression.

Critiquing the Culture of Poverty

El Barrio and the Puerto Rican experience in the United States has generated a disproportionally large literature. Puerto Ricans have been called the "most researched but least understood people in the United States."[21] The last major ethnographic work in El Barrio to receive national attention was Oscar Lewis's *La Vida* in the mid-1960s, and it illustrates perfectly the problems inherent in ethnographic method and in life history case studies more specifically. In fact, *La Vida* as well as Daniel Patrick Moynihan's 1965 report on the Negro family are frequently cited as the studies that scared a generation of social scientists away from studying the inner city.[22] Lewis collected thousands of pages of life-history accounts from one extended Puerto Rican family in which most of the women were involved in prostitution. The "culture of poverty" theory that he developed out of this – and other – ethnographic data from Mexico, focused almost exclusively on the pathology of the intergenerational transmission of destructive values and behaviors among individuals within families. Lewis's approach is rooted in the Freudian culture and personality paradigm that dominated anthropology in the 1950s. He fails to note how history, culture, and political-economic structures constrain the lives of individuals. With the advantage of thirty years of hindsight, it is easy to criticize Lewis for his overly simplistic theoretical framework. Class exploitation, racial discrimination, and, of course, sexist oppression, as well as the subtleties of contextualized cultural meanings are not addressed in Lewis's psychologically reductionist descriptions of desperately poor Puerto Rican immigrants. Nevertheless, despite its lack of scholarly rigor, Lewis's compellingly written book on daily life in El Barrio and the shantytowns of Puerto Rico became a best seller in the United States, where it resonated with Protestant work ethic notions of rugged individualism and personal responsibility. Despite the author's progressive political intent and his personal sympathy for the socially marginal, critics interpret his volume as confirming the deep-seated contempt for the "unworthy" poor that permeates U.S. ideology.

It is no accident that it was an anthropologist who coined the concept of the culture of poverty and focused data collection on individual behavior. The simple practical fact of the discipline's methodology – participant–observation – gives it access to documenting individual actions in minute detail. Structures of power and history cannot be touched or talked to. Specifically, in the New York City Puerto Rican context, the self-destructive daily life of those who are surviving on the street needs to be contextualized in the particular history of the hostile race relations and structural economic dislocation they have faced. Embroiled in what seemed like a whirlpool of suffering during my ethnographic research, it was often hard for me to see the larger relationships structuring the jumble of human interaction all around me. In the heat of daily life on the streets of El Barrio I often experienced a confusing anger with the victims, the victimizers, and the wealthy industrialized society that generates such an unnecessarily large toll of human suffering. For example, when confronted with a pregnant friend frantically smoking crack — and possibly condemning her future baby to a life of shattered emotions and dulled brain cells — it did no good for me to remember the history of her people's colonial oppression and humiliation, or to contextualize her position in New York's changing economy. Living in the inferno of what the United States calls its "underclass," I, like my neighbors around me and like the pregnant crack addicts themselves, often blamed the victim.

Political economy analysis is not a panacea to compensate for individualistic, racist, or otherwise judgmental interpretations of social marginalization. In fact, a focus on structures often obscures the fact that humans are active agents of their own history, rather than passive victims. Ethnographic method allows the "pawns" of larger structural forces to emerge as real human beings who shape their own futures. Nevertheless, I often caught myself falling back on a rigidly structuralist perspective in order to avoid the painful details of how real people hurt themselves and their loved ones in their struggle for survival in daily life. Again, this analytical and political problem can be understood within the context of the theoretical debate over structure versus agency, that is, the relationship between individual responsibility and social structural constraints. The insights from cultural production theory — specifically, the notion that street culture's resistance to social marginalization is the contradictory key to its destructive impetus — is useful to avoid reductionist structuralist interpretations. Through cultural practices of opposition, individuals shape the oppression that larger forces impose upon them.[23]

The difficulty of relating individual action to political economy, combined with the personally and politically motivated timidity of ethnographers in the United States through the 1970s and 1980s have obfuscated our understanding of the mechanisms and the experiences of oppression. I cannot resolve the structure-versus-agency debate; nor can I confidently assuage my own righteous fear that hostile readers will misconstrue my ethnography as "giving the poor a bad name." Nevertheless, I feel it imperative from a personal and ethical perspective, as well as from an analytic and theoretical one, to expose the horrors I witnessed among the people I befriended, without censoring even the goriest details.[24] The depth and overwhelming pain and terror of the experience of poverty and racism in the United States needs to be talked about openly and confronted squarely, even if that makes us uncomfortable. I have documented a range of strategies that the urban poor devise to escape or circumvent the structures of segregation and marginalization that entrap them, including those strategies that result in self-inflicted suffering. I have written this in the hope that "anthropological writing can be a site of resistance," and with the conviction that social scientists should, and can, "face power."[25] At the same time, as already noted, I continue to worry about the political implications of exposing the minute details of the lives of the poor and powerless to the general public. Under an ethnographic microscope everyone has warts and anyone can be made to look like a monster. Furthermore, as the anthropologist Laura Nader stated succinctly in the early 1970s, "Don't study the poor and powerless because everything you say about them will be used against them."[26] I do not know if it is possible for me to present the story of my three and a half years of residence in El Barrio without falling prey to a pornography of violence, or a racist voyeurism – ultimately the problem and the responsibility is also in the eyes of the beholder.

1

VIOLATING APARTHEID IN THE UNITED STATES

We love listening to you talk. It makes us laugh. You sound just like a
television advertisement.

> giggling eight-year-old

My research on the streets of Spanish Harlem almost came to a disastrous
end just after the halfway point when I inadvertently "disrespected" Ray,
the man who owned the crackhouses where I spent much of my time
between 1985 and 1990. It was just after midnight, and Ray was visiting
his most profitable sales point to make sure the manager of the late-night
shift had opened punctually. Business was booming and the heavyset,
thirty-two-year-old Puerto Rican crack entrepreneur was surrounded by
his coterie of employees, friends, and wanna-be acquaintances — all eager
for his attention. We were on the corner of 110th Street by the entrance
to the Lexington Avenue subway station right in front the abandoned
four-story tenement building occupied by Ray's dealers. He had camouflaged the ground floor as an after-hours bootleg social club and pool hall.
Ray and many of his employees had grown up in this very tenement
before its Italian owner burned it down to collect its insurance value.
Their corner has long been nicknamed "La Farmacia" because of the
unique diversity of psychoactive substances available: from standard products like heroin, Valium, powder cocaine, and crack to more recherché,
offbeat items like mescaline and angel dust.[1]

Learning Street Smarts

In retrospect I wince at my lack of street smarts for accidentally humiliating the man who was crucial not only to my continued access to the crack

19

scene, but also to my physical security. Perhaps, despite my two and a half years of crackhouse experience at that point, I was justified in being temporarily seduced by the night's friendly aura. Ray was leaning on the front bumper of his gold Mercedes smiling and chatting – happy with life. His followers and employees were also happy because Ray had just treated us all to a round of beers and had promised to order some lobster takeout from the lone surviving hole-in-the-wall Chinese restaurant down the block. We all loved it when Ray was in one of his good moods; it made the man capable of unpredictable largesse, which contrasted dramatically with his usual churlishness. The night was young, and comfortably warm. The emaciated junkies, crackheads, and intravenous coke freaks who gather on La Farmacia's corner twenty-four hours a day, seven days a week, had retreated respectfully across the street, occasionally eyeing our closely knit group enviously. We controlled the space.

Perhaps it was also only normal for me to want to bask in my increasingly close and privileged relationship with the "main man." Earlier that week Ray had confided to me the intimate details of his stickup artist past. According to his account, he had specialized in holding up drug spots until he was ambushed by a hidden lookout while fleeing with $14,000 from a high-volume heroin outlet. It ended with a rooftop shoot-out and a four-and-a-half-year prison sentence for him. His sister posted bail following his arrest by recovering the $14,000 wad of bills that he had managed to stuff into a half-empty can of roofing tar just before his arrest.

Perhaps my guard was also down because Ray had just made a point, in front of everyone, of buying me a bottle of Heineken's instead of the fifteen-cents-cheaper can of Budweiser that everyone else had received. He had said loudly and clearly for everyone to hear, "Felipe, you drink Heineken's don't tcha'?" I felt even more privileged when I saw that he had purchased a Heineken for himself as well, as if to distinguish us from the run-of-the-mill street drinkers by our distinctively green imported bottles.

Surrounded by all this good feeling and security, I thought it might be a good moment to share my minor media coup from earlier that day: a photograph of me on page 4 of the *New York Post* standing next to Phil Donahue following a prime-time television debate on violent crime in East Harlem.[2] I hoped this would impress Ray and his entourage, raising my credibility as a "real professor," capable of accessing the mainstream world of white-dominated daytime television. I was eager to legitimize my presence because there were still a few people in Ray's network who suspected that I was an imposter – nothing more than a fast-talking closet drug addict, or a pervert – pretending to be a "stuck-up professor." Worse yet, my white skin and outsider class background kept some people convinced to the very end of my residence in the neighborhood that I was really a narcotics agent on a long-term undercover assignment.

I noticed Ray stiffen uncharacteristically as I proudly pushed the newspaper into his hands – but it was too late to stop. I had already called out loudly for everyone to hear "Yo! Big Ray! Check out this picture of me in the papers!" A half-dozen of the voices surrounding the large man were already urging him to read the caption on the photo. There was an eager silence as he fumbled awkwardly with the newspaper, not quite knowing how to hold the pages open without having them flap loudly in the gentle breeze. I tried to help by pointing directly to the lines where the caption began. Flustered, he feigned indifference and tried to throw the newspaper into the gutter, but the voices of his admirers were calling out aggressively now for him to read the blurb under my picture. "Come on Ray! What's the matter? What's it say? Read it! Read it!" Unable to save face, he desperately angled the paper to get a fuller beam from the streetlight above us, and screwed his face into an expression of intense concentration. I suddenly realized what the problem was: Ray did not know how to read.

Unfortunately, he tried. He painfully stumbled through the entire caption – ironically entitled "The Calm After the Storm" – his face contorted into an expression akin to that of a dyslexic second-grader who has been singled out for ridicule by his teacher. The eager silence of his followers was broken by embarrassed, muffled giggles. Ray's long-buried and overcompensated childhood wound of institutional failure had burst open. He looked up; regained his deadpan street scowl, threw down the paper, and screamed, "Fuck you Felipe! I don't care about this shit! Get out of here! All of you's!" He then somewhat clumsily pushed his oversized body into his Mercedes, revved the motor, and screeched his tires as he sped away from the corner impervious to the red light, or to the Auschwitz-like survivors on La Farmacia's far curb who dodged his flying wheels and continued to hawk Valium, adulterated heroin, co-caine, and animal tranquilizers.[3]

Primo, my closest friend on the streets – the central character of this book and the manager of Ray's other crackhouse, known as the "Game Room," located in a bogus video arcade two doors down from the rat-infested tenement where I lived with my wife and infant child – turned to me with a worried expression, "Yo, Felipe! You dissed the fat nigga'." Someone else picked the crumpled newspaper out of the gutter and started to read the offending article and to comment on the quality of the photograph. Most of the other hangers-on simply lost interest, disappointed that there would be no more freebees from the head drug dealer that night. They straggled back inside the crackhouse to listen to rap music, play pool, and watch anxious addicts pour through the doors clutching handfuls of dollar bills.

The Parameters of Violence, Power, and Generosity

Ray recovered his dignity by redefining his anger as a legitimate concern over the potential breach of security that my exposure in the press represented. The next time I ran into him as he was delivering a fresh shipment of crack vials and picking up the midshift's sales at the Game Room next to my house, he pulled me aside gruffly, speaking in a loud voice for all to hear:

> Felipe, let me tell you something, people who get people busted – even if it's by mistake – sometimes get found in the garbage with their heart ripped out and their bodies chopped up into little pieces . . . or else maybe they just get their fingers stuck in electrical sockets. You understand what I'm saying?

He then hurried out to his double-parked Lincoln Continental with black-tinted windows, stumbling clumsily over a curled linoleum fragment in the Game Room entrance. To my dismay, his teenage girlfriend, who was waiting impatiently chewing gum in her powerful lover's car, chose this moment to look up from her scowl and eyeball me intensely. Terrified lest Ray think that on top of everything else I was flirting with his new girlfriend, I stared at the ground and lamely hung my head.

Primo was worried. He had known Ray all his life. As a child, Ray, who is ten years older than Primo, had been the leader of two loosely knit youth gangs that Primo and most of Ray's other employers had been involved with in their early teens: the TCC (The Cheeba [marijuana]

22

Crew)[4] and *la Mafia Boba* (the Sly Mafia).[5] He had taught Primo how to steal car radios and burglarize downtown businesses. I tried to laugh off Ray's warning and recover some of my flustered dignity by cracking one of the misogynist jokes they frequently used to dismiss their boss's nasty mood swings: "The fat yak is on the rag. He'll get over it. Chill out man." But Primo shook his head somewhat apologetically; he pulled me out of the Game Room onto the curb to tell me in a hushed voice, that I should make myself scarce around the Game Room for the next few weeks. "You don't understand Felipe, that nigga' is crazy. He's respected on the streets. People know about him. He was wild when he was a kid. He's got juice." When I interrupted Primo somewhat confrontationally in a loud voice with "You mean you're scared of Ray?" Primo responded with what at that stage in our friendship was still a rare admission of vulnerability,

> Hell yeah! I know that nigga' since I was little. He was weird man. Used to think he would rape me or something. Because he's a big nigga', and I'm a little guy back then. I'm only fifteen, boy. And he used to talk crazy shit like, "One of these days I'm gonna get that ass." And I used to wonder if that was true. I never used to dare to be alone with him.

To press his point Primo camouflaged his memories of childhood terror by proceeding casually with an account of how Ray and his best childhood friend, Luis, once raped an old male transient in the empty lot next to the Game Room. I had turned my tape recorder off, unconsciously enforcing the taboo on public discussions of rape. Caesar, however, Primo's best friend who was working as lookout at the Game Room, joined us outside and insisted I document the tale. He mistook my expression of shock to be a sign of fear that someone passing by on the street might be suspicious or angry at seeing a "white boy" holding out a tape recorder to two Puerto Rican men.

> *Caesar:* Take the recorder out, ain't no one going to do nothing to you here Felipe.
> *Primo:* Yeah! They fucked some dirty old man bum in the butt. They followed him in the yard over there [pointing to the garbage strewn rubble to our right].

23

Caesar: Yeah! Yeah!

Primo: Ray and Luis takes turns boning the man in the ass right over there [walking halfway into the lot to mark the spot].

Caesar: Real crazy. Yeah! Ray's a fuckin' pig; Ray's a wild motherfucker. He's got juice. You understand Felipe? Juice! . . . On the street that means respect.

Ignoring Caesar's outburst, Primo proceeded to explain how Ray at that very moment was debating whether or not to have Luis — his fellow rapist, childhood friend, and employee — killed rather than having to spend money on legal fees following Luis's recent arrest while delivering a bundle[6] of crack to the Game Room crackhouse. Coincidentally, the cost of a murder contract was the same as the fee demanded by Luis's lawyer: $3,000. Even though Luis — who was also Primo's first cousin — had grown up as Ray's best friend, he was no longer trusted because of his crack habit. He hustled money compulsively from everyone around him, and, worse yet, he had a reputation as a *chiota,* a stool pigeon. It was rumored that several years earlier he had broken down under police interrogation following an arrest for burglary and reported his own godmother's husband for fencing stolen objects.

These assertions and rumors of Ray's ruthlessness and even cruelty were an integral part of his effectiveness at running his network of crackhouses smoothly. Regular displays of violence are essential for preventing rip-offs by colleagues, customers, and professional holdup artists. Indeed, upward mobility in the underground economy of the street-dealing world requires a systematic and effective use of violence against one's colleagues, one's neighbors, and, to a certain extent, against oneself. Behavior that appears irrationally violent, "barbaric," and ultimately self-destructive to the outsider, can be reinterpreted according to the logic of the underground economy as judicious public relations and long-term investment in one's "human capital development."[7] Primo and Caesar explained this to me in less academic terms early on in my relationship to them.

Primo: It's not good to be too sweet sometimes to people, man, because they're just gonna take advantage of you. You could be a nice and sweet person in real life but you gotta have a little meanness in you and play street. Like, "Get the fuck outta my face." Or "I don't give a fuck." That way you don't let nobody fuck with you later.

Caesar: Yeah, like me. People think that I'm wild.

Primo: Out here, you gotta be a little wild in the streets.

Caesar: You've got to be a little wild for this neighborhood, Felipe. [gunshots] What did I tell you?

You can't be allowing people to push you around, then people think that you're a punk and shit like that. And that's the whole point: making people think you're cool so that nobody bothers you.

You don't really want to be a bully or violent or nothing. But you can't let people push you around, because when the other guys see that, they want to do the same thing too. You get that reputation, like, "That nigga's soft."

And there's a way of not having really big fights or nothing, but having the rep — like "That dude's cool; don't mess with him" — without even having to hit nobody.

And then there's the other way of just total violence.

Fully aware of the potential consequences of Ray's public warning in front of the crackhouse, I gave him a wide berth. Primo and his lookout Caesar cooperated fully to protect me. We worked out a modus vivendi so that I could continue visiting them at the Game Room during working hours without risking a confrontation with Ray. Primo "hired" one of the addicts on the corner to warn with a whistle whenever he saw Ray's car approaching so that I could slip out of the crackhouse to the safety of my apartment building two doors down.

After several weeks of maintaining this cautious low profile at the Game Room, I was still not rehabilitated. Primo warned me that Ray had foreboding dreams about me:

> Ray dreamt you was some kind of agent — like an FBI or CIA agent — no it was more like you was from Mars or something, that you was sent here to spy on us.

Everyone took this symbolic warning seriously because dreams have a powerful significance in Puerto Rican culture. Meshed with the Afro-

Caribbean religious practices of *Santería,* their import may even be greater in the hybrid "Nuyorican culture" of second- and third-generation New York–born Puerto Ricans in the inner city.

My camouflaged visits to the crackhouse continued for almost three more months until finally one night Ray arrived on foot instead of by car, surprising us all in the midst of an uproarious conversation. Primo and I were trying to calm the lookout, Caesar, who had drunk too much rum and coincidentally was venting his resentment of Ray's authoritarianism. Caesar, who was nicknamed "C-Zone" because of the frequency of his drug and alcohol binges, had to be watched closely and taken seriously because of his propensity for gratuitous violence. In our attempts to quiet Caesar down, we had been ineffectively warning him of Ray's rules against obstreperous behavior in his crackhouses.

Caesar: Ray's been riffin' [complaining]? He's gonna come in and say I'm not allowed no more to associate?

Primo: Don't worry. Just don't make no noises. Don't worry about it.

Caesar: I'll tell you about Ray. He's the fattest, laziest, son of a bitch in the fuckin' East. 'Cause he's a drink-Budweiser, be-fat-motherfucker. [pausing to vomit in the trash can at the entrance] He's one of those motherfuckers that whenever the fuck, he feel good, everybody else gotta watch out.

He don't wanta let anybody make money. Well, I teach that nigga' . . . Ah' kill that fat-assed Michelin man. The only reason I don't kill that fat son of a bitch is because I'm going to fuck him up.

[facing me] You recording this shit, Felipe? Fuck you man!

[turning back to Primo] You talking a lotta shit too, Primo, because you're scared of that fat motherfucker. But ah' kill him. Ah' kill that fat motherfucker. I kill him. . . . He's just a black, ugly nigga', a black-a-claus, a fat yak.

[spinning back to me again] I'm scared if I'm sober. I wouldn't talk this shit . . . [pointing to the tape recorder] but since I drunk, I kill that fat son of a bitch.

Understand? [screaming directly into the microphone] Ah' kill that motherfucker!

Primo: [changing his tone somewhat aggressively] You wouldn't
do shit.

Caesar: [in an almost sober tone] I would too. I would even
murder someone. That shit is like wild. Ah'm'a nut case man.
What's the matter? You never thought about that shit, man?

Primo: You must be a simpleton to do something like that.

Caesar: Just think! I should become a wild murderer, man.

Primo: You believe that shit, Philippe?

Philippe: Yes. I believe it. I just don't want to be around when
he does the killing.

Right at this point, just as we were on the verge of coaxing Caesar
into laughing to defuse his mounting rage, Ray stepped into the Game
Room unannounced. My racing adrenaline immediately subsided when
Ray merely smiled at me and cracked an insignificant, hostile joke about
how skinny I looked and how awkwardly my pants fit. We all laughed
with relief – even Caesar, who had suddenly become as subdued and
bewildered as me.

Over the next few months my relationship with Ray gradually improved until by the end of a year I had achieved the same levels of
confidence with the man that I had originally enjoyed prior to my gaffe
in exposing his illiteracy. I remember with relief when he began greet-
ing me, once again, with his usual question, "How's that book
comin' Felipe? Finished yet?" thereby communicating to everyone within
earshot that I had his formal permission to be prying into his personal
business.

Ray's followers did not remain loyal to him solely out of fear and
violence. Some of the older members of his network genuinely liked him.
He was capable of reciprocating friendship. For example, Candy, an old
childhood friend of his and one of only two women who sold for him
during the years I frequented his crackhouses, described him affectionately:

He was like a Gumby Bear as a kid. He was always a nice kid.
[pausing thoughtfully] He was wild; but not wild in the sense
for you to hate him.
We were like brothers and sisters. He always helped me out.

And don't get me wrong, when he gave me money he always did it out of the goodness of his own heart.

The Barriers of Cultural Capital

Whether Ray was a Gumby Bear, a violent pervert, or an omnipotent street don "with juice," my long-term relationship with the man ultimately uncovered a vulnerability that he kept hidden in his street persona. In his private conversations with me over his aspirations for the future, he often seemed naive or even learning-disabled. He was completely incapable of fathoming the intricate rules and regulations of legal society despite his brilliant success at directing a retail network for crack distribution. To borrow the French sociologist Pierre Bourdieu's analytical category, Ray lacked the "cultural capital" necessary to succeed in the middle-class – or even the working-class – world. Ironically, by the time I left New York in August 1991, my relationship to Ray became problematic once again, but this time because he trusted me too much. He expected me to serve as his cultural broker to the outside world, ultimately demanding that I help him launder his money. It began with a harmless phone call: "Felipe, do you know how I can get a picture I.D.?"

Despite all his cars, and the wads of cash padding his pockets, Ray did not even have a driver's license or any other form of legal identification. He was helpless outside the cocoon of El Barrio's streets. He had no concept of how to deal with bureaucracies. New York City's Department of Motor Vehicles rejected the photocopy of his birth certificate when he applied for a license, insisting that he needed a picture I.D. I explained to him what a passport was, and how to obtain one. Soon he was asking me to accompany him through all the bureaucratic hoops that kept him from being able to operate as a legal entrepreneur. He wanted me to come with him to police auctions to review the lists of tax-defaulted and drug-bust confiscated buildings that the City of New York sponsors several times a year. His dream was to buy an abandoned building, renovate it, and establish a legal business. Careful not to offend the man in any way, I always concocted excuses to avoid unwittingly becoming a facilitator to his money-laundering schemes, which inevitably failed miserably as soon as he encountered institutionalized bureaucracies or any kind of formal paperwork.

Violating Apartheid in the United States

The first legal business Ray attempted to establish was a Laundromat. He was unable to wade through the bureaucratic maze of permits, however, and gave up after a few weeks. He then bought the lease on a bodega, a corner grocery store, and thought he had obtained the rights to its secondhand liquor license and health permit, but ran afoul of the bureaucracy once again and abandoned the project. His most successful foray into the legal economy was his purchase of the lease on a former garment factory a few blocks uptown from the Game Room. He converted it into a "legitimate" social club, renting the space out for parties and selling beer without a liquor license. He was proud of this new operation and considered it legal because he kept it rigorously "clean." He expressly forbade drugs from being sold on the premises. New York City closed the social club down in 1992, following the implementation of the Peoples with Disabilities Act, as it was not wheelchair accessible.

Confronting Race, Class, and the Police

Ray represented only one of the many complex personal relationships and ethical contradictions I had to balance while living in the crack-dealer scene. Before I even was able to establish my first relationship with a crack dealer I had to confront the overwhelming reality of racial and class-based apartheid in America. When I first moved into my irregularly heated tenément opposite a massive conglomeration of high-rise, subsidized housing projects sheltering more than five thousand families,[8] I was painfully aware of my outsider status whenever I initially attempted to access any street-dealing scenes. The first time I walked home from the subway station I went down a side street that happened to be a heroin "copping corner" where a half dozen different "companies" competed with each other to sell ten-dollar glassine bags with official, ink-stamped logos. I was greeted by a hail of whistles and echoing shouts of "*bajando* [coming down]" – the coded alarms that lookouts posted on dealing corners use to announce the approach of a potential undercover agent to the "pitchers" who make the actual hand-to-hand sales. Everyone began scattering in front of me as if I had the plague; all of a sudden the block was desolate. I felt as if I was infested with vermin, as if my white skin signaled the terminal stage of some kind of contagious disease sowing havoc in its path. On this occasion my feelings were hurt; I had been feeling lonely and had walked a block out of my way to reach this particularly busy corner precisely because of the exciting bustle of activity surrounding it. In my hopeful naiveté I had thought that the eager knots of pedestrians coming and going signaled the location of one of the street fairs that often grace East Harlem streets like a splash of charm in springtime – relics from a small-town past.

In the long run it was not my conspicuous profile as a potential undercover narcotics agent that became my biggest obstacle to accessing crackhouses and copping corners but, rather, my white drug addict profile. I was almost never harassed by the street sellers; at worst, they simply fled from me or ignored me. On the other hand, I was repeatedly stopped, searched, cursed, and humiliated by New York City police officers on the beat. From their perspective there was no reason for a white boy to be in the neighborhood unless he was an undercover cop or a drug addict, and because I am skinny they instantly assumed the latter. Only one time was I able successfully to impersonate a narcotics officer when stopped by angry police officers. I was in a corner grocery store-cum-numbers joint on my block, buying an ice-cream sandwich and a beer with one of Primo's part-time crack dealer lookouts, when a heavyset white undercover police officer pushed me across the ice-cream counter, spreading my legs and poking me around the groin. As he came danger-ously close to the bulge in my right pocket, I hissed in his ear, "It's a tape recorder." He snapped backward, releasing his left hand's grip on my neck, whispering a barely audible "Sorry." Apparently he thought he had inadvertently intercepted an undercover officer from another unit because before I could get a close look at his face he had exited. Mean-while the marijuana sellers stationed in front of the bodega, observing that the undercover had been rough with me when he searched through my pants, suddenly felt safe and relieved, confident that I was a white drug addict rather than an undercover; and one of them – the tallest and burliest with flashing eyes that suggested recent ingestion of angel dust – promptly came barreling through the door to mug everyone waiting in line at the cash register.

Many of my approximately bimonthly encounters with the police did not end so smoothly. My first encounter with the police was my worst. It was 2:00 a.m. and I was on a notorious crack-copping corner three blocks from where I lived, chatting with a street dealer who was the former boyfriend of one of my neighbors. He had told me to wait with him because his shift had just ended and as soon as the night manager collected the receipts he was going "to go party" and he wanted me to accompany him. I was eager to please him; happy that I had finally found an entrée into this new and particularly active crack scene. He was already introducing me to his colleagues and competitors as a long lost friend and neighbor of his "ex-girl," thereby finally dispelling their conviction that I was a police officer. All of a sudden a patrol car flashed its lights, tooted its siren, and screeched to a halt next to us. To my surprise the officers called out to me and not to my crack-dealing acquaintance: "Hey, white boy! Come ovah' hea'h." For the next fifteen minutes I found myself shouted at, cursed, and generally humiliated in front of a growing crowd of crack dealer/addict spectators. My mistake that night was to try to tell the police officers the truth when they asked me, "What the hell you doin' hea'h?" When they heard me explain, in what I thought was a polite voice, that I was an anthropologist studying poverty and marginalization, the largest of the two officers in the car exploded:

> What kind of a fuckin' moron do you think I am. You think I don't know what you're doin'? You think I'm stupid? You're babbling, you fuckin' drug addict. You're dirty white scum! Go buy your drugs in a white neighborhood! If you don't get the hell out of here right now, motherfucka', you're gonna hafta repeat your story in the precinct. You want me to take you in? Hunh? . . . Hunh? Answer me motherfucka'!

After ineffectual protests that merely prompted further outrage, I was reduced to staring at the ground, mumbling "Yes sir" and shuffling obediently to the bus stop to take the next transportation downtown. Behind me I heard: "If I see you around here later, white boy, ah'm'a' take you in!"[9]

I eventually learned how to act appropriately. By my second year on the street my adrenaline would no longer pump in total panic when police officers pushed me against a wall and made me stand spread-eagled to be patted down for weapons and drugs. My accent proved to be a serious problem in these encounters because patrol officers in East Harlem are almost always white males from working-class backgrounds with heavy Irish- or Italian-American dictions. In contrast to the Puerto Rican and African-American children on my block, who used to marvel at

31

what they called my "television advertisement voice," the police officers assumed I was making fun of them, or putting on airs when I spoke politely to them in complete sentences. I learned that my only hope was to shorten my encounters with the patrol officers by staring at the ground, rapidly handing over my driver's license, and saying "yes-sir-officer" or "no-sir-officer" in minimalist, factual phrases. When I tried to sound sincere, friendly – or even polite – I risked offending them.

Conversely, on the occasions when the police tried to be polite to me their actions only reinforced my sense of violating hidden apartheid laws. On one occasion a squad car overtook me as I was riding my bicycle, to make sure I was not lost or insane: "You know where ya' going? This is Harlem!" Another time as I was sitting on my stoop at sunset to admire the spectacular colors that only New York City's summer smog can produce, a patrolman on the beat asked me, "What're you doing here?" I quickly showed him my driver's license with my address to prove I had a right to be loitering in public. He laughed incredulously. "You mean to tell me you live here! What'sa' matter with you?" I explained apologetically that the rent was inexpensive. Trying to be helpful, he suggested I look for cheap rent in Queens, a multiethnic, working-class borough of mixed ethnicity near New York City's airports.

Racism and the Culture of Terror

It is not merely the police who enforce inner-city apartheid in the United States but also a racist "common sense" that persuades whites, and middle-class outsiders of all colors, that it is too dangerous for them to venture into poor African-American or Latino neighborhoods. For example, when I moved to East Harlem, virtually all of my friends, whether white, black, or Latino/a, berated me for being crazy and irresponsible. Those who still visited me would often phone me in advance to make sure I would meet them downstairs as they descended from their taxis. Indeed, most people still consider me crazy and irresponsible for having "forced" my wife and infant son to live for three and a half years in an East Harlem tenement. When we left the neighborhood in mid-1990, several of my friends congratulated us, and all of them breathed a sigh of relief.[10]

Most people in the United States are somehow convinced that they would be ripped limb from limb by savagely enraged local residents if they were to set foot in Harlem. While everyday danger is certainly real in El Barrio, the vast majority of the 110,599 people – 51 percent Latino/Puerto Rican, 39 percent African-American, and 10 percent "other" – who lived in the neighborhood, according to the 1990 Census, are not mugged with any regularity – if ever. Ironically, the few whites residing in the neighborhood are probably safer than their African-American and Puerto Rican neighbors because most would-be muggers assume whites are either police officers or drug addicts – or both – and hesitate before assaulting them. Primo's primary lookout at the Game Room crackhouse, Caesar, was the first person to explain this to me:

> Felipe, people think you're a *fed* [federal agent] if anything. But that's good; it makes them stay away from you.
>
> Think about it: If you was selling shit on the street and you see a white guy coming by, you wouldn't really want to bother with him.
>
> But then again, some people also think, "he's white and he's in the neighborhood, so he must be crazy." If they didn't, they'd just come up to you and crack you in the face and take your wallet.
>
> You're lucky. Look at me, I'm Puerto Rican. If I was to walk into Bensonhurst,[11] they would figure, "we could beat the shit out of this dude." They might think that I got to be crazy or something but they will test me or kick my ass.

During all the years I spent on the streets of El Barrio walking around at all hours of the night, I was mugged only once – and that was at 2:00 a.m. in a store where everyone else was also robbed at the same time. My wife, who is Costa Rican, was never mugged and she circulated freely throughout the neighborhood – although she was cautious after dark. During the span of these same years, at least a half-dozen of our friends living downtown in safer neighborhoods were mugged. I do not mean to overstate the safety of El Barrio; my seventy-year-old Filipino landlord was mugged in the hallway of our apartment building in broad daylight while walking out of his ground-floor apartment. As I noted in the Introduction, everyone is conscious of the real possibility of assault. Even the toughest of the drug dealers in Ray's network would ask a friend to accompany them for protection when they were carrying money or drugs after dark.

Violence cannot be reduced to its statistical expression, which would show that most murders and beatings in any given inner-city neighborhood remain confined to a small subgroup of individuals who are directly involved in substance abuse and the underground economy, or who are obviously vulnerable, such as frail, elderly persons. Street culture's violence pervades daily life in El Barrio and shapes mainstream society's perception of the ghetto in a manner completely disproportionate to its objective danger. Part of the reason is that violent incidents, even when they do not physically threaten bystanders, are highly visible and traumatic. For example, during my first thirteen months of residence in El Barrio I witnessed a slew of violent incidents:

- A deadly shotgun shooting outside my apartment window of a drug-dealing woman (who also happened to be the mother of a three-year-old child).
- A bombing and a machine-gunning of a numbers joint by rival factions of the local Mafia – once again, within view of my window.[12]
- A shoot-out and police car chase in front of a pizza parlor where I happened to be eating a snack with my wife.
- The aftermath of the fire-bombing of a heroin house by an unpaid supplier around the block from where I lived.
- A half-dozen screaming, clothes-ripping fights.

None of these particular incidents came close to threatening me physically, but their traumatic nature and prominent public visibility contributed to a sense of an omnipresent threatening reality that extended far beyond the statistical possibility of becoming a victim.[13] To analyze the very different contexts of South America and Nazi Germany, anthropologist Michael Taussig has coined the term "culture of terror" to convey the dominating effect of widespread violence on a vulnerable society.[14] In contemporary Spanish Harlem one of the consequences of the "culture of terror" dynamic is to silence the peaceful majority of the population who reside in the neighborhood. They isolate themselves from the community and grow to hate those who participate in street culture – sometimes internalizing racist stereotypes in the process. A profound ideological dynamic mandates distrust of one's neighbors.[15] Conversely, mainstream society unconsciously uses the images of a culture of terror to dehumanize the victims and perpetrators and to justify its unwillingness to confront segregation, economic marginalization, and public sector breakdown.

I had a professional and personal imperative to deny or "normalize" the culture of terror during the years I lived in El Barrio. Many local residents employ this strategy. They readjust their daily routines to accommodate the shock of everyday brutality in order to maintain their own sense of sanity and safety. To be successful in my street ethnography, I had to be relaxed and enjoy myself on the street. I had to feel comfortable while hanging out surrounded by friends and basking in relaxed conversation. This is not difficult during daylight hours or even during the early evening, when El Barrio streets often feel warm and appealing. Children are running every which way playing tag and squealing with delight; one's neighbors are out strolling and often pause to strike up a friendly conversation; a loudspeaker pulses salsa music from a tenth-story housing project window so that everyone on the street below can step in tune for free. In short, there is a sense of community in the neighborhood despite the violence. In fact, most residents even know the nicknames of their more hostile or suspicious neighbors.

Having grown up in Manhattan's Silk Stocking district just seven blocks downtown from El Barrio's southern border delineated by East 96th Street, I always appreciated the shared sense of public space that echoes through Spanish Harlem's streets on warm sunny days. In the safe building where I grew up downtown, neighbors do not have nicknames, and when one shares the elevator with them, they usually do not even say hello or nod an acknowledgment of existence.[16] I enjoyed the illusion of friendly public space that the working-class majority in El Barrio are often able to project during daylight hours. It was the dealers themselves who frequently shattered my sense of optimism and insisted that I respect the violent minority who really controlled the streets when push came to shove. In one particular instance toward the end of my residence I had commented to Caesar in the Game Room that the neighborhood felt safe. His outraged comical response was particularly interesting in that it traced the full ambiguous cycle of the culture of terror by demonstrating the instrumental brutality of the people who were supposed to be protecting us. Both the criminals and the police play by the rules of the culture of terror:

Caesar: Yo Pops [waving Primo over], listen to this. [turning to me] Felipe thinks the block is chill.

Well let me tell you Felipe, what happened earlier today, because all day it was wild on this block. I didn't even have to watch HBO

35

today. I just had to look out the window and I had a full array of murder and beat down and everything. There was even a fire. I saw an assortment of all kinds of crap out there.

It all started when two crackheads – an older man and a black dude – yoked this girl. They beat her down and took her jewelry. Punched her in the eye; just cold bashed her. She was screaming and the old guy kicked her some more. It was in the daytime like around two.

Then the cops came and caught the muggers and beat them down. There was at least twenty cops stomping out them two niggas because they resisted.

And they should never have attempted that shit because they got the beat-down of their lives. The cops had a circus with the black kid's face. Hell yeah! They were trying to kill that kid. That's why they needed two ambulances.

Homeboy got hurt! Both of them was in stretchers bleeding hard. It wasn't even a body there. It was just a blob of blood that was left over. The cops had pleasure in doing it.

It was not a normal beat-down like: throw-you-up-on-a-car extra hard. I'm talking about "take your turn, buddy" [grinning]; hold 'em right here [punching] and BOOM and BOOM. And this guy goes BOOM [pretending to fall unconscious].

Even 'Buela [grandma] saw it from the window next to me. And she was yelling and someone else was yelling, "Abuse! Abuse! Police brutality!"

If I woulda had a little video camera I woulda sent it to Al Sharpton.[17] Because it was a black dude that they did that beat-down to. Coulda caused a major political scandal and Sharpton woulda been right up here with that wack perm he's got.

Philippe: How does it make you feel to see the cops doing that?

Caesar: I was feeling really sorry for myself because I was thinking about getting hit. I could feel the pain they was feeling 'cause I know what it is to be beat down by cops. They don't let up; they be trying to kill you, man! They do it with pleasure [grinning].

That's stress management right there. That's release of tension. That's my-wife-treated-me-dirty-you'll-pay. That's terrorism with a badge. That's what that is.

The cops look forward to that. They get up in the morning and go, "Yeah, Ah'm'a' gonna kick some minority ass today." [rubbing his hands together and licking his lips]

I could tell that attitude, because I would be the same if I was a police officer. 'Cause you take the badge for granted. The badge gets to your head. You know what I'm saying? Makes you feel like you're invincible; like you could do whatever you goddamn well please.

I would have the same attitude. I'm going to hurt somebody today. I don't care if he's white or Puerto Rican. And I'm going to have pleasure in doing it. I'm full into it. And I would be a happy married man because I wouldn't fight with my wife.

I don't even know why they have human police officers. They should just put animals out there patrolling the streets. Word up! 'Cause they're worse than animals. It's like they're animals with a mind.

Internalizing Institutional Violence

Although we did have to worry about the danger of police brutality, it was not one of our primary daily concerns. There was always a strong undercurrent of anxiety over the risk of arrest, but we were considerably less worried about being brutalized by the police if they raided the crackhouse compared to what we risked at the hands of our fellow inmates in the holding pen. Judges in Manhattan almost never send anyone to prison for selling or buying small quantities of drugs the first time they are arrested. A hand-to-hand sale of crack to an undercover officer usually results in a two- to four-year suspended felony sentence. I have never even heard of a simple customer being brought to trial – much less being convicted of anything. The problem in an arrest is that one usually has to wait in a municipal jail holding pen for forty-eight to seventy-two hours before being arraigned by the judge in the special Narcotics Court.[18]

Our fate in these overcrowded "bullpens" was a frequent subject of anxious discussion. I captured one such debate on my tape recorder. Caesar's non-drug-using cousin, Eddie, was reminding all of us in the Game Room that we risked being sodomized in jail if the police picked us up in a sweep that night. Eddie's father was African-American, and Caesar made sure to racialize his retort as well as demonstrate his superior technical knowledge of the likelihood of sexual assault in a New York City holding pen.

Eddie: Yo Caesar, don't you come crying to me when they take that ass a' yours downtown and bust your cherry. [laughter]

Caesar: [businesslike] Unnh-uhh! They don't rape niggas in the bullpen no more 'cause a' AIDS. You don't even get raped on Riker's [New York City's biggest municipal jail] no more.

You get raped when you go upstate where they got them big, black, brick-Georgia, Georgia-Tech Bulldog, Black Muslim ham hocks that been in the slammer twenty years.

They be runnin' that little ass a' yours. [jumping to within an eighth of an inch of Eddie's face] Because they bigger than you. They been lifting weights. They big and they take your shit. [spinning around into my face] And they take your arm like this [twisting my arm] and they put it down and they dog it. [spinning around and seizing Eddie in a full nelson] And they jerk it around. [pumping his crotch against Eddie's rear] And you like: [switching roles to grab at his head and pull his hair, shrieking] AHHUUHH.

Because they got their large mammoth, lamabada-blada, Alabama black snake with its magnets out plunging you. Alabama black snake found its way to the assets boy!

[pausing to gauge our hesitant laughter] And they black. And they cruddy. And they smell black. And they big. And they smell like James Brown. And they spit their stuff in your shit. And you gotta be like a lamb and wash drawers and shit, and socks. And you get juiced because you give the biggest niggas' *bolos* [penises] blow jobs. And that's your man [hugging Eddie violently].

And if you're a new nigga' [jumping into my face] and you're a fag and you like it and he want to dog you, you get the big black bogeyman and shit. And they take your ass and stuff it with some mad concrete. They fill your canyon. Word!

And if the faggots like you, they get you in trouble. [spinning back around to face me] And they try to mush 'em, "All right motherfucker, you don't wanta fuck me? I'm back with the black bohemians."

[swinging around again into Primo's face] And they're taking that ass and they make you a fag. And people out on the street, be recognizing *you*! [swinging his face around yet again to within an eighth of an inch of my nose]

I was especially sensitive to Caesar's harangue that night because the New York City police had just deployed their new elite Tactical Narcotics Teams – appropriately nicknamed TNT – in El Barrio.[19] TNT was founded in 1989 to assuage popular outrage during the height of the national just-say-no-to-drugs hysteria.[20] TNT's specific directive was to bust the small, street-level dealer rather than the wholesale supplier. A week earlier, at 2:00 a.m., TNT had arrived in U-Haul trucks to block off both ends of a notorious crack-copping block a few streets down from the Game Room. They rounded up everyone loitering on the sidewalk and even dragged people out of private apartments in the few still-inhabited tenements on the block.

The night of Caesar and Eddie's jousting over jailhouse rape, I had forgotten my driver's license. Not carrying a picture identification is a sure guarantee for inciting police wrath. The recording from this session ends with my voice cursing Caesar through cackles of nervous background laughter:

> *Philippe:* Outta' my face Caesar! What the fuck's the matter with you! You'a fucking pervert, or what?
>
> Primo, I'm outta here. You guys have made me *petro* [paranoid]. I'll be right back though, I'm just going upstairs to get my I.D.

Accessing the Game Room Crackhouse

In my first months on the block, I was not debating complex theoretical points about how the United States legitimizes inner-city segregation, or how victims enforce the brutality of their social marginalization. I was primarily concerned with how to persuade the manager of the crackhouse on my block that I was not an undercover police officer. I remember vividly the night I first went to the Game Room. My neighbor Carmen – a thirty-nine-year-old grandmother who I had watched over the past three months become addicted to crack and transform herself into a homeless ninety-nine-pound harpie abandoning her two-year-old twin grandchildren – brought me over to the manager of the Game Room and told him in Spanish, "Primo, let me introduce you to my neighbor,

Felipe; he's from the block and wants to meet you." Excited at the possibility of finally accessing a crackhouse scene, my heart dropped when Primo shyly giggled and turned his back on me as if to hide his face. Staring out into the street, he asked Carmen in English, loud enough for me to hear clearly, "What precinct did you pick him up at?" I hurriedly mumbled an embarrassed protest about not being "an undercover" and about wanting to write a book about "the street and the neighborhood." I had the good sense not to impose myself, however, and instead slunk into the background onto the hood of a nearby parked car after buying a round of beers. Even in my largesse I managed to prolong the awkwardness by purchasing the wrong kind of beer – an unstreetwise brand whose taste Primo did not like. He was only drinking 16-ounce bottles of a new brand of malt liquor called Private Stock, which was being marketed on Harlem billboards featuring beautiful, brown-skinned women draped in scanty leopard skins and flashing bright, white teeth, to attract a fresh generation of young, inner-city street alcoholics.

Despite my inauspicious first evening, it took less than two weeks for Primo to warm up to my presence. I was aided by having to pass the Game Room literally every day, and usually several times a day, in order to reach the supermarket, the bus stop, or the subway. Primo would usually be standing outside his pseudo video arcade surrounded by a little clique of teenage girls vying for his attention. At first we just nodded politely to each other, but after a week he called out, "Hey guy, you like to drink beer, don't you?" and we shared a round of Private Stocks with Maria, his fifteen-year-old girlfriend, and his current lookout, Benito – anglicized and commodity fetishized into "Benzie" – a short, loud-voiced twenty-year-old whose exaggerated street swagger hid the limp caused by the dumdum bullet lodged in his left femur.

A few hours, and beers, later my pulse quickened when Primo invited me into the back of the Game Room to where the crack supply was hidden behind a false linoleum panel, and he laid out a dime bag of powder cocaine. It was the "We Are the World" brand, which was sold across the avenue under a half-block-long mural celebrating the late-1980s rock concert of the same title for famine relief in Ethiopia. "You like to sniff too?" Worried that I was going to ruin rapport – or, worse yet, confirm my suspected police officer status – for turning down his offer, I discovered to my surprise that both Primo and his lookout, Benzie, were thrilled to be hanging out with someone who was "such good people" that he did not even "sniff." This was my first encounter with the profound moral – even righteous – contradictory code of street ethics that equates any kind of drug use with the work of the devil, even if almost everybody on the street is busy sniffing, smoking, shooting, or selling.

Primo, Benzie, Maria, and everyone else around that night had never been tête-à-tête with a friendly white before, so it was with a sense of relief that they saw I hung out with them out of genuine interest rather than to obtain drugs or engage in some other act of *perdición*. The only whites they had ever seen at such close quarters had been school principals, policemen, parole officers, and angry bosses. Even their schoolteachers and social workers were largely African-American and Puerto Rican. Despite his obvious fear, Primo could not hide his curiosity. As he confided in me several months later, he had always wanted a chance to "conversate" with an actual live representative of mainstream, "drug-free" white America.

Over the next few weeks, I regularly spent a few hours at the Game Room crackhouse chatting with Primo and whoever else was on duty that shift – either little Benzie or Caesar. To my surprise, I became an exotic object of prestige; the crackhouse habitués actually wanted to be seen in public with me. I had unwittingly stepped into a field of power relations where my presence intimidated people. My next challenge, consequently, was to break through the impressions-management game playing that inverse power relationships inevitably entail. For example, I had triggered within Primo a wave of internalized racism whereby he enthusiastically presented himself as superior to "the *sinvergüenza mamao'* [shameless scum] all around us here." He kept trying to differentiate himself "from all these illiterate Puerto Ricans" who "work in *factorías*." I was especially embarrassed when he began letting me know how good he thought it was for the development of his mind to be talking with me. At the same time, however, he still thought I might be an undercover police officer. Almost a month after I met him, he said, "I don't care if tomorrow you come and arrest me, I want to talk to you. You're good people." It was not until three years later that Primo would casually describe me to others as "the white nigga' who always be hangin' with me." As a matter of fact, I still remember the night when I first graduated to "honorary nigga' " status. Primo had imbibed more alcohol than usual, and I had walked him up to his girlfriend Maria's sister's high-rise project apart-

41

Tape-recording Primo in his mother's housing project stairwell. Photo: Susan Meiselas.

ment to make sure he would not get mugged in the stairway, because the elevators were broken as usual.[21] Upon our safe arrival, swaying in the doorway, he grabbed me by the shoulders to thank me: "You're a good nigga', Felipe. You're a good nigga'. See you tomorrow."

It was not until two years later at 2 a.m. in the stairwell of Primo's mother's high-rise project, where Primo and Benzie had gone to sniff a "speedball" (combination of heroin and cocaine), during New Year's week that they told me what their first impressions of me at the Game Room had been. Primo had ripped open a $10 glassine envelope of heroin and dipped his housekey into the white powder in order to lift a dab to his left nostril. He sniffed deeply, repeating the motion deftly two more times to his right nostril before sighing and reaching out for me to hand him the 40-ounce bottle of Ole English malt liquor I was swigging from.

Benzie, meanwhile, was crushing the contents of a $15 vial of cocaine inside a folded dollar bill by rolling it between his thumbs and forefingers, which gets rid of any clumps and crystals and makes it easier to sniff. He then dipped a folded cardboard matchbook cover into the inch-long pile of white powder and sniffed dryly twice before laying it down gently in the corner of the stair he was sitting on:

Primo: When I first met you, Felipe, I was wondering who the hell you were, but, of course, I received you good because you sounded interesting; so, of course, I received you good. [reaching for the cocaine] *Te recibí como amigo, con respeto* [I welcomed you as a friend, with respect].

Benzie: [interrupting and handing me the malt liquor bottle] Felipe, I'm going to tell you the honest truth – and he knows it. [pointing to Primo] The first time I met you I thought that you was in a different way. . . . But I would really rather not tell you. [sniffing from the heroin packet with Primo's key]

Philippe: [drinking] It's all right don't worry; you can tell me. I won't get angry.

Benzie: Yeah . . . well . . . [turns to Primo to avoid eye contact with me, and sniffs again] yeah, you remember? I used to tell you, you know, the way he used to talk. The way he used to be. That I thought maybe . . . you know, . . . How you call it? That some people are bisexual. Even though you had a wife, I thought you was like . . . dirty.

It was really 'cause of the way you talk and 'cause of the way you act. You always asking a lot of questions, and a lot of gay people be like that – you know, trying to find out the way you are.

But then after a while, when I got to know you [grabbing the bottle from me], I saw the way you was hanging; and I got to know you better; but still, I always had that thought in my head, "Man, but, but this nigga's a faggot." [drinking]

Primo: [cutting Benzie short] Damn, shut up man! You're going to give Felipe a *complejo* [complex]. [putting his arm over my shoulder] It was just 'cause you was white. He was thinking, *"Quién es éste blanquito?"* [Who is this white boy?]

Philippe: So was it my accent? My voice? The way I move my body?

Benzie: Yeah, like your accent . . .

Primo: [interrupting] I told him you were an anfropologist, and that the way you speak is just like intelligent talk. I mean you just speak your way. And maybe, we don't understand a few words, but it's all right.

But when you talk Spanish, then you really be sounding different. Then you really be sounding different. You know, when you talk Spanish, you sound like an *Español* [Spaniard].

Even my mother thought you was gay, but that was because she was only talking to you through the phone. [gunshots] One day she asks me [in Spanish], "Who's this little white boy who's always calling here? Is he a *pato* [faggot] or something?" [*Quién es este blanquito que siempre llama aquí? Es pato o algo así?*]

And I said [once again in Spanish], "No! What are you talking about? He is a professor. He speaks Spanish and English and French." [*No! De qué tú hablas? El es profesor. Habla español, inglés, y francés.*]

At the time I heard this, I could not stop myself from feeling some kind of vain personal pique at having been misidentified sexually, because by that time I fancied myself to be at least minimally streetwise. In retrospect I am relieved that during the first few years of my fieldwork I thoroughly misread street cues and did not suspect I was giving off "dirty sexual pervert" vibes. Being self-conscious about my sexual image in the homophobic context of street culture might have interfered with my ability to initiate comfortable relationships with the crack dealers.

African-American/Puerto Rican Relations on the Street

Racial tension in El Barrio is not just focused around whites. Ray's network was intensely internally segregated. It was almost exclusively composed of second-generation, New York–born Puerto Ricans.[22] Although Ray himself would be classified as "black" by Anglo society – as would almost half of his employees – most were explicitly hostile to African-Americans. Only two of the approximately two-dozen dealers I met working for Ray were African-American. Both had hispanicized their nicknames: Sylvester, for example, was called Gato, the Spanish word for cat. The other African-American dealer, who went by the name Juan, confided to me in private that he found the atmosphere at the social club crackhouse on La Farmacia's corner distinctly hostile:

Blacks and Puerto Ricans really don't get along here. See that plaque there, that says "Latin Family"? Well, some people take that seriously. It's a lot of racism. When I come through the door I have to have an aim and a purpose. If I go and I sit in a seat and I cross my legs, all of a sudden they'll be gathering together, speaking in Spanish, like "Yo, who's that?" They'll even tell you in English, "Yo, you better be chill."

Caesar was more explicit about racial tension in the Game Room – at least when he was drinking.

I'm Klu Klux Klan. Ah' kill black people. You know why I hate black people? Because they're black; they stink; they smell like shit. And they're lazy motherfuckers. I swear to God I hate their fucking guts.

I even hate Puerto Ricans that afro. I hate them like any other black man. [running his hands through Primo's hair] Fuck Primo too, because he's got an afro and he's black. I kill him.

[facing me] I hate whites too. I kill them all. But not you Felipe. You all right, you a good nigga'. But if you didn't hang out with us I'd kill you.

You know why I hate *moyos* [racist Puerto Rican term for blacks] because it was a black man who killed my sister – stabbed her eighteen times in the projects.

They get me pissed off, because why did they got to do these things to me? I'm already fucked up as it is. I hate everybody.

For all his explicit racism, Caesar emulated African-American street culture, which has an almost complete hegemony over style in the underground economy.

I used to want to be black when I was younger. I wanted to be with that black style. 'Cause they're badder. Like *malos* [bad]. Yeah! *Malo malos!* More rowdier.

I liked'ed evil black kids the most because I was learning how to be schemish and steal fruit from the fruit stand and stuff like that.

Plus black people like to dress hard — like rugged. You know what I'm saying? Look wild, like *black*. Black, just being *black*. Cool.

'Cause the Spanish people I used to hang with, their style was kind of wimpy, you know.

Look, right now, it's the *moyos* be bringing in the marked necks and the A.J.'s.

That be the *moyos* with the fly clothes.

Regardless of the complexities of racial tension, class polarization, and everyday street style, in the long term everyone in Ray's network came to accept me — and most people appeared genuinely to like having me around. Of course, there were dozens of other people on the periphery of Ray's scene, or in other dealing networks, who never grew to trust me. This was especially true of African-American sellers and younger Puerto Rican teenage dealers, whose relationship to white society is more self-consciously oppositional—hostile than that of their parents or even their older brothers. Nevertheless, I felt comfortable in my role as "professor" and "anthropologist" writing a book. On several occasions it almost became problematic when marginal members of Ray's network, and even outsiders, accosted me angrily for never tape-recording them, claiming that they "deserved to be at least a chapter" in my book. I had originally worried that the main characters in this book might resent the fact that an outsider was going to use their life stories to build an academic career. My long-term goal has always been to give something back to the community. When I discussed with Ray and his employees my desire to write a book of life stories "about poverty and marginalization" that might contribute to a more progressive understanding of inner-city problems by mainstream society, they thought I was crazy and treated my concerns about social responsibility with suspicion. In their conception everyone in the world is hustling, and anyone in their right mind would want to write a best seller and make a lot of money. It had not occurred to them that they would ever get anything back from this book project, except maybe a good party on publication day. On several occasions my insistence that there should be a tangible political benefit for the community from my research project spawned humiliating responses:

Caesar: Felipe, you just talking an immense amount of shit. Because we talk huge amounts of crap that don't mean a goddamned thing – into the air.

Like, like we on Oprah Winfrey or the Donahue Show – which doesn't mean shit. That's not going to help the community. It's not going to help us. It's not going to change the world in an eensy-weensy bit at all. It's just talk. Flap the lip.

Of course, I hope Caesar is wrong; but maybe his cynicism is more realistic than my academic idealism.

About halfway through my research, the main characters in this book, with whom I have developed deeper relations, began following the details of my writing habits and urging me to make speedier progress. They wanted to be part of "a best seller." For example, when I came down with a debilitating tendinitis in my wrists and forearms from spending too many hours at my word processor, Caesar and Primo became genuinely worried and disappointed. I realized that our relationships had developed an almost psychotherapeutic dimension.

Caesar: [grabbing my arms and twisting them] Don't be giving up on us, Felipe. Don't be fuckin' up. We could beat you up for this.

[turning to Primo] I think Felipe is going out of his mind. I think we're going to have to put pressure on him.

[giggling] You're our role model here. You can't be fuckin' around. We could beat you down for shit like that. Word up!

I ain't lettin' you leave us until I get something in writing with your name on it, as a lifetime reference. You gonna have to give me at least a chapter, regardless. I know my words is going to be in your chapters because my stories is so good that you can't leave them out.

[hugging me] I think the students are becoming more advanced than the teacher here, educational-wise. I think Felipe's in a deep depression. I think he's got a writer's block thing.

2

A STREET HISTORY OF EL BARRIO

[East Harlem is] a nursery of all kinds of law-breakers; there are nests of narcotics, thieving, stealing, cheating and every conceivable kind of law-breaking. The country is flooded with criminals from here. A taxi driver would not dare go through 113th Street east of Second Avenue after dark: an armored car would be the only thing safe.

Catholic priest, 1930s[1]

The intimate details of the lives of the crack dealers and their families revealed in this book cannot be understood in a historical vacuum. Second- and third-generation Puerto Rican immigrants in New York City need to be placed in the context of their grandparents' and great-grandparents' oppressive colonial history. The strategic physical location of the island of Puerto Rico in the middle of the Caribbean at the very heart of the most important trans-Atlantic shipping routes has always made world superpowers covet the territory jealously – almost ever since Christopher Columbus first set foot on the Island in 1493 and Ponce de León conquered it in 1508. Dogmatic strategic-military concerns that have nothing to do with economic logic or with the welfare of Puerto Rico's residents have arbitrarily distorted the political and economic administration of the Island for almost five hundred years. Although the original Spanish conquerors imported African slaves and established sugar cane plantations, Puerto Rico was never an economically profitable colony. It was always, above all, a locus for military control; hence the reactionary tenacity with which Spain held on to the territory through the entire nineteenth century, long after the rest of the Americas had been decolonized in the 1820s. More recently, the failure of Puerto Rico to achieve a viable form of political and economic development over the past century has spawned what is proportionately one of the most massive population dislocations of the twentieth century.

When the United States invaded Puerto Rico in 1898, it continued the Spanish pattern of putting military concerns above economic logic. Since 1952 the Island has held the ambiguous political title of "Free Associated Commonwealth." It is subject to U.S. rule, but its residents are not allowed to vote in presidential elections and have no enfranchised representatives in the U.S. Congress. The territory's colonial status is regularly denounced in the United Nations. Ironically, Puerto Rico continues to be a financial liability to its political overlord. Like the Spanish crown one hundred years ago, the U.S. federal government spends money to maintain military and political control of the territory and to subsidize its insolvent economy. Since the 1970s, federal transfers in the form of food stamps and social security insurance have accounted for almost a third of Puerto Rico's personal income. In 1992, more than 50 percent of the Puerto Rican population qualified for food stamps.[2] Caesar insightfully summed up the political basis for Puerto Rico's relationship to the United States late one night while on duty at the Game Room:

> *Caesar:* The only reason the U.S. acknowledges P.R., is because it's close to Cuba — a shorter distance to destroy communism. I mean we don't have nothin' to offer. There's no natural resources. There's no oil; there's no gold; there's not even good water there. They have nothing.
>
> What they got? Rum? The U.S. already got Kentucky, Tennessee, all the southern states make moonshine.

From Puerto Rican Jíbaro to Hispanic Crack Dealer

In the early 1900s, the United States actively transformed Puerto Rico's economy, rendering it even less responsive to local needs and culture than it had been under Spanish domination. Immediately following the U.S. military occupation, land and power were concentrated under the ownership of large U.S.-owned agro-export companies. Hundreds of thousands of small farmers were forced to leave their plots of land in the Island's central highlands to seek wage-labor employment on the immense sugar plantations that soon covered much of Puerto Rico's most fertile coastal plains. Since World War II, these uprooted farmers and their descendants have often been referred to as "jíbaros," a term that could be translated in English as "hillbillies." The term *jíbaro* conveys a stereotypical image of a ruggedly independent subsistence farmer who wears a straw hat, wields a wide machete, and squats [*ñangotea*] on the packed-earth patio [*batey*] of his country home to receive visitors at the end of a hard day's work in the fields. Although bearing an ambiguously pejorative connotation, the jíbaro has emerged as a symbol of Puerto Rican cultural integrity and self-respect in the face of foreign influence, domination, and diaspora. The original Spanish meaning of the word *jíbaro* was "wild." Jíbaros were supposed to have been the descendants of escaped African slaves, Taino Amerindians, and European and Moor stowaways who refused to work as sugar cane cutters on Spanish colonial plantations. Instead, throughout the eighteenth and nineteenth centuries, they home-steaded on their Island's rugged interior hills and rejected the laws and social conventions of Spanish-dominated high society. They lived outside the jurisdiction of the urban-based state.[3]

There is an appealing parallel between the existence of a former jíbaro society that refused colonial plantation wage labor and rejected elitist Spanish cultural forms out of a sense of indomitable self-respect, and the oppositional content of street culture's resistance to exploitation and marginalization by U.S. society. At the same time, the concept of jíbaro should not be reified into a simple culturalist category as a traditional relic from the rural past. Jíbaros have been repeatedly reinvented and redefined by rapidly changing political and economic contexts. The cate-gory now sometimes includes not only sugar plantation laborers, but also factory workers and even second-generation U.S.-born inner-city residents. Primo, for example, occasionally referred to himself and to his friends as jíbaros, but he burst out laughing when I told him about the post–World War II image of jíbaros *ñangoteando* in their *bateys* to discuss the day's events. He not only did not know what the word *batey* meant, but he assured me that

> the only time I've ever "*ñangoteado*" was in the [prison] bullpen. But yeah, a whole bunch of us Puerto Ricans got down, *ñangoteando,* and we talked a lotta shit for hours.[4]

Primo may not be aware that his grandfathers and certainly his great-grandfathers had probably been small farmers who were forced to become seasonal sugar cane laborers when U.S. multinational companies took over Puerto Rico's rural economy. He is well aware, however, of the massive emigration that followed Puerto Rico's economic transformations. The figures are impressive: In the fifteen years following World War II, an average of 40,000 people left Puerto Rico annually. More than 75,000 left in 1953 alone. Coincidentally, this is the same year that Primo's mother, at the age of seventeen, abandoned her plantation shack in the cane fields of the coastal village of Arroyo to rent an apartment in East Harlem and find work in an inner-city sweatshop as a seamstress. Another 586,000 Puerto Ricans followed in her footsteps in the 1960s seeking new homes and jobs in the ghettos of New York City.[5] Few other countries in the world have exported such a large proportion of their population over such a short period of time to such a culturally hostile and economically alien host. Even the 2 million Irish who emigrated and the 1 million who starved during the potato famine of the late 1840s do not exceed in proportional numbers the 1.5 million Puerto Ricans – fully one-third of the total population of the Island who were wrenched from sugar cane fields, shantytowns, and highland villages to be confined to New York City tenements and later to high-rise public housing projects in the two decades after World War II.[6] At the time of the 1980 Census, 36 percent of all Island-born Puerto Ricans between the ages of twenty-five and forty-four were living in the mainland United States.[7]

Most Puerto Rican immigrants in the 1940s and 1950s found work in light manufacturing – specifically, garment factories – precisely at the historical moment when these jobs were beginning to leave the city in large numbers as the global economy was being restructured.[8] Service positions replaced manufacturing jobs as New York City became the logistical nodal point for the multinational corporations that have been closing their local production plants to relocate overseas where labor is cheaper. In the twenty years following Primo's birth in 1967, in East Harlem's municipal hospital, almost half a million factory workers lost their jobs as manufacturing employment dropped by 50 percent in New York City.[9]

To summarize, New York–born Puerto Ricans are the descendants of an uprooted people in the midst of a marathon sprint through economic history. In diverse permutations, over the past two or three generations their parents and grandparents went: (1) from semisubsistence peasants on private hillside plots or local haciendas; (2) to agricultural laborers on foreign-owned, capital-intensive agro-export plantations; (3) to factory workers in export-platform shantytowns; (4) to sweatshop workers in ghetto tenements; (5) to service sector employees in high-rise inner-city housing projects; (6) to underground economy entrepreneurs on the street. Primo captured the pathos of these macrostructural dislocations when I asked him why he sometimes called himself a jíbaro:

> *Primo:* My father was a factory worker. It says so on my birth certificate, but he came to New York as a sugarcane cutter. Shit! I don't care; fuck it! I'm just a jíbaro. I speak jíbaro Spanish. *Hablo como jíbaro* [I speak like a jíbaro].

One particular economic sector has benefited greatly from Puerto Rico's repeated social and economic metamorphoses: the U.S.-based multinational corporations who dominate its local economy. They have taken advantage of the Island's generous tax concessions to convert Puerto Rico into a haven for inflated corporate profits. This economic distortion was, once again, largely fueled by military strategic considerations. Following the Cuban revolution in 1959, the United States wanted to convert Puerto Rico into a free world showcase for capitalist economic development. The result has been a development strategy based on promoting private sector initiative through a policy of ten-year tax exemptions on investment in productive facilities. These tax giveaways have encouraged multinational corporations to manipulate transfer pricing schemes via local subsidiaries. The Island has the highest corporate profit rate of any country in the western hemisphere. As Puerto Rico's secretary of state boasted in 1990, "There is no single country in the world that produces as much net income for U.S. companies as Puerto Rico."[10]

The economic imperatives shaping the lives of Puerto Ricans have been compounded ideologically by an overtly racist "cultural assault." This is symbolized by the U.S. colonial administration's English-only policy in Puerto Rican schools until 1949.[11] For those who emigrated from the Island, culture shock has obviously been more profound. Literally overnight, the new immigrants whose rural-based cultural orientation and self-esteem was constructed around interpersonal webs of *respeto* [respect] organized around complex categories of age, gender, and kinship found themselves transformed into "racially" inferior pariahs. Ever since their arrival in the United States they have been despised and humiliated with a virulence that is specific to North America's history of polarized race relations and ethnically segmented immigrant labor markets.

The overwhelming changes imposed so rapidly on the formerly rural-based Puerto Rican population translate statistically into high rates of unemployment, substance abuse, broken families, and deteriorated health in New York's inner city. Few other ethnic groups, except perhaps Native American Indians, fared more poorly in official statistics than the 896,753 Puerto Ricans who lived in New York City at the time of the 1990 Census. They have the highest welfare dependency and household poverty rates, as well as the lowest labor force participation rates, of any other ethnic group in the city. In fact, in 1989 their poverty rate (38 percent) was double that of New York City's (19 percent). One statistical survey showed their family poverty rate in the late 1980s to be 500 percent higher than New York City's average. [12]

Although the 1990 Census documents significant improvement for several major cohorts of the Puerto Rican population – especially those who do not live in New York City – epidemiological health indexes reveal that Puerto Ricans suffer disproportionate hardship. This ranges from having the fastest growing HIV infection rates, the highest rates of bedridden disability, the most deaths caused by cirrhosis of the liver, and the highest rates of suicide attempts. In March 1993, Puerto Rican median household income in the United States was over $14,000 less than that for whites ($33,355 versus $18,999), and over $4,000 less than that of other latino groups. [13]

Confronting Individual Responsibility on the Street

From the safety of a desk or a reading chair, the Puerto Rican population's history of economic dislocation, political domination, cultural oppression, and large-scale migration easily accounts for why street culture in El Barrio might be so brutally self-destructive. On the street, however, faced with violent, substance-abusing individuals, a political-economy explanation for cause and effect is not so evident. To put it in more moralistic terms, when face to face with individuals like Ray,

Primo, or Caesar, one feels that no amount of "historical apology" and "structural victimization" exempts them from the consequences of their often violent, self-destructive, and parasitical actions. On a daily basis in their interpersonal interactions they impose suffering on their families, neighbors, and friends.

I discussed this complex theoretical issue of the relationship between structure and agency with most of the crack dealers I befriended. They, like most people in the United States, firmly believe in individual responsibility. For the most part, they attribute their marginal living conditions to their own psychological or moral failings. They rarely blame society; individuals are always accountable. Perhaps this comes from blending the stubborn individualism of a jíbaro past with the pioneer puritanism of the Anglo-immigrant legacy of the United States, and then pressure-cooking the syncretic result in the survival-of-the-fittest pragmatics of New York City's underground economy. At the same time, there exists in El Barrio an alternative, younger-generation variant of street culture that is almost political in its opposition to mainstream society. This tension was frequently manifest between Primo and his friend Caesar, who was five years younger:

> *Philippe:* So you see what I'm saying about your not having money, and there being racism, and . . .
>
> *Primo:* [interrupting] Felipe it's not only the white man . . . that makes it harder for us. We're poor, that's true, but we're supposed to struggle and make something of ourselves. It's just a harder struggle 'cause we're poor.
>
> *Caesar:* [interrupting] We're never gonna inherit nothing, unless we hit the Lotto.
>
> *Primo:* [ignoring Caesar] You have to do good for yourself in order to achieve, and you have to achieve in life in order to get somewhere. If you lay back, it's 'cause you want to lay back, and then you want to cry out for help later. The struggle's harder for the poor, but not impossible; just harder.
>
> When you're poor, you gotta have faith and respect for your own self.
>
> If I have a problem it's because I brought it upon myself. Nobody gotta worry about me; I'm gonna handle it. It's my problem.
>
> *Caesar:* That's a lotta bullshit man. This country's based on

making your money. Everybody wanna make money, live in the suburbs, and die.

Primo: Shut up Caesar. I hate it when you talk shit.

East Harlem's Immigrant Maelstroms

Ultimately, much of the analytical tension in this book focuses on how individuals deal with the forces that oppress them. In the case of El Barrio there is a another historical legacy of social marginalization that has nothing to do with Puerto Rico's colonial quandaries. When one situates Ray's crack dealers within the microhistory of East Harlem – and, more specifically, within the ten-square-block easternmost corner of their neighborhood – an almost ecological explanation for their lives of crime, violence, and substance abuse emerges. In short, the streets of East Harlem have always produced violent, substance-abusing felons no matter what immigrant ethnic group happened to be living there at the time.

The very first foreign immigrants, of course, were the Dutch, who stole Manhattan Island from the indigenous peoples who used to hunt and fish there. The only contemporary legacy of the Dutch is the neighborhood name for the post office, Hell Gate, on 110th Street, around the corner from Ray's Social Club crackhouse. It is an anglicized version of the Dutch name for the bay, *Hellegat* [sinkhole],[14] that is formed by the curve in the East River just above 96th Street. Three hundred and fifty years later, the lowland marshes along the bay of Hell Gate became the easternmost section of El Barrio where I lived and where Ray's crackhouses flourished. During the early 1600s, the area was the site of repeated bloody skirmishes between the encroaching Dutch Calvinist farmers and the original indigenous inhabitants. The last Amerindians forced out of what was to become the Hell Gate postal district were the Reckgawawanc in 1669. Soon after, East Harlem was covered with profitable Dutch-owned tobacco farms.[15] During the eighteenth and nineteenth centuries, before becoming one of the epicenters of immigrant poverty and substance abuse in New York City, East Harlem passed through a fashionable period as a countryside retreat for wealthy New Yorkers. Downtown Manhattan was a full hour and a half away by stagecoach. Even Franklin Delano Roosevelt's great-grandfather owned property in the patchwork of bucolic stream valleys and small farms that crisscrossed the district.[16] East Harlem's pristine rural isolation ended in the late 1800s with the ambitious construction of a massive network of inexpensive, privately owned public transportation arteries, coupled with large public sector investments by the City of New York in basic municipal infrastructure: The Harlem River Railroad along Park Avenue in the late 1830s; the Third Avenue Horse Railroad in 1870; the First Avenue Trolley in the 1880s; and, finally, the IRT Lexington Avenue Subway, which opened in 1903.[17]

Shortly after the turn of the century, consequently, East Harlem had convenient and inexpensive public transportation making it accessible to all of Manhattan, the Bronx, and parts of Brooklyn. These large-scale infrastructural construction projects inaugurated the arrival of the first wave of immigrant wage laborers in the 1880s and 1890s, converting East Harlem into one of the poorest and most culturally diverse neighborhoods in the history of the United States. The first permanent urban residents in the late 1800s were German and Irish Catholic construction workers who laid the trolley tracks and dug the subway tunnels that eventually crisscrossed all of Manhattan Island. They were followed by Central and Eastern European Jews who were fleeing the already overcrowded Lower East Side of Manhattan. East Harlem's cheap tenement apartments and its efficient public transportation made it an ideal locale for factory workers from downtown Manhattan sweatshops. The turn-of-the-century Jewish immigrants were accompanied or followed by a significant presence of African-Americans and Scandinavians. By 1920, in addition to two thriving Greek Orthodox churches, the neighborhood boasted New York City's highest concentration of Finns and Norwegians.

All accounts of East Harlem from this period grope for adjectives to describe its ethnic diversity. It was variously dubbed a "League of Nations" and a "kaleidoscopic sequence of racial additions."[18] The 1920 census cites the presence of 27 different nationalities: "Perhaps in few other spots throughout the world are so many races to be found in so small an area. The life in many parts of the Old World is reenacted here."[19] Social scientists in those years almost automatically interpreted national and ethnic diversity to be a negative, prime-moving sociological force: "Always, where so many tongues are found, Old-World mores of mothers and fathers temper the New World habits of their boys and . . . retard their progress."[20]

The Italian Invasion of East Harlem

It was in this multicultural working-class context that tens of thousands of rural southern Italians arrived at the turn of the century. They rapidly converted the neighborhood into what the Mayor's Committee on City Planning called in 1937 "probably the largest Italian colony in the Western hemisphere."[21] The very first Italians who arrived in the 1880s were brought by the management of the First Avenue Trolley to break a strike of Irish track layers.[22] The Italian immigrant shantytown coexisted tensely with an older conglomeration of shanties only two blocks away on 104th Street, which remained occupied by the striking Irish workers who had all been fired. Over the next three decades, competition for jobs and housing expressed itself in extreme ethnic segregation. Ethnic hostility penetrated even the most personal and spiritual dimensions of daily life. Local churches, for example, closed their doors to the new immigrants. A neighborhood study sponsored by a local Protestant church in 1910

Fifth Avenue between 116th and 117th Streets, 1889. Photo courtesy of the Museum of the City of New York.

somehow calculated that 79.5 percent of the community's residents were "nonassimilable."[23] When the German and Irish Catholics celebrated their first mass on December 4, 1884, in a large new church, Our Lady of Mount Carmel, built to minister to the same Hell Gate corridor served by Ray's crackhouses, the resident priest made the new Italian parishioners sit in the basement. Not until 1919 were Italian immigrants allowed to mingle freely with the rest of the parishioners.[24]

The handful of octogenarian Italian residents still living in the neighborhood along Pleasant Avenue – the five-block-long easternmost avenue of East Harlem – could still remember the names of the warring Irish and Italian gangs from that transition period. They enjoyed enumerating the blocks, and even the precise buildings, occupied by each different nationality group. During these first few decades, the Italian new-immigrants were pushed into the dirtiest, poorest avenues closest to the East River, whose banks – where Pleasant Avenue is now located – were described in 1900 as "all dumps, broken cars, broken wagons . . . junkyards, broken bottles, and rags."[25] This easternmost upper corner of the neighborhood is the exact same territory where Ray's network operated during my residence in El Barrio.

The racist uproar that accompanied the turn-of-the-century influx of rural southern Italians – mostly from Sicily – reverberated throughout larger New York City. Alarmed politicians denounced East Harlem's newest residents as being of "African racial stock." They were contrasted unfavorably to northern Italians living in other parts of the city, who were said to be "Germanic."[26] As early as 1893, the *New York Times* condemned the "lawlessness and vindictive impulses of the many immigrants from southern Italy living in East Harlem."[27]

Perhaps the most insidious manifestation of this ideological assault on the sense of cultural dignity and individual self-worth of the Italian immigrants was the practices and attitudes of those representatives from mainstream society who were supposed to be assimilating the immigrant children into Anglo-American culture. Schoolteachers reported that "the Italians are not eager to learn . . . they are very slow," and that "they . . . keep to themselves." A social worker complained that when she "asked an Italian family what they missed most here in America," the reply was " 'Living with our animals.' " Social science researchers from the period, despite their generally progressive orientations and their concern for writing socially responsible reports on behalf of the poor, could not help but reproduce the contemporary stereotypes that were so hostile to working-class immigrant Italians: "There is much delinquency and there are many feeble-minded and morons in the neighborhood."[28] In fact, Frederick Thrasher, the scholar generally credited with pioneering gang research, reported matter-of-factly in the 1930s that "all boys in the district were found to be on a lower intelligence level than the norms for their ages."[29] We now have sensitive autobiographical accounts of these years confirming the effects of prejudice on Italian-American adolescents living in the neighborhood.

> We soon got the idea that "Italian" meant something inferior, and a barrier was erected between children of Italian origin and their parents. This was the accepted process of Americanization. We were becoming Americans by learning how to be ashamed of our parents.[30]

The Puerto Rican "Invasion" of El Barrio

Predictably, when rural Puerto Rican immigrants began entering the neighborhood in the 1930s and 1940s, they received as negative a reception as had the Italians one or two generations earlier. Replacing Italians and Jews in the garment factories in the mid-1900s – just as Italians had replaced the Irish on the trolley track construction sites in the late 1800s – Puerto Ricans became the butt of physical and ideological assault. Leonard Bernstein's classic musical *West Side Story*, from the 1950s, captured for popular consumption an adolescent street-gang version of the structural antagonisms existing at the time between Italians and Puerto Ricans. In a less romanticized vein, the now classic autobiographies of Nuyorican literature – Piri Thomas's *Down These Mean Streets* and Edward Rivera's *Family Installments* – document in eloquent detail how newly arrived twelve- and thirteen-year-olds from rural Puerto Rico felt as they fought the Italian-American youths who were defending their traditional turf from the newest, darker-skinned immigrants. All the members of Ray's network who were more than twenty-five to thirty years old, vividly remembered being beaten up by Italian gangs from "Vinnie-land," which is what they called the easternmost blocks along the East River – First Avenue and Pleasant Avenue. Caesar's thirty-seven-year-old cousin, who moved out of the neighborhood and became an insurance agent in suburban Connecticut, summarized to me this historical transition:

> I remember when the whites moved out. I lived on 112th and we used to have fights with the Italians all the time. Those were the gang years. There was a lot of mafiosos around there – they still there.
>
> We used to have a lot of fights with the Italians down over here on First Avenue [pointing out the window].
>
> I even remember seeing an Italian beat a guy to death. You know, like with bats.
>
> [gunshots] but it wasn't with guns . . . maybe some zip guns.
>
> [more gunshots] Now it's Uzis.

At the street level, opposition to the metamorphosis of Little Italy into El Barrio during the post–World War II period was not limited to adolescent youth gangs. Local members of organized crime syndicates forced local landlords to maintain white segregated buildings. This was particularly true for the easternmost corner where I lived and where Ray maintained his crackhouses. For example, according to middle-aged residents, the first Puerto Rican immigrants were not able to move onto the particular block I lived on until Joe Rao, a hit man for the Genovese crime family, passed away in the early 1970s. Shortly after I moved into the neighborhood a real estate agent with dreams of gentrification complained to me that one of the lieutenants of the Genovese family had warned her to "think about who you want to rent to" when he saw a middle-class African-American couple visit a tenement she had just renovated.

Popular memory emphasizes the violence of the Italian–Puerto Rican confrontation, but in fact the very first link in East Harlem's latest chain of ethnic succession in the 1930s was the flight of upwardly mobile Jews, who left for more middle-class, homogeneously white neighborhoods. This was noted on the opening page of a report commissioned by the Jewish Welfare Board in 1931.

> The influx of Puerto Ricans (among whom there is a considerable Negro element) . . . into East Harlem has been a significant factor

in displacing the Jewish population which is moving largely to the Bronx and Brooklyn.[31]

The African-Americans who already populated isolated blocks within the neighborhood and represented 14 percent of the population, according to the 1930 Census, aroused less ire.[32] They may have been tolerated because of their restriction to segregated buildings and blocks. Perhaps their more profound socialization into North American–style racism resulted in more accommodating or self-effacing behavior. Hence, a researcher in the late 1920s noted with approval that barriers between black and white children were being broken down by the local librarian who "reads to them about little Black Sambo and tells them stories."[33] Less than twenty years later, however, the community was experiencing three-way race riots: African-American versus Italian-American versus Puerto Rican. In 1946, the neighborhood inspired a virulent *Time* Magazine editorial: "[It] is a venomous, crime-ridden slum called East Harlem, [populated] by hordes of Italians, Puerto Ricans, Jews, and Negroes."[34]

In general, however, it was the new Puerto Rican immigrants who generated the most antipathy on the part of mainstream society. They were poorer than everyone else. In fact, according to a 1929 hospital study, they were literally starving: "The large majority of Puerto Rican children examined were suffering from malnutrition."[35] Their health problems were, of course, expressed in a racist idiom. For example, from the 1920s through the 1940s public health hysteria erupted over the epidemics of tuberculosis and venereal disease that Puerto Rican immigrants were supposed to be infesting New York with. The nation's top medical specialists on tropical diseases "scientifically" legitimized the pariah status of Puerto Rican immigrants in New York:

Dr. Haven Emerson, a Columbia University expert on tropical diseases, says . . . that every Porto Rican[36] has within him germs of tropical diseases, venereal diseases and those which are looked on as minor "dirt diseases." This health problem does not worry the Porto Rican as much as it does New Yorkers for he has acquired an immunity to it. Pulmonary diseases show an increase in rate due to the prevalence amongst these people. They have primitive notions of child care due to conditions in which they lived in Porto Rico.

Many never saw a cow and do not know about the use of canned milk. . . . The Italian mother is more intelligent for she at least can use goat's milk.[37]

Once again, as in the case of Italian immigrants a generation earlier, academic discourse reflected the contemporary prejudices. One master's thesis completed by a second-generation Italian-American in 1931 refers to Puerto Ricans as "Spics," and notes that they are "invading" East Harlem.[38] Another thesis completed in 1930 describes Puerto Ricans as "bringing . . . low morals and low standards of living."[39] A 1935 study commissioned by the Chamber of Commerce of the State of New York claims that Puerto Ricans in East Harlem have "a marked and serious inferiority in native ability." Their average IQ scores were said to be 20.5 points lower than that of native-born Americans. The researchers complained that "few bright or even average Puerto Ricans were found."[40] With less academic and institutional legitimacy, a popular guidebook in the post–World War II period stated matter-of-factly:

Puerto Ricans were not born to be New Yorkers. They are mostly crude farmers subject to congenital tropical diseases, physically unfitted for the northern climate, unskilled, uneducated, non-English speaking, and almost impossible to assimilate and condition for healthful and useful existence in an active city of stone and steel.

. . . The Puerto Ricans all look alike, their names all sound alike and if an inspector calls in one of the swarming flats in the teeming tenements, nobody speaks English.

. . . Not only are many of these Puerto Ricans on relief [welfare] within an hour after their feet land on a dock or a secondary airport, but some are already booked on the dole in advance, while they are in the air or on the water.[41]

Poverty and Ecological Disrepair

Regardless of which ethnic group has prevailed in East Harlem since the 1880s, researchers and commentators have virtually unanimously decried the neighborhood's concentrated poverty, condemning it judgmentally.

East Harlem is one of the worst districts in the city. The boys have no respect for learning law or discipline . . . poverty and social maladjustment prevail.[42]

About one-half of the residents in the neighborhood may be classed as poor, and the other half as very poor.[43]

Physically, the neighborhood is repeatedly described as "congested and filthy" with deficient public sector infrastructure. Hence, the categorical criticism by a journalist in 1946: "Every service . . . is strained to the utmost . . . quite inadequate to care for such a population load."[44] Street descriptions from 1930 ethnographers could as easily apply to the 1890s as they do to the 1990s:

The street was very dirty, refuse of various kinds such as watermelon rinds, banana peelings, broken glass, old boxes and papers was everywhere in evidence . . . an empty store [had a broken window]. The sidewalks, the doorsteps, the windows, all showed people in great numbers.[45]

The exceptionally concentrated and segregated poverty of East Harlem has historically generated a denunciatory literature, both academic and artistic. This may be due to the visible proximity of this poorest neighborhood in Manhattan to the city's richest residential district, and because East Harlem is within walking distance of the most powerful art galleries and publishing companies in the United States. Most of the social science research on the neighborhood has involved some level of participant–observation fieldwork, usually around the poverty–pathology theme. In the 1920s and 1930s, the influential criminologist Thrasher, mentioned earlier in this chapter, devoted the last decade and a half of his life to studying juvenile delinquency in Italian Harlem. Through his institute at New York University he funded dozens of master's and doctoral dissertations, all premised on his ecological diffusionist notion of "interstitial areas." He posited that crime and social pathology emerged in expanding concentric circles from out of core urban poverty areas.[46] As simplistic or atheoretical as Thrasher's approach may appear half a century later, his research represented a progressive intellectual critique of the social Darwinist and racialist thinking of his era.

In the Introduction I discussed the next major theory on poverty to emerge, at least in part, on the basis of fieldwork in El Barrio. Known as the "culture of poverty theory" and developed by the anthropologist Oscar Lewis in the early 1960s, it was also originally intended to contribute to a national call for attention to the plight of the urban poor. Limited by the psychological-reductionist "culture and personality" school that dominated U.S. anthropology at that time, however, Lewis's theory backfired. By focusing on the poverty-reproducing psychological traits that are socialized into children by dysfunctionally poor families, his material is often interpreted as confirming the conservative, blame-the-victim individualistic interpretations of the persistence of poverty that dominate most popular thinking in the United States.

The artistic, literary, and multimedia productions the neighborhood has inspired have better withstood the test of time than have the social scientific theories. James Agee, the New York–based author who immortalized sharecropper poverty in the deep South during the Depression, made his way uptown to El Barrio during World War II accompanied by the photographer Helen Levitt. They made an experimental film on the energy of the children swarming the streets that is still occasionally presented in major museum exhibitions. Of more popular renown, El Barrio inspired Ben E. King's 1961 hit single, "A Rose in Spanish Harlem."[47] Finally, and most important, much of the Nuyorican literary genre is specifically set on East Harlem streets. This literary movement continues to be highly productive and to receive international worldwide recognition. In fact, it has emerged as a symbol of dignity and cultural resistance to poverty and social marginalization in the Puerto Rican diaspora.[48]

The Reconcentration of Poverty in Easternmost East Harlem

Public-policy makers and social scientists have not shared in the literary and artistic celebrations of East Harlem's inhabitants. On the contrary, as noted throughout this chapter, virtually all written accounts, from the turn of the century through the 1950s, are overwhelmingly negative in their portrayal of living conditions. Ironically, many of the academic or policy-oriented reports specify that the precise blocks where I lived and where Ray's network of crack dealers operated were the poorest and most delinquent section of Harlem. For example, a 1935 ethnographic report notes, "The nearer one comes to the East River . . . the more marked the deterioration."[49]

Presumably it was this persistent hypermarginalization that prompted in the late 1950s a massive, multimillion-dollar "urban renewal" program in the microneighborhood where the Game Room was located in the early 1990s. Typical of the public sector poverty policies from the period, the result was the physical destruction of several dozen square blocks of a functioning, working-poor community. Despite several denunciations in the local press, tens of thousands of the last remaining working-class Italian-Americans in the neighborhood were displaced by bulldozers in the name of "slum clearance."[50] Subsequently, several thousand poor Puerto Rican and African-American families were moved into the newly constructed red-brick high-rise housing projects to make it one of the most concentrated foci of dislocated poverty and anomic infrastructure in all of New York City.

In the early 1990s, according to the official statistics, 15,736 of the 40,162 families who lived in East Harlem resided in Housing Authority projects. This figure does not include the additional 20 percent who illegally overcrowded project apartments, or the several thousand families who relied on other forms of subsidized housing, such as Section-8. It is precisely this kind of physically concentrated and ethnically segregated poverty that allows violently self-destructive street cultures to engulf public space and vulnerable lives in so many inner-city, marginal, working-class neighborhoods throughout the United States.[51]

As urban renewal bulldozers were physically implementing economic and racial segregation in the 1950s and 1960s, despairing social workers filled the files of philanthropic aid societies with Pollyannaish reports on the dramatic decay of community life in Italian Harlem – slated to become El Barrio:

Basic requirements for even minimal living [are] lacking. . . . Robberies are frequent. The looting of water pipes, radiators, toilets, and bathtubs cause hardship to the remaining tenants. . . . Litter fills vacant apartments and hallways. Rats are a serious health menace. They occupy demolished buildings, and multiply and flourish in the buildings that remain.

. . . Derelicts congregate in vacant apartments to drink or use drugs, and people are fearful of entering or leaving their homes.

Nobody, not even an angel, can avoid trouble here! I feel sorriest
for the little kids – they've never known what a decent neighborhood is like![52]

With the advantage of historical hindsight these apocryphal social
worker reports confirm the cliché "plus ça change plus c'est la même
chose." (The more it changes the more it remains the same.) As a matter
of fact, I was able to find a 1956 Community Service Society report
describing a semi-inhabited tenement going up in flames on precisely the
same corner where I was living in 1990:

On a day in August, at the corner of [X]th street and [Y] Avenue,
we joined a group of recreation workers watching a bonfire almost
two stories high, burning the last traces of a house. . . . Smoke
was blackening the wall of an adjacent, partially-occupied dwelling,
where a woman gazed in consternation.
   . . . Dust from falling brick covered everything.
We became aware of an isolated window here and there – one
with a flower box or curtains, one framing a child's face.[53]

Twenty-four years later, I, too, found myself gazing in consternation
from my decrepit tenement apartment window at "a bonfire almost two
stories high, burning the last traces" of one of the few remaining tenements across an empty lot, catercorner from mine.

From Speakeasy to Crackhouse

Most relevant from the perspective of the street dealers this book ana-
lyzes, East Harlem has always been "one of the outstanding crime breed-
ing areas in greater New York City," according to the experts on delinquency.[54] Consistent with the first cash crop of the valley's original
Dutch tobacco-growing settlers, purveying addictive substances has been
an important source of income generation for local residents. Thrasher's
students, who combed the streets for their master's and doctoral theses in
the late 1920s, denounced the proliferation of "speakeasies on every
side."[55] They portray a filthy, demoralized community unable to control
its dens of iniquity.

Old brick buildings row on row, dingy, dreary, drab, wash flying like strings of pennants from the fire escapes, garments of a none too selected choice; streets littered with rubbish from push carts, busy curb markets of the district; "mash" in dark heaps in the gutter, silent evidence of a flourishing illegal industry; garbage in piles, thrown from kitchens where heavy, oily fare is prepared for gluttonous gourmands; pencilled or chalk lines on walls and side walks, indecent expressions of lewd minds; ground floor shops, unattractive warehouses of dusty stock; cellar pool rooms, "drink parlors," many curtained or shuttered, suggestive of their real business; human traffic busy about nothing in this squalid congestion.[56]

Sixty years later it is crackhouses and shooting galleries rather than speakeasies that are "on every side." While walking down my block, instead of tripping over "mash heaps" (the prime ingredient for bootleg liquor) I crunch under my feet plastic crack vials and an occasional hypodermic needle.

Once again, many of the details of crime and vice in the microneighborhood served by Ray's network have remained the same since the turn of the century. For example, La Farmacia's corner, where Ray's most profitable social club crackhouse was located, has always been a central locale for retail narcotics distribution. This is evident from the paper trail left by the embattled public library serving the Hell Gate corridor. It happens to be located a hundred yards from La Farmacia's corner, and during my residence the administrator of the library was the head of the neighborhood's Drug Busters Coalition. They spent an unsuccessful year and a half attempting to shut a shooting gallery that operated in an abandoned, city-owned building adjacent to the library in full view of the only window in the library's young-adult section. Unable to pressure the public authorities to shut down the shooting gallery, the Drug Busters Coalition negotiated a publicity agreement with the Coca-Cola Company to provide funds to demolish the shooting gallery tenement and build a children's park. This private sector–community collaboration, however, never materialized.

In the 1930s, instead of coke freaks, crackheads, and heroin junkies parading in front of the local library, it was alcoholics who were harassing patrons. In fact, the very same abandoned shooting gallery tenement from the early 1990s appears to have been a speakeasy in the late 1920s:

In the winter the janitor is called upon everyday or so to get drunk men out of the library. In the morning drunken men are seen lying around on the sidewalks so that policemen come and gather them up by the wagon load. The house directly back of the library . . . was raided and locked up for a year.[57]

These details of the historical continuity of speakeasies, brothels, crackhouses, and shooting galleries would be incidental if they did not profoundly affect the quality of day-to-day interactions among the majority of individuals who attempt to lead "healthy lives" in the neighborhood. Once again, this is encapsulated by the hostile relationship of the Hell Gate library to its surrounding blocks. The librarians are angry about their working conditions and distrust their patrons. Hence, early in my residence when I still had illusions about a functioning public sector in the neighborhood, I took Angel, an eleven-year-old neighbor, to the branch to get him a library card and to introduce him to "the miracle of free books." Not only were we unsuccessful but we were humiliated in the process by a hostile librarian. At the time, I assumed I fit the profile of a "dope fiend" engineering a scheme to steal library books by manipulating the image of an innocent child. In retrospect, I realized they might have thought I was a pedophile trying to entrap a new victim.

The Omnipresence of Heroin and Cocaine

Within the neighborhood's long heritage of a substance abuse–driven underground economy, heroin and cocaine have been the most disruptive to the daily quality of life. When the full economic effect of the new federal government policies of criminalizing narcotics in the United States were just being felt in the 1920s and 1930s, Thrasher's students already marveled at the remarkable profits to be made in the neighborhood by selling morphine and cocaine. Forty years later an undercover narcotics detective published a second-rate best seller, *The Pleasant Avenue Connection,* on exactly the same subject.[58]

Periodically, public opinion in the United States is swept by waves of concern over the prevalence of drug use.[59] La Farmacia's corner has often been featured prominently in the spate of photojournalistic essays that inevitably accompanies these almost cyclically recurring national drug scares. This happened, for example, in 1990.[60] The blocks surrounding La Farmacia's corner were also described in detail in a 1951 social worker's report commissioned by New York City's Welfare Council, entitled "The Menace of Narcotics to the Children of New York: A Plan to Eradicate the Evil." A junior high school youth is cited in the report describing 110th Street as a place where "men line up to get their injection . . . [and] almost go crazy."[61]

Thirty-nine years later, on October 19, 1990, Ray's clients made the front page of one of New York City's largest tabloids[62] for doing the exact same thing on the exact same corner, except that they were mixing Ray's cocaine with heroin in order to inject speedballs.

A plume of blood squirted into the dropper, mixing quickly with the heroin solution. He squeezed the dropper pushing the blood into his vein. . . . When he finished the others began the same dance of death.

. . . The junkies buy crack and heroin [and powder cocaine] on the corner of 110th Street and Lexington Avenue — one of the busiest drug locations in the city — and duck into . . . the lot to shoot.

For four decades, junior high school students have complained about the maelstrom of drugs overwhelming these same East Harlem blocks: " 'There's always people out there putting needles in their arms,' [said] sixth grader Karima Sappe. 'They don't care who comes around.' "[63] The situation was so bad in 1990, the teachers at the middle school on 111th Street covered the windows of their classrooms with black construction paper in order to block the view of the city-owned vacant lot where Ray's clients injected speedballs. The teachers had their students draw a make-believe sky with white chalk on the darkened windows.

Mafia Legacies in the Underground Economy

Once again, the historical continuity of visible substance abuse on the blocks where Ray and his workers grew up and worked would be an irrelevant coincidence if it did not have the profound effect of repeatedly socializing new generations of ambitious, energetic youngsters into careers of street dealing and substance abuse. Yet again, much of a 1951 social worker's report could have been written without any changes in 1991:

> Here is the way one boy put it: "Everybody is doing it. It is almost impossible to make friends who are not addicts. If you don't want to buy the stuff, somebody is always there who is ready to give it to you. It is almost impossible to keep away from it because it is practically thrown at you. If they were to arrest people for taking the stuff, they would have to arrest practically everybody."[64]

The same applies to Thrasher's simple insights from the early 1930s that the neighborhood's "criminal traditions" initiated "a vicious cycle" among youth:

> The organization and operation [of] underworld crime in East Harlem serves . . . to promote and encourage the juvenile demoralization which has later to eventuate in more crime.
> The names of successful gangsters and racketeers have become by-words in the mouths of the residents of the area and these men have often been canonized by the juvenile and adolescent community of the streets and by the gangs and clubs of boys and young men.[65]

Thrasher's students worried about the inappropriate reaction of Italian children to crime films in local movie theaters. In other words, an oppositional street culture was already being celebrated in the late 1920s:

> There is one characteristic typical of these Italian child audiences which has been noted by observations at various movies by social workers and patrolmen in the area. Enthusiastic applause greets the success of the villain and the downfall of any "cop" or representative of the "Law."[66]

A material logic explains much of the uninterrupted historical appeal of a criminally rooted oppositional street culture in East Harlem. The extraordinary profit-making potential of the neighborhood's underground economy was first institutionalized by the Italian Mafia, who converted the community into a supermarket for drugs and rackets. As early as

1893 a *New York Times* headline denounced organized crime in Italian Harlem: "Mafia Code in New York . . . Assassination a Favorite Penalty for Real or Fancied Wrong."[67]

Over the past century, organized crime has affected many intimate facets of daily life in the neighborhood, redefining "common sense" in favor of crime and violence. Journalists in the 1940s treated the corruption of the local police force as an obvious statement of fact.[68] One of Thrasher's students during Prohibition was reprimanded by an exasperated police officer for her naiveté: "Don't you know the police are too well paid to answer your questions."[69] A 1946 *New York Herald Tribune* article on the accessibility of weapons on East Harlem streets reads, once again, much like a 1990s newspaper article, describing "arms ranging from . . . sub-machine gun[s] to homemade rubber band pistols that police say can fire a .22 caliber cartridge with sufficient force to kill."[70] In the same vein, Thrasher's students documented the almost routinized experience of murder in a manner that would be very familiar to El Barrio residents in the 1990s. Indeed, it is interesting to compare the following two fieldwork excerpts. The first fieldwork note dates back to the late 1920s; I wrote the second in 1990:

> A man sat outside in a chair by the door. He pointed to [building] 234 and said, "Two men killed here. Hands up. Sunday night. Men played cards inside. No get money. Got away." The floor was strewn with broken glass from the doors and windows.[71]

> [June 1990] Waiting bored for Ray outside the Social Club crackhouse, Primo's cousin Luis began chatting about the childhood memories the block evoked. "Right there, right there on the wall [pointing]. Not inside the Club, but outside towards the Avenue. Yeah, right on that wall next to the fish store. I seen brains splattered right there."

Dramatic public assassination is normalized throughout the neighborhood by numerous "in memoriam" spray-paint graffiti paintings celebrating fallen friends. On an abandoned building around the corner from my tenement, a two-story graffiti "piece" advertised the famous Mafia hit squad Murder Inc., reputed to have been based in the neighborhood in the 1970s and early 1980s.

Through the 1980s, most youths growing up in East Harlem knew that the Genovese crime family — one of the five Sicilian "families" that run organized rackets in New York City — traditionally controlled their neighborhood. More concretely, local residents could point to the individuals who publicly flaunt the economic success they have achieved through violent crime. Coincidentally, "Fat Tony" Salerno, who was the don of the Genovese family, kept a residence on the corner of the same block where the Game Room and my tenement were located. My wife was the first of us to discover this when she complained to a friend that the produce stocked by the fruit store on our block was always rotten. Through a barrage of laughter, she was advised not to shop there anymore because her rotten-fruit sellers were really "Fat Tony's boys." They were overseeing his still active numbers-running bank.[72] These were the same men who rushed down to the court to pay his $2 million cash-up-front bail when he was arrested on February 25, 1985, exactly three days before I moved into my apartment down the block. Halfway through my residence, seventy-eight-year-old "Fat Tony" had 5 years added to the 170-year sentence he was already serving in prison.[73]

Despite his terminal incarceration, Fat Tony's organization continued to maintain several offices on the blocks surrounding me. Most were old-fashioned whites-only social clubs. The most important one was opposite the Our Lady of Mount Carmel Catholic church, where I baptized my son. Geraldo Rivera put it on prime-time television, jumping up and down outside the club, waving his finger at the black limousines double-parked in front of the church, and stabbing his microphone into the sullen faces of the tattooed Italian-Americans in their mid-twenties standing guard on the curb. Another block farther down was Rao's, one of New York's most exclusive restaurants in the 1980s. It was owned by Vince, the eighty-year-old brother of Joe Rao mentioned earlier as the person who obliged landlords to respect racial segregation through the early 1970s.[74] His restaurant had a three-month waiting list — presumably to screen the FBI officials who might be trying to pass as downtown yuppies excited about genuine Italian food served in a unique Mafia ambience. My "connected" Italian-American baby-sitter noted that the floors above the restaurant were the official meeting hall for high-level members of the Genovese clan. The windows on the top half of the building were covered with corrugated metal to make it appear semi-abandoned.

Out of fear of being killed, I made no concerted attempt to penetrate what was left of the ranks of traditional organized crime on my surrounding blocks. My caution was reinforced when a local real estate agent – once again named Vinnie – was assassinated in a bank lobby two days after I had applied for an apartment in one of his tenements. To make their message clear to whichever faction of organized crime was being sanctioned, the killers walked slowly out of the bank and left Vinnie's attaché case, which was stuffed with hundred-dollar bills, lying on his bloodied stomach. I decided to limit myself to interacting with Ray's network. As a matter of fact, I did not even bother requesting a refund of my application fee from Vinnie's secretary lest she surmise there was more than a coincidence between my visit to his office and his subsequent murder.

I occasionally encountered one of Fat Tony's loyal street lieutenants in the Chinese takeout restaurant next to his produce shop on my block. Even though he was always very friendly to me – obviously happy to see a new white face in the neighborhood – I never dared ask him why he sometimes made telephone calls at the pay phone on the corner while flanked by two men carrying army-issued mobile communications knapsacks and walkie-talkies. Nor did I ask him what was delivered to the basement of his produce store by the young African-American man wearing a cowboy hat and matching orange-pink leather outfit, who supervised the unloading of dozens of "plaster of paris" sacks from the trunk of his maroon Jaguar.

Although the Genovese family is said to be especially powerful in union rackets, such as the New York City District Council via the United Brotherhood of Carpenters and Joiners, there was something pathetic – and at times comic – about the way their operations were decaying in East Harlem during my years of residence in the neighborhood.[75] It is as if they resisted the logic of upward mobility and ethnic succession that the other four families have taken advantage of in New York City's underworld. One can detect a distinct lack of respect for the East Harlem–based Genovese clan among the other New York City godfathers. According to the FBI, when Paul Castellano, the head godfather of New York's infamous Mafia Commission, was arrested along with the four other Mafia clan heads, he burst out laughing over how badly dressed Fat Tony was.[76] The ultimate local humiliation of the Genovese family occurred halfway through my residence when the studio apartment above

Fat Tony's fruit stand–numbers bank was burglarized. Our Italian-American baby-sitter was visibly shaken. "I says, 'Where am I? The dark ages?' I says, 'This can't be!' " Even at the height of the race riots in the 1960s no one had dared touch any of the Italian-owned businesses in Fat Tony's vicinity, "There was respect for us back then."

A local real estate agent who thought I was interested in purchasing East Harlem tenements admitted that petty street crime had increased since Fat Tony's indictments in the late 1980s. She reassured me, however, that the problem could be solved by installing steel doors – as she had done on the building she herself had bought from Fat Tony several years ago. She also noted that the federal racketeering indictments had artificially depressed the local real estate market because Fat Tony and his associates were hastily selling their tenements to pay their lawyers' fees. The real estate agent also assured me that since the demise of the mob:

> There's just not a lot of negativity anymore about renting to a black tenant. Back in 1985, you had to have a certain respect for the lay of the land – if you understand what I mean. Now, they just don't pay as much attention to the neighborhood.

Once again, on the positive side, she explained that Fat Tony's "political clout" in City Hall had lasted long enough to ensure that the blocks east of Second Avenue were not overwhelmed by city-financed social welfare programs that were renovating abandoned tenements in the late 1980s and early 1990s to resettle homeless families.

The Free Market for Crack and Cocaine

The demise of Mafia hegemony on the street occurred just as the underground economy was redefining itself around cocaine and crack in the mid-1980s, which were supplanting heroin as the undisputedly most profitable product. The vigor of the crack–cocaine economy during the late 1980s and early 1990s was largely the result of an aggressive federal drug policy prioritizing the criminal repression of smuggling. Sometime in the early to mid-1980s, marijuana importers working the Latin American supply routes adapted to the escalating levels of search-and-seizure they were facing at U.S. borders by switching from transporting marijuana to trafficking in cocaine. Cocaine is much easier to transport clandestinely because it takes up only a fraction of the physical space occupied by the equivalent dollar value of marijuana. U.S. inner cities consequently were flooded with high-purity cocaine at bargain prices shortly after the federal government increased drug interdiction efforts. According to the Drug Enforcement Administration, the kilo price of cocaine dropped fivefold during the 1980s from $80,000 to $15,000.[77]

The Colombian organized crime cartels who have historically maintained a monopoly over cocaine production and transport, responded vigorously to the new market opportunities in the early 1980s and violently bypassed the traditional networks of the Italian-dominated Mafia that specialized in heroin. The Colombians tapped directly into the entrepreneurial urge that is such an integral facet of the American Dream. The magic of a highly competitive market spawned a new, more profitable product – crack, which is, as noted in the Introduction, merely an alloy of cocaine and baking soda. The admixture of baking soda, however, allows the psychoactive agent in cocaine to be released when smoked. Powder cocaine, on the other hand, can only be sniffed or injected. The capillaries in the lungs have a greater absorption capacity than the arteries of the musculoskeletal system or the veins in the nostrils. Consequently, crack delivers the psychoactive effects of cocaine to the brain with maximum efficiency and speed. Furthermore, within minutes of smoking, crack users crave another exhilarating rush of 2 minutes and a half. They are not content with the subtler, longer-term high that comes from sniffing powder cocaine. This makes crack a perfectly flexible consumer commodity. Even though individual doses are inexpensive and therefore accessible to the poor, a user with money can spend virtually infinite sums in a single extended session of binging. This technological and marketing breakthrough of alloying cocaine to baking soda unleashed the energy of thousands of wanna-be mom-and-pop entrepreneurs who were only too eager to establish high-profit, high-risk retail crack businesses. Hence, in late 1985, the Game Room, which had been a struggling candy store selling nickel bags of marijuana, upgraded itself to become a video arcade purveying $10 vials of crack.

Crack and cocaine inaugurated the next phase in the long tradition of ethnic successions in East Harlem's underground economy. New, energetic networks like Ray's filled the vacuum left by the Italian Mafia's upward mobility, and its clumsy fumbling of cocaine–crack marketing. Even on the last two easternmost blocks of the Hell Gate corridor, where the Mafia had once so proudly and violently ruled, upstart Puerto Rican, African-American, and Dominican entrepreneurs began struggling for control of sidewalk crack-sales points.

Although no longer as powerful as it once was locally, the old-fashioned Mafia has left a powerful institutional and ideological legacy on East Harlem by demonstrating decisively that crime and violence pay. This, of course, is periodically reinforced by mainstream society with the recurring financial scandals on Wall Street and in the banking world. Caesar certainly absorbed the message, and put it into practice in his job as lookout at the Game Room.

Caesar: The only way you could survive in this world is to be connected or to be connected dirty. You got to be making your money dirty like the Eye-talians.

And if you're clean, you still got to be gettin' over white-collar dirty. Because you're dirty. You're already rich but you're conniving, sca-niving deals.

Like that thing they had on the news about them [savings and loan] banks . . . like that Silverado shit that, that dude – that the taxpayers have to pay billions of dollars 'cause of that.

Why do these people get away with that? That's what I want to know.

3

CRACKHOUSE MANAGEMENT: ADDICTION, DISCIPLINE, AND DIGNITY

Hell, yeah, I felt good when I owned the Game Room. In those days everybody be looking for me; everybody needed me. When I drove up, people be opening the door for me, and offering to wash my car. Even kids too little to understand anything about drugs looked up to me.

Felix

The logistics of selling crack are not dramatically different from those of any other risky private sector retail enterprise. Selling high-volume, inexpensive products is an inherently boring undertaking that requires honest, disciplined workers in order to be successful. Such businesses are inherently rife with traditional management versus labor confrontations, as well as internal jealousies or rivalries within employee hierarchies. It is only the omnipresent danger, the high profit margin, and the desperate tone of addiction that prevent crack dealing from becoming overwhelmingly routine and tedious. The details of how the Game Room was run during the years I lived next to it provide a good example of these dynamics.

Living with Crack

Ray did not found the Game Room. The person who actually established the 250-square-foot video game arcade as a crackhouse was a childhood friend of his named Felix, who was also Primo's first cousin. Felix did not run a tight operation; he reveled too much in street-corner glory and consequently did not insulate himself from the police by hiring a manager, or at least some intermediary worker-assistants, to make the actual

The Game Room crackhouse. Photo by Philippe Bourgois.

hand-to-hand sales. Instead, for the first year after opening shop he ran every detail of his crackhouse operation with the exception of the "cooking" of the crack – its processing – which he delegated to his wife, Candy, in traditional patriarchal style. The bulk of Felix's energy at the Game Room was devoted to cultivating sexual liaisons with addicted women – especially teenage girls.

During this early phase of the crack epidemic in late 1985, Primo was one of Felix's steadiest customers. He had lost his job as a messenger-clerk at a typesetting shop, had broken up with his wife, and had abandoned all pretense of supporting their two-and-a-half-year-old son. Instead, he had returned home to his fifty-year-old mother's nineteenth-floor housing project apartment, where he shared a cramped bedroom with one of his three older sisters. While his mother sewed all day in the living room for an off-the-books garment subcontractor to supplement her welfare payments, Primo dedicated himself full time to hustling and robbing for his crack habit.

In later years, in front of his friends, workers, and even his customers, Primo enjoyed reminiscing about the desperate year he spent as a crack addict:

Primo: I was in my own habit world. I didn't give a fuck about anything.

Let me tell you about one time when I was on a mission [crack binge]. I wanted a blast [catching the eyes of his crack-addicted lookout Caesar].

Caesar: [spinning around from his position in the doorway] Yeah, yeah. Your only worry was making a cloud in your *stem* [glass crack pipe].

Primo: One time I was with my homeboy and his girl. We saw this Mexican sleeping on the floor in the lobby of my aunt's building. He was just probably drunk. He looked like he had a job, maybe, because a homeless would not have had a gold ring.

As soon as I saw him, I just went, *"Tú times la hora"* [You got the time]? And as he got the time [making the motion of looking at a wristwatch], I grabbed him by the back of the neck, and put my 007 [knife]¹ in his back [grabbing me in a choke hold from behind], I put it in his back — right here [releasing me to point to his lower spine]. And I was jigging him *hard!* [grinning, and catching his girlfriend Maria's eye].

Caesar: Them Mexican people get drunk like real crazy man. Everybody be ripping them off; they easy prey 'cause they illegal most of them.

Primo: I said: *"No te mueva cabrón o te voy a picar como un pernil"* [Don't move motherfucker or I'll stick you like a roasted pig]. [we all chuckle.]

Yeah, yeah, like a piece of *pernil* – a pork shoulder . . . like how you stab a pork shoulder when you want to put all the flavoring in the holes.

Caesar: Everybody take Mexicans like a joke. It's a little crime wave. Mexicans be fucked-up with crime in New York. That's like the new thing to do.

Primo: The Mexican panicked. He looked like he wanted to escape, but the more he tried to escape, the more I wouldn't let go and the more I was jigging him.

And I had a big 007. I wasn't playing, either, I was serious. I would have jigged him. If he would have made an attempt, I would have went like CHKKK [grimacing painfully while twisting his wrist forward in a slow-motion stab].

And I'd regret it later, but I was looking at that gold ring he had. [chuckle].

I put the Mexican to the floor, poking him hard, and my homeboy's girl started searching him.

I said, "Take everything, man! Search for everything!"

She found his chain. I said, "Yo, take that asshole's fucking ring too."

He was going: [imitating a high-pitched whine] "Oh no! Por favor, por favor!"

It must have been like a thing he treasured, maybe. He was saying "Take whatever else, but not the ring." I said, "Fuck that shit, you don't have enough money homeboy. [gruffly barking his words like a foreman at a construction site] Take the fucking ring off his finger!"

After she took the ring we broke out. We sold the ring and then we cut out on her to go get a blast.

Caesar: Yeah, yeah. You was smoking heavenly.

Primo: We left her in the park, she didn't even get a cent.

Caesar: Smokin' lovely.

Primo: She helped for nothing – got jerked.

Caesar: [frazzled by his images of smoking crack] The only reason I get high is because I love it. The first blast is the best'est one. It's like a Ruffle potato chip. You just can't have one. You need more, 'cause it's good.

It's a brain thing. It's thick. Once you take that first blast, then the whole night is going to be a total adventure into madness. It's just a thing, you have to have more.

Primo: Chill the fuck out Caesar! Why you always be interrupting me when I'm talking with Felipe?

At the height of his own crack-smoking days, Primo's life took a dramatic turn when Felix's out-of-control machismo provided him with a brand-new, well-paid job opportunity.

Felix was hanging around with some woman in a hotel in New Jersey. It was on the second floor, and Candy – his wife – had found out about it and came looking for him.

And so Felix jumped off from the second floor landing and he fucked up his foot, so he couldn't work.[2]

The next day Felix asked me if I would help him out. From that day on, I just stood working here.

Once Felix's ankle recovered, he maintained Primo as manager of daily sales in order to devote even more time to hanging out on the street. He came frequently to the Game Room to display his "sexual conquests" – usually crack-addicted young women. Felix's antics allowed Primo to keep his job, which provided the stability and sense of self-worth that finally allowed him to kick his crack habit after twelve months of steady smoking.

Primo's dream of going straight almost came to a crashing end when Felix's wife, Candy, who was six months pregnant at the time, shot Felix in the stomach to punish him for sleeping with her sister. As soon as Felix recovered from his hospital stay, he was sent "upstate" to prison to serve an unrelated two- to four-year prison sentence for weapons possession. Candy immediately sold the rights to the Game Room for $3,000 to Ray, who himself had just completed a four-year sentence upstate for assault with a deadly weapon, following his $14,000 rooftop shoot-out above the heroin den he was holding up.

Restructuring Management at the Game Room

After a tense week or two of negotiations, which temporarily drove Primo back to binging on crack, Ray maintained Primo as manager of the Game Room on an eight-hour shift from 4:00 p.m. to midnight. The price of vials was dropped to five dollars to make them more competitive with two new teenage outfits operating in the stairwells of the housing project opposite the Game Room where vials were selling for three dollars and even two dollars on discount nights. Primo was to be paid on a piece-rate basis, receiving one dollar for every five dollars he sold. Primo had been held up at shotgun point several weeks earlier and obtained the right from Ray to hire any lookouts or assistants he wanted, so long as he paid them out of his own piece-rate wages. Ray imposed stricter limits, however, on the behavior of noncustomer visitors in order to reduce crowding and noise levels on the stoop in front of the crackhouse.

Ray proved to be a brilliant labor relations manager. Over the years, I watched him systematically extract higher and higher profit margins from his problematic workers. Having grown up in El Barrio as a gang leader in the early 1970s, he knew how to discipline his workforce firmly without overstepping culturally defined rules of mutual respect. He knew exactly where to set violent limits, and when to express friendship and flexible understanding without ever revealing vulnerability.

Ray was particularly skillful in his manipulation of kinship networks to ensure the loyalty of his often addicted and violent workers. The majority of his employees were blood-related kin, or were affiliated through marriage, or had been incorporated through a fictive kinship arrangement. He asked Primo, for example, to be the godfather of one of his sons, thereby establishing a *compadre* relationship. The institution of *compadrazgo* is a powerful tradition in Puerto Rican culture that sanctifies solidarity and reciprocal obligations between men. Ironically, several generations earlier, back in the mountains of rural Puerto Rico, local landlords had probably manipulated this same paternalistic godfather institution to coerce the indebted day-labor of Ray and Primo's grandfathers or great-grandfathers.[3] In his more modern context, Ray also benefited from the contemporary street-culture kinship arrangements that oblige women to establish serial households with different men through their life cycles. Hence, his childhood friendship with his employee, Luis, was cemented into a quasi kin-relationship by their having fathered children with the same woman.

In the first few weeks following his takeover of the Game Room, Ray's business acumen – specifically his lowering of prices and his raising of the quality of the product – made business boom. The Game Room easily outcompeted the low-quality powder cocaine sold out of a grocery store four doors down as well as the budget-rate crack hawked by teenage crews in the project stairwells across the street. An immediate crisis for control of the site erupted, however, when a police offensive against drug dealing in public school playgrounds pushed several Dominican-run heroin companies onto the block. All of a sudden our sidewalk was swarmed by half a dozen four-man teams, each with two lookouts, one pitcher, and a runner. After some tense face-offs, Ray pressured the Dominican managers to respect his space and move across the avenue.

Within a few months, Ray had invested his Game Room profits into opening two new franchises: one — which was relatively short-lived — in the second-floor apartment of a condemned building being renovated by New York City funds to become subsidized public housing; and the other, the Social Club on La Farmacia's corner by the Hell Gate post office. During this initial period of expansion Primo basked in a distinctly privileged position within Ray's budding network of crackhouses:

> I was the first one of the regular crew to start working with this guy [Ray]. I was saving money; I wasn't getting high — only a few beers occasionally. And I used to hang out with Ray. At that time, he didn't have no cars yet. He use to be on foot. And I use to stay with him, hanging around every night.
>
> Both of us used to go home with a knot [wad of bills] and save a coupla' hundreds. The next day, I used to come down with change — you know, thirty or forty dollars — money in my pocket to spend while I was working.

As a formal, founding member of Ray's growing organization, Primo was eligible for the benefits that are part of a crack dealer's pay — such as bail money and lawyer's fees, bonus payments during special holidays (Christmas, Easter, and Father's Day), periodic gifts for his son, and an occasional lobster dinner at Orchard Beach, Coney Island, or Far Rockaway. Primo's lookouts, on the other hand, were a step lower in the hierarchy. There is probably no work site in the legal economy where Primo could ever aspire realistically to becoming a manager, or even a privileged employee within his first year of being hired. Toward the end of my residence on the block, I frequently asked Primo to give me retrospective accounts of the half-dozen workers he had hired over the five years I knew him at the Game Room.

> *Primo:* [sitting on a car hood in front of the Game Room] The first one that worked for me was Willie. I used to feed him and give him a coupla' dollars at the end of the day.
>
> After him came Little Pete — I used to give him a hundred and fifty dollars a week. Strictly one fifty — plus beers — things like that. After Little Pete came Benzie because Little Pete got promoted fast by Ray to the Club [on La Farmacia's corner].

I used to pay Benzie daily. I used to give him thirty-five or forty dollars, sometimes fifty on a good night – which is not a lot – but I was treating Benzie better than the others. So after a while I let Benzie keep half and half. Me and him, we used to split everything.

I hired Caesar permanently because of problems between Benzie and Ray. Before that Caesar was only part time because he was always acting too stupid. He used to get jealous because of Benzie. But I told Caesar, "You can't sell, 'cause you're a crackhead and you fuck up."

There's always a problem paying Caesar. I don't know what to do with that nigga' [waving dismissively at Caesar, who was standing in the doorway]. He's been acting stupid. I gotta talk to him.

Philippe: You sound like a fuckin' hard-ass boss, complaining about your workers' attitude problems.

Primo: Nah Felipe. I don't act like no boss. I don't bitch. I have never succeeded with power in here. Even when I had little thirteen-year-old Junior helping me out – you know, Felix's son – he would say "Okay, okay, shut up already" to me when I would tell him to do something.

The only time I have full authority is when I'm really pissed off, but I don't really want to boss you around just to boss you around.

I have to keep things from getting too fucked up here because I'm responsible. If anything is missing, I'm gonna hear it from Ray.

All of them [waving disdainfully at Caesar again] used to like to take over the whole show.

[loud gunshots]. Yo! Chill out Felipe. Why you so *petro?*

So . . . after I put Benzie to work, he used to act like he owned the whole show. It's like he feels power just because he's dealing, so he feels like he could *diss* [disrespect] all the customers. He used to *dish* [mispronunciation of diss] some good people, especially all the men.

He dissed them, like . . . like they were kids – like shit. And these guys, they do what they do, but they're human beings and they're cool, you know. I used to tell him lots of times to "cool the fuck out." I'd have to tell him "I know this guy; talk to him nicely. *Respétalo,* bro!" [respect him]. But he wouldn't play by the rules.

He was treating people like shit. So I brought Caesar back, but *también* [also] he thinks he's running the whole show.

Philippe: Isn't Caesar worse than Benzie?

Primo: Bohf [both] are bad. But Caesar is worser because he don't give a fuck about anybody. I don't even trust him anymore.

Indeed, I vividly remember Benzie chanting triumphantly to oncoming customers, "That's right, mah' man! Come on! Keep on killing yourself; bring me that money; smoke yourself to death; make me rich." Of course, Primo ultimately was not much more courteous to his clients. He sometimes joined his colleagues in ridiculing the walking human carcasses that so many street-level crack addicts become after several months of smoking. In the Game Room, this was often conjugated by an explicitly racist and sexist dynamic:

Caesar: Felipe, you shoulda seen these two dirty *moyo* motherfuckers who came by here earlier. It was a *moreno* [African-American][4] and his girl.

Primo: [laughing] She slipped on her ass walking out the door.

Caesar: And she musta broke that ass, 'cause she tripped and fell face first.

Primo: I saw her limping . . .

Caesar: She got damaged, man, because she hit that iron thing that we got there stuck in the cement.

She limped off. She limped away real fucked up. But homeboy didn't give a fuck that his woman fell down; he just walked away.

[perhaps noticing my silence, he shook his head righteously] It was wrong, boy.

Primo: [ignoring me and laughing at Caesar's righteousness] No man, he was thirsty!

Caesar: Yeah! Yeah! He was like, "Fuck her. Ah'm'a' smoke." [inhaling deeply with a blissful grin, and then spinning around to face me] I don't care what you think Felipe, *morenos* be more fucked up and eviler than Puerto Ricans. Because when she fell I said, "Oh, shit, you all right there?"

But her man, he was like . . . he jumped over her and walked out in front of her.

Curbing Addiction and Channeling Violence

Primo's close friendship with Caesar was a complicated one. Caesar's drinking often unleashed uncontrollable outbursts of aggression and when he binged on crack – which was almost every time he got paid – he ended up borrowing or stealing from everyone around him. Nevertheless, for the last three years of my residence on the block Caesar and Primo were inseparable. Caesar lasted the longest of all the lookouts and other crackhouse assistants whom Primo hired.

Sometimes I thought Primo tolerated Caesar's poor work discipline because he sympathized with Caesar's crack addiction. He seemed to be providing Caesar with the same kind of supportive environment for quitting that he had been afforded by Felix when he was first hired to sell at the Game Room. At other times I suspected that the reason all of Primo's subcontracted employees – Willie, Benzie, Little Pete, and Caesar – were crack addicts was because this enabled Primo to pay them lower wages and to impose more dependent working conditions. Often he substituted payments-in-kind (vials of crack) for cash remuneration at the end of the shift. Of course, Primo did not have much choice since most of the people in his world were crack users. On a few occasions, Primo acknowledged his manipulation of the addiction of his workers as well as his own dependence on Ray for steady cash to buy powder cocaine and alcohol for himself.

> *Primo:* It was stupid slow tonight. The shit we're selling is whack. I've only got thirty dollars for me, and I gotta give half to Caesar.
>
> But since it's so slow we just don't give each other money, we just spend it together.
>
> Plus, you see, we had already borrowed money from Ray from before so we have to pay him back little by little.

As if to illustrate his words, almost without breaking stride, Primo handed a ten-dollar bill to an emaciated coke seller who happened to be standing in our path, and pocketed a half-inch-long vial of white powder. Caesar had walked ahead of us and did not hear Primo whisper to me:

Primo: Caesar doesn't really keep track of it. I can jerk him. It's not no fifty-fifty thing.

Despite regularly drinking liquor and sniffing cocaine with Caesar, Primo genuinely tried to wean his friend and worker away from his more destructive and uncontrollable crack binging. Over the years, he experimented with half a dozen different schemes to rehabilitate Caesar and convert him into a more disciplined worker.

Caesar was always fucking up. He always wanted me to pay him each night, but then he'd take the money and break out to smoke. He'd come find me later, begging me for more money.

I'd say, "You stupid? I paid you already. Don't do that shit to me. You crazy, boy? Don't ask me for no money. I gave you your fucking pay."

Then the next day, he wouldn't show up for work or he'd come late. So then I didn't use to pay him daily. I used to pay him at the end of the week when Ray pays me.

Even that didn't work. [pausing to sniff out of a folded dollar bill full of powder cocaine] I was tired of him doing that to me. So one day, when I paid him, I said, "If you go and fuck this up and don't come in tomorrow. I'm not going to keep on working with you no more, because I'm getting tired of you."

Shortly after that is when I hired Benzie, who was still one of my customers at the time.

A year or so earlier, Primo had fired his friend Willie – nicknamed "O.D." because of his overdose-style of binging – for exactly the same reason. According to Primo, O.D.'s addiction was even more unacceptable since he smoked during work hours. Under pressure from his father, Willie joined the army. He was the only person in Ray's network able to enter the military because he was the only one to have a high school degree – which he had obtained on a fluke affirmative action program in a downtown elite private high school that has since declared bankruptcy. Trained as a tank driver, he miraculously escaped the Gulf War in January 1991 when he happened to be on furlough in East Harlem binging on crack. He simply prolonged his binge and went AWOL.

Despite Primo's perennial complaints – compared to an addict like OD or a street culture prima donna like Benzie – Caesar did an excellent job as lookout. He personified the personal logic of violence in the street's overarching culture of terror by intimidating everyone around him with his reputation for unpredictable outbursts of rage. The only person who ever disrespected the Game Room premises while Caesar was on duty was a jealous young man high on angel dust. He was subsequently carried away from the premises with a fractured skull. I cannot forget hearing the nauseating thump of the baseball bat that caught the offending man squarely on the forehead just as the Game Room door behind me shut as I was fleeing the scene. Primo later confided in me that he had to restrain Caesar after three blows to keep him from killing the man while he lay unconscious on the floor. Caesar loved to remind me and anyone else within earshot of the event. It was good public relations for ensuring the security of the premises.[5]

> *Caesar:* That nigga' was talking shit for a long time, about how we pussy. How he fuckin' control the block and how: [putting his hands on his hips and waving his head back and forth, imitating a spoiled child's taunts] "I can do whatever I want."
>
> And we were trying to take it calm like until he starts talkin' this'n'that, about how he gonna drop a dime on us [report us to the police].
>
> That's when I grabbed the bat – I looked at the ax that Primo keeps behind the Pac-Man but then I said, "No; I want something that's going to be short and compact. I only gotta swing a short distance to clock the shit out of this motherfucker."
>
> [shouting out the Game Room door] You don't control shit, because we rocked your fuckin' ass. Ha! Ha! Ha!
>
> [turning back to me] That was right when you ran out the door Felipe. But the bottom line, Felipe, is survival of the fittest – or survival with a helmet, because I had got wild.
>
> Now I gotta try to get Ray to lend me his Lincoln.

Another benefit Caesar derived from his inability to control his underlying rage was a lifelong monthly social security insurance check for being – as he put it – "a certified nut case," which he periodically reconfirmed by occasionally attempting to commit suicide.

In Ray's judgment, Caesar was too out of control to be trusted, and he was never formally hired into the network. Ray was much more cautious than Primo about whom he hired. Only in exceptional cases did he give breaks to full-blown addicts or excessively violent individuals. Caesar was acutely aware of Ray's rejection of him, but nevertheless continually aspired to formal inclusion in his organization.

> *Caesar:* Ray don't pay me directly, I'm subcontracted by Primo.
>
> If I go to jail, I'm Primo's responsibility but Ray will look out for me, 'cause he likes to keep me around too, for security reasons. He wants to slide me into the organization.
>
> Plus I don't got no felony arrests. I got the cleanest [criminal] record out of anybody working for Ray. If I got busted, he knows I wouldn't jerk him for the bail money like Benzie did. I'd keep going to court and I wouldn't drop a dime.

Benzie, the lookout who replaced Caesar, was also a crack addict, but unlike Caesar he followed Primo's example and used his position as drug dealer as a trampoline for overcoming his crack addiction by substituting it for a less virulent powder cocaine habit occasionally supplemented by heroin. This allowed for a less hierarchical relationship and Primo promptly promoted him to partner. Particularly interesting in Benzie's case is that he had originally been holding a permanent legal job as a janitor's assistant at an exclusive men's club in midtown Manhattan at the time that Primo offered him the position of lookout. It was only once he fully immersed himself in street culture's underground economy as a powerful figure – a dealer – that he was able to stop using crack. In other words, Benzie started using crack while working legally, and not until he quit his legitimate job to work full time as a crack dealer was he able to kick his crack habit. The responsibilities of his new position as a street seller forced him to straighten out.

> *Primo:* After I fired Caesar I started working by myself again until, somehow, some way, this guy [pointing to Benzie] started giving me hints that he wanted to work, and I liked'ed him. [pausing to sniff again]
>
> So I started asking him, "You wanna work here?" 'Cause I

wanted to take it easy. [sniffing from the tip of a key dipped into a ten-dollar glassine packet of heroin and passing it to Benzie]

Benzie: [sniffing] At the time I was working legit with my Pops at the Yacht Club as a maintenance engineer. I used to come over here [to the Game Room] after work.

When Primo hired me that gave me two jobs.

You know at what time I used to get up to get to the Yacht Club? Five o'clock in the mornin' because I used to have to be there at seven – and right on the dot! From seven until three-thirty I be at the Yacht Club. Then at four I had to be at the Game Room [sniffing heroin].

Primo: So I told him, "Thirty dollars a day, six days a week. 'Cause I don't work Sundays."

He said, "Yeah, yeah, that's good." So he hung out.

And after that, time went by. I saw he was cool – that he wasn't smoking so much. I used to take him to the [Social] Club and buy a bottle of Bacardi and feed him food, and we'd be sniffing. [pausing to crush a fresh vial's worth of cocaine in a dollar bill]

So one time, I told him, "Go ahead, serve." Then after a while [sniffing cocaine], I told him, "Whatever we sell, we gonna divide equally each day. That way, you could make some money."

Because I was gettin' paid back in them days. [throwing his head back and sniffing heavily] I used to get like two hundred, two-fifty, three hundred, even four hundred dollars a night for eight hours work. The least I would get is two hundred – two-fifty dollars a night.

Benzie: Yeah, we was *making* money then, boy! Bohf making two-something a night.

Primo: We used to clock, man. This shit [pointing to the back of the Pac-Man machine, where the crack vials were stashed] used to sell like hotcakes.

I'm a fuckin' idiot man. I should have bought something so that my money would have been still here.

But as soon as Benzie started working with me it was all party. And my money is history. That money just flew, boy. I spent it [spitting the words] on hotels, coke, liquor. It was easy come, easy go. I used to treat for everything with everybody – Benzie, Caesar,

O.D. – everybody. I just wanted friends. Everyday we was hoteling it. Hotels cost money, man.

It's too bad I didn't see you a lot in those days Felipe. We could've really enjoyed you. [grabbing my arm with the instant affection that a sudden rush of cocaine can generate in the roller-coaster ebbs and flows of a speedball – heroin-cum-cocaine – high] And we probably would have been more cool if you would've been there. 'Cause you can't get into no trouble. Instead we used to break everything in the room.

I was hanging out so roughly trying to be a, Mr. Big Star. [sniffing and catching Benzie's eye] 'Cause we had cash and we used to enjoy it. [slapping five with Benzie and erupting into loud mutual laughter]

Minimum Wage Crack Dealers

I finally solved the mystery of why most street-level crack dealers remain penniless during their careers, when I realized that their generous binge-behavior is ultimately no different from the more individualistic, and circumscribed, conspicuous consumption that rapidly upwardly mobile persons in the legal economy also usually engage in. The tendency to overspend income windfalls conspicuously is universal in an economy that fetishizes material goods and services. Crack dealers are merely a caricaturally visible version of this otherwise very North American phenomenon of rapidly overconsuming easily earned money. Their limited options for spending money constructively in the legal economy exacerbate their profligacy.

A more complex dimension of the crack dealers' relationship to the mainstream economy is their interaction with the legal labor market. A systematic discussion of this complex, antagonistic relationship is the basis for Chapter 4. I shall explore briefly here, however, how this tension with the legal economy affected day-to-day operations at the Game Room, because the appeal of the crack economy is not limited to a simple dollars-and-cents logic.

Street dealers tend to brag to outsiders and to themselves about how much money they make each night. In fact, their income is almost never as consistently high as they report it to be. Most street sellers, like

Caesar displaying cash and three bundles of crack inside the Game Room. Photo by Susan Meiselas.

Primo, are paid on a piece-rate commission basis. In other words, their take-home pay is a function of how much they sell. When converted into an hourly wage, this is often a relatively paltry sum. According to my calculations, Ray's workers, for example, averaged slightly less than double the legal minimum wage – between seven and eight dollars an hour. There were plenty of exceptional nights, however, when they made up to ten times minimum wage – and these are the nights they remember when they reminisce. They forget all the other shifts when they were unable to work because of police raids, and they certainly do not count the nights they spent in jail as forfeited working hours.

It took me several years to realize how inconsistent and meager crack income can be. This was brought home to me symbolically one night as Primo and Caesar were shutting down the Game Room. Caesar unscrewed the fuses in the electrical box to disconnect the video games. Primo had finished stashing the leftover bundles of crack vials inside a hollowed-out live electrical socket and was counting the night's thick wad of receipts. I was struck by how thin the handful of bills were that he separated out and folded neatly into his personal billfold. Primo and

Caesar then eagerly lowered the iron riot gates over the Game Room's windows, and snapped shut the heavy Yale padlocks. They were moving with the smooth, hurried gestures of workers preparing to go home after an honest day's hard labor. Marveling at the universality in the body language of workers rushing at closing time, I felt an urge to compare the wages paid by this alternative economy. I grabbed Primo's wallet out of his back pocket, carefully giving a wide berth to the fatter wad in his front pocket that represented Ray's share of the night's income – and that could cost Primo his life if it were waylaid. Unexpectedly, I pulled out fifteen dollars' worth of food stamps along with two twenty-dollar bills. After an embarrassed giggle, Primo stammered something to the effect that his mother had added him to her monthly food stamp allotment, and now gave him his thirty-dollar share each month to spend on his own.

Primo: I gave, my girl, Maria, half of it. I said, "Here, take it, use it if you need it for whatever." And then the other half I still got it in my wallet for emergencies.

Like that, we always got a couple of dollars here and there, to survive with. Because tonight, straight cash, I only got garbage. Forty dollars! Do you believe that?

At the same time that wages can be relatively low in the crack economy, working conditions are also often inferior to those found in the legal economy. Aside from the obvious dangers of being shot, or of going to prison, the physical work space of most crackhouses is usually unpleasant. The infrastructure of the Game Room, for example, was much worse than that of any legal retail outfits in East Harlem: There was no bathroom, no running water, no telephone, no heat in the winter, and no air-conditioning in the summer. Primo occasionally complained.

Primo: Everything that you see here [sweeping his arm at the scratched and dented video games, the walls with peeling paint, the floor slippery with litter, the filthy windows pasted over with ripped movie posters] is fucked-up. It sucks, man [pointing at the red forty-watt bare bulb hanging from an exposed fixture in the middle of the room and exuding a sickly twilight].

Indeed, the only furnishings besides the video games were a few grimy milk crates and bent aluminum stools. Worse yet, a smell of urine and vomit usually permeated the locale. For a few months Primo was able to maintain a rudimentary sound system, but it was eventually beaten to a pulp during one of Caesar's drunken rages. The same thing happened to a scratchy black-and-white television set that Primo had bought from a customer for the price of a five-dollar vial. Of course, the deficient infrastructure was only one part of the depressing working conditions.

> *Primo:* Plus I don't like to see people fucked up [handing over three vials to a nervously pacing customer]. This is fucked-up shit. I don't like this crack dealing. Word up.
>
> [gunshots in the distance] Hear that?

Why then did Benzie ecstatically forfeit his steady job as maintenance engineer to work with Primo under these conditions?

> *Benzie:* I lost my job for hanging out with you [pointing to Primo and sniffing more cocaine].
>
> At first even if we broke night [stayed awake partying all night], the next day I went to my job. I was chilling and I just walked in like nothing. Nobody – my boss, my supervisor – said nothing to me, because I was a maintenance engineer and I did everything.
>
> Everything! No matter what it is, you do it. You got to fix everything in the hotel. They call and complain, you gotta go and fix it, no matter what it is.
>
> You know, like when the john leaks – whatever it is. Pipes – all that shit – you gotta go up and fix it.
>
> And I had union and everything man, because when you're in the New York Yacht Club Union, you get union shit – I mean, you know, all the benefits.
>
> That's a high-class place over there! I saw Mayor Koch eating there! Yeah I saw what's his name . . . you know, that guy from the news! Man, I seen a lot of people eating there.
>
> It's like a membership shit. You gotta be a member of a yacht ship or some yacht shit! Those are people who got yatch'es. They rich! They got like little models of yatch'es all over the place. It's only whites eating there, like I seen alot'a' whites there.

I never had no problem with white people. It was always: [bowing and imitating an upper-class accent] "How you doing?" [bowing again deeply, but then pausing to sniff] "Good morning." They're nice people though.

I lasted there. A long time. Like a year and a few months. I was making four bills [$400] man! For five days work.

[continuing soberly] Now, the way I lost my job: I never forget that day: it was me, you [pointing to Primo], Candy, and Flora and we stood at Candy's house and we broke night.

In a way, it was my own fault. I started messing around with Flora. And I was still with her in the morning.

I didn't go to work. I fucked up. I was *sniffed up* and I didn't call or anything the next day. I stayed with Flora.

Ultimately, Benzie pushed his macho street culture identity to its logical conclusion. He could not tolerate Ray's authority and ended up stealing money from him and forfeiting a court date for an arrest in a stolen car that was unrelated to crack dealing, but for which Ray had posted $2,500 worth of bail. After a brief stint in prison, "on Riker's," Benzie came full circle and found just above minimum wage employment in "food prep" at a health food cafeteria in a fitness gym – once again, surrounded as a subordinate by powerful whites. He managed to limit his alcohol and cocaine-cum-heroin binging to weekends. He enjoyed coming to the Game Room for visits to lecture Primo on the glories of legal employment. On cold nights after the Game Room was closed, we would often take refuge in a housing project stairwell where Primo and Benzie would sniff speedballs and we would all drink malt liquor until well past daybreak, tape-recording our conversations.[6]

Benzie: The best way to be, is legal. Survive. Make your money and make everybody love you [opening a ten-dollar packet of heroin and handing me a quart of malt liquor to open].

I want you to be like that, Primo. I've been doing it a year, Primo. Look at this, box, [holding out a small plastic object] look what it says here. One year, this is a tie tack, this is a tack that goes on a tie. But it's because I've made a year. That's what it says there.

Do you know why I've made a year at this place? [sniffing heroin]

Because I've been through fuckin' coke; [pointing to the cocaine Primo was crushing into sniffable powder in a folded dollar bill] I've been through fuckin' crack; I've been through marijuana; I've been through fuckin' every drug. I always was troubulated. But now I'm finally getting mines – my *capacidad* [self-worth] – I've finally got to that stage that I won't do something. [pointing again to the cocaine] I'm tired of fuckin' crack living. [waving his arm at the vials littering the stairway] Serious, man.

Like right now [pausing to sniff cocaine] I do not do drugs. Fuck! Look at my face. [moving it aggressively to within an inch of mine and taking the malt liquor bottle] I got a round face. When you do drugs you could tell by someone's face. [sniffing delicately from the packet of heroin, using Primo's key as a dipper].

All of a sudden as if a cocaine rush in his speedball high had triggered some particularly aggressive pathways in his brain, Benzie defensively addressed the difficulty of maintaining respect in the entry-level legal economy.

> *Benzie:* But don't you ever disrespect me or dish me.
> *Primo:* [soothingly] You're a working nigga' and I respect you the way you are right now. [turning to me] I respect him.
> *Benzie:* [unmollified] I don't want someone to respect me. I want to respect myself.

I respect myself, man. [jabbing both forefingers into his chest] I changed. I'm a different person. I love myself. I'm not trying to brag or anything, you know. [swigging from the quart of malt liquor]

> *Primo:* [to me reassuringly] It's like an outburst, Felipe. 'Cause Benzie feels so great, he feels so wonderful.
> *Benzie:* [calmer, passing me the bottle] Man, I'm making eight dollars a fuckin' hour. I'm a prep. I'm an assistant chef. I make eight dollars an hour. I make close to three hundred dollars a week. Okay, they take almost a hundred dollars, you know, in taxes and . . . I get, like, two seventy-five – shit like that.

If you was to go home later on, you could see that I'm telling you the truth. And after taxes – they take like ninety, eighty dollars out of my shit. Like I would come home with my two seventy-five.

Primo: [proud of being privy to legal working-class hustles] That's because you only have one dependent. I always used to put three dependents.

Benzie: But yo, I love myself. I'm proud of myself. You know, who's really fuckin' proud of me and who loves me, bro? My father, bro. He loves the shit out of me now.

My father's been a working man all his life. He came from PR when he was twenty-one. Right now, he's fifty-three years old. He's been a waiter all his life.

Primo: [in a low voice] Man! I don't want a job that's supposed to last you for your whole life. Man! I don't want to work for tips. I wanna work the way I wanna work.

[abruptly changing the subject] Let's go get another beer.

In private, especially in the last few years of my residence, Primo admitted that he wanted to go back to the legal economy.

Primo: I just fuck up the money here. I rather be legal.

Philippe: But you wouldn't be the head man on the block with so many girlfriends.

Primo: I might have women on my dick right now, but I would be much cooler if I was working legal. I wouldn't be drinking and the coke wouldn't be there every night.

Plus if I was working legally I would have women on my dick too, because I would have money.

Philippe: But you make more money here than you could ever make working legit.

Primo: Okay. So you want the money but you really don't want to do the job.

I really hate it, man. Hate it! I hate the people! I hate the environment! I hate the whole shit, man! But it's like you get caught up with it. You do it, and you say, "Ay, fuck it today!" Another day, another dollar. [pointing at an emaciated customer who was just entering]

But I don't really, really think that I would have hoped that I can say I'm gonna be richer one day. I can't say that. I think about it, but I'm just living day to day.

If I was working legal, I wouldn't be hanging out so much. I wouldn't be treating you. [pointing to the 16-ounce can of Colt 45 in my hand] In a job, you know, my environment would change . . . totally. 'Cause I'd have different friends. Right after work I'd go out with a co-worker, for lunch, for dinner. After work I may go home; I'm too tired for hanging out – I know I gotta work tomorrow.

After working a legal job, I'm pretty sure I'd be good.

The problem – as discussed in detail in Chapter 4 on the relationship of the crack dealers to the legal market – is that Primo's good intentions do not lead anywhere when the only legal jobs he can compete for fail to provide him with a livable wage. None of the crack dealers were explicitly conscious of the linkages between their limited options in the legal economy, their addiction to drugs, and their dependence on the crack economy for economic survival and personal dignity. Nevertheless, all of Primo's colleagues and employees told stories of rejecting what they considered to be intolerable working conditions at entry-level legal jobs. Benzie's case, for example, illustrates the complex role that subjective notions of dignity play in the process of rejecting legal employment and becoming a crack addict and then a dealer. Another one of Primo's lookouts, Willie, also had a legal-labor trajectory before being hired by Primo that illustrates the forces propelling a young man to seek refuge in the world of crack. Contradictorily, while Willie rejects the brutality of the working conditions he encountered in the legal labor market, he embraces an even more violent alternative that has him wreaking destruction on his neighbors and community.

In my whole life, I never got paid over six dollars an hour. The most I ever got was my last job when I worked at the ASPCA [American Society for the Prevention of Cruelty to Animals]. It was like two hundred and thirty dollars a week straight – then there was the taxes.

I remember my first day on the job. I had went there pretty well dressed and I'm working with this good-looking girl, so I'm like,

I'm gonna rap with this chick. And then they pull out the carts full of gassed animals.

So I'm standing there with these rubber gloves, right? But I'm trying to stand back, you know, because I can't deal. I love animals . . . you know, I got three chihuahuas upstairs.

But the boss knew there was going to be trouble so they had overhired — that's how they always do it. They get rid of one person. So when the boss said, "You and her, do this," I did it.

But then I looked at this dead animal, and I got sick. And I've got on a button-down shirt, slacks, and I'm at this job in this big garage-type room with rubber gloves on, putting these laundry carts full of dead dogs, cats, baby dogs, baby cats that have all been gassed into a garbage truck.

I couldn't do it for long.

So one day they call me into the office and tell me, "You're not right for this job." So I got fired.

Management–Labor Conflict at the Game Room

Primo's options in the legal job market were no better than those of any of his employees, but on the stoop of the Game Room his vulnerability was not visible — especially when contrasted with that of his crack-addicted customers and workers. He looked and behaved like an effective boss. Ultimately, however, Primo's relative autonomy and importance within Ray's network was eroded when Ray expanded his franchises. The Social Club's prime retail location on La Farmacia's corner made it far more profitable than the Game Room. Ray instituted a double shift at the Social Club, keeping it open for sixteen hours every day except Sunday. Perhaps also because of his own personal fondness for the spot — having grown up in the building — he invested in renovating the physical infrastructure. Soon the Social Club had a pool table, a powerful sound system, a flush toilet that worked some of the time, an air conditioner, and a heater. Ray also established an after-hours bar at the site, serving beer and Bacardi. For the upscale customers and for hard-core intravenous cocaine users, in addition to the nickels of crack, he offered half-grams of relatively unadulterated cocaine for twenty dollars.

The expansion and diversification of Ray's network allowed him to be more manipulative in his management of labor relations. He began leveraging increased levels of discipline and higher profit margins from Primo at the Game Room. This initiated a protracted juggle for power between Primo and Ray. Ray's first action was to supersede Primo's right to hire assistants. He imposed his own choice of secondary employees to work as lookouts and sellers side by side with Primo. Primo rebelled against Ray's encroachment on his operational autonomy. He did not want to be demoted from manager to senior salesperson.

Ultimately, Primo lost out in this struggle for workplace autonomy, and his position as "manager" became increasingly ambiguous, until by the last two years of my residence on the block, Primo had lost all fiction of control over Game Room operations. Ray even managed to lower his piece-rate commissions from $1.00 to 75 cents per vial sold, although he did maintain an extra incentive by increasing the commission to $1.75 per vial on nights when seven bundles [175 vials] were sold. Ray claimed that Primo had precipitated the changes because of his tardiness, absenteeism, and ineffectiveness in curbing violence and noise at the Game Room. For one ten-month period, Primo became so marginal that another three-quarters-time senior salesperson, Tony, was hired and Ray limited Primo to only working two night shifts per week.

Primo responded to his lowered wages, reduced work hours, and lost managerial autonomy by escalating his alcohol and substance abuse. He became an even less punctual and more undisciplined worker, provoking Ray on several occasions to lay him off in retaliation for probationary two-week stretches. Part of the problem was rooted in the laws of supply and demand. The competition across the block in the project stairwells had permanently dropped the prices of their vials from three dollars to two dollars, and a conglomerate of companies located on another crack corner two blocks away had cut its prices from five dollars to three dollars, while simultaneously increasing the quality of its product.

Ray made a last-ditch effort to retain market share by upgrading the Game Room's locale. He moved operations upstairs to the newly vacated premises where three licensed doctors had formerly operated an illegal Medicaid-funded pill mill. This temporarily raised morale among his workers but did not affect sales significantly. We critiqued and debated the boss's management strategies in much the same mundane way that anxious employees in a retail enterprise in the legal sector who are in danger of being laid off, will speculate on the reasons for declining

Primo feeding cocaine to Caesar on the benches of a housing project courtyard, after closing the Game Room. Photo by Susan Meiselas.

business. Relaxing after the end of the night shift in my apartment living room with Primo and Caesar, I tape-recorded one particularly anxious conversation. For the preceding two weeks, the Game Room had been shut down because of intensified police sweeps, and upon reopening that night, Ray had introduced a lower-quality product. (The Dominican wholesaler who formerly supplied him with cocaine at the kilo level had been arrested and his new connection had provided him with inferior cocaine.)

Before speaking morosely, Caesar opened a glassine envelope of heroin, sniffed from it, and then tossed the packet onto my coffee table. He then immediately reached for the folded dollar bill containing cocaine that Primo had just crushed. Primo pulled the cocaine away from him, saying, "Chill man, let me feed you!" and turned to me for emphasis: "I hate it when this nigga' gets thirsty." Primo then scooped a folded matchbook corner into the pile of cocaine and held it up to Caesar's nose for him to sniff with a grimace that effectively closed off one nostril while opening the other one wide. He repeated the motions three more times until Caesar finally sat back calmly on my couch, nodding a thanks to Primo.

Caesar: [speaking slowly] Tonight was slow, we only made twenty-two dollars and fuckin' fifty cents. And I be risking getting snatched and dirtyin' my [police] record for chump change from that fat-assed nigga'.

Ray's gonna lose a lotta business with no light up there. And no one wants to walk up those stairs.

Primo: No, it's not the place of the business. It's just that we're selling two-dollar bottles for five bucks [sniffing].

Caesar: Yeah, the bottles are too small. [gravely] Lately Ray's been fucking up with the product, man. He's like switching product. It'll be good; then it'll be fucked up; then it'll be good; then it'll be fucked up.

Primo: The real problem is that they be small bottles.

Caesar: Plus it was a major mistake to be closed all that time and then the first time we open we be selling shit.

How you gonna open up and sell fire? 'Cause that's what the customers said it is. The cracks taste like fire. That shit is nasty!

He's fucking us up because a lot of people don't come back, man. And people be complaining that we are selling fire.

[picking up his tempo, feeling a rush of energy from the cocaine] I done told Ray, "What's up? This shit is garbage." But he's like, "Fuck you! I sell it like that."

Primo: [sniffing] I never tell him shit, especially tonight. I think he had a roach up his ass, 'cause it's slow. He was pissed off 'cause the electrician from Con Ed [New York City's electrical utility company] didn't show up today.

When I pushed the conversation into a discussion of how they could tolerate being minimum wage crack dealers, they responded with self-congratulatory, glorifying reminiscences of nights of record sales. Perhaps the same types of dialogue could be tape-recorded after-hours among heavy-drinking used-car salesmen during a recession in the local economy.

Caesar: [sniffing more cocaine from Primo's upheld matchbook] Nah, Felipe, it's not so bad. It's slow tonight because it's Monday, and the end of the month, and nobody ain't got no money.

[excited] Primo left out of here the other day with almost three hundred bucks all by himself.

Primo: [smiling] It was the first of the month and everybody had got paid.

Caesar: [taking more cocaine] It was a huge day for selling. Everything comes on the first of the month: all the checks.

Primo: Yeah! Everybody got paid [grinning]. Because the first of the month is like when welfare checks, rent checks, social security checks, all come. The first of the month is definitely *monneeey* [licking his lips].

Caesar: For everybody! Veterans' checks, pensions, social security, welfare, Jew checks . . . [noting my raised eyebrows] You know, Jews be into crazy scams, making money with papers . . . you know, insurance, real estate, shit like that. The Jews be picking up checks. [wiggling his forefingers greedily with a devious grin]

On the first of the month, money flows.

Primo: Everyone was coming. Welfare recipients and workers. I sold twelve bundles.

Ray's sales remained slow for the next several months and morale among his workers continued to plummet, while tensions mounted. Ray ordered Primo to fire Caesar following a series of loud drunken arguments, but Primo refused. Ray retaliated by switching Primo's schedule to working on Monday and Tuesday nights instead of Thursday and Friday nights. Thursday is an especially coveted night to sell on because it is payday for municipal employees.

In a classic example of the internalization of labor–management antagonisms, Primo and Caesar redoubled their hatred for Tony, the replacement employee whom Ray had hired a few months earlier to discipline Primo and Caesar. Tony reciprocated their antagonism. This escalated into a potentially lethal confrontation when three bundles of crack disappeared from the stash inside the Pac-Man video machine during the interval between Primo's Tuesday night shift and Tony's Wednesday shift. Everyone professed innocence, but there was no sign of forced entry and Tony and Primo were the only two people besides Ray to have keys to the locale. Ray wanted to kill – or at least break the legs – of the culprit, but he could not decide whom to punish.

The following Thursday, another three bundles were stolen from the overnight stash, which had been rotated to a live electrical socket for protection. Ray was not only furious but also helpless – a condition that made him even more dangerous than he normally is. To save face he began deducting the value of the stolen bundles from both Primo's and Tony's wages on a fifty-fifty basis. Sales on Primo's Monday and Tuesday night shifts, however, were so low that Ray had to set up an installment plan for his reimbursement. Primo and Caesar were allowed to keep their full Monday night commission in return for surrendering all of Tuesday night's receipts until their share of the $450 worth of missing merchandise was accounted for.

Sensing that he was the prime suspect, Caesar was especially vocal in denouncing Tony as the thief. He repeatedly advocated "wasting the motherfucker." Those of us who frequented the Game Room regularly were convinced that Caesar had stolen the crack. Primo could not help but share this suspicion. It depressed him that his best friend and employee – his "main nigga' " – could have disrespected him so profoundly. It was during these tense weeks that I tape-recorded many of Primo's most insightful denunciations of how he was trapped in the crack economy.

The mysterious disappearance of the six bundles was finally resolved with the anticipated life-threatening beating, but neither Tony nor Primo nor even Caesar were the victims. The thief was Gato, Ray's jack-of-all-trades maintenance worker who had renovated the new locale upstairs from the Game Room. In the process he had hollowed out fake paneling under the floor, to which he had access after hours via the abandoned building behind the Game Room. He knew the kinds of places where Ray kept his stashes because he repaired all his video games and maintained his electrical systems. In fact, he was the one who had pirated the electricity to the new crackhouse out of a neighboring bodega. We could not help but feel sorry for Gato when Ray brought him back to the Game Room three days later to start working off the debt he owed by fixing some newly acquired broken machines. Gato climbed awkwardly out of Ray's Lincoln Continental limping heavily from the beating he had received three days earlier. He avoided eye contact with all of us. We all left the premises hurriedly when he started unscrewing the back of a broken video game because he reeked from the acrid smell specific to homeless crack bingers who have no access to showers or clean clothes. That he was still alive with no bones broken was a testimony to his childhood friendship with Ray, whom he had faithfully followed as a teenage member of "The Cheeba Crew" (TCC) some dozen years earlier.

Ray took advantage of the tensions generated by this incident to renegotiate Tony's salary from a piece-rate commission to a set wage of $100 per shift, regardless of how many bundles were sold. This was especially profitable for Ray because Tony worked on the nights when sales were at their highest volume, Wednesday through Saturday. Relations were too strained between Tony and Primo for them to coordinate their demands for a higher proportion of Ray's profits. In fact, in a classic divide-and-conquer scenario, neither worker even knew what kind of payment arrangement his nemesis had negotiated with their mutual boss.

The Crackhouse Clique: Dealing with Security

Primo's subordination to Ray was not immediately visible to the clique of parasitical friends, acquaintances, and wanna-be employees who congregated in front of the Game Room on most nights. When Primo was on duty, he appeared to his hang-out crowd to be well in control. He was exceptionally generous, and he regularly treated his friends to beer, liquor, and occasional sniffs of cocaine. I had assumed originally that Primo cultivated a large hang-out crowd to fulfill a psychological need for power and domination, especially vis-à-vis the teenage women competing for his sexual attention.

It took me several months to realize that the people reclining on car hoods, squatting on neighboring stoops, or tapping their feet to the ubiquitous rap or salsa playing on someone's radio, served several different useful roles for the crackhouse. They provided strategic business information on competing drug spots and on the changing trends in tastes and market shifts in the underground economy. As long as they did not become too rowdy, they also served to camouflage the comings and goings of the emaciated addicts, making the crackhouse look more

Hanging out in the Game Room. Photo by Oscar Vargas.

like a youth center than a place of business. A subtle touch of "normalcy" was added by the presence of Primo's adopted grandfather, Abraham, who was responsible for collecting the quarters from the video machines. Whenever potential undercover narcotic detectives entered the Game Room, this hopelessly alcoholic seventy-two-year-old man pretended to be senile. He exuded an aura of helplessness and gentleness that was accentuated by the homemade black patch covering his left eye, which he had lost when a mugger stabbed him while he was home from his job at the cafeteria of Lenox Hill Hospital in the early 1980s.[7]

Most importantly, the hang-out crowd complemented the lookout's job by protecting the Game Room from excessive violence and aggression. Primo's best and cheapest insurance against physical assault was to surround himself with a network of people who genuinely respected and liked him. His crowd of friends became an effective army of detectives for investigating foul play; for warning him of potential stickup artists who might be casing the premises; or for shielding and witnessing when an attack actually occurred. Indeed, assault by thieves represented Primo's greatest physical danger. Whenever two people walked into the Game Room at the same time or at a fast pace, he always tensed up. He also usually suspected new people who joined his hang-out crowd of being emissaries gathering intelligence for a future holdup crew.

Primo's fears were well founded. During the five and a half years that I documented the Game Room's operations, it was robbed twice by masked men bearing sawed-off shotguns. Primo confided to me that during the first robbery he had urinated in his pants with his attacker's shotgun pressed against his temple while he lied about not having a stash of cash. Nevertheless, when he reported the theft to his boss later that night, Primo had exaggerated how much money and crack was stolen in order to keep the difference.

Primo considered somewhat insulting my functionalist interpretation of why he treated his friends and acquaintances so generously. Nevertheless, in his counterexplanations he reaffirmed the sense of tension and imminent danger he was forced to endure every night. More subtly, he made me realize that the hang-out crew was more than physical protection, it provided a stabilizing social atmosphere for him to counterbalance the anxiety that constantly threatens to disable a lonesome seller. His peers distracted and relaxed him from the dangerous reality of his work site:

> *Primo:* I don't need anyone to protect me, Felipe. Naah. I can handle myself alone. It's just like I want my people to be there for me.
>
> It don't have to be O.D. here. [pointing to Willie, who was working lookout that night] It could be anybody that's keeping me company. It could even be Jackie [his girlfriend at the time].
>
> See, just so long as there's someone I could talk to, to keep me company. It could even be just Maria [his former girlfriend, whom

he had temporarily broken up with]. But Ray don't like Maria hanging out; he don't know her all that well. She's not from the block.

You understand? I just want someone to accompany me . . . just for the company. You know, it's hard to just be in this dump by yourself.

Because if you're by yourself you know you feel . . . you be more edgy. It's boring and I need to be more relaxed.

And if anything, you always want a witness or somebody to be there . . . you know.

Ironically, it took me several years to realize that Primo's enthusiastic friendship with me was part of the unconscious logic for why he maintained a hang-out crew in front of the Game Room. The disconcerting presence of a white face at night in an El Barrio crackhouse was probably an even better deterrent to potential stickup artists than Willie's large frame, Caesar's reputation for irrational violence, or any one of the teenage girls flirting with Primo. Stickup artists are simply not willing to take the risk of assaulting anyone who could possibly be confused as an undercover police officer. There are too many other easy targets around.

Another crucial service fulfilled by Primo's hang-out network as well as his lookouts was to screen for narcotics agents. Crack dealers have to have organic ties to the street scene in order to be able to recognize the bona fide addict or user from the undercover impostor. The best lookouts and street sellers are those who have hung out in the streets all their lives and know everyone in the neighborhood. When Primo did not recognize someone or sensed something suspicious about a customer, he checked first with his lookout, or with one of his friends outside on the stoop, before serving them. The most frequent confusion arose over men who had just been released from prison and had not yet destroyed their bodies on crack.

Primo: Yo Caesar, who were those two *morenos?* I didn't even know the motherfuckers. They could be *la jara* [the police].

Caesar: Yeah, it's okay. They were good-looking and dressed well, but I know that big black Alabama. He's cool. I know him. He's walked in the Game Room before, it's just that you don't remember,

He musta just came outta jail because that nigga' looked fresh
union. That nigga' was healthy. He was like a Buster Douglas size.

In the five years that I knew Primo he must have made tens of
thousands of hand-to-hand crack sales; more than a million dollars probably passed through his fingers. Despite this intense activity, however, he
was only arrested twice, and only two other sellers at the Game Room
were arrested during this same period. No dealer was ever caught at Ray's
other crackhouses, not even at the Social Club on La Farmacia's corner,
even though its business was brisker. Ironically, the Social Club was
raided half a dozen times, because it doubled as a pool hall and bootleg
bar. The large clientele of omnipresent regulars confused the police; they
never knew whom to arrest. They could not expropriate the landlord,
because the City of New York was the owner. The original proprietor
had long since defaulted on his taxes. Instead, on two occasions the police
smashed the pool tables into kindling wood, ripped out the electrical
fixtures, and boarded over the entrance. On one raid, they ticketed Candy
for serving unlicensed liquor to an undercover officer, but they were never
able to apprehend the primary seller-manager in the act of a hand-to-
hand narcotics sale. The biggest threat to the Social Club came from the
New York City fire marshals, who sealed the place on several occasions
for violating fire codes following the much publicized arson of a social
club in the South Bronx that took the lives of eighty-four people.[8]
The invulnerability of Ray's crackhouses to police control was largely
owing to the generalized public sector breakdown of the neighborhood.
Inner-city police forces are so demoralized and incompetent that for the
most part they do not have to be systematically corrupt – although they
often are – in order for street-level drug dealing to flourish in their
precincts.[9] The attitude of honest officers is too hostile toward the local
community for them to be able to build the networks that would allow
them to document the operations of the numerous drug-dealing spots in
the neighborhoods they patrol. For example, after five and a half years of
being practically the only white person out on the street after dark on a
regular basis on my block, which hosted almost a half-dozen drug-selling
spots, the police never learned to recognize me. Even after I began
attending their community outreach meetings for combating drugs, they
continued to fail to recognize me on the street.[10]
Ray and his workers took certain basic precautions to minimize their

risk of arrest. They never made sales outside the door on the street, and they usually asked customers to step behind a strategically placed Pac-Man machine at the back of the establishment before touching their money and handing them the vials of crack, in case the police were watching with binoculars from a neighboring apartment building. Most importantly, at no point was there more than twenty-five vials — one bundle — visibly accessible. Depending on the night and the season, additional bundles might be strategically hidden in rotated stashes, such as the live overhead electrical socket, the linoleum wall paneling, or the entrails of one of the video games. Depending on supply and demand, runners periodically delivered extra bundles and picked up cash receipts.

Sellers have to develop the crucial skill of judging when it is necessary to stash their vials in the event of a raid. This was what saved Primo, for example, from four years of incarceration on his last arrest. As the police were battering down the Game Room door with their portable ram he flicked thirteen vials from his current bundle into the back of a Mario Brothers video machine. The police found nothing in their search of the premises. At the same time, if a seller becomes overly paranoid — *petro* — of every suspicious siren and revving car motor, the smooth operations of the crackhouse become excessively disrupted. Dealers have to juggle between relaxation and acute premonition. In Primo's case, strategically dispensing beer and cocaine to his friendly hang-out clique was crucial to maintaining this delicate balance of calm alertness.

Primo, Caesar, and other dealers provided me with dozens of accounts of close calls with the police. They had developed complex, risk-minimization strategies.

Caesar: [drinking from a 16-ounce can of malt liquor] I'm not gonna get caught with the stash on me. I'll pitch it or hide it fast. I got a clean slate. So I don't even think I would even get bail. They'll call it being in the wrong place at the wrong time.

I don't sell to people I don't know, never. Pops only made that mistake a coupla' times in the Game Room, but that was when it was wild man.

Primo: [also drinking from a separate 16-ounce can of malt liquor] Yeah, I only got caught once like that, in a buy-and-bust. But there's been times when cops came to buy but I knew it and I was cool.

Way back when my grandfather Abraham was still hanging out here. I was reading in the newspapers about that guy, Larry Davis, who killed those cops. I was chilling, reading.

Caesar: My cousin's in jail with Larry Davis in Louisiana on some wild federal charge.

Primo: Shut up Caesar, let me finish.

So I was reading that Larry Davis thing out loud to Abraham, because he can't read English, when this guy in an army jacket came in — but he was white.

I don't even know why they sent him. He looked like an obvious cop. I pretended I didn't see him, when he walked in. I kept reading like that [peering deeply into an imaginary newspaper]. So he walked past me, to the back and asked Abraham for the shit. But Abraham realized quick what was up and he just went, *"Wahhhh?"* [imitating a senile old man slobbering at the mouth]. And I was in the front, reading the paper like this [crossing his legs awkwardly perched on a milk crate] and there were kids playing, and it was cool.

Then he said to me, "They still sell crack here?" but I just went, "I don't know," and kept reading my paper.

He was a cop because I seen the man in the day, with the regular blue suit on.

Primo attributed to carelessness the one time he was successfully arrested and convicted.

Primo: I got my [criminal] record back when O.D. was hanging with me. Oh man, I got jerked! I was outside with a mirror, trimming my hair like that. It was early in the day; it was like four o'clock. I used to open earlier in them days. Like one or two, because Felix was like, "Gotta be there, boy!" I used to hate that.

So Abraham calls me, because I didn't notice the guy go in because I was talking with O.D., trimming my shit.

So I went in and he was pretending he was playing Pac-Man. So then I didn't even bother to look at him, it was like he had a gold chain, short pants, and everything.

So I took the shit from where we kept it right there in a little thin box [pointing in the direction of the current stash]. He tells me he wants five. And when I was serving him, was when I looked at his face; I said to myself, "Shit, I don't know this motherfucker!" He looked like so clean-cut, *y gordito* [and chubby]; I was like [waving his arms in confusion].

So I tell him, "How do you smoke this? Put it in the pipe; or do you smoke woolas [a crack and marijuana mixture]?" He said, "You got that too?" and I said, "No, I'm just asking." So he left.

And when he left, I told O.D., "Yo, wait a minute. Let me stash the shit." Because I didn't trust that dude. But O.D. followed me. He was talking to me so much shit about his problems that I got distracted [drinking].

And when I turned to put the vials away, like that [going through the motions], right there they pushed me [coming over to me and throwing me against a video machine in a half-nelson]. I thought it was Eddie just fucking around so I continued; but when I finished I looked and the cop was already ready to blow me away like that [holding an imaginary gun up to my temple] – or whatever. He was taking precautions. Them niggas just rushed us, boy [drinking]. He pulled the shit out and said "This is what we're looking for" [holding out a handful of crack vials and grinning cruelly].

I got jerked for selling five vials – two-to-four years probation [shaking his head sadly, drinking, and handing me the bottle].

A year later, as the New York state penal system spiraled into a crisis owing to overcrowding following the precipitous increase in drug arrests and the toughening of drug-sentencing rules, an exasperated judge declared Primo's suspended sentence to be completed a year early, in order to clear his overburdened docket. Primo had been arrested for failing to report to his probation officer, a violation that under normal conditions might have resulted in his incarceration for the full term of his probation sentence.

Following his second arrest for a hand-to-hand sale of ten dollars' worth of crack to an undercover officer, once again the mayhem of New York's drug enforcement strategy in the early 1990s saved Primo from becoming a predicate felon and having to serve four to six years in jail.[11] In their disorganized haste to boost arrest statistics, the Tactical Narcotics Team officers who engineered the buy-and-bust operation on the

Game Room confused the identities of Primo and Caesar in the court-room. The jury was forced to free Primo when Caesar derailed the prosecution's case by insinuating under oath – but with the protection of the Fifth Amendment – that he had actually been the one who had sold the crack to the undercover officers. Ray and several of the crackhouse habitués had the pleasure of watching the judge rebuke the district attorney for having wasted the court's time with a sloppy case. Primo was fully vindicated, and the Game Room stayed in business for another year with no police raids.

4

"GOIN' LEGIT": DISRESPECT AND
RESISTANCE AT WORK

I really wanna work legal.

Primo

Everyone in Ray's network – including Ray himself – has had extensive experience working honestly. Most entered the legal labor market at exceptionally young ages. By the time they were twelve, they were bagging and delivering groceries at the supermarket for tips, stocking beer off the books in local bodegas, or running errands. Before reaching twenty-one years of age, however, virtually none had fulfilled their early childhood dreams of finding stable, well-paid legal work.

The problem is structural, as outlined briefly in Chapter 2: From the 1950s through the 1980s second-generation inner-city Puerto Ricans were trapped in the most vulnerable niche of a factory-based economy that was rapidly being replaced by service industries. Between 1950 and 1990, the proportion of factory jobs in New York City decreased approximately threefold at the same time that service sector jobs doubled. The Department of City Planning calculates that over 800,000 industrial jobs were lost from the 1960s through the early 1990s, while the total number of jobs of all categories remained more or less constant at 3.5 million.[1]

Economists and sociologists have documented statistically that the restructuring of the U.S. economy around service jobs has resulted in unemployment, income reduction, weaker unions, and dramatic erosions in worker's benefits at the entry level. Few scholars, however, have noted the cultural dislocations of the new service economy. These cultural clashes have been most pronounced in the office-work service jobs that have multiplied because of the dramatic expansion of the finance, real estate, and insurance (FIRE) sector in New York City. Service work in professional offices is the most dynamic place for ambitious inner-city youths to find entry-level jobs if they aspire to upward mobility. Employment as mail room clerks, photocopiers, and messengers in the high-rise office corridors of the financial district propels many inner-city youths into a wrenching cultural confrontation with the upper-middle-class white world. Obedience to the norms of high-rise, office-corridor culture is in direct contradiction to street culture's definitions of personal dignity – especially for males who are socialized not to accept public subordination.

Resistance, Laziness, and Self-Destruction

Contrary to my expectations, most of the dealers had not completely withdrawn from the legal economy. On the contrary – as I have shown in Chapter 3, in discussing the jobs that Willie and Benzie left to become crack dealers and addicts – they are precariously perched on the edge of the legal economy. Their poverty remains their only constant as they alternate between street-level crack dealing and just-above-minimum-wage legal employment. The working-class jobs they manage to find are objectively recognized to be among the least desirable in U.S. society; hence the following list of just a few of the jobs held by some of the Game Room regulars during the years I knew them: unlicensed asbestos remover, home attendant, street-corner flyer distributor, deep-fat fry cook, and night-shift security guard on the violent ward at the municipal hospital for the criminally insane.

They were usually fired from these jobs, but they treated their return to the world of street dealing as a triumph of free will and resistance on their part. A straightforward refusal to be exploited in the legal labor market pushes them into the crack economy and into substance abuse. At the same time, however, becoming a crack seller is by no means the voluntarily triumphalist decision that many street dealers claim it to be. Primo repeatedly confided to me his frustration over not being able to find steady legal employment. He initially admitted this to me when his probation officer ordered him to go to an employment agency following his first felony conviction for selling crack. Beneath his outrage over the bad working conditions he was offered, lay a deep fear that his biggest problem is incompetence and laziness.

Primo: [while crushing cocaine in a dollar bill in the back of the Game Room] That fuckin' lady counselor I got; she's a stupid bitch. She wanted me to be like a security guard, you know. I don't wanta be no guard. I don't wanta deal with some crazy son of a bitch outside. I let them rob anything. Word! All I got is a stick in my hand. And I'm only getting paid once a week. I let them rob anything, man.

That fucking counselor she tells me [imitating a bureaucratic whine], "The better your qualifications, the better the work." Well fuck her, I'll just keep searching on my own.

I had an appointment yesterday, a company that I was supposed to check out that takes care of like sheets and stuff, like from hotels – rooming service. So I went to see, just to take a look at it; but there's a lot of Mexicans in there, and I'm not a fucking Mexican.

My cousin's got a job where he's been working for like three years. He told me last week, "Come with me tomorrow morning to talk to the boss." But it didn't work out. I overslept. I had even set up the clock, but I didn't hear the alarm [sniffing cocaine].

Philippe: Why don't you just take any old bullshit job just for right now? Like what your sister's got at McDonald's.

Primo: You know why I don't fly to work real quick? I am twenty-six years old, and if I was to fly out of my way and get a McDonald's job and not no union job, it just shows that you're flying to get a McDonald's to cover your ass.

Twenty-six-year-old guy at McDonald's! Every time you go to McDonald's, you don't see anybody twenty-six years old.

Every time that you see someone that's older, it's probably because they don't have no education; no high school; no nothing. They don't speak English. I mean my English is very bad, but I can go further than at Burger King.

Philippe: Man! You're just making up excuses.

Caesar: [interrupting, almost angry at me] You know what I call working at a Burger King or a McDonald's? That's what I call slavery-ing.

I know, because I worked there, and working at McDonald's is overworked and underpaid. You could work full time – a week, five days a week – full time, and you only come home with like a hundred forty, one thirty.

And you know why it's fucked up? It's not only because it's overworked and underpaid; it's that you have to – I mean when I talk about overworked and underpaid! – you have to fuckin' fry burgers; scrub the floors; because you have to do so much work for bullshit money

[suddenly reaching for the dollar bill with cocaine and changing his serious tone to a smirk] The only reason why I don't get a decent job is because *I'm lazy*. I don't want to go through the processes.

I don't want to go looking for no bullshit job and be all frustrated and be getting paid weak and shit like that, until something else comes along.

'Cause think about it; if you got a bullshit job; how you gonna go look for another one? 'Cause you gonna be there at the job all the time. And why you wanna be missing a day of your work to go see an interview so they could tell you, "We'll call you."

[motioning to Primo to dip his key in the pile of cocaine] Yo! Feed me Primo!

And then you lose a day's pay which makes you move more to the brink of hell 'cause then you don't got money for drugs. [grinning wildly before sniffing from the key tip full of cocaine that Primo was holding up to his left nostril] And if I can't get high the way I want to be on the weekends . . . [sniffing again, loud mutual laughter]

Philippe: Okay! Okay! C-Zone, I hear you. But seriously Primo, you got a court case coming up.

Primo: [sniffing and recomposing himself] Yes, I am making excuses, but I'll go to the job center on Monday and follow up. I think I had just got used to the street scene, because it's been a while since I've held a legal job that's been there.

I didn't like the tuxedo place they sent me to last week. I didn't want to be measuring men. It's not for me to be touching men all over the place like that. That's wack!

At the same time I shoulda stayed for more than two weeks. That was just not the whole excuse. My problem was that I was hanging out late at the Game Room and I've got to wake up in the morning to get to work.

Caesar: [reassuringly] Naah. I visited the store, it wasn't no place to make a career.

Primo: [morosely] I was just fucking up. I made a choice from there to here and I'm still here.

Caesar: Yeah, I'm lazy right now, 'cause I just want to get up at any fucking chosen time of the day. Wash my balls and go outside with a fat belly from all the grub in my house and go hang out and write [rap] rhymes and bug out upstairs and make my little bullshit money.

See, I stay out of trouble in a way by selling crack, 'cause I chill with Primo. [motioning to Primo to serve him more cocaine] See, what fucked me up before when I was working legal was, I was *using* the crack. That was the only thing that fucked me up.

'Cause really, I'm happy with my life. [sniffing] Like no one is bothering me. I got my respect back.

Buela [grandma] likes me. I got a woman. I got a kid. I feel complete now. I don't really need nothing. I got money to get wrecked. [sniffing again] I just go downstairs and work for Pops, and I ain't taking none of it home because tomorrow I don't need no money. So I'll go get wrecked, but then tomorrow I don't need no money, 'cause I go back to the Game Room: I work; I get the money; and then I can go get wrecked again. [pointing to Primo, who was dipping his key back into the cocaine]

Philippe: [laughing] That's why your sneakers are so dirty?

Caesar: Only reason I ain't got nice new sneakers is 'cause I have a decision: I could either save the money to buy the sneakers, or I could get wrecked. And right now, I'm going to get wrecked. [sniffing again]

The money I make in the Game Room is for my personal madness; for my personal drug-addiction and self-destruction. It's something only I could control. No one could tell me what to do with it.

[breaking into a tirade] So I could hurt myself on the inside; so I could wake up every morning with my stomach twisted all in knots and throwing up and sick; and I can't eat; and I can't breathe and I'm fulla' diarrhea; and I'm shitting all over the place; and I'm fucked up; and my one eye is pink; and one eye is white; and my hair stinks; and I'm dirty; and I don't bathe; and I'm fucked up; and I stink; and I hate my woman; and I hate everybody in the morning. That's what happens to me after I get wrecked. [sniffing again]

But then I'll chill; and I'll be sick; and I'll puke; and then I'll be cool by the time I get to the Game Room. Then we're having a good time; we're breaking shit [pointing to where the television used to be, then opening the door of the Game Room for a customer who had knocked]. We're hassling customers; we're cursing customers. Cursing customers in Spanish in front of them; fucking with their minds; selling them garbage drugs so we can make our money [collecting ten dollars and handing over two crack vials]; and so we can go out and buy garbage drugs [pointing to the folded dollar bill full of cocaine balanced on Primo's knee]; and get ripped ourselves; and talk immense amount of shit [pointing to my tape recorder].

Philippe: What about all the money you could be making steadily if you was legal?

Caesar: My woman takes care of me with her food, 'cause she got, she got welfare and food stamps. In a few months I start getting my social security again – three hundred dollars every month, and that's enough for all my gear.

My problem started because they found out that I had worked legal and they had to tax me a thousand five hundred dollars. So they been jerking me now for a couple of months until my SSI pays it all back.

First Fired – Last Hired

None of those in Ray's network considered themselves to be victims. Their niche in the underground economy shielded them from having to face the fact that they were socially and economically superfluous to mainstream society. I watched Primo struggle with the glimmering realization of his profound economic vulnerability when one of his episodic attempts to reenter the legal economy coincided with the deepening of the recession that afflicted the U.S. economy from late 1989 through 1991. At first Primo was totally confident. "I've had like ten jobs before in my life. I dropped out of school at sixteen and I've been working ever since. Any asshole can find a job out there." He almost enjoyed taking the subway downtown during daylight hours, marveling at the "full cheeks" and "cut hair" of the healthy-looking legally employed commuters.

When a half-dozen employers abruptly refused to hire him, Primo was able to blame his inability to find a job on his employment counselor, even though the newspapers were running euphemistically worded articles about the "temporary interruption in America's growth" and "the softening in the labor market."[2] He defiantly "fired" his counselor:

> *Primo:* I got a feeling this son of a bitch guy at the job center, my job counselor, was high. His eyes were always red. He lost my whole files. He was helping me without even knowing who the fuck I was. He sent me to so many fucking places, and nothing.
>
> That nigga' must have been on drugs. He was looking for my file all over his office. He's an idiot because that file was thick. It had all of the test'es I took.
>
> I told him, "Maybe you're not supposed to be my supervisor. Why don't you look around to some other counselor?"
>
> He said, "No, I had your file. I don't know where it's at."
>
> He had a whole bunch of files, and I was hoping he would like look through the files and find mine, but mine wasn't there at all. It was like I never existed.

A month later, after another half-dozen employment rejections, Primo's self-confidence plummeted and his substance abuse escalated. He was living in flesh and blood the sense of personal powerlessness that impersonal market forces of supply and demand impose on vulnerable laborers during recessions:

> *Primo:* It's become hard to get a job now, I guess. It used to be easy to get a job, or maybe this TAP [Testing Assessment and Placement] Center I'm going to is sending me to the wrong places.

I keep telling my job counselor, "Why don't you send me to a place you haven't sent someone the day before, so that when they see me, it's definitely that they'll take me? Because when you send them a few people, then they're just not going to take me."

But I think my counselor agreed with the bosses to send them a few people, and "whoever you like better you can keep." Which is bad!

I told him, "Why don't you just tell them, just say, 'We can only send you one person because we lack more people. We lack clients.' "

Instead this guy was sending me and everyone else. That makes your chances fucked up. Its like you got to battle it out to get a job.

In the old days the TAP centers were better. Everytime they sent me to some company, boom! I'm hired, because they're not sending a whole bunch of people. Word!

The dramatic deterioration in 1990 of the number of jobs available in the entry-level legal labor market caught Primo by surprise. Not only did the recession make it hard to find a job, but Primo also had to confront his life-cycle developmental constraints: He was rapidly becoming too old to compete for the kinds of jobs that had been available to him when he had been an eager, teenage high school dropout just entering the legal labor force. Now that Primo was in his mid-twenties he had a several-year-long hiatus of unemployment that he was unable to justify to prospective employers. Primo internalized his structural marginalization. He panicked and spiraled into a psychological depression.

Primo: I guess I was wrong, Felipe, about how easy it is to get a job.

I was hearing on the news that there's a depression . . . an economic recession — or something like that. And I was thinking to myself, "Damn! That's going to fuck up not only city, state, or federal workers, but it also fucks up someone like me . . . I guess — people that don't have skills, like me. This is fucked up."

It makes me feel fucked up, not being able to get a job. Because sometimes it seems like I like to be lazy.

But you get tired of sitting around and not doing shit. I like to make myself useful, really – like I'm worth something. Not having a job makes me feel really fucked up, man.

Perhaps realizing that jobs are often found through personal connections, Primo began inviting his only legally employed ex-Game Room associate, Benzie, to hang out with him more often. Sure enough, Benzie began telling Primo about a possible opening in the kitchen of the downtown health club where he worked. The night before Christmas Eve he even motivated Primo to come to the office Christmas party to meet his supervisor. Primo arrived late, however, long after the upper-echelon administrators had left. He managed to meet only a few of the custodial workers, who were finishing off the leftover punch. Later that night, in his mother's housing project stairwell surrounded by beer, cocaine, and heroin, Benzie berated Primo for having ruined his chances of getting a job. During the conversation, however, Primo discovered the limitations of the job he had been so eagerly pursuing, and also whom he was competing with:

Benzie: You remember El Gordo – that fat guy – at the party? Well, he's the one that I'm trying to get my supervisor to fire so that you can get the job.

Primo: But all he be doing is washing dishes.

Benzie: [a little flustered] I know . . . I'm in the back with him. I'm in charge of him. He's always fucking up. I keep trying to get him on point, but he doesn't take the job seriously.

I keep telling my supervisor I know someone who really wants to work. But she's not hard on him. She feels sorry for him. And I feel sorry for him too, 'cause I know how he is.

Primo: [suspiciously] What do you mean "how he is"?

Benzie: [ignoring the question] So Pops, your responsibility would be to wash dishes; but it's at six dollars an hour; and there's no place you could go to wash dishes that they'll start you off at six dollars an hours. They'll start you off at four or five.

And after you work for a year you get a week vacation . . .

Primo: [interrupting] Answer me. What's with El Gordo? Why everyone feel sorry for him?

Benzie: [embarrassed] I mean he's slow, so he takes the job in a funny way.

At Work: Disrespect and Resistance

Primo: [worried] What do you mean he's slow?
Benzie: I mean he's slow in the mind. He's got like a handicap.
[defensively] Listen man, I'm only trying to help you out.

Benzie's mentally retarded colleague outcompeted Primo for the dish-washing job. Meanwhile, the logistics of Primo's personal life began falling apart. He had been squatting with his girlfriend, Maria, in her sister's project apartment opposite the Game Room. Maria's sister had fled to Connecticut with her husband and three children when her husband's drug-selling partner was found shot to death in their car. Primo and Maria were supposed to take charge of the continuing rent payments, but this was the same period when Ray had limited Primo to working two nights a week at the Game Room, and sales were slow. Maria found a job at a fast-food franchise, but this still did not provide them with enough money to meet their bare necessities. Primo was reduced to begging from his mother and sisters.

Primo: Maria just started this week at Wendy's but she makes — net pay — about eighty something, ninety something bucks a week. Her welfare is a fucking piece of shit. She gets like not even forty dollars every other week. It's thirty-seven and some change because the cashiers keep something. Jesus that's bullshit money.

But me and Maria never starve, because if I don't have anything to eat at Maria's, I go to my mother's, or my other sister's, who just lives down the block.

Sometimes my mother looks me out. Twenty dollars, here and there. Sometimes she gives me food stamps, like once a month.

Within a few weeks of this conversation, failing to meet the Housing Authority rent payments, Primo and Maria were evicted. They were forced to separate, each returning to their own mother's high-rise Housing Authority apartment located in different projects in the neighborhood.

Internalizing Unemployment

Over the next few months Primo's main strategy was to keep from facing the fact that he was locked out of the legal labor market. He escalated

123

his alcohol and narcotics use, and lashed out at the one person he still had power over: his girlfriend Maria. He lectured her righteously, for example, when she lost her job at Wendy's. Somehow, he managed to invert the traditional gender roles of who should be gainfully employed in a household, even while retaining the patriarch's prerogative of imposing family discipline.

> *Primo:* I have to abuse that bitch verbally, because she doesn't do nothing for herself – like with school or nothing like that. She'd always rather be hugging me and kissing me, and not doing nothing.
>
> But I handle it well. I talk to her. I'll get her sick with my lectures.
>
> I think Maria should work at a McDonald's. Just to get that good work experience. But she doesn't want to do it. I've threatened that if she doesn't start working, I'm going to leave her.
>
> I tell her "Go to a job center. Make a call." But instead she just misses her call; she just forgets about it.

Primo's longer-term defense mechanism was to take refuge in the ranks of what the economists euphemistically call "discouraged workers," the ones who are no longer registered as unemployed in the national statistics. He became just one more person contributing to what the statisticians described in the mid-1980s as "the spiralling decline" in the labor force participation rates of Puerto Ricans in New York City. Although the labor force participation rates of Puerto Rican men stabilized by the 1990 Census, New York–based Puerto Ricans continued to have some of the lowest rates of any ethnic group in the United States, with the exception of certain Native American peoples.[3]

> *Primo:* My job searches have been fucked up. I didn't get hired nowhere. Not even as a porter at Woolworth's for four-forty an hour. Four dollars is wack and that's a union job.
>
> So I don't think I'll find a job in a while, because I don't want to work for minimum wage. And I really won't honestly take a five dollars-an-hour job either, and they won't give me one anyhow.
>
> I don't want to talk about it, Felipe.
>
> I didn't see the point of me wasting a lot of money on train fare

going to interviews, and then not getting a place. I went to a lot of places, Felipe, and I got sick and tired of it. So that's how I ended up back here in the Game Room.

In fact, Primo did want to talk about it, except that he was only able to do so when he had drunk enough alcohol and sniffed enough cocaine and heroin to admit his deepest problems and anxieties. Primo's former lookout, Willie, happened to come home on furlough from the army during this difficult period, and at dusk we used to go to a nearby public school playground to share our problems with one another. We would crouch by one of the jungle gyms sheltered from gusts of wind and occasional police floodlights in order to lay out ten-dollar packets of cocaine and heroin side by side on the fat logs originally built for elementary school children to play on. As a friend of Primo's, I was worried about his escalating alcohol and narcotics consumption and I wanted him to confront his problems. Ironically, my tape recordings of Primo and Willie's depressed, almost stream-of-consciousness confessional dialogues, are punctuated by the background sounds of steerers calling out the brand names of the heroin they sold in the elementary playground: "Terminator," "Black Power," "DOA" [Dead on Arrival], "Rambo," "Poison." Not only was this particular schoolyard one of Manhattan's most active retail heroin markets, but it is also the site for the headquarters of the East Harlem School District.[4]

> *Primo:* Okay, Okay, Felipe, I hear what you're saying. And so I drink and I sniff, and everything.
>
> You say I'm depressed. But when I'm under the influence it's like "fuck that." Maybe I spill my guts out. But I know that there's always tomorrow. Tomorrow is the next day. I'm gonna be sober, so I got time to think [sniffing from the pile of heroin and passing me a quart of Bacardi].
>
> *Willie:* You know what it is Primo. [sniffing] You don't have nothing to look forward to. No job. You gotta have something to look for.
>
> *Primo:* [continuing] Tomorrow man . . . tomorrow is another day . . . [pointing to the cocaine and heroin]
>
> *Philippe:* Tomorrow you're gonna have a hangover.
>
> *Primo:* You know, I think I'm gonna be an alcoholic. Yeah, you

know, I gotta stop drinking, man. I gotta stop drinking. I'm gonna kill myself. I'm not getting anywhere. Yeah. Not getting anywhere.

Philippe: What does your mother think of your situation? Does it bother her? [passing the quart of Bacardi]

Primo: Hell yeah! [swigging] But this bothers me too Felipe! Mainly because I'm not getting any . . . any younger; I'm getting old and it would be like, "What if mommy ain't there?" And if mommy ain't there, my sisters definitely ain't with it. And if they don't want to look me out, then you know, I'll be like . . . like a bum . . . *un bón todo aborchornado* [a down-and-out bum].

If I was to live in the City, I would have to be homeless. And if I don't find any work, how would I provide for myself to pay for an apartment to live in. You know they're so expensive now. I would have to sell drugs . . . or . . . or do something to be able to live.

Because if I wouldn't do that, I would be on welfare. I don't like to ask nobody for money, you know. I don't wanna ask anybody for nothing. I want to earn my money.

Willie: [interrupting] Yeah! Before it used to be everybody works, and welfare is like the lowest thing. But now it's like the style. Now practically everybody is on it, you know. But my family works. We never be on welfare.

Primo: Besides, welfare would put me into something. I would have to go to school, you know, or take some kind of training in order to keep getting the check.

So how would I be able to live by myself, support myself, and go to school, with the little bit of money I'm gonna get from welfare? I would have to do something to get the extra money to be able to live.

Willie: No Pops. [sniffing, then swigging] You know what your problem is? Your problem is that fast money. You got used to it . . . to being a lazy person and having somewhere to live; somewhere to eat; and somewhere to go at night.

Primo: You know why I didn't get a job? 'Cause I really got used to being a lazy person. I really got used to just . . .

Willie: Sleeping.

Primo: I really got used to getting fed at home . . . and not doing nothing to enhance my life. [sniffing and drinking]

Philippe: So how do you feel about that? How about helping your mother with some of the money you make at the Game Room? [swigging from the bottle]

Primo: That's it. My mother feeds me and gives me a room. I just take advantages of those things. [sniffing]

But I realize it. It makes me think, and I get upset, and I say, maybe if I don't hang out — like right now — I could just deal with the things I have to do.

Philippe: So why did you spend the money tonight on this shit? [pointing to the cocaine and heroin and then drinking from the quart of Bacardi and waving it]

Primo: And my mother be *dishing* me hard. Not for eating her food, because she don't want me to starve, but nobody likes to see somebody just living for free. [in Spanish] "You don't go to school. You don't do nothing. Why don't you go look for a job. You're not a little baby man. [throwing up his arms to imitate his mother's exasperation in an imaginary conversation with a friend] *El es un hombre ya* [He's a man already]."

Philippe: And how does that make you feel?

Primo: It makes me feel like she's right; and I have to get my act together; and make some money; and then be clean, and work.

To tell the truth, if I was to be working, man, my mother would even iron my clothing. I'd be walking around in ironed clothes. My mother wouldn't even bitch if Maria was to come over and maybe even spend the night.

Instead my mother makes it hard on me. "*Para que yo aprenda* [So that I learn]."

She works; my sisters work; everybody works! They been leading a nice quiet life. She wants to see me working and being somebody.

That's the way my mother is. She hates it when she gets up in the morning, and I'm sleeping. And then when she comes from work all tired and she sees me sitting like a king in a rocking chair in front of the television like a fucking *turista*. [splaying out his body like someone lounging in a hammock] She gets mad bro! [drinking]

And she's right. I have to make something of myself. I got to start, even if I don't have a job. I just gotta get my life back into the working world . . . and look for what I want.

Right now, to tell you the truth, I've just been a *vago* [lazy bum] – drunk and naked.

Willie: I'm just like you Primo. [drinking] I grew up with you at the same time. My mom's always worked too. She worked hard; she busted ass. She was a nurse's aide. You know she didn't make a lot of money; but we never be on welfare. And I feel like you.

But damn, man! It's hard. It is hard. I mean the fucking shit that I done been through. [sniffing from the heroin]

Primo: [sniffing from the cocaine] Okay, it's hard, but it's not impossible.

Willie: [reaching for the cocaine] But it's hard Pops. I been through such fuckin' dilemmas in my life.

Primo: Forget the past. Think about today; and then get to tomorrow.

I mean, if I'm living wrong I wanna be corrected. You and I are fucking up today, right? But tomorrow, you wake up. Even if it's with a hangover, you eat breakfast, or whatever, and you recover. 'Cause you have to do something to enhance your life for that day, and continue with tomorrow – if it has to be continued.

Willie: But, Primo, Primo, I'm so god damn lost in my life.

This particular night ended disastrously for Willie. Somehow he managed to beg ten dollars from both Primo and me, which set him off on an all-night crack binge.

During these particular months at the height of the recession in 1990, I was just cementing my friendship with Primo's mother. We spoke over the telephone and I could hear a tremendous frustration in her voice as she helplessly watched her son degenerate into open alcoholism and depression. To make matters worse, the water main in their project apartment had burst, and she and her daughters had to run back and forth to their neighbors' with buckets to fetch water. This plumbing crisis lasted for two weeks because they were always out at work when the building maintenance crews came to fix the pipes during the day. Primo was supposed to open the door for them, but he kept sleeping through their knocks.

Primo's mother: [in Spanish] He's always passed out on the couch like a drunk dog, coming home from the street at seven in the morning.

What a shame that at twenty-six he is still living with his mother. He should go find a woman and move out with her. I threw my husband out twenty-three years ago and Primo is just like him. He comes drunk from the street every morning.

He's always had bad friends. His teachers in school told me that; and he stopped going to school at fifteen because of bad friends.

He never really held a job for a long time. Just last month he only lasted two weeks at a job [the tuxedo rental store]. I lost money giving him money for car fare and food for lunch. He never even went back to pick up his paycheck.

I can't even leave beers in the refrigerator, he takes them for his friends.

And what would happen to me if I got sick and couldn't work? We'd lose the apartment!

To make matters worse, Primo and his mother fell victim to a $2,400 job-training racket that preys on the false hopes of the unemployed. In a bogus mail-promotion scam, she "won" a half-price coupon to a so-called maintenance engineering training program that normally cost $4,800. She immediately made the remaining down payment and forced Primo to go to classes. It turned out that the half-price deal depended on the client's qualifying for a federally guaranteed student loan grant for the "discounted" amount. Completely unaware of the implications and responsibilities involved, Primo signed himself up for a $2,400 student loan. He enthusiastically threw himself into the program, bragging to Caesar and me about the "nineties and eighties" he was "making" on the weekly "test'es." He began fantasizing about finding a stable job as a janitor, adding a classic rural Puerto Rican refrain, *"Si Dios quiere"* [God willing] – the Latino version of the Anglo expression "knock on wood" – every time he mentioned graduating from the training program or finding a job.

Primo's dream was dashed when his school declared bankruptcy before he had a chance to graduate from the program. Not only did his mother lose her $2,400 cash-down payment, but he suddenly found himself responsible for the $2,400 matching federal loan the job training program had processed for him. To make matters worse, Primo was in the midst of his second year-and-a-half-long trial, for a hand-to-hand sale of two vials of crack to an undercover narcotics officer. I remember vividly

watching with surprise as Primo lowered his eyes submissively while his
legal aid lawyer screamed at him on the courthouse steps.

> What kinda fucking asshole are you? Just get a job! Any kind of
> bullshit job! So I can tell the judge you're a good man. Jesus Christ!
> Can't you understand what I'm telling you?

The fact was, of course, that in the midst of the national recession,
Primo was unable to find "any kind of bullshit job." Caesar became his
only source of solidarity and understanding. He empathized with Primo's
depression and attempted to cheer his friend up with tirades embracing
the ecstasy of substance abuse and celebrating the street-defined dignity
of refusing to work honestly for low wages.

The most persuasive dimension to Caesar's oppositional celebration of
street marginality was his cultural redefinition of crack dealing and
unemployment as a badge of pride – even if ultimately self-destructive.
For example, one Tuesday night right after the end of a busy shift at the
Game Room, I accompanied Primo and Caesar on their way to buy a
twenty-dollar bag of El Sapo Verde [the green toad], a new brand of
cocaine with a growing reputation for quality that was sold a few blocks
downtown from the Game Room. This was their first time purchasing
from this outfit, so Caesar and I waited around the corner to avoid "*petro-
lyzing*" [rendering paranoid] the sellers while Primo made the actual
purchase. I struck up a conversation in Spanish with three undocumented
Mexican immigrants from Piaxtla, a rural municipality in the state of
Puebla. They were drinking beer on the stoop of their tenement watching
with disdain as El Sapo Verde's customers passed by.

One of the immigrants had arrived two years ago and was earning
$500 a week fixing deep-fat fry machines. I put my arm around Caesar
and asked the successful immigrant how it was possible that he was doing
"so good" when my friend Caesar, an articulate, native-born, fluent-
English speaker, could not even find a $200-a-week position. His re-
sponse was straightforwardly racist:

> Okay, Okay I'll explain it to you in one word: Because the Puerto
> Ricans are stupid! Stupid! Do you understand? They're stupid
> because look at that guy [pointing to Caesar] he knows English.

And look at his body. He's got a body that at least should get him a job as good as mine. And he doesn't have it because he's a brute. That's all.

They like to make easy money. They like to leech off of other people. But not us Mexicans! No way! We like to work for our money. We don't steal. We came here to work and that's all.

A wave of fear swept over me as I looked at the expression on Caesar's face, convinced I had irresponsibly provoked a bloody confrontation. Instead, Caesar waited for Primo to return and then responded loudly in English, turning the Mexican's racist humiliation into a generationally based assertion of street culture pride.

Caesar: That's right my man! We is real vermin lunatics that sell drugs. We don't wanna be a part of society. It's like that record: "Fight the Power!"[5]

What do we wanna be working for? We came here to this country, and we abused the freedom, because Puerto Ricans don't like to work. We rather live off the system; gain weight; lay women.

Okay, maybe not all of us, 'cause there's still a lot of strict folks from the old school that still be working. But the new generation, no way!

We have no regard for nothing. The new generation has no regard for the public bullshit. We wanna make easy money, and that's it. *Easy* now mind you. We don't wanna work hard. That's the new generation for you.

Now the old school was for when we was younger, and we used to break our asses. I had all kinds of stupid jobs . . . scrap metal sorting, dry cleaning, advertising agencies.

But not no more. [putting his arm around Primo] Now we're in a rebellious stage. We rather evade taxes; make quick money; and just survive. But we're not satisfied with that either, ha!

Crossover Dreams

Despite his public assertiveness, Caesar was ridden with self-doubt over his exclusion from mainstream society. At times, he too shared Primo's

A neighborhood bodega. Photo by Philippe Bourgois.

fantasies of being a "normal working nigga'." His tolerance of exploitation, however, was lower than Primo's, and his sensitivity toward personal disrespect at work was much more acute. Furthermore, his social skills – or his cultural capital – that might have enabled him to interact credibly with middle-class society were even more limited than Primo's. Nevertheless, he too allowed himself to fantasize about "goin' legit" when opportunities presented themselves in contexts that were not completely anathema to the norms of street culture. For example, when Ray made his first concerted attempt to launder his crack profits by purchasing the lease on a bodega, Caesar jumped at the opportunity to work there. Ray had hired Primo to clean and renovate the premises, and Primo, once again, subcontracted Caesar to be his assistant. It was a perfect opportunity for the two crack dealers to ease a transition to stable, legal employment. Not only would they maintain the same boss, but they would remain in the same immediate neighborhood vicinity. The bodega was located only half a block away from Ray's Social Club crackhouse next to the Hell Gate post office. In other words, they merely had to substitute lard, cigarettes, potato chips, sandwiches, beer, ice cream, and so forth for the crack they formerly purveyed to their neighbors.

Ray himself was also excited about his attempt to open a "legit place" for much the same reasons. In the early phase he proved to be an astute businessman, negotiating a discounted price for the storefront lease from the previous owner, who had been forced to flee the neighborhood after the "numbers" [gambling] racketeers who used the site as their bank torched the place following a dispute over profit shares. Primo's first tasks were to kill the rats, throw out the charred and decaying waterlogged merchandise, and eventually repaint the premises. Caesar was especially effective at killing the gigantic rats that had multiplied exponentially (as only rats can multiply in a New York City grocery store abandoned for more than a month following a fire). He relished crushing them with well-aimed bricks, broomsticks, and work boot kicks.

Despite the filth and the Hitchcockesque size and quantity of the rats infesting their new work space, both Caesar and Primo were thrilled at the prospects of "workin' clean" under Ray's auspices. During these weeks after finishing work, they would come over to my living room in their stinking clothes, with their wet sneakers caked in powdered rat poison and rotten grocery grime, in order to sniff speedballs, drink beer, and tape-record fantasies of their future stable careers at Ray's soon-to-be-opened bodega. Their enthusiasm over their imminent metamorphosis to legality once again expressed itself semantically in their internalization of the polite superstitions of their parents' jíbaro past.

Caesar: I haven't told 'Buela [grandma] yet. I ain't tellin' no one nothing until I be coming home paid every week. [slamming his fist into his palm and then bending over to sniff from the key-tip laden with heroin that Primo was serving him]

I'm not going to *salal*[6] [jinx] but I think – *si Diós quiere* – this is the one thing that's going to work for me. I'm going to get off hard-core drugs. [grinning and sniffing heroin again] Well, except maybe dope and coke.

And my career in here is going to escalate, because the more money the store makes, the more money I make, 'cause I'm the sandwich man. That means I'll probably have to be pulling a double shift.

This is good for us; this is good for Primo; we're close. No more of this bumming around. [waving his arm at my living room]

On this particular night, Caesar and Primo had also taken purple microdot capsules of synthetic mescaline. If, as some psychotherapists claim, hallucinogenic drugs unleash the anxieties, obsessions, and fantasies of one's unconscious, then Caesar's babbling reveals how profoundly excited he was over the possibility of finding legal employment.

I'm the sandwich- , the clean-up- , and the hurt-the-customer-man. And [flashing his eyes deviously] the scam-some-money-on-the-side-man.

Yeah! Yeah! Yeah! I'm also The Man – the bouncer. Because if I catch a shoplifter, when the cops come they're not going to have to handcuff him. They're going to have to bring a stretcher, because me and Primo are going to *stretch* someone right open.

[Grabbing my tape recorder and speaking into the microphone as if it inspired a brilliant idea] We make it a social club for informants, for Felipe. A club!

Dropping the tape recorder, Caesar began imitating the sounds of a cashier barking orders, and of change dropping in a cash register drawer while, at the same time, he made the deft motions of handing out imaginary sandwiches.

Caesar: Sandwich man! Here! Yo! Take yours! Ring! Clink! Next! [sitting back on my living room couch wide-eyed] Wow, this is a weird . . . Primo, check this out. [waving his hands to admire the mescaline-induced visual tracers] It's like wavy blue. [spinning around and pointing in the opposite direction at the ceiling] These are like purple.

[turning abruptly again to face me as if I were a customer at the deli] Got money? [raising his arms like He-Man] I work! [waving his hands, once again, to admire the color tracings, but then switching back and forth between the personas of a customer and a deli clerk] I want light blue. Sandwich! Sandwich man, how you doin'?

[sitting back again relaxed with a happy smile] All right! We're gonna open a deli! [reaching out to hug Primo]

Caesar's ecstatic legal dream never materialized. Ray was unable to negotiate the complicated New York City paperwork for health inspections and outstanding tax forfeitures. He never even managed to open his enterprise legally for a single day. He began selling without official permits for about ten days and soon realized there was not enough of a local demand for his grocery products. The final insult occurred when the man he hired to do inventory stole from him and escaped to Puerto Rico. Ray gave up and returned Primo and Caesar to their part-time positions at the Game Room selling crack on Monday and Tuesday nights.

The contrast between Ray's consistent failures at establishing viable, legal business ventures – that is, his deli, his legal social club, and his Laundromat – versus his notable success at running a complex franchise of retail crack outlets, highlight the different "cultural capitals" needed to operate as a private entrepreneur in the legal economy versus the underground economy. As the preceding chapter on crackhouse management demonstrates, Ray's mastery of street culture enabled him to administer his businesses effectively in the drug economy. He skillfully disciplined his workers and gauged the needs of his customers. He mobilized violence, coercion, and friendship in a delicate balance that earned him consistent profits and guaranteed him a badge of respect on the street. In contrast, in his forays into the legal economy, Ray's same street skills made him appear to be an incompetent, gruff, illiterate, urban jíbaro to the inspectors, clerks, and petty officials who allocate permits and inventory product, and who supervise licensing in New York City.

Similarly, when Primo attempted to establish a legitimate enterprise by pasting photocopied flyers at bus stops advertising his "Mr. Fix-It Services" for repairing domestic electronic appliances, he too failed miserably despite his own obvious entrepreneurial skills as a crackhouse manager. When potential customers with broken appliances managed to reach him on the telephone at the project apartment of his girlfriend, Maria, they balked at the address he gave them and then usually declined his offer to come to their homes. Those who did not hang up on him were suspicious of his precapitalist, jíbaro way of setting prices. It ultimately became a forum for racist humiliation for Primo who was already feeling especially vulnerable in his attempt to "go legit."

> *Primo:* It's like they hear my voice, and they stop. . . . There's a silence on the other end of the line.
> Everyone keeps asking me what race I am. Yeah, they say, like, "Where're you from with that name?" Because they hear that Puerto Rican accent. And I just tell them that I'm Nuyorican. I hate that.
> Plus I tell them they can pay me whatever they feel is right once I fix their shit. But they don't even want me to come over.
> I hate that shit, Felipe.

Primo encountered further stereotyped barriers when he did manage to meet his legal customers face to face. For example, after arranging for him to fix three broken Dictaphone machines and a cable television box at a foundation where I had an affiliation, I received an apologetic computer E-mail from one of the administrators advising me not to bring Primo onto the premises anymore for fear patrons "might think we're turning the place into an electronic repair shop."

Not all of Primo's failures as a private entrepreneur were imposed by distrustful or racist customers. Some of his inability to run a profitable private enterprise was caused by his own jíbaro definitions of proper decorum and reciprocal obligation to friends and relatives. For example, when my mother asked him to examine her broken stereo system, he mysteriously missed several appointments to meet her at her apartment. He finally accompanied me to her apartment one evening at my insistence. He later admitted that it had not seemed proper to him to go alone to the apartment of a woman he did not know well. Finally, after successfully fixing her stereo, he did not know how much to charge her since she was my mother, and besides, she had prepared dinner for us in the process.

At Work: Disrespect and Resistance

Pursuing the Immigrant's Dream

Mainstream society easily evokes racial stereotypes to dismiss Primo, Caesar, and even Ray as pathetic losers, or as lazy, pathological, self-destructive drug addicts. My examples framed by cultural production theory have emphasized the disjuncture in cultural styles of communication and the allocation of power around symbolic markers. A more political-economy understanding of the crack dealers' failures in the legal world would point to how they and their parents had been channeled into the most marginal economic sector almost since birth. I pursued this structural economic argument by asking them to talk extensively about their first "real" jobs. It became clear to me that in their early teenage years they had been energetically pursuing the immigrant's working-class dream of finding a tough, macho factory job and working hard for steady wages. One standard scenario emerges from the dozens of accounts I collected: With their mothers' permission they dropped out of high school – or even junior high school – to work in local factories. Usually within a year or two, their factories had closed down to seek cheaper labor elsewhere. They then began the treadmill of rotating from one poorly paid job to the next, with little education or social skills to allow them mobility outside of the marginal factory enclaves that trapped their entire social network.

Once again, Primo's and Caesar's cases are particularly illustrative of these dynamics. Primo was so highly motivated and energetic in pursuit of his mother's immigrant working-class dream that in his early teenage years he actually dropped out of junior high school to find a job through family connections.

> *Primo:* I was playing hooky and pressing, like, dresses, and whatever they were making on the steamer. They was cheap, cheap clothes.
>
> I was just a kid, and it used to be stupid hot behind the steamer, but I liked'ed that job. The best job I had was in that factory. Wish I would've lasted there, but they moved out of the neighborhood.
>
> My mother's sister was working there first, and then her son, Luis' brother – the one who's in jail now – he was the one they hired first, because his mother agreed, "If you don't want to go to school, you gotta work."

He was young, he was . . . like sixteen or fifteen, I guess, and I was younger. So I started hanging out with him. Just hanging out, but then at the factory, sometimes he needed help with some rush work, and I used to go out and help him. And the boss used to look me out at the end of the week. I wasn't planning on working in the factory; I was supposed to be in school; but it just sort of happened.

I wanted to get paid and I hated school. I rather just work.

Predictably, Primo was working for a garment subcontractor – one of the most vulnerable niches in the manufacturing sector.

Primo: The boss was Spanish, and shit, but I don't know if she was the main man. She just ran the whole factory.

Her husband was a dope fiend, but he was the one that picked the payroll money up. We used to go downtown to do that shit, and it used to be white people who used to have a huge amount of money.

Primo and his cousin became the agents who physically moved their jobs out of the inner city. In the process they became merely two more individuals out of the 445,900 manufacturing workers in New York City who lost their jobs as factory employment dropped 50 percent from 1963 to 1983.[7] Of course, instead of seeing themselves as the victims of a structural transformation, Primo remembers with pleasure, and even pride, the extra income he earned for clearing the machines out of the factory space:

Primo: Them people had money, man. Because we helped them move out of the neighborhood.

It took us two days – only me and my cousin. Wow! It was work. They gave us seventy bucks each, and back in them days that was money, boy! Plus, we were stupid little niggas.

Not coincidentally, Caesar interrupted this particular reminiscence of Primo's that I was tape-recording in the Game Room to give me an almost identical story. Like Primo, Caesar had obtained his first job through his family connections and their social network. Instead of the garment industry he was channeled into metallurgy, another one of the least desirable and most unstable niches within New York City's manufacturing sector:

Caesar: I worked in a factory before too. That was my first job. My uncle got me the job when I dropped out of school. My moms told me I either get a job or go back to school.

I liked'ed it at that time, but I lost a lot of weight, because it used to be stupid hot in there. They used to give us these salt pills and shit.

They used to plate metal, like paint fake jewelry. But the company moved too.

Like Primo's aunt, Caesar's uncle subscribed to the same working-class ideologies about the dignity of hard work versus education. These are working-class rather than lumpen childhood memories. They are not yet imbued with the hopeless nihilism of the unemployable crack dealer. Objective conditions, however, prevented Primo and Caesar from achieving working-class stability. In Caesar's case, the limitations of tough, hard factory labor were driven home by the subsequent experience of his role-model uncle.

Caesar: Damn, man, that was my uncle's trade, metal salvaging and metal plating. That nigga' worked in there for about forty-five years, man. On one job. For forty-five years. Can you imagine that shit? Forty-five years and he's only a foreman.

And he fell in the acid one time and it was crazy, boy – the acid that they dip the metal in. I saw it. Yeah, it was fucked up. I saw it when he slipped.

That nigga' was out of work for at least like about seven, eight months, man. He burned his skin tissue off, man. I saw him all red, with, like, his muscles exposed. It was bugged.

He can't even sue, man. It was his own negligence, because he was the one that slipped in. You see, it was like an assembly line, and they have to be cleaning out these big tanks where they be dunking the metal pieces. So the nigga' was going in over the tanks one day, and he slipped. He fell in it, and jumped out real quick, less than five seconds, but his fuckin' clothes turned into rags,

HHIISSS, HHIISSS. He got dogged man. That nigga' screamed real loud.

After that he lost weight. He got like, REAL THIN, and he was all muscle before.

Significantly, in Caesar's uncle's case, the ultimate outcome of a lifetime of assembly line employment was sexual impotence and sterility, a theme the crack dealers often elaborated on when they talked of the powerlessness they experienced in their legal jobs.

Caesar: That's my uncle Joe, he's still fucked up. His whole, like, legs is all like, like, a burn victim whose skin is all burned.

He can't have no babies, man. Just dogs. Because he burnt his joint and everything, man.

He lives in Cincinnati now, 'cause the company moved, and they got him another position as a foreman at a factory that makes bathroom fixtures, and shit like that.

[snapping to attention and motioning for Primo to hide the purse with crack vials as a roving police car slowed down in front of the Game Room] Yo-yo-yo-yo! Static-static-static!

Retrospectively, Caesar's decision to drop out early from school with his family's blessing to find employment in a dead-end niche of New York's shrinking manufacturing sector appears tragically self-destructive. At the time it was taking place, however, fifteen-year-old Caesar looked and felt like a king within the confines of his second-generation immigrant's working-class universe. For a poor adolescent the decision to drop out of school to become a marginal factory worker was attractive. In separate conversations, Willie, the only member of Ray's network to have graduated from high school, confirmed how powerful and macho Caesar had appeared to him in his early teenage, hardworking glory:

Willie: I was fourteen and Caesar's like fifteen and the motherfucker dropped out of school and during this whole year he was working with his uncle chroming.

Mah' man was making himself some money, and I was going to school. I was so jealous. I was so jealous.

Caesar was always working. By eighth, ninth, . . . no by my

tenth, eleventh, and twelfth grades, Caesar was working. He was a nice dresser 'cause he had money, and he used to get pussy, and everything.

After school I'd come home, and I'd say, "Yeah, Caesar's getting fucked, 'cause he ain't going to school, and he's got money."

Caesar was so bold. He didn't have like no fear. This was before we met you.

He was the first one who came out with fly clothes. Primo, you remember how C was in those days?

He always had a big box. And he used to hook me up outta sight, because I was always with Caesar out on the streets after school. Me and Caesar were so dope . . . so dope, that I never had to run the same coat each year.

Caesar used to wear a burgundy leather jacket and a burgundy Kangol. And we used to have these crowns, these gold crowns – right – that you put on a jacket – like those little things that you pin on your shirt and all that.

And we would be "king of the crew." That was the best time of my life.

Shattered Working-class Fantasies in the Service Sector

It almost appears as if Caesar, Primo, and Willie were caught in a time warp during their teenage years. Their macho-proletarian dream of working an eight-hour shift plus overtime throughout their adult lives at a rugged slot in a unionized shop has been replaced by the nightmare of poorly paid, highly feminized, office-support service work. The stable factory-worker incomes that might have allowed Caesar and Primo to support families have largely disappeared from the inner city. Perhaps if their social network had not been confined to the weakest sector of manufacturing in a period of rapid job loss, their teenage working-class dreams might have stabilized them for long enough to enable them to adapt to the restructuring of the local economy. Instead, they find themselves propelled headlong into an explosive confrontation between their sense of cultural dignity versus the humiliating interpersonal subordination of service work.

Formerly, when most entry-level jobs were found in factories, the contradiction between an oppositional street culture and traditional working-class, shop-floor culture – especially when it was protected by a union – was less pronounced. I do not wish to romanticize factory work. It is usually tedious, tiring, and often dangerous. Furthermore, it is inevitably rife with confrontational hierarchies. On the shop floor, however, surrounded by older union workers, high school dropouts who are well versed in the latest and toughest street culture styles function effectively. In the factory, being tough and violently macho has high cultural value; a certain degree of opposition to the foreman and the "bossman" is expected and is considered masculine.

In contrast, this same oppositional street-identity is dysfunctional in the service sector, especially among the office-support workers who serve the executives of the FIRE sector, where most of the new entry-level jobs with a potentially stable future are located. Street culture is in direct contradiction to the humble, obedient modes of subservient social interaction that are essential for upward mobility in high-rise office jobs. Workers in a mail room or behind a photocopy machine cannot publicly maintain their cultural autonomy. Most concretely, they have no union; more subtly, there are few fellow workers surrounding them to insulate them and to provide them with a culturally based sense of class solidarity. Instead they are besieged by supervisors and bosses from an alien, hostile, and obviously dominant culture. When these office managers are not intimidated by street culture, they ridicule it. Workers like Caesar and Primo appear inarticulate to their professional supervisors when they try to imitate the language of power in the workplace, and instead stumble pathetically over the enunciation of unfamiliar words. They cannot decipher the hastily scribbled instructions – rife with mysterious abbreviations – that are left for them by harried office managers on diminutive Post-its. The "common sense" of white-collar work is foreign to them; they do not, for example, understand the logic in filing triplicate copies of memos or for postdating invoices. When they attempt to improvise or show initiative, they fail miserably and instead appear inefficient – or even hostile – for failing to follow "clearly specified" instructions.

Their interpersonal social skills are even more inadequate than their limited professional capacities. They do not know how to look at their fellow service workers – let alone their supervisors – without intimidating them. They cannot walk down the hallway to the water fountain without unconsciously swaying their shoulders aggressively as if patrolling their home turf. Gender barriers are an even more culturally charged realm. They are repeatedly reprimanded for offending co-workers with sexually aggressive behavior.

The cultural clash between white "yuppie" power and inner-city "scrambling jive" in the service sector is much more than superficial style. Service workers who are incapable of obeying the rules of interpersonal interaction dictated by professional office culture will never be upwardly mobile. In the high-rise office buildings of midtown Manhattan or Wall Street, newly employed inner-city high school dropouts suddenly realize they look like idiotic buffoons to the men and women for whom they work. This book's argument – as conveyed in its title – is that people like Primo and Caesar have not passively accepted their structural victimization. On the contrary, by embroiling themselves in the underground economy and proudly embracing street culture, they are seeking an alternative to their social marginalization. In the process, on a daily level, they become the actual agents administering their own destruction and their community's suffering.

Getting "Dissed" in the Office

Both Primo and Caesar experienced deep humiliation and insecurity in their attempts to penetrate the foreign, hostile world of high-rise office corridors. Primo had bitter memories of being the mail room clerk and errand boy at a now defunct professional trade magazine. Significantly, the only time he explicitly admitted to having experienced racism was when he described how he was treated at that particular work setting. The level of racially charged cultural miscommunication at his work site is nicely illustrated by his inability to identify the name and ethnicity of his boss, just as she might have been unsure of what Latin American country he was from, and how to spell or pronounce his first name:

Primo: I had a prejudiced boss. She was a fucking "ho'," Gloria. She was white. Her name was Christian. No, not Christian, Kirsch-man. I don't know if she was Jewish or not.

She would like to talk about me to whoever was over visiting in the office – you know, like her associates who would come over for a coffee break.

When she was talking to people she would say, "He's illiterate," as if I was really that stupid that I couldn't understand what she was talking about.

So what I did one day – you see they had this big dictionary right there on the desk, a big heavy motherfucker – so what I just did was open up the dictionary, and I just looked up the word, "illiterate." And that's when I saw what she was calling me.

So she's saying that I'm stupid or something. I'm stupid! [pointing to himself with both thumbs and making a hulking face] "He doesn't know shit."

The most profound dimension of Primo's humiliation was not being called illiterate but, rather, having to look up in the dictionary the words used to insult him. In contrast, in the underground economy Primo never had to risk this kind of threat to his self-worth.

Primo: Ray would never disrespect me that way, because he wouldn't tell me that because he's illiterate too, plus I've got more education than him. I almost got a GED.

Worse yet, Primo genuinely attempted to show initiative at Gloria Kirschman's magazine-publishing company, but the harder he tried, the stupider he felt when he inevitably failed. As he explains, "It only gets worse when they get to know you."

Primo: So you, you know, you try to do good, but then people treat you like shit.

Man, you be cool at first, and then all of a sudden, when they get to know you, they try to diss you.

When I first got to my jobs, I was busting my ass and everything, but after a while, it's like, you get to hate your supervisor.

I was disrespected a few times at that job when I didn't follow, like, the orders. When my supervisor told me to do a job one way, but I thought it was best to do it another way. She dissed the shit out of me a coupla' times. That lady was a bitch.

Quite simply, Primo was being exposed to the fact that he did not have the cultural or symbolic capital that would have allowed him to step out from behind the photocopy machine or the mail meter. He was claustrophobically surrounded by overseers from an alien but powerful culture:

> *Primo:* I had to be cool. Even when we used to get our lunch breaks, when we were supposed to be able to just hang, even then, the supervisors were right there.

Primo was both unwilling and unable to compromise his street identity and imitate the professional modes of interaction that might have earned him the approval and respect of his boss. It is precisely in moments like this that one can see institutionalized racism at work in how the professional service sector unconsciously imposes the requisites of Anglo, middle-class cultural capital. His boss forbade him to answer the telephone, because objectively a Puerto Rican street accent will discourage prospective clients and cause her to lose money. Ironically, the confrontation over Primo using the telephone occurred because he had been attempting to show initiative and good faith by answering calls when he saw that his supervisors were busy or out of the office.

> *Primo:* I wouldn't have mind that she said I was illiterate. What bothered me was that when she called on the telephone, she wouldn't want me to answer even if my supervisor – who was the receptionist – was not there and the phone be ringing for a long time.
>
> So when I answered it, my boss sounds like she's going to get a heart attack when she hears my voice. She'd go, "Where's Renee?" – Renee Silverman – that's the receptionist, my supervisor.
>
> I'd say, "She's out to lunch" – or whatever.
>
> And she would go, "Is Fran there?"
>
> I'd say, "Yes she is."
>
> But, you see, it wasn't Fran's job to answer the phones. She was taking care of the bills and always busy doing some work. So I just said, "She's probably out to lunch too."
>
> That boss was just a bitch, because I answered the phone correct. There are so many different kinds of people out there in New York City that've got a crazy accent. They could be into real estate; they

could be into anything. They just got their own accent. But that bitch didn't like my Puerto Rican accent.

I don't know what was her problem; she's a fucking bitch.

Okay, maybe I don't have the education to type; so I will not type. But don't diss me for answering the phones instead of letting it ring forever. Maybe it's important! Bitch!

I used to answer it pretty well, man. But then after that — after she dished me — when I did pick up the phone, I used to just sound Porta'rrrrican on purpose. Fuck it.

The Gender Diss

The contemporary street sensitivity to being dissed immediately emerges in these memories of office humiliation. The machismo of street culture exacerbates the sense of insult experienced by men because the majority of office supervisors at the entry level are women. Hence the constant references to bosses and supervisors being "bitches" or "ho's" [whores], and the frequent judgmental descriptions of their bodies. On numerous occasions in the Game Room, or after hours in my living room, or on the street, Caesar interrupted Primo's accounts of legal employment with his own memories of workplace humiliation. For example, in the middle of Primo's "telephone diss" story he launched into a tirade of male outrage at having been forced, in the legal labor market, to break the street taboo against public male subordination to a woman:

Caesar: I had a few jobs like that where you gotta take a lot of shit from fat, ugly bitches and be a wimp.

My worst was at Sudler & Hennessey — the advertising agency that works with pharmaceutical shit. I didn't like it but I kept on working, because "Fuck it!" you don't want to fuck up the relationship. So you just be a punk.

Oh my God! I hated that head supervisor. She was a bitch, Peggy MacNamara. She was an Irishwoman. She was beautiful, but that bitch was *really* nasty.

She used to make me do fucked-up errands for her — wack shit. One time I had to go all the way to Staten Island and find this fuckin' place, and go collect two paintings for her. And shit like that. That bitch just didn't like me.

She got her rocks off on firing people, man. You can see that on her face, boy. She made this fucking guy cry – he was Eye-talian – and beg for his job, and shit. And then she gave him his job back and put him on probation, like that. [snapping his fingers and shaking his head in disgust]

And then I heard her, like, laughing about it with the other supervisors, like, joking about it.

Ultimately the gender disses respond to economic inequality and power hierarchies. The crack dealers' experience of powerlessness is usually expressed in a racist and sexist idiom. For example, even though Caesar, like Primo, is incapable of reading the white ethnic markers of his supervisors, he is clearly aware of the economic and racial facts of his marginal niche in the labor hierarchy:

Primo: I lasted in that mail room for like eight months. They used to trust me. I used to go to the bank, get the checks, the payroll, and hand out the payroll to all the executives.

Damn, there was this one bitch, her name was Inga . . . Hoffman . . . no, it was Hawthorne, 'cause she was Jewish. Well, that bitch used to get paid well, boy! I used to put the fuckin' check up to the light to see.

That bitch was making about five thousand dollars a week, man! You could see [squinting at an imaginary envelope] like, five thousand three hundred and forty three dollars and change.

I was like, "Oh, my God!" Yeah, Hoffman, that bitch, was well paid, man.

Mine's was the lowest paid job there. Shit, that was what drove me out of it. I was just scum-a'-the-earth Porta' Rican nigga'.

In the lowest recesses of New York City's FIRE sector, tens of thousands of messengers, photocopy machine operators, and security guards serving the Fortune 500 companies are brusquely ordered about by young white executives – often female – who sometimes make bimonthly salaries superior to their underlings' yearly wages. The extraordinary wealth of Manhattan's financial district exacerbates the sense of sexist–racist insult associated with performing just-above-minimum-wage labor.

Work Site Wars

The remarkable profitability of New York's financial service companies allows management to pay arbitrary bonuses to even the most lowly employees. This co-opts whatever solidarity and resistance might have been fomented in the mail room or behind the photocopy machines as the low-wage workers involute their energies, backbiting one another in a jealous scramble for tips and extra perks.

> *Caesar:* My supervisor was a greedy nigga'. He's always wanting to know how much I get paid 'cause they give you bonuses on holidays – like at Christmas – and the bonuses go up by the years. My bonus was three hundred dollars.
>
> *Primo:* [gasping] That's a lot of money. I never got more than twenty-five, fifty dollars.
>
> *Caesar:* So when my supervisor found out how much I got, the nigga' got on the phone, and started complaining hard:
>
> "Ah, why, uhum" [clumsily imitating an office telephone voice] – that's the way they spoke there – "Why did the mail room clerk get a three hundred dollar bonus, and he only been here eight months, and I've been here nine years, and I only got four hundred dollars. I think you made a mistake."
>
> You see he was telling them he should get more, and I should get less. I never shoulda told him how much I got.
>
> This son of a bitch was pissed off. I don't know if they gave him more, but after a while he started complaining to me about everything. He was on my case.

In the less-well-established FIRE service sector industries the infighting among the entry-level workers and their immediate supervisors results in job loss. This had been Primo's experience in the highly specialized and vulnerable desktop-publishing industry. Despite learning some computer skills, he still lacked the cultural capital to be able to compete effectively according to professional workplace rules. When a fluctuation in the demand for annual reports or for merger and acquisition agreements occurred, he was the first fired. Once again, his anger over losing his job fixates misogynously on the humiliation of having been the victim of a more powerful female supervisor. He redundantly punctuates his sentences with the term "bitch" and makes repeated references to his nemesis' body. In fact, he even concludes with the classic, violent fantasy of following his supervisor after work to dominate her physically in the most traditional patriarchal setting of all – her home. His repeated sniffs from a ten-dollar bag of cocaine while he was talking seemed to fuel his ire and frustration at the unpleasant memories.

Primo: My problem was that my supervisor was just a bitch who liked to make sure I'm doing my job all the time, even when it used to be slow, and she didn't need to be hawking me that way.

I was responsible there. The worst thing I did was fall asleep, 'cause they switched me onto the night shift. That's what got me fired. [sniffing cocaine]

That bitch – I hate her. She was a big, fat woman, and they hired her after me. She was just working there months too, man – that bitch – before she got me fired.

I used to do telecommunications too. [enthusiastically] On this other Kaypro computer I'd be sending files over to Boston [pointing officiously into the distance]. I took care of all those things, the computer, cleaning the machines – even bringing up the system when it locks down. Crazy shit! I used to have my own file, too.

But I was falling asleep, man, sometimes I used to fall asleep, like on the chair, with a terminal right there, and running.

And when I used to wake up, there's people doing my work, and I'd just get up real quick, and send them back, like, "No, no, it's okay – okay, shit! I could lose my job. I have to do my job." [sniffing again]

But the supervisor of the night shift – the fat bitch – was already writing me down.

I used to find her letters about me in the terminal. 'Cause I know, when you have a file on the terminal in the system, you have a password. So I used to just figure out their password.

I would go [squinting with feigned concentration], "They probably used their last name, their first name, their nickname." I used to keep trying all those names until I get into their files. So I knew the file of the main supervisor from that section. I used to find all her letters she used to write about me. [sniffing again]

I used to look at her and want to kill her; wanted to burn her.

She used to live in a little trailer thing, I used to want to catch her and — I used to think of all the most miserable shit to do to her.

I could tell she didn't like me.

I told the company that she falls asleep on the job too. Sometimes she goes to the back and falls asleep on the floor.

But they told me, "Yeah, but she signs out for that time. She signs out, and signs back in when there's work."

They should have told me to sign out when they see me asleep, then sign back in. But I guess she's a supervisor and I'm just a nobody.

Primo's white-collar enemy was obviously invulnerable to his attempts at revenge. Ultimately, he realized that his fundamental vulnerability at the work site was structural rather than merely the result of his negative personal relationship with his immediate supervisor.

Primo: I had been there a long time. The problem was that they were really coming down on a lot of the employees. I was one of the lucky ones. They were waiting for any little mixup that we might do. They were looking for reasons to let people go, just like that. [snapping his fingers]

They weren't hiring nobody. The only ones that stayed were the ones that were working there first, which was John, and Art Schwartz, and this other tall white guy.

Philippe: And how did that make you feel?

Primo: [sniffing cocaine in each nostril pensively] When I found out I wanted to cry, man. My throat got dry, I was like . . . [gasping and waving his arms as if suffocating, then sniffing more cocaine]

You see, I had went to pick up my check, but before getting my check, there was a little hassle, and they called me to the office.

I was like, "Oh *shit!*" [sniffing again]

But I couldn't get through to them. I even told them, "I'll let you put me back to messenger, I will take less pay, just keep me employed. I need the money; I need to work; I got a family.

They said [feigning dismissive authority], "Nope, nope, nope."

So I said, "Okay." I left.

My friends were waiting for me outside. I was fucked man. All choked up.

Relationships with supervisors and bosses do not have to be malicious to be humiliating or otherwise intolerable by street culture standards. In Primo's previous job at the trade magazine publishing house, for example, his boss, Gloria Kirschman, had probably been a well-meaning liberal. Reading between the lines of Primo's vilifying account, one suspects that she cared about the future of the bright, energetic high school dropout working for her. At one point, she took him aside to advise him to "go back to school." This is how her well-intentioned – and objectively accurate – advice sounded to Primo, however:

Primo: If you're young, you're a fucking idiot if you're working.

My boss, she wanted me to go to school too. Well fuck her, man! I'm here and I'm working. I want my money.

And they talk about that school shit 'cause they're pampered, they lead pampered lives. Everybody can't go to school a lot. Some people have to live, man. They got to eat – you know what I'm saying? People got to eat, man. Especially if you got a son, you got to . . . people got to do things.

I was eighteen then and Papito, my son, was already born. I mean, you want things in the world. You can't wait for some fuckin' degree.

She had no business worrying about my schooling.

Caesar: I don't see how learning about George Washington crossing the fucking Delaware is going to help you in this fucking world.

Primo: Like, teach me how to write the letters to other companies. English – [turning to Caesar] that's what they call English – and reading and writing.

Primo had no frame of reference to interpret and understand the office work tasks that Gloria Kirschman insisted he perform.

I didn't like working there at all, anyway. I didn't want to be doing no collating, or no mail shit.

Plus, she used to have me look in this closet and put everything together . . . I forgot the names of those things . . . oh yeah, she would call it, "Make an inventory."

I didn't even know what the hell those things were — an inventory? Anyway, the closet was a mess. So I just like thought, "I should throw some of this shit away. Just to make it look neater."

So I just threw it all out, 'cause I knew she was never gonna use any of that stuff again.

In his confusion over the ostensibly irrational mysteries of office work, Primo worried about a repeat of the illiteracy insult. He was constantly on guard lest Gloria Kirschman disrespect him without his being immediately aware of what was happening. Consequently, when she ordered him to perform mysteriously specific tasks, such as direct mailings of promotional materials that required particular conjugations of folding, stuffing, or clipping, he activated his defense mechanisms. His mother's inner-city apartment project mailbox address is only rarely targeted by direct-mail campaigns, and consequently Primo had no frame of reference for understanding the urgency of the precision with which Gloria oversaw the logistics of her direct mailings. Instead, she appeared overbearingly oppressive and insulting to him. In fact, he even suspected Gloria was superstitious and arbitrary in the rigor and anxiety with which she supervised every detail of the direct-mailing packets he was preparing.

Weapons of the Weak

Primo refused to accept the "flexibility" that these delicate, targeted mailing campaigns required — that is, late-night binges of collating and recollating to make bulk-rate postage deadlines coincide with the magazine's printing and sales deadlines. It was offensive and sexually inappropriate to Primo to have to bring over the assembled promotional packets to Gloria's home for last-minute, late-night inspections.

Primo: It would be late, and I would be at the office to do these rush jobs: collate them, staple them, fold them in the correct way . . . whatever way she said. It was always different.

And it had to be just the way she wanted it. I'd stuff them just the right way [making frantic shuffling motions with his hands] and then seal the shit.

I used to hate that. I would box it and take it to the Thirty-eight Street post office at ten-thirty at night.

But then sometimes she would call me from home, and I would have to bring papers up to her house on Seventy-ninth Street and Third Avenue [Manhattan's Silk Stocking district] just to double-check my work. She had to check every single envelope. And she always used to find a paper that I had folded just wrong.

And she would try to offer me something to eat and I would say firmly, "No, thank you." Because she would try to pay me with that shit; 'cause she's a cheap bitch.

She'd say, "You want pizza, tea, or cookies." She had those Pepperidge Farm cookies.

But I wouldn't accept anything from her. I wasn't going to donate my time man.

She thought I was illiterate. She thought I was stupid. Not me boy! Charge *every penny*. [grinning] From the moment I leave the office, that's overtime, all the way to her house. That's time and a half.

I used to exaggerate the hours. If I worked sixteen, I would put eighteen or twenty to see if I could get away with it — and I would get away with it. I'm not going to do that kind of shit for free.

And that bitch was crazy. She used to eat baby food. I know, 'cause I saw her eating it with a spoon right out of the jar.

If Primo appeared to be a scowling, ungrateful, dishonest worker to Gloria, then Gloria herself looked almost perverted to Primo. What normal middle-aged woman would invite her nineteen-year-old employee into her kitchen late at night and eat baby food in front of him? Ironically, it was precisely by showing eager flexibility during these emergency late-night binges to complete direct-mailing campaigns that Primo might have earned a promotion — or at least job stability — at Gloria's magazine. She probably saw herself as bending over backward to be trusting and friendly to her shy, moderately hostile employee by inviting him into her kitchen and offering him a friendly snack.

In any case, Primo's working-class victories over his employer proved to be Pyrrhic. His definition of worker rights was still based on the conceptions that emerged out of generations of factory floor confrontations where self-respecting hourly wage earners always demand time and a half once they have completed their eight-hour shifts. In the cross-cultural confrontation taking place in the corridors of high-rise office buildings, one never gets promoted if one requests overtime. The "paper trail" rather than collective-bargaining contracts predicates survival.

Entry-level inner-city workers are also hindered by the fact that the vocabulary used in office work performance evaluations has no counterpart in street culture. When someone like Primo or Caesar is "terminated," the personnel report might contain a series of notations: "lack of initiative," "inarticulate," or "no understanding of the purpose of the company." Primo realizes that in street English these evaluations mean "she's saying to her associates that I'm stupid." He cannot improve his performance at work, however, without jeopardizing the basic foundations of his definition of personal dignity. Consequently, at Gloria's trade magazine Primo was the first person to fall victim to one of the periodic economic retrenchments characteristic of this highly specialized subsector, which fluctuates with the changing whims and fashions of upper-class culture.

> *Primo:* I had to leave that job because my hours were cut down. I think it was four and a half hours a day, and then some days she would cut me out the whole full day. There was like less work to do.
>
> I already had my son, Papito, and expenses. Sandra, my son's mother, was on public assistance. But that's not enough. She worked off the books; but she was just surviving. Her cousin . . . or somebody . . . the next-door neighbor used to baby-sit while she worked.
>
> Sandra would look them out, but it was hard because she was giving them half of her . . . whatever-she-makes-a-day, to whoever was baby-sitting. It was like minimum wage.
>
> She was working hard for bullshit.
>
> So that's why I had to find a new job. My boss had me on restricted hours, and I can't even work overtime.

Although Primo and Caesar were at the very bottom of the office service-work hierarchies of the FIRE sector, they were not completely powerless. Nonunion service workers in high-rise office buildings can draw on much the same repertoires of work site resistance that masses of dominated people from agricultural serfs to apprentice artisans to modern-day housekeepers have always engaged in: foot dragging, attitudinal opposition, and petty theft.[8] This kind of purposeful disgruntlement, however, is particularly unacceptable in the new office service sector, where "attitude" – enthusiasm, initiative, and flexibility – often determines who is fired and who is promoted. Oppositionally defined cultural identities that were legitimate on the factory shop floor – and even served to ritualize and stabilize management–worker confrontations – are completely unacceptable in the FIRE sector, where upper middle-class Anglo modes of interaction prevail with a vengeance.

In contrast to the unionized factory worker, low-echelon service sector employees in the FIRE sector have no formal institutional channels to legitimize or to render productive their dissatisfaction with their working conditions. The result is an alienated "working-class culture" isolated within the extremely limited autonomous confines that entry-level office employees are able to carve out for themselves. Caesar noticed this right away in the mail room of his pharmaceutical advertising agency:

> *Caesar:* I used to get there late, but the other workers wasn't never doing shit. They was *lazy* motherfuckers – even the supervisor.
>
> They all be sitting, asking each other questions over the phone, and fooling with video games on the computer. And that's all you do at a place like that.
>
> My boss, Bill, be drinking on the sneak cue, and eating this bad-ass sausage.

Both Primo and Caesar, however, preferred to engage in a more instrumental and personally satisfying form of powerless revenge: stealing on the job.

> *Primo:* I used to do all the Express Mail. Yeah, it was nine dollars and thirty-five cents and they would give me ten dollars to take it to the post office. But instead, I would just slide the envelope through the Pitney-Bowes [postage-meter machine] and drop it in the nearest mailbox.

Primo was particularly proud of how effectively he pilfered from his employer, Gloria Kirschman, who had called him illiterate. Indeed, within a few months of being hired, Primo excelled at concocting scams that manipulated double invoicing and interchanging receipts – skills not usually associated with illiteracy:

> *Primo:* One time, I just took eighty dollars from this petty-cash money box that they kept with the receptionist in the front office. [sniffing heartily from a packet of heroin that he had placed on my living room coffee table]
>
> I didn't just steal the eighty dollars. I knew the ropes to the place. I was doing everything ahead of time.
>
> You see, when I first started working there, I used to bring all the receipts from everything. And, I used to borrow money sometimes from petty cash, and I would have to pay it back when I get paid. Gloria was so fucking cheap, always bitching because the receipts' not in the right place, and then complaining, 'cause I'm answering the phones, and I'm illiterate.
>
> Well, she didn't keep good inventory. Nothing was accurate there. So she would send me to get Xeroxes, but I would already know the price, because I had already called the Xerox place to see how much they going to charge me for how much she was going to give me. Like, how much copies, whatever size, eight and a half by eleven.
>
> And then I told the lady at the front office, the receptionist, to give me eighty bucks so I'll be able to pay for the stuff.
>
> So I asked Gloria [sniffing more heroin], the bitch, my boss, "Do you want this paid by cash or check?"
>
> She told me, "By check." [giggling] So I got a check for eighty bucks and kept the cash and put the receipt from the Xerox place into the petty-cash box. Nobody figured it out. [chuckling]
>
> That bitch was stupid. She bitches so much, and she wasn't even doing anything correct. [laughing hard]

Primo's laughter was cut short in this particular conversation when he suddenly lurched in the direction of my apartment's bathroom, vomiting on my living room rug, prompting Caesar to call with protective concern:

Self-portrait of a crack dealer wearing his gold chain and medallion. This particular dealer competed directly with the Game Room, and he marked his sales site with his graffiti art. Photo by Philippe Bourgois.

Caesar: Oh man! You all right, Primo? I keep telling you, man, you're a light nigga'. You can't be sniffing so much dope all at once. [dipping his house key into the packet of heroin and sniffing dryly into each nostril]

"Fly Clothes" and Symbolic Power

Not all forms of resistance to marginal legal employment are so instrumental and practical. On a deeper level, the entire foundation of street culture and the unwillingness of people like Primo and Caesar to compromise their street identity is a refusal to accept marginalization in the mainstream professional world. The oppositional identities of street culture are both a triumphant rejection of social marginalization and a defensive – in some cases terrorized – denial of vulnerability. The ways office dress codes become polarized provide insight into this complex dynamic because clothing is a concretely visible arena encapsulating symbolic, or cultural, conflict. To my surprise, many of the crack dealers cited their inappropriate wardrobes and the imposition of demeaning dress codes as primary reasons for shunning legal employment. At first I dismissed the issue as trivial. It took me several months to realize how centrally this symbolic expression of identity articulates with power relations in the labor market.

The oppositional meaning of "subcultural style" among youths and marginalized sectors of society has long fascinated sociologists.[9] Much of that material romanticizes and exoticizes the real pain of social marginalization. In contrast, of course, seen through the eyes of mainstream America, an inner-city youth's preoccupation with "fly clothes" only confirms a stereotype of immaturity, petty irrationality, or even personal pathology.

When young inner-city men and women are forced to submit to powerful white women in the entry levels of the office-worker labor force, physical appearance becomes a fierce arena for enforcing or contesting power. Of course, on a more general level, this occurs whenever the crack dealers or anyone engrossed in street culture venture into the middle-class white world that dominates most public space beyond inner-city confines. Caesar, for example, highlights his experience of this tension in his angry reminiscences of office workplace confrontations. He had no idea when his clothes would elicit ridicule or anger. His vulnerability and powerlessness outside the street context is clearly expressed in his anger over the "flexible" job description of his FIRE service-sector position. He mediates his objective powerlessness at work, through his preoccupation with the confusing office dress code.

Caesar: When I worked at Sudler & Hennessey, the pharmaceutical advertising agency, they had a dress code and shit like that. I wore the tie for about three weeks, but, uhum . . . Bob – I mean Bill – he was my supervisor, an Irish son of a bitch, an old white guy – he told me I didn't really have to wear a tie if I didn't want to. So I didn't.

Because for some reason, since I was new, like the new mail clerk there, and they was remodeling and shit, they wanted me to do like, all this wild work. I'd be taking down shelves, clearing dust, sweeping – dirty work.

I mean I didn't wanna really do construction work in my good clothes. But I couldn't come in bummy, because my supervisor would tell me, "Why you coming in like that?" Or "Why you dressed like that for?" He meant, "Like a hoodlum." But I dressed good, like in nice baggies, and fancy shoes, and nice paisley shirts.

But what I didn't like was that construction wasn't in my job description. I got hired to be a mail room clerk right. They never told me that they were going to be remodeling shit.

But then they had that dress code right. I hated that shit. You see I didn't have no clothes back then because I was still goin' on mission [crack binges]. So really, like my first paycheck went for clothes, but then I had to replace the clothes I had fucked up at work.

In much the same way that Primo was humiliated by having to look up the word "illiterate" in the dictionary, Caesar was hurt when his supervisor accused him of "looking like a hoodlum" on the days when he thought he was actually dressing well. His problem was not merely that he did not have enough money to buy clothes but, rather, that he had no idea of which clothes to choose when he went to buy them. Losing this particular struggle over cultural capital has to be profoundly disorienting to the kind of person whose fly clothes on the street have always made him "king of the crew," as Caesar's teenage friend Willie had assured me in a conversation cited earlier in this chapter.

In the same vein, several months earlier, I had watched Primo drop out of a "motivational training" employment program in the basement of his mother's housing project, run by former heroin addicts who had just received a multimillion-dollar private sector grant for their innovative approach to training the "unemployable." Primo felt profoundly disrespected by the program, and he focused his discontent on the humiliation he faced because of his inappropriate wardrobe. The fundamental philosophy of such motivational job-training programs is that "these people have an attitude problem." They take a boot camp approach to their unemployed clients, ripping their self-esteem apart during the first week in order to build them back up with an epiphanic realization that they want to find jobs as security guards, messengers, and data-input clerks in just-above-minimum-wage service sector positions. The program's highest success rate has been with middle-aged African-American women who want to terminate their relationship to welfare once their children leave home.

I originally had a "bad attitude" toward the premise of psychologically motivating and manipulating people to accept boring, poorly paid jobs. At the same time, however, the violence and self-destruction I was witnessing at the Game Room was convincing me that it is better to be exploited at work than to be outside the legal labor market. In any case, I persuaded Primo and a half-dozen of his Game Room associates – including Candy and Little Pete, who was then managing the Social Club crackhouse on La Farmacia's corner – to sign up for the program. Even Caesar was tempted to join.

None of the crack dealers lasted for more than three sessions of the job training program. Primo was the first to drop out after the first day's registration and pep talk. For several weeks he avoided talking about the experience. I repeatedly pressed him to explain why he "just didn't show up" to the free job-training sessions. Only after repeated badgering on my part did he finally express the deep sense of shame and vulnerability he experienced whenever he attempted to venture into the legal labor market. In the particular case of the motivational employment program, clothes and appearance – style, once again – were the specific medium for resisting the humiliation of submission to a menial position in the service sector labor market.

Philippe: Yo Primo, listen to me. I worry that there's something taking place that you're not aware of, in terms of yourself. Like the coke that you be sniffing all the time; it's like every night.

Primo: What do you mean?

Philippe: Like not showing up at the job training. You say it's just procrastination, but I'm scared it's something deeper that you're not dealing with. Like wanting to be partying all night, and sniffing. Maybe that's why you never went back.

Primo: The truth though – listen Felipe – my biggest worry was the dress code, 'cause my gear is limited. I don't even got a dress shirt, I only got one pair of shoes, and you can't wear sneakers at that program. They wear ties too – don't they? Well, I ain't even got ties – I only got the one you lent me.

I would've been there three weeks in the same gear: T-shirt and jeans. *Estoy jodido como un bón!* [I'm all fucked up like a bum!]

Philippe: What the fuck kinda bullshit excuse are you talking about? Don't tell me you were thinking that shit. No one notices how people are dressed.

Primo: Yo, Felipe, this is for real! Listen to me! I was thinking about that shit hard. Hell yeah!

Hell yes they would notice, because I would notice if somebody's wearing a fucked-up tie and shirt.

I don't want to be in a program all *abochornado* [embarrassed]. I probably won't even concentrate, getting dished, like . . . and being looked at like a sucker. Dirty jeans . . . or like old jeans, because I would have to wear jeans, 'cause I only got one slack. Word though! I only got two dress shirts and one of them is missing buttons.

I didn't want to tell you about that because it's like a poor excuse, but that was the only shit I was really thinking about. At the time I just said, "Well, I just don't show up."

And Felipe, I'm a stupid [very] skinny nigga'. So I have to be careful how I dress, otherwise people will think I be on the stem [a crack addict who smokes out of a glass-stem pipe].

Philippe: [nervously] Oh shit. I'm even skinnier than you. People must think I'm a total drug addict.

Primo: Don't worry. You're white.

Obviously, the problem is deeper than not having enough money to buy straight-world clothes. Racism and the other subtle badges of symbolic power are expressed through wardrobes and body language. Ultimately, Primo's biggest problem was that he had no idea of what clothes might be appropriate in the professional, service sector context. Like Caesar, he feared he might appear to be a buffoon on parade on the days when he was trying to dress up. He admitted that the precipitating factor in his decision not to go back to the job training program was when he overheard someone accusing Candy of "looking tacky" after she proudly inaugurated her new fancy clothes at the first class. As a matter of fact, Primo had thought she had looked elegant in her skintight, yellow jumpsuit when she came over to his apartment to display her new outfit proudly to him and his mother before going to class.

Unionized Travesties: Racism and Racketeering

Isolating oneself in inner-city street culture removes any danger of having to face the humiliations Candy, Caesar, or Primo inevitably confront when they venture out of their social circle to try to find legal employment. At the same time, there is a persistent awareness held by even the bitterest, most alienated of the crack dealers that a unionized job represents a positive, legal alternative to the drug economy. This was especially true for construction work, the single most accessible and relatively abundant, unionized entry-level job in New York City. A job in construction coincides even better than factory work with street culture's definitions of masculinity.[10] Even Caesar rebuked me when I accused him of being too lazy to work in construction. Framed by the Game Room door where he was standing at his lookout position, he puffed out his chest and raised his fists, reminding me of a television advertisement for Captain Planet.

> *Caesar:* Naah man. Fuck you! Construction is good.
> Look at my body. I got a body that's good for construction.
> Mines' isn't like Primo's. [pointing to Primo, who was serving a customer] He's got a body that's more for shipping and receiving. [distant gunshots]

To my surprise, Caesar admitted to failing in his attempt to become a construction worker before being hired by Primo at the Game Room. The experience had been less humiliating to him than his failure at the advertising agency, Sudler & Hennessey, because it is common knowledge in New York City that the construction industry is a racist preserve for well-paid white workers ensconced in Mafia-controlled unions.[11] Since the 1970s, inner-city-based affirmative action organizations have attempted to force local construction sites to hire laborers from their communities. Ironically, they utilize the same strong-arm techniques pioneered by the old-fashioned Italian Mafia. Men with Caesar's muscular stature and rage-filled disposition are recruited systematically by these affirmative action employment organizations in order to act as violent pickets to intimidate the construction companies and force them to integrate Latinos and African-Americans onto their work sites. The most effective picketers are rewarded with positions as full-time, unionized day laborers at the same construction sites where their strong-arm tactics were successful.

With his hulking bravado and affinity for public displays of violence, Caesar earned one of these rare union jobs after only a week of picketing for one of the more legitimate and famous of these race-busting employment organizations, known as "Harlem Fight-Back." Although brilliantly successful on the picket line, Caesar fell apart when he left the protective cocoon of Harlem Fight-Back's street culture tactics. He found himself all of a sudden confronting the racist stonewalling of his new, exclusively white, union colleagues.

It was good pay. They was paying me fourteen dollars an hour. But I was the only Puerto Rican; they were all like Eye-talians and shit like that. And I never got paid.

What happened was they started jerking me around. I was working in demolition, but everytime I would go to the site the foreman wouldn't know nothing about their hiring me, and they be sending me from one job site to another.

And these big Eye-talian dudes – like forty years old – be asking me [gruffly], "Who send you here?"

And I was like [shrugs his shoulders helplessly].

And they would be [gruffly again], "Who hired you?"

I would tell them who hired me. But my problem was that the main union office didn't send me no papers. And I didn't get no time card or nothing like that. So I was just working wildly.

I would go to the job site and everybody would be there waiting for the bosses to go, "All right now, everybody start working." Then they'd be working, and I just join in the work.

But nobody knew who I was. It was like "Who hired you?" and "Where's your time card?"

So they kept jerking me around. I was stupid. I just never went back. 'Cause at that time I was smoking, so I said "Fuck this man, they giving me a hard time." And I went off on a mission.

In other words, crack colluded with a racist labor market and with Caesar's personal vulnerabilities to keep him from having to face his structural exclusion from even the most traditional, macho niche of the working-class labor force.

Two subsectors within the unionized construction industry were relatively more open to El Barrio's African-American and Puerto Rican population: building demolition and high-rise window replacement. These particularly dangerous enclaves of the industry abound in New York City's poorest neighborhoods, where they thrive on landlord gentrification schemes and rampant public sector corruption. Most blatantly, in demolition, tough El Barrio high school dropouts, proud of working legally, clear away the hulks of arsoned and abandoned working-class tenements to make room for the construction of new, luxury structures that they, and their families, will never be able to afford. Economists and real estate agents call this gentrification. On the street, I heard it referred to as "bleachification."

The abundant supply of window-replacement jobs is only slightly more subtly the result of the competition over affordable housing in Manhattan. According to New York City's housing regulations, window replacement counts as a capital improvement that landlords are allowed to pass on to their unsuspecting tenants at several times the real cost through strategic – but perfectly legal – bookkeeping. It represents one of the only ways for landlords to bypass New York's strict rent stabilization and family eviction laws, and force poor tenants out of their buildings by raising their rents rapidly. Fringe areas between very wealthy and very poor neighborhoods, like East Harlem's southern border with New York's Silk Stocking Upper East Side around East 96th Street, are precisely the kinds of interstitial zones most vulnerable to these gentrification schemes. Ironically, in El Barrio young men experience as positive their long-term residential displacement from their natal neighborhoods because they are provided in the short term with well-paid construction jobs renovating buildings that will no longer be affordable to the working poor.

The periodic "renovations" of Housing Authority project buildings that are sponsored by organized crime provide another abundant source of high-altitude window-replacement jobs. Several of the crackhouse habitués, including Little Pete, the manager of the Social Club, participated proudly and unknowingly in these Mafia-controlled window scams. Little Pete's tenure replacing the several thousand windows on the housing project buildings opposite the Game Room was cut short when a pane fell on his head, lodging glass splinters in his left eye. He was forced to apply for indigent medical aid at Metropolitan Hospital, East Harlem's public municipal facility, because his subcontractor had never paid any medical insurance or workers' compensation policies. Worse yet, the hospital social worker's investigation revealed that Little Pete's subcontractor had hired him illegally through an arrangement with a corrupt union official that allowed them to collect the full union wage of $18 for each hour worked by Little Pete at $10. Little Pete had been so proud of earning $10 an hour, it had never occurred to him that his labor could be valued at $18 according to union regulation.[12]

The New-Immigrant Alternative

Despite these consistently negative experiences on the fringes of the unionized labor market, everyone acknowledged that union employment was the ideal. "I gotta find a union job" was one of Primo's most common refrains during his intermittent periods of concerted job search. In fact, for a brief two-month period he fell prey to the illusion that he had found a unionized position with a nighttime janitorial services company that cleaned hotel conference rooms and theaters in Times Square. At first, despite his $6.50-an-hour starting wage, Primo was thrilled. He confided to me that he felt terrific, "like a normal working nigga' "; although he did note, "You know the weird thing? They're all fuckin' immigrants there except for the bosses." He also complained that the company refused to pay them overtime; nevertheless, he accepted their explanation that hotel management insisted the workers leave the premises before the guests awoke: "I guess they don't want to be seeing scum like us around. So we try to bust out a lotta work from eleven [p.m.] to six-thirty [a.m.]." He disliked the "bald, white Jewish boss" for berating them everytime he inspected their work, but he was impressed by the unionized workers on his shift who militantly cursed the "bald white guy" back. After his second biweekly paycheck he noticed that several nights' worth of work were missing and that none of the native-born Americans were lasting through the two-and-a-half-month probation period that all workers had to pass before being allowed to join the union.

Sure enough, when Primo was two weeks short of qualifying for union tenure, he was laid off.

Primo: I figured it was gonna happen 'cause I was just working there for two or three months. So I'm the one at the most risk to get laid off, because of that wack union business. Besides you don't get no Blue Cross/Blue Shield at that job, and they mess up your money.

The older guys working there for years, they told me, "You don't get no union on this job. By the time you're three months here, they'll lay you off. Watch it."

They still owe me hours. That job is wack. Its gonna be all wetbacks, Jamaicans and Central Americans, soon.

Caesar was particularly enraged by Primo's accounts of management's union-busting. Nevertheless, both he and Primo succumbed to a classic racist, divide-and-conquer logic. They channeled their anger over their structural vulnerability within management–labor confrontations into scapegoating the new immigrants entering New York City's low-wage labor market, and in this process, further crushed their own dreams of ever having access to well-paid unionized jobs.

Caesar: Mexicans get jerked in these places man. They not getting paid well, and they takin' all the jobs. You know what I'm saying? They cheap labor.

People will hire Mexicans before they hire a white man, or a Puerto Rican, because they know they could jerk them more.

Primo: They getting paid like, two or three dollars an hour in a job that I coulda had.

Caesar: That gets me mad too man!

Primo: They take up jobs that other people could have that are citizens of the United States.

Caesar: 'Cause we belong to America.

Primo: And then I could probably get paid the right amount — five, six, or eight dollars.

Caesar: And Mexicans be bringing a lotta partners with them. They be having buildings full of Mexicans now.

Primo: The building on 116th is packed with Mexicans boy.

Caesar: This whole block is getting to be fuckin' full of a lotta different types of races. And they be like a whole bunch of them living all crazy-like in one crib.

Especially the Africans – those people look dirty to me.

Primo: They treat you like shit, and they live better than us.

Caesar: They look like unclean people for some reason.

Philippe: Aw, come on!

Caesar: They really black. Like real dark black. They look dirty to me. They not the same kind of blacks as the Americans that be around here. They're like a real hard-core suntan black.

Primo: And then there's the Dominicans.

Philippe: Man! You guys should read my book[13] about how stupid it is for poor people to be racist against each other. Let me go get it and read out loud – It's about a plantation in Costa Rica where blacks and Latinos be riffin' at each other. The companies love it; they just laugh all the way to the bank.

Caesar: [ignoring my comment] It's like Dominicans who are most fucked up. They come in and they either sell drugs or buy a store.

I hate Dominicans the most, man.

In a classic replay of the historical process that brought their parents and grandparents to El Barrio – but with the roles reversed – Primo, Caesar, and virtually everyone in the Game Room entourage detested the new immigrants moving into their neighborhood. During the last years of my fieldwork this expressed itself in random predatory violence against the rural Mexicans who were arriving in increasing numbers and moving into the most decrepit tenements on the worst drug-copping corners surrounding us. Several of the Game Room habitués – including Nestor, a seller directly employed by Ray to occasionally replace Primo and Caesar – were arrested for mugging, stabbing, and, in one fatal case, shooting their new Mexican neighbors.

Three or four decades earlier, it was Italian-Americans who were lashing out at Puerto Ricans whom they accused of "stealing" their factory jobs and "invading" their neighborhood. The same third world desperate poverty faced by Mexicans in the 1990s was the driving force rendering new-immigrant Puerto Ricans more "exploitable" in the 1940s and 1950s than the progeny of the previous immigrant group, New York–born Italians. This is clearly expressed, for example, in Primo's mother's childhood memories of her rural youth.

> *Primo's mother:* [in Spanish] I loved my life in Puerto Rico. We always ate, because my father always had work, and in those days the custom was to have a garden in your patio to grow food and everything that you ate.
>
> We only ate meat on Sundays, because everything was cultivated on the same little parcel of land. From there we got our eggplant, our beans, our cilantro, our . . . [lists several more traditional Puerto Rican subsistence vegetables and herbs] That way we saved our money.
>
> We didn't have a refrigerator, so we ate *bacalao* [salted codfish], which can stay outside, and a meat that they call *carne de vieja* [shredded beef], and sardines from a can.
>
> But thanks to God, we never felt hunger. My mother made a lot of cornflour. And to save money, whenever there were beans left over, she would strain them; mash them; make a little soup; and add a little cornflour. So we were never hungry.

In the 1950s, Leonard Covello, the Italian-American principal of El Barrio's public high school, was dismayed over the racism that his neighbors directed against people like Primo's mother. In his autobiography he reports an argument he had with a group of Italian-American men on an El Barrio street corner:

> [Man on street corner] They're not like us. We're American. We eat meat at least three times a week. What do they eat? Beans!
>
> [High school principal] What do you think your parents ate when they came to America? . . . *Pasta e fasul* . . . Beans and macaroni — and don't forget it. Don't forget that other people used to say the same things about your mothers and fathers that you now say about the Puerto Ricans.[14]

The violence and racist tensions of the 1990s between young, unemployed New York–born Puerto Ricans and the new immigrants "invading" their neighborhoods and labor markets is the human underside to the latest phase in the restructuring of New York's economy. The real value of the minimum wage declined by one-third during the 1980s at the same time that the federal government decreased by more than 50 percent its proportional contribution to New York City's budget. Under normal conditions this would precipitate a crisis in the reproduction of the entry-level labor force.[15] Instead, new immigrants provide a fresh source of below-subsistence-cost workers tolerant of exploitative labor conditions. Specifically, in East Harlem the majority of the new immigrants are Mexicans from the rural states of Puebla and Guerrero. The poverty of their natal villages makes them a highly disciplined, inexpensive workforce capable of fulfilling the enormous needs that well-paid FIRE sector executives have for personal services: housekeepers, office cleaners, delivery personnel, boutique attendants, restaurant workers.[16] Furthermore, their impoverished rural backgrounds where running water and electricity are considered a luxury make them tolerant of the crushing public sector breakdown endemic to U.S. inner cities. Native-born New Yorkers of any ethnicity are simply not exploitable enough to compete with rural new immigrants for low-wage menial jobs.

In addition to the material fact of tolerating lower standards of living and of accepting more exploitative working conditions, new-immigrant Mexicans experience racism and subordination at work in a very different manner from Puerto Ricans or African-Americans. Their sense of self-respect does not articulate as closely with the ethnic hierarchies and definitions of self-worth constructed by native-born North Americans. Many of the subtler expressions of racism and disrespect that are routinely directed against Latinos in New York are simply irrelevant to them. Of course, this partial insulation from "gettin' dissed" by other ethnic groups will decrease with time as new-immigrant Mexicans develop greater personal and emotional stakes in local society, and as a second generation of New York–born Mexicans comes of age. Presumably, similar dynamics mediated by different cultural and economic parameters occur among undocumented new-immigrant Asians in lower Manhattan, Dominicans on the Upper West Side, and West Indians in Brooklyn.[17]

The Bicultural Alternative: Upward Mobility or Betrayal

Given the structural dynamic of ethnic succession by new immigrants at the lowest echelons of New York's labor force, the primary hope for upward mobility among New York–born Puerto Ricans lies in the expanding FIRE sector's need for office support workers – mail room clerks, photocopiers, and receptionists. Not only is this one of the fastest-growing subsectors of the city's economy, it also has the greatest potential for upward mobility as messengers get promoted to clerks, who get promoted to administrative assistants, and so on. Of course, these are also precisely the kinds of jobs that require subservient behavior anathema to street culture.

As noted earlier, success in the FIRE service sector requires an inner-city office worker to be bicultural: in other words, to play politely by "the white woman's rules" downtown only to come home and revert to street culture within the safety of a tenement or housing project at night. Thousands of East Harlem residents manage to balance their identities on this precarious tightrope. Often, when they are successful, their more marginally employed or unemployed neighbors and childhood friends accuse them of ethnic betrayal and internalized racism.

I collected several righteous condemnations by Game Room habitués of their successfully employed neighbors who work downtown and adapt to high-rise office culture. Leroy, another cousin of Caesar's, who ran his own private crack operation, was especially adamant on the subject.

Leroy: When you see someone go downtown and get a good job, if they be Puerto Rican, you see them fix up their hair and put some contact lens in their eyes. Then they fit in. And they do it! I seen it.

They turnovers. They people who wanna be white. Man, if you call them in Spanish, it wind up a problem.

I mean like, take the name Pedro – I'm just telling you this as an example – Pedro be saying, [imitating a white nasal accent] "My name is Peter."

Where do you get Peter from Pedro?

Just watch how Spanish people fix up their hair. When they get nice jobs like that, all of a sudden, you know, they start talking proper.

The bicultural alternative is not an option for Leroy, whose black skin and tough street demeanor disqualify him from credibility in a high-rise office corridor. I learned later that part of his articulate anger on the night I tape-recorded his denunciation of "turnovers" was the result of his most recent foray into office work. He had just quit a "nickel-and-dime messenger job downtown" (in order to return to crack dealing full time in his project stairway) shortly after a white woman fled from him shrieking down the hallway of a high-rise office building. Leroy and the terrified woman had ridden the elevator together and coincidentally Leroy had stepped off on the same floor as she did, to make a delivery. Worse yet, Leroy had been trying to act like a debonair male when the woman fled from him. He suspected the contradiction between his inadequate appearance and his chivalric intentions was responsible for the woman's terror:

> *Leroy:* You know how you let a woman go off the elevator first? Well that's what I did to her, but I may have looked a little shabby on the ends. Sometime my hair not combed, you know; so I could look a little sloppy to her, maybe, when I let her off first.

What Leroy did not quite admit until I probed further is that he too had been intimidated by the lone white woman. He had been so disoriented by her taboo, unsupervised proximity that he had forgotten to press the elevator button when he originally stepped into the elevator with her:

> *Leroy:* She went in the elevator first, but then she just waits there to see what floor I press.
>
> She's playing like she don't know what floor she wants to go to, because she wants to wait for me to press my floor. And I'm standing there, and I forgot to press the button.
>
> I'm thinking about something else — I don't know what was the matter with me. And she's thinking like, "He's not pressing the button; I guess he's following me!"

Leroy struggles to understand the terror his mere presence inspires in whites:

Leroy: It's happened before. I mean after a while you become immune to it.

Well, when it first happens, it like bugs you, "That's messed up. How they just judge you?" You know, they be thinking, "Guys like that, they're a lot of dark guys running around." It's like crazy.

But I understand a lot of them. How should I say it? A lot of white people . . . [looking nervously at me] I mean Caucasian people – [flustered, putting his hand gently on my shoulder] If I say white, don't get offended because there are some white people who live in this neighborhood.

But those other white people they never even experienced black people. They come from wealthy neighborhoods, and the schools they go to . . . no black kids there. The college they go to . . . no black kids there. And then they come to office buildings, and they just start seeing us.

And you know, we don't have the best jobs. You know, how it is. I call them nickel-and-dime jobs. You know, we are not always as well adjusted or as well dressed.

Sometime I come in a little sloppy. So automatically they think something wrong with you. Or you know, they think you out to rob them or something. So I like, . . . I don't pay it no mind. Sometime it irks me. Like, you know, it clicks my mind. Makes me want to write. I always write it down.

Sometime I write down the incident, what happened. I try to make a rhyme [rap lyrics] out of it.

Of course, as a crack dealer Leroy no longer has to confront this kind of confusing class and racial humiliation.

I pursued this issue with another, older cousin of Caesar's – one who had actually "made it" in the legal economy. He maintained a stable white-collar job in an insurance agency and had moved his family to the suburbs. His experience was particularly interesting as he had grown up in the neighborhood and had passed through a phase of heroin addiction. He still maintained acquaintanceships with some of his old street friends. At first he assured me that his escape from street culture had not necessitated any ethnic compromise. He saw it as part of a religious conversion. He and his family were devout Jehovah's Witnesses. At the same time, he did admit he had to hide the extent of his economic success when he returned to visit friends and family in El Barrio.

Caesar's cousin: Half of my friends died: killings, overdose. But I stay in touch with the ones who are still alive. As a matter of fact, I just seen one tonight. He's still on methadone.

My friends though, they don't see me as looking down on them, because I don't ever do that. They really don't know how I really live. They know I "peddle insurance," but I don't get heavy about it with them. It might make them feel uncomfortable. I never do that to them. So they don't see me as someone who's betrayed.

The tightrope of class and ethnicity is not quite as easy to balance in his new upwardly mobile world governed by a deeply institutionalized racism. The solution in his case has been to internalize the legitimacy of apartheid in the United States.

Caesar's cousin: My kids' future is much brighter than mines' ever was. We live in a suburban situation. As a matter of fact, we may be one of the three Hispanic families in that general area.

When I jog down the neighborhood, people get scared; people get nervous about me. It's not a problem for me, because I have self-confidence. I don't worry about it. It doesn't faze me at all.

Every once in a while, I used to get a crank call in the house, saying, you know, "Hey spic," you know, "spic" and other stuff, but I don't worry about that. [he giggles]

In a sense, I've learned to be in their shoes. You see what I mean? Because I've seen what minorities as a group can do to a neighborhood. I've seen great neighborhoods go down. So I step into their shoes and I understand; I've learned how to be sympathetic. I understand their thinking.

Caesar and Primo are not capable of such sympathy and understanding; instead, they take refuge in the underground economy and celebrate street culture.

5

SCHOOL DAYS: LEARNING TO BE A BETTER CRIMINAL

I was chillin' out most of the time in junior high. But they had like a wild war out there – blacks against Puerto Ricans – and the Puerto Rican kids used to get beat up real crazy.

This guy killed this one kid, so we used to not want to go to school because of that. We used to cut school and go downtown and rob.

Caesar

The complex interfaces among family, school, and peer group are crucial to the construction and enforcement of social marginalization, especially in one's pre-teenage years. Consequently, I purposely collected the childhood, school-age reminiscences of the crack dealers in Ray's network in an effort to explore their early institutional relationships with both mainstream society and inner-city street culture. This also led them to talk about their intimate home lives. Much of this material is presented in this and the following three chapters, where I address changing gender-power relations and the transformations in family arrangements with respect to emotional nurturing and economic stability. In this chapter I focus on the quintessential early-socializing institution of mainstream society in the inner city: the public school. This leads fluidly into street culture's alternative to school – the peer group or the proto-criminal youth crew – gang – which effectively fills the formal institutional vacuum created by truancy. When the crack dealers began confiding to me about their earliest teenage experiences of violence and crime on the street, I was also forced to confront the brutal phenomenon of sexual violence that was central to both their formal and their informal schooling. Consequently, the chapter ends with an analysis of how street-bound, school-age boys learn to enforce the misogyny of street culture through gang rape.

Kindergarten Delinquencies: Confronting Cultural Capital

Most elementary school teachers assert that up through second grade, the majority of their students desperately want to please their teachers, even when they are prone to acting out their personal problems in the classroom. Primo's and Caesar's very first school memories, however, are overwhelmingly negative.

> *Primo:* I hated school. I just hated it. I used to fuck up all the time in school. I never did homework in my life. I just didn't want to do it.
>
> From first grade to my last year that I dropped out, I only did two or three homeworks.
>
> Never in my life did I do homework. Never!

Primo's institutional alienation was compounded by the cultural and generational gap that had destabilized the traditional power relations of his household. His monolingual Spanish immigrant single mother was embroiled in a cultural confrontation with her New York City–born toddlers, whose very first delinquency was to refuse to answer her in Spanish.[1] Her children's enrollment in kindergarten exacerbated this crisis. Following the insights of Bourdieu, if forms of cultural interaction – and literacy, more specifically – are the basis for the "symbolic capital" that structures power in any given society, then one can understand from the perspective of a new-immigrant mother and her second-generation progeny the trauma of first contact with the public school system.

The inability of Primo's mother to speak English and her limited literacy skills were a recipe for institutional disaster in her very first opening-day interactions with her kindergarten child's homeroom teacher. No precocious, healthy five- or six-year-olds can stand witnessing the instantaneous transformation of the mother – the authority figure in their lives – into an intimidated object of ridicule. Worse yet, over the next few years, this hostile, alien institution proves itself to be much more powerful in determining one's future fate than all of a mother's caresses, criticisms, or beatings.

In his kindergarten homeroom, Primo inherited the instantaneous onus of his mother's identity as former rural plantation worker, and now new-immigrant inner-city sweatshop employee. Her functional illiteracy and her inability to communicate with the educational bureaucracy condemned Primo to appear uncooperative and slow-witted to his teachers. Perhaps right away he had to protect himself by resisting his teachers lest they unconsciously insult or hurt him should he make the mistake of trying to please them – and inevitably failing. Despite his anxious mother's admonishments that he respect his teacher and do well in school, success in the classroom would have betrayed his love for her.

Theorists working at the intersection of the fields of education, anthropology, and sociology have built a body of literature – sometimes called cultural production theory – to document the way teachers unconsciously process subliminal class and cultural messages to hierarchize their students. Tangible markers like accent and clothing combine with subtler forms of expression such as eye contact, body language, play styles, and attention spans to persuade the agents of a mainstream, middle-class, white-dominated bureaucracy that a particular child is a disciplinary problem, emotionally disturbed, or of low intelligence. Imagine how Primo must have looked to his teachers by second grade:

> *Primo:* I never wanted to do nothing in class. I never raised my hand. I would just sit there.
>
> I used to wanta really hide. I was really a shy kid, like, sitting in the back of the class and like, "Leave me alone."
>
> So I started drawing – my whole table was all decorated – like graffiti.
>
> Sometimes I used to feel fucked up and just started making noises. They'd throw me out of class.
>
> But when the citywide test'es used to come, I would pass them.

Primo's behavior and demeanor in the classroom inspired the symbolic judgments of his teachers and peers that on a macrolevel constitute the glue that maintains class and economic inequality in any given society. I have already occasionally referred to the exclusionary power of cultural capital – for example, the inability of Ray, the semiliterate head of the franchise of crack houses I frequented, to obtain a driver's license, or, more important, Primo, Caesar, or Leroy's experiences of disrespect in high-rise office corridors – but it is in school that the full force of middle-class society's definitions of appropriate cultural capital and symbolic violence comes crashing down on a working-class Puerto Rican child.

> *Primo:* When the teacher used to dish me for talking a lot, or not paying attention, I'd probably curse the shit out of her.
> Like if she said, "Shut up!" or something. I'd say, "Fuck you asshole!"

Caesar's delinquent status was almost physical in its immediacy.

> *Caesar:* The teachers used to hate me. They used to say, "He's big and mean." And I used to be the class clown.
> I was wild. I was a delinquent. [laughing]

The enforcement at school of the symbolic parameters of social power is an unconscious process for everyone involved. It poisons the most intimate facets of a vulnerable child's life. For example, when Primo achieved minimal literacy and an understanding of grade school conventions, he was able to manipulate the system against his mother and betray her trust. The normal channels of mother–child authority were subverted. She lashed back at him helplessly with beatings, anger, and distrust.

> *Primo:* My whole first-grade notebook was marked red. And my mother had to sign anyway. I never used to tell her nothing about why it was red so that she would sign it.
> Then the teachers told her about the red, and she went like, "AAAAGGGH!" [flailing both arms in rage]
> So then I used to draw a lot, and I was always tracing things, so when they wrote her a letter about my homeworks that she was supposed to sign, I just traced her signature right over where it was supposed to be.
> I was a kid. I was probably like my son Papito, six or seven years old, yeah that's second grade.

Primo's elementary school resistance escalated into truancy, petty crime, and substance abuse as he reached pubescence. His mother tried to save her son by sending him to live with her parents in Arroyo, the same Puerto Rican plantation community where she had grown up. Primo moved into his grandparents' household in the newly constructed federal housing projects on the edge of the sugar plantation owned by a U.S. multinational corporation, which at one time had employed his grandfather and all of his uncles and great-uncles. His mother's desperate attempt to compensate for her child's traumatic experiences in the U.S. inner city backfired. Fourteen-year-old Primo became a legal truant in Puerto Rico when the East Harlem school district failed to forward his papers. More devastating, however, from a psychological developmental perspective, the rural plantation community of Primo's grandparents immediately rejected him. Puerto Ricans born and raised on the Island are acutely aware of the breakdown of community and social control among return emigrants, and Nuyoricans are generally distrusted. Primo discovered that he straddled two cultures – both of which rejected him.[2] Rural Puerto Rico confronted him with the classic uprooting experience faced by the adolescent children of immigrants whose dreams of upward mobility and full citizenship have been crushed in segregated inner cities.

Primo: [sipping beer] My mother sent me to P.R. when I was fourteen, because I was fucking up out here [waving out the Game Room window].

I was just a kid, and so were the girls I was trying to get next to. They would stand far away from me, like from here to the other side of the room. Like they was scared.

I had never met their fathers, but still they used to speak to me, *"No te puedo hablar mucho, porque mi papá no quiere."* [I can't talk to you much, because my father doesn't want me to.]

And I would say, "Who's your Father?" thinking like I met him already, and he don't like me.

But they had just been warned about me. You see, in those small towns news spreads like this [snapping his fingers], and 'cause somebody's from Nueva York he's probably *fresco* [oversexed].

Caesar: Yeah, that happened to me too. Puerto Rico is wack. I done went plenty of times too. They don't really like Puerto Ricans from New York. They call us "gringos." They say people from New York are like slicker, wilder. [grinning and wiggling his finger] Manipulative.

They try to say, "You be coming here and trying to make us look like hicks and shit." You know, like jíbaros.

You gotta be careful in Puerto Rico or you be getting into problems.

Primo: Yeah, I fucked up over there too.

I mean I'm a real *condenao'* [damned person]. With my cousin we stole five hundred dollars from my grandmother who was selling lottery tickets. We just went into her purse in her room. And that woman [morosely lowering his head], she loved me.

Her husband caught us and gave us a beating. So it was back to New York for me.

Violence: Family and Institutional

Caesar's school experiences were more profoundly violent and negative than Primo's. Like Primo, he is the son of a woman who immigrated as a teenager, but Caesar's mother came from an urban shantytown rather than a rural plantation village, and she was more literate and acculturated. This translated into even more violent personal disruptions in her life: serial teenage pregnancies with different men, heroin addiction, petty crime, and eventually murder and incarceration. Hence, the personal and institutional discontinuities and hostilities in Caesar's life.

Caesar: I wasn't that dumb in school. I was violent. The only reason I came out wild is because . . . I didn't have no guidance.

I'm the oldest. I had no pops, nor mom. I mean, my mother used to live with me a little bit, but I was always with my grandmother.

My moms was all over the place. She was only sixteen when she had me. She was like a beauty queen in P.R. at the time, and she got a lot of raps. My pops was young, he was about twenty.

She also used to sniff coke and dope, and drink. My mother, she had problems, man.

I mean she couldn't take care of me because she was taking care of my little brother and my little sister, so I was with my grand-mother.

We was moving a lot from El Barrio to Chicago to Connecticut, and all that.

I lived'ed with my grandmother, because my moms had already done what she had to do, and was in jail.

Several weeks later, in private, Primo explained in greater personal detail Caesar's relationship to his mother.

Primo: Caesar's mother was a wild bitch. She was a dope fiend, and he used to get treated like shit. She was a son of a bitch with him.

His mother was so fucked up that she killed a doctor. And that was premeditated murder. It was some doctor who was writing scrips for her, that she was fucking.

Caesar might even have been born addicted to heroin.

Caesar: I was born sick. I had to stay in the hospital a coupla' months. And my mother she had problems.

Later my moms killed some man, 'cause he got wild on her. I think she was trying to defend herself; that's what she told me; she wind up killing a man.

My mom had a wacked public defender and they jerked her. They really dogged her. The judge gave her twenty-five years. That's all of my life practically.

Philippe: Do you keep in touch with her? How's she doing?

Caesar: I done went plenty of times to visit her. I don't like to go up there.

She's in jail with Jean Harris. [grinning] You know that Scars-dale Diet doctor. Well, my moms is in jail with her. I met her, Jean Harris. She's kind of cranky, though. I got a picture of them. They hang out together in an honor prison. Big time.

Caesar claims that the repeated moves he made with his grandmother from one extended family member to another were the precipitating factors for his dropping out of school at an early age.

Caesar: The first move was to my cousins in Connecticut, 'cause I was getting into too much trouble in New York.

And from there, I went to Chicago. 'Buela [grandma] got real sick. She was going to the hospital to have an operation, and I was getting in trouble, making it worse.

I was in trouble with the law, and they told me, if I don't go back where I came from, that I was going to go to jail. And I was scared, so we left back to New York.

I would move, because I would have family in those places, who would tell me to go with them.

But every time I had moved, I would come into the next school, and then you gotta wait a long time for papers, and it was like when I came back to New York, I just didn't go back to school; I went to work.

I wasn't so little, I was like eleven, twelve, up to sixteen.

I don't even remember how many times I changed school. Six, seven, eight times, ten times.

Violence organized daily life in school to become his primary memory of formal education. It is necessary for youths to cultivate violent personas when they are repeatedly shifted from one school to another.

Caesar: I went to a whole bunch of schools before I dropped out. I went to 113, 117, 102, 109. I was all over the place. Ward's Island. Upstate. Downstate.

I used to fight so wild that they wouldn't bother me for a while. I would go real crazy! Real crazy, every time I would fight, so they'd thought I was wild and real crazy. I remember one nigga', I had rebuilt his face, but I broke my wrist.

Primo: I always got into fights. Even if I lost, I always started fights.

Caesar: You see, I remember whenever I came to a new school, the first days, all the older niggas would wanta like initiate you. And they be in the hallway calling out, [eerily] "Roookieees."

They stand right there [bumping into me and almost knocking me over], just to start trouble with you.

Yeah, they would slap you on the back of your neck [slapping me].

They be sitting on the stairwell banister, but the first nigga' that slapped me on the back of my neck, I tried to throw him off the banister, you know, like off the steps to break his head . . . [lifting me up in the air] 'Cause I was scared.

But they were *biiig* niggas, though. Like bully niggas. But we were ready, man.

Primo: Everybody used to get bullied; but nobody fucked with me because I used to pick up a chair, or pencil, or something, and fuck them up.

That let me relax more.

Caesar: Yeah, and then later I used to run up on niggas too, when I got big.

I mean, Felipe, you' rich. You didn't have to handle this shit, but me and homeboy [pointing to Primo], we was all jumpin'. And there used to be a lot of us like that.

It was worser in Connecticut, because there it was like blacks against Puerto Ricans.

This violence conflates with a machistic focus on sexual conquest as a central parameter for schoolyard respect.

Caesar: I never even got bullied that much because I used to always be like rappin' to girls and shit. So the niggas wouldn't bother me. I didn't have too much violence.

Despite his triumphal celebration of street culture's violence, Caesar did acknowledge his ultimate vulnerability in the institutionalized school setting.

Caesar: My only problem was when I was sent to reform school upstate. There, all the kids would get beat down well by the counselors. They used to do wild shit to us.

Plus, we'd get *beat* down by other kids and shit. I was getting my ass kicked. I used to get hurt.

Niggas has me mopping floors for them and shit. I used to be out there [a dominated victim].

It was a nasty reform school. I used to see the counselors holding down the kids naked outside; and the counselor beat him down;

stripped him up; and threw him outside in the snow and shit. It was fucked up.

I was about twelve or thirteen. It was fucked up, man. When I saw that shit, I said, "I'm outta here." The counselors was too wild and shit.

Surprised at Caesar's unusual expression of vulnerability I probed into this period of his life. I was able to collect several alternative, complementary accounts of his reform school experience from his younger cousin Eddie, who, coincidentally, was also interned as a juvenile delinquent with Caesar at age nine in the same institution: "One of them schools where you used to have to fight to survive." Both their families were in such a state of crisis at the time that no one told the children that they would be confined to the same reform school.

Eddie: I didn't even know Caesar was in there, until one day they took us all out swimming, and I saw him. Once we was together, it was a little bit better. Niggas had to be respectin' us more, because we would be watching each other's back.

Eddie provided me with his own painful account of being "a disturbed little nigga' " who "got in a lot of trouble all the time" at school. By seven years of age, he had already tried to commit suicide; and at nine, he attempted to throw himself out of a third-floor school window when a teacher "roughed me up for not paying attention in class." Like Caesar's mother, Eddie's mother was abandoned by her alcoholic husband, "a stingy, cheap, nongiving, just-making-babies-type person." She also used heroin and "had to split the family up among other relatives." Unlike Caesar, Eddie was able to admit, "I missed my mom. I used to cry every day; be a big sucker. I was thinking suicide." The school authorities interpreted the nine-year-old's paralyzed depression at being rejected by his mother as a violation of classroom discipline. They sent him to reform school.

Eddie: They told me, "You not gonna be seeing your mom, 'cause you need that seclusion." I was in the treatment ward. I had to get separated for a while.

Eddie's uncharacteristically emotional portrayal of how the trauma of his preadolescent family life meshed with institutionalized violence in the public school system, encouraged me to delve deeper into Caesar's home life during these same tender childhood years. Eddie politely limited his descriptions of Caesar's battered youth, however, to sympathetic generalities, stressing the special humiliation of Caesar's public beatings.

> *Eddie:* Caesar's been through some wild shit. 'Cause I remember when he was a little nigga', 'Buela used to abuse him in front of everybody in the streets — like with bats and sticks for being one minute late — or some shit like that. She was like abusive: Go to your school, and beat you down.

At first, Caesar simply denied any youthful vulnerability, but the terrors and anxieties of his youth emerge between the lines of his reconstructed memories. Finally, in later conversations, he poured out the classic battered-child rationalizations and denials of his early childhood abuse:

> *Caesar:* Nah, my grandmother never hit me. I was like a God. My grandmother is my moms'. She loves me.
>
> *Philippe:* How about your mother? Did she used to hit you?
>
> *Caesar:* My mother never hit me, 'cause I wouldn't do nothing around her. 'Cause I was scared of her.
>
> I seen my mother having a few fights when I was little. That made me nervous a couple of times. One time I seen my mother throw one of these black ladies that had attacked her through a store window. And I was always scared of my mother after that. That was why my mother never hit me.
>
> The only one that ever hit me, was my grandmother, but I liked'ed it, 'cause it didn't hurt. She hit me, and it'd be funny, but it never hurt me. I liked'ed to get hurt.
>
> *Philippe:* What was the worst beat down you got?
>
> *Caesar:* 'Buela threw a knife at me. Yeah, it cut me. Right here on my chest, but I don't got no scar or nothing.
>
> I remember the knife went WSSHHHT. If I wouldn't have weaved, I probably would've been jigged a little bit.

That's really the only wild time I ever . . . it was 'cause I was being real bad.

Philippe: What do you remember about it?

Caesar: I remember that I was scared, and I didn't mess with 'Buela for a long time after that.

I was bad though, I deserved to have been hit a lot of the time. She had to beat me with wires, but it didn't hurt man.

I mean I was always looking forward to getting beat down by 'Buela. Sometimes she'd even throw a punch. And she would hit hard. But mostly she might just give me like a *cocotazo* — you know, tap me on the head with a broomstick.

'Buela always treated me with formal respect when I visited Caesar at home: Before running into the kitchen to fetch us all food and drink, she would turn up the volume on the oversized floor-model color television in the center of the room, and motion us to sit. The overstuffed couches that were part of a fuchsia-colored and gold tinsel–striped living room set were surprisingly comfortable, despite still being covered by the original plastic factory-wrap. The whole ensemble was wedged into the undersized project living room space, forcing us to slide sideways around the orange-pink plastic-laminated coffee table in order to sit down. Despite her traditional, polite demeanor, even the toughest of the dealers gave 'Buela a wide berth. I once saw the manager of a sex-for-crack den in the apartment across the hall from 'Buela warn an unruly customer, "Shut the fuck up! If you don't chill, that old lady across the hall is gonna come at you with her cane and hit you upside the head."

Given his family background, it is not surprising that Caesar might have attempted to resolve his school problems violently in his earliest youth. I took advantage of our occasional bouts of drinking and sniffing in the solid concrete playground of the junior high school both he and Primo had been thrown out of some ten to fifteen years earlier, to tape-record their schoolyard reminiscences. That particular school's recreation yard was encased on all sides by solid cement walls, two to five yards high, offering an Alcatraz-like prison ambience. As if to drill home the infrastructural irony of apartheid segregation in the urban United States, a suburban commuter train cuts through the center of El Barrio's stretch of Park Avenue precisely at this point, casting its shadow onto the edge

Inside the Graffiti Hall of Fame. Photo by Henry Chalfant.

of the concrete playground. Every school day, this particular commuter line whisks thousands of New York's highest paid finance, insurance, and real estate executives to their suburban homes in Connecticut and "up-state" New York. The train serves some of the wealthiest census tracks in all of the United States. If the commuters were to look out the window, they might catch a fleeting glimpse of the whirlwind blaze of aerosol spray paint that covers the cement walls of the schoolyard. Artists from all the inner-city neighborhoods of New York City have converted these particular walls into the self-styled "Graffiti Hall of Fame." They compete for the artistic control of the hundreds of square yards of highly visible smooth concrete space to exhibit their painting skills with psychedelic representations of fire-breathing monsters in combat, cryptic hip-hop initials, or renditions of Bart Simpson in triumphantly resistant poses. The best artists are able to maintain their "pieces," some of which cover up to half a dozen square yards, for several weeks before they are defaced by competitors or jealous wanna-bes. The aesthetics of street culture have assertively triumphed in this otherwise infrastructurally and institution-ally hostile environment. It is as if the miracle of human creativity and aesthetic genius has to assert itself in the face of despair and oppression. Not a single inch of cold, gray concrete remains visible in the schoolyard.

From the perspective of the students and the teachers in this junior high school, Caesar was an agent of personal terror and institutional decay. His truancy must have been a relief for everyone. The problem was that he actually spent time at school, even as a truant:

Caesar: Oh yeah, I came in late one morning, and this teacher – I think his name was Mr. Washington – he got wild on me.

So I got mad, and I think about it:

"Ah'm'a' pick up this chair, and . . . and Ah'm'a' bash his head in."

I thought about it for a while, until I saw this other kid named Toto. He was crazy too.

Jaycee, Primo's girlfriend at the time: [interrupting] He's dead now. I heard they killed Toto.

Caesar: [nodding at Jaycee] So I said, "Fuck it, I'm going to jail, 'cause I'm a criming thief."

I picked up that chair, and I went up to the teacher – he was writing on the blackboard – and I went up to him, and I hit him with the chair on the back, and I broke his arm. [burst of laughter from all four of us]

Primo: You were a sick little nigga'. I never broke no chair over no teacher's head.

Caesar: I just cracked it. I didn't break the chair. I hated that teacher.

Primo: I hated teachers, and I used to wanta cut, but I wasn't really that wild.

Caesar: You remember that tap-dancing teacher? That skinny bitch? Stupid bitch! We tried to rape her.

Jaycee: Yeah, boy! You was really bad.

Caesar: There was this one bowlegged, bastard, science teacher. His name was Mr. Poole. He was like a nervous wreck, and we used to rob him every day. We used to wait in the park for him.

He never used to rat us out neither. He didn't suspend me or nothing.

We made a fire in his classroom, and we burned it down.

Me and some black dudes. The whole student body had to leave the school.

Primo: Nobody wanted my class. They gave us substitute teachers and we used to throw them with erasers, spitballs. We used to diss the shit out of them.

That's when I went AWOL. I never used to show my mother my report card in junior high school, 'cause I didn't want her to see all those absences and *stuuuupid* latenesses.

Caesar: I never went to school neither. I used to go in for gym, and lunch, and then to play with the girls and shit like that in the afternoon – but I never used to go in the morning.

No, I'm lying. We used to come to school to fuck Special Ed niggas up – kick their asses. Because they had the retarded here, and the ones that used to walk like this [scraping his toes, inflecting his knees, and pronating his arms to imitate someone with cerebral palsy]. We used to beat the shit out of them. We used to hurt them, because we didn't like them.

There was this one little kid named Lucas that used to walk *fucked up* [exaggerating his cerebral palsy motions], who we used to love to kick the shit out of. [Primo and Jaycee giggle]

Everybody used to come in the morning, see him, and smack him, like PAAA [hitting me hard on the back of the head]. Real crazy! [noting my scowl] We was really mean to that kid.

One day, we had a rope and we pretended that we were going to hang him in the gym. We pull't him up a little bit, but then we dropped him when he started coughing.

Another time, we stole a rubber hammer from the science class, and we hammered his head.

Primo: [concerned by my facial expression] You was fuckin' dumb Caesar!

Caesar: [also looking at me with concern] We kicked his ass so hard around, that he started walking normal, and he started being in the posse after a while.

Primo: [perhaps remembering that only two months earlier my one-year-old son had been diagnosed with cerebral palsy] He . . . got . . . he got . . . [putting his arm around my shoulder] he got initiated, Felipe!

Philippe: [fighting back tears and clearing my throat] Wha' . . . what happened to him?

Caesar: [confused by the emotions] He walked a little bit fucked up, [scraping his toes delicately] but not that bad. He started smoking cheeba and shit . . . getting girls.

[reaching out reassuringly to grab my shoulder as well] The nigga' even took my girl, Felipe!

I remember this 2:00 a.m. schoolyard conversation clearly because it was one of the first times on the street that I personally confronted the contradictions of anthropology's methodological caveat of suspending moral judgment. At the time, I was still in shock over having to deal with my own son's physical challenges, and I never forgave Caesar for his cruel brutality. Significantly, his unusual attempt to comfort me via macho bonding immediately uncovered another Pandora's box of gender-based brutality that the cultural relativism of my anthropological training was, once again, incapable of accommodating. Before this conversation was over, he shocked my already numbed ears and spinning emotions with boasts of schoolyard rape. I vividly remember trying to persuade myself that he was speaking metaphorically, or was exaggerating. It was not until several years later that I had the courage or the *confianza* and respect of the Game Room dealers to collect systematic accounts of adolescent gang rape.

Caesar: We used to break the lock and go out on the roof; rape bitches; and have some sex.

Jaycee: You'a fuckin' asshole Caesar!

Philippe: Word! Schmuck!

Primo: [coaxingly] Nah, you exaggerating Caesar. You didn't really rape them, but just fuck around with them.

Caesar: [laughing, and smashing an empty quart of malt liquor against a ten-foot-tall spraypainted dragon] My bitch was raped, troop!

Primo: [looking worriedly at me again] Nah, come on, man.

Caesar: [changing his tone] I mean we used to finger these bitches and go all out. And smoke *cheeba* and everything.

Yo Pops, I'm thirsty, let's get some brews.

In Search of Respect

Learning Street Skills in Middle School

Primo's resistance to school tracked him into the "low-IQ" undesirable classes; Caesar's rage, on the other hand, interned him in an experimental Special Education facility at a hospital for the criminally insane on Ward's Island where psychiatrists were pioneering psychotropic treatments with tranquilizers. It also initiated his dependence on social security insurance. Caesar has been receiving this monthly federal subsidy ever since, with the exception of the three or four intervals in his life when he has found steady legal employment.

> *Caesar:* They called me "emotionally disturbed" because my violence was a little wild, so they put me in Special Ed.
>
> [almost puffing out his chest] Ah'm'a Special-Ed-person, Felipe. That's how come I be getting SSI and all that shit — because I was violent.
>
> But shit, I learned more in Special Ed than in public high school. We'd finish books and shit in Special Ed.
>
> The way I got into Special Ed, was because one day, I had got high, and my science teacher kept fuckin' with me; I was cheeba'd up, and my posse was with me, and everything was all wild: so I took a scissor, and I grabbed his tie, and I *cut* the shit.
>
> It was funny, 'cause afterwards the principal told me, "Why you gonna do something crazy like that?" And I told him, "'Cause . . ." — What did I tell him? — oh yeah, I told him something crazy, like, "I heard voices." I said I was hearing voices and that's when they put me on Thorazine.
>
> They had us in a school on Ward's Island for Special Education. Ward's Island is where they keep all the lunatics. They had everybody on Thorazine there. They used to experiment with Thorazine on the Spanish and black kids. They had us all on Thorazine. That was the testing ground for those drugs. They had kids on all kinds of drugs. Word up!
>
> That lasted for like three years and then I was mainstreamed. I came back here.

Caesar's "future career" as a mentally and emotionally disabled SSI recipient was forged and legitimized in his earliest school years. Of course, in Caesar's case – as in most people's – a conjunction of personal and sociological factors overdetermined his qualifications for being certifiably crazy. His remorseful response to my berating him for being too lazy to work illustrates this well.

> *Caesar:* Yeah, you're right, Felipe. I always use excuses not to work: 'cause of the hospital stuff [he had recently been released from Metropolitan Hospital's psychiatric ward following his third suicide attempt];[3] and because of my moms [who was in jail on a twenty-five-year sentence for murder]; and then my sister [who was stabbed seventeen times in their project stairwell].

Caesar was not socially isolated by his disability; on the contrary, he felt it gave him honorary middle-class status. Of the three men who had had children with Caesar's mother, his father, who was a salsa singer, was the only one who did not qualify for SSI disability payments.

> *Caesar:* We live pretty good – like middle-class. My grandmother's retired and she gets her social security. My little brother, he gets money from his father's SSI. And then my sister – when she was still alive – was getting money from her pop's SSI. So we never had no problem.
> Poor people they can't afford nothing. They short on groceries. They got to buy cheap products. But I'm more middle-class. Whatever I want, I can get it on time [monthly credit payments].

Primo's future career in the underground economy was also established – or learned – at school. He spent most of his time in the hallways avoiding classrooms because they are the only physical space still under a modicum of teacher control in tough inner-city schools. His most important lessons revolved around selling, and using, drugs. In another class and ethnic setting, alcoholized autobiographical reminiscences in childhood schoolyards would probably elicit tales of playful mischief with only occasional overflows of offensive violence. In the courtyard of the Graffiti Hall of Fame, however, this balance between "normal" adolescent rebellion and serious delinquency was reversed.

> *Primo:* I was always in the hallways because they'd throw me out of class, 'cause I was a son of a bitch. I talked too much in class;

bothered the girls; wrote on the tables – my whole table was all decorated.

We had fun in the hallways. One day, we was smokin' pot, and we see this box, and it was clay. They had just made a delivery of clay. We said, "Oh shit! Clay." And we clay'ed the whole school.

Caesar: [aggressively] We used to go in posses, and bum rush through the hallways. One time at exit sixteen, we saw two niggas. They was men from the street, and they was giving each other a blow job . . . sixty-nine on the floor. We kicked the shit out of them.

Primo: We used to do everything in school. We got the special keys that you needed for the light switches. And we turned off all the lights in the basement. We had the whole entire basement to ourselves.

Everybody started hanging out in that basement. I used to sell smoke, so everybody was smoking. We was hiding in the lockers, smoking pot.

I used to go to school with like ten joints a day. And sell four or five. I wasn't making much in those days, because I used to smoke all of the rest. Whatever money I had, I would take and buy more for the next day. It was just for me.

Philippe: What about you Jaycee? Did you graduate from junior high? Tell us some of your stories.

Jaycee: Naah, I fooled around too. I had to leave the school when I got pregnant.

Caesar: [interrupting] I never used to throw joints. I was a Special Ed nigga', a big stupid nigga'. But I was doing a lot of drugs at that time. I became a playboy, because I just didn't give a fuck no more. I had women: Ah'm' a man.

I had a posse. We used to play dice.

Primo: Me, too. I loved to play dice. One time we got up on the roof, and we used to throw apples on the street at people.

Caesar: [interrupting] I used to throw bottles up there. And one time, I took a shit off the roof. 'Cause we was moonin' people, so I said, "Let me make it more dramatic."

There was nine of us, and we all mooned, and I took a shit. Then the whole school chased us.

Looking into the Graffiti Hall of Fame. Photo by Henry Chalfant.

All of a sudden, with no logical transition except for the theme of "acting stupid," Caesar launched into a series of stories about turning pigeons into "Halley's comets" and "running roasts" by setting them on fire after dousing them with lighter fluid; drowning a dog in the East River by tying bricks to its tail; and throwing cats off roofs. He seemed to be calling clinical attention to his "personality disorder" around violence and aggression. Indeed, at the time I tape-recorded this I worried that instead of analyzing the social context of violence in street life in my book, I would be forced to address individual psychopathology. When Caesar ended this particular tirade with "What's the matter, Felipe? You never murdered an animal, or try to throw a cat off of a high building to see it smack down hard on its feet [grinning]?" all I could muster was "As a matter of fact, no; I never have. That shit is sick, Caesar!" To my disappointment, neither Primo nor Jaycee seconded my condemnation; they just laughed.

As we left the schoolyard that night to drink more beer, I could not help wondering, once again, at the extraordinary skill and creative energy that was sprayed on the concrete walls all around us. Over the past two generations, this school has effectively channeled hundreds of children like Primo, Caesar, and even Jaycee, into careers of drug dealing, violent substance abuse, social security insurance, and single motherhood. Primo learned the entrepreneurial skills necessary for drug dealing when he stole the keys that controlled the basement's electrical system and set up shop "throwing joints." Caesar learned to take Thorazine and explain away his rage and violence by claiming to hear voices. Even Jaycee learned the survival skill of escaping failure, meaninglessness, and unemployment by becoming pregnant.

The Peer Group

School is obviously a powerful socializing force, but it is by no means the only institution pushing marginal children into street culture and the underground economy. When asked how they ended up on the streets, most of the dealers blamed their peer group. Indeed, one of the messages to come out of my schoolyard conversations with Caesar and Primo was that they spent almost no time in class. They learned a great deal during their school days — but almost none of it was academic. Most important, they spent their time cultivating street identities both inside and outside the physical confines of school.

> *Caesar:* We used to cut school and go downtown and rob. You know anything, you know, like cars, and tires, and shit like that.
> Everybody was wild, and I wanted to be with the wild crowd, because I liked it. I didn't want to be a nerd, or nothing like that. I figured it was wise, so being wild became a habit. I used to get into trouble and do atrocities.
> I was trying to look for an image, and it was like black. We wear kangos, earrings, jewelry; wear leather blazers, straight legs and shit, leather pants, big radios, and shit like that. We be smoking cheeba; drinking brew; hanging out on the Deuce [Times Square]; just being wild; being black; rapping on the mike, shit like that.

Primo was more instrumentally criminal than Caesar. He was not merely pursuing an image of "evilness" and playful delinquency. This is reflected in the almost apprentice-like manner in which his older peer group incorporated him into street crime.

Primo: You see, it was me and my older cousins. I was a little nigga' and they was already thieving.

I was like eleven − no, I'm lying − when I was like ten that was my first one. I was an ignorant idiot. It was me and my older cousin Hector. We was shitting in the same place where we eat − stealing right in our neighborhood.

My mother used to warn me not to, and stuff like that, but I liked'ed it out on the street with my cousins; and they taught me the tricks as to how to get into cars; how to break into places; how to pick locks. Ray used to key us on the techniques.

Back in the days, it was mostly car radios. Me and Luis together, we got good at it. By then we don't shit where we eat. Instead, we used to go downtown . . . rob *all* the niggas with big cars.

I was part of the epidemic of car stealing. Me and my cousin, added to it. We were part of it. It was a thing downtown.

That's why they came out with the Bensi box, man, and they'd have a sign, "No Radio."

The cops already knew all about us downtown, and we were known on the block [La Farmacia's corner] by all the cops. We even talked to them sometimes.

The only time Primo broke the invisible apartheid line between El Barrio and the Upper East Side was to steal. I remember how surprised I was when in the course of a random conversation when he revealed that he knew the address of the Whitney Museum. I asked him what he thought of the highbrow modern art institution, but he had never been inside: "I used to go down there with Luis to steal car radios. It was a real good spot." Naive suburbanites would park their luxurious cars at angles that offered car burglars camouflaged hiding places.

Car thieving was a memorable rite of passage into teenagehood for an enterprising youngster. It also offered a modicum of revenge against the rich white neighborhood hemming and tantalizing El Barrio at its southern border on East 96th Street:

Primo: Luis used to have me as a lookout because I was so inexperienced, so I wanted to graduate and do my own cars.

So one time when Luis be in the back taking out the speakers in this big car, he said, "Okay, you take the radio out this time."

That first time, it was too hard. I couldn't do it. As a matter of fact, I'm thinking now that probably Luis maybe gave me a radio that was hard to take out just to test me.

So what I just did was, I took the long-nosed pliers – which is the basic tool that you need to steal the car radio – and since I couldn't have that radio, I pushed the pliers inside the cassette hole, and just started ramming it in there real hard, and fucked the whole car system up. And I kept the buttons [knobs], you know, the radio buttons, even though, I eventually just ended up throwing the buttons away.

It was a good radio that I fucked up. It was a Blunt Point [Blaupunkt] – I don't know if you ever heard of that brand – so that the normal guy who owned the car probably said [shaking his head in disgust], "Damn, son of a bitch!"

But I was like, "If I can't have it, they can't have it." I was a young, ignorant, stupid idiot. You know, *estupido*. We just broke out of the car and laughed.

Although Primo's mother was quick to blame her son's demise on the "bad influences" of his friends, there was a powerful economic imperative, coupled with a gender-based definition of dignified male adolescent behavior, that propelled him into petty crime before he was even a teenager. As noted in the preceding chapter, Primo's mother's earnings as a seamstress – despite the supplements she received from welfare and food stamps – could not supply Primo during his childhood years with the sneakers, candy, or occasional comic book that most ten- or eleven-year-olds in suburban North America take for granted. The economic logic of stealing from wealthy neighbors melded into a street culture identity. In fact, Primo was AWOL from his mother's home as much as he was from school.

Primo: I was just thinking about mahahahni [money]. 'Cause I just wanted to get the little things that I wanted. You know, like . . . just like, little things. Anything that you can't have, that you wanta get for yourself, and shit.

It was just like, junk shit. Like a bag of Vicks cough drops. I forgot really, but it wasn't for drugs. [pausing to sniff cocaine]

Maybe I wanted a new pair of sneakers . . . or something to eat; or just to have money in the pocket.

My money used to last. It used to go a long way, because mostly we used to buy food or clothes. We wasn't drug addicts, but we needed money.

We would be selling the stuff we stole, little by little. Asking people whether they wanted this, or whether they wanted that.

Everybody always wants a radio, man. And the prices we used to have! Cheap! Cheap! We were stupid little niggas and we'd get jerked.

Philippe: Your mother couldn't buy you the shit you needed?

Primo: My mother didn't give me allowances. I wasn't the type to ask. Gotta get money on my own.

I mean my mother would see if my sneakers were really crazy-looking, but I wasn't the one to beg. My sisters used to ask for an allowance, but not me.

Philippe: And would she notice that you had money to buy things?

Primo: I didn't like the idea of my mother knowing. I used to always come in when she was sleeping. Or else come in with a bag, and stash the shit. If I come in in the morning, I'd go to my room quick.

But she used to see the stolen goodies, and she used to hate it. I used to have a lock on my room. She would scold me and bitch the shit out of me. But I didn't listen.

Philippe: Would she worry when you were out all night?

Primo: Hell, yeah. My sisters – everybody – used to tell me, "You better go home Primo. You've been gone for three or four days. At least go home and change your clothes."

Philippe: Where would you break night?

Primo: Anywhere. With girls. We always had a crib. The top of the club. We used to run that building back in the days. We had apartments everywhere; bitches all over the place. It was wild, man.

Caesar's attachment to his home was even more fragile, but he did not focus on the skill and art of petty thieving. In fact, it is not clear that he was stable enough to be integrated into a solidary peer group or youth

gang. Consistent with his adult crack-binging behavior, as well as his
propensity for uncontrollable rage as a young teenager, Caesar celebrated
the public, rowdy dimensions of street culture. He excelled at conspicu-
ous consumption, for example.

> *Caesar:* Yeah, that's when I started being like a pre-teenager. I
> wanted to dress well; I wanted like fresh sneakers, and have my hair
> combed good; and go dancing, and stuff like that. I liked'ed it.
>
> I didn't get high; it was just like I had money; and I was
> spending it on things. Like tapes for my radio.
>
> I was addicted to tapes for my radio. Music! That was my first
> addiction. I grew up real close to a radio.
>
> My second addiction was clothes. I needed to buy stuff every
> week.
>
> *Philippe* [Turning to Primo]: This is what you were like as a
> little kid too?
>
> *Primo:* I wasn't really brought up to do that. I was only doing
> what the big boys were doing. Because I was hanging out tough.
> My mother used to care.
>
> When I was stealing from the cars, there was always that thing
> goin' in my head: "My Moms don't like this"; and that when I was
> going to take it home, she'd know I didn't really earn it; and then,
> I got to hide it; and that it's not accepted.
>
> I knew I did something that I wasn't supposed to do. I knew I
> was going to get my ass beat when I got home, if she found out.

Adolescent Mischief and Inner-City Rage

Despite claims to an ex post facto sense of guilt, crime was a part of
youthful common sense to a precocious junior-high-school eleven-year-
old like Primo. The boundary between stealing car radios and playing,
for example, was intangible. In another class and ethnic setting, Primo's
activities might have confined themselves to harmless mischief; his
mother would simply have scolded "the boys for being boys." Indeed,
this is illustrated in her accounts of growing up on a sugar plantation.

> *Primo's mother:* [in Spanish] Boy, we really did bad things [*mal-
> dades*]! One time a group of us boys and girls went to a farm where
> there was lots and lots of mangoes. I think there were ten mango

trees there, and we didn't have a single tree in our house. It was far away.

It was a private farm, but you know how boys and girls are. We would get together as a group, and walk over there, and hide.

We would hide from my grandfather to do it, because it was stealing. We also had to hide near the mango trees, because the guy had a dog. One time we even got shot at.

And those were good mangoes, they were pink mangoes that had a real good smell. And I would throw rocks at them to knock them down, and the boys would be picking them up under the tree. But then, when the man would come out, we would all run away.

Boy, we really did bad things! Sometimes we'd even steal sugar cane too. We'd wait until it was dark, and one person would look out.

We'd have to eat it in hiding. If my grandfather found out about it, he'd be angry. He was strict, and he would give me one heck of a beating, because he was strict.

So you see, we weren't little saints, we did our mischief. We'd even steal fresh corn from our neighbors. We'd make a little fire and put ears of corn right on top of the charcoal.

But then they'd find the eaten ears of corn and they'd get angry at us.

This was when I was fourteen, fifteen, sixteen years old, 'cause I came here at seventeen.

The social control and repression exerted by the family and the community on unruly children was obviously qualitatively very different in rural Puerto Rico during the 1930s and 1940s from inner-city New York in the 1970s. Most important, the consequences for a fourteen-year-old are tremendously different from being barefoot and stealing pink mangoes for their "sweet taste" versus wearing dirty sneakers and stealing car radios for money to buy Vicks cough drops or "fly clothes." The acts themselves, however, are symbolically the same: precocious childhood mischief. The difference in the long-term outcomes between children raised in the relatively subsistence-oriented and commodity-poor plantation economy and those born into the fetishism of urban cash needs in the industrial decay of the U.S. inner city, becomes even greater when, by the ages of fifteen or sixteen, drugs become easily available, prized objects for recreation. As a teenager, Primo excelled in his second-generation urban immigrant context. He rapidly graduated from pre-teenage car-stereo thieving, to bona fide apartment burgling:

Yeah, then I became a burglar. The first apartment I ever robbed I was eleven years old. I remember that first time. I loved'ed it and liked'ed it.

I never got caught out there. I even robbed a dance studio, a liquor store, and two different pharmacies . . . burglarized it all. Took cash, liquor . . . the most expensive shit they had.

You know that pharmacy right there on 103rd Street and Third Avenue? I burglarized it before; robbed it.

On top of the pharmacy there's a dead building – an abandoned building. We climbed through from another building with flashlights; made a hole through the floor [illustrating with hand motions], PPKKKKK, PPKKKK; and went in through the ceiling, GGWSSSSHHH; the alarm rang; the cops came; the owner came.

It was a silent alarm; the owner was there with a gun! And we were kids! [throwing his arms up in mock astonishment] I was shaking. I saw the cops and the gun.

But we jumped outta there and by the time they opened the store and looked through the hole, we were already buildings away.

And they didn't really want to go in that building in the *dark* because it's like a whole abandoned building, empty. The shit is real old inside. Like a landmark. It was antique.

It took hours, but we came out with some good shit, and stashed it in my cousin's crib. But it was wack. We got jerked selling it, because we were little niggas. I was twelve or maybe thirteen.

Philippe: Man! You were a little kid!

Primo: The last baddest thing I did was when I was sixteen, with Luis and this other guy named Papito – which is Ray's present wife's brother. We went downtown for the purpose of stealing from a pharmacy that was connected with an electronic goods store.

I don't know whose idea was it. These guys had really scoped the store before. It was downtown, so we went in a small car.

But we kept hesitating. I was like, "I don't want to do this; it doesn't seem right."

And then, when we got there, they couldn't break the locks. But by coincidence we bumped into Ray. He was walking from downtown on Lexington Avenue.

So Ray said, "What you up to?"

We told him, and then I was saying, "Damn, these guys can't even bust the locks."

So Ray said, "Watch it, watch it." And he came with a police crowbar. [making full body arm motions] POW! POW! Busted those locks like *butter*. PSSSHHHT [grinning widely]; open the gate; [making deliberately efficient hand motions] and took the boards out — because the windows were boarded and gated — put them to the side; and he got a big rock; wrapped it up with cloth. [more full body hand motions] PFFFF. Bashed up the windows.

[pausing to remember] I wanted to do it though — I mean throw the rock — I don't know for what reason, but that's the way I was back in them days.

But they told me, "No." 'Cause I was little, and skinny, and I wouldn't't've even break'ed it; 'cause the first time Ray bashed it, the window didn't even break. It just went, like, PSHHHWT. [making hand motions to mime vibrating plate glass] It cracked. It just like shook.

So then he came, the second time, PGHHHHWWWW! And it's a thing that, when you rap a brick with cloth, the impact doesn't sound hard. The only thing that you're going to hear, is just the glass going SHHZZZT. So the second bang was just like, PSSSHT.

And then the alarm started ringing, so we just started grabbing every kind of shit that we could grab from the window and everything. And as I grabbed; I was going to grab some — what was it again — oh yeah, a radio-cassette TV, a beautiful color TV set. But Ray grabbed it real quick from under me, [hand motions] WSSSHHHHT.

So I just grabbed this other one. It was just like a radio and TV, but when I grabbed [moving his arm in slow motion to exhibit the long scar stretching from his wrist to forefinger], my hand got cut up with glass, SKKKKTT. And I knew my hand banged the glass, but I didn't realize that I was cut.

Then we had to run. And when I was running, I saw the top of my hand was flipped over. I was like, "Oh my God! There was no skin."

My tendons were still holding on — as a matter of fact, they locked because I couldn't open my hand anymore. So they locked onto the radio and this other shit I had in my hand.

I went into the car to throw this shit in, CSSSSHHH. And I got into the car and flipped my skin back over my tendons, and pressed and said, "Luis, take me to the hospital, I'm cut."

So he said, "Yeah, Papito too." Papito was sitting in the front seat. It was me, Ray, Papito, and Luis was driving.

It was raining real hard. Pouring real hard that night. Papito was moaning and groaning. I like looked over, and he had his muscle split right here [pointing to the top of his other hand]. You could see his muscle meat fresh, ahhhh [wincing].

So what we did, was, we went to 110th Street where Ray lived, and we dropped all this shit off before we went to the hospital, in case they investigate.

Lucky it was raining, because nobody was present. It was crazy.

I was bleeding like crazy, but this guy wasn't even bleeding, but he was fainting. I don't know why. Maybe he was just fainting at the sight of his muscles, which were sticking out, and shit.

They couldn't take care of me in the hospital, 'cause I was under age. And Luis and these guys looked'ed too wild, and they didn't want to put them down as responsible. So I just kept holding on to my shit. [grasping tightly in mock pain at the scar above his wrist]

I didn't really know what was going on, I was scared. I saw my bones in there. The skinny bones in your hand. My man [Papito] burst out crying, but I told him "Shut the fuck up. You gettin' me nervous, you son of a bitch."

I started cursing. I was thinking, "Oh my God Jesus this is punishment. I should not have done this shit." I knew it from the whole get-go. It was like; I knew I deserved it, and I didn't want to steal no more.

The hospital people had to call my mother, so we invented a story. We just said that we had a fight at 111th Street with some people. You know, some guys with knives cut us up. Plus we had to just write that down on the report at the hospital. And that's the way the story stood to my mother and sisters until I just decided to say the truf after a while.

At the hospital they say, "Your tendons are cut; they're splitting." I didn't know anything about tendons, but it was like definitely operation time.

They set up a date; they operated me; they had a cast. And to this day, this hand ain't even right; it can't go down. [demonstrating the limited mobility]

Philippe: So you stopped stealing after that?

Primo: After a while, I just stopped. I got stuck with my son's mother. We were teenagers going steady; found a job, and stuff like that.

But this guy [Ray], was always into something, working on his own thing. He was a big guy, and probably would bash somebody and take theirs – or whatever.

My other cousin Papito used to work in New Jersey burglarizing, but he got locked up.

Automatic gunfire rang out from the project's courtyard just as we were about to cut diagonally through it to reach a grocery store to buy more beer. We abruptly stopped and turned around to walk the long way around the projects along the avenue. Three teenage girls came running past us giggling, "These niggas be crazy."

Caesar's stories of being initiated into the common sense of crime in his early teens were suffused with a more violent rage. They lacked the obvious instrumentality and the extensive, almost ritualistic, peer group solidarity of Primo's burglaries and car break-ins. This expressed itself symbolically in their different opinions on mugging, which Primo roundly condemned, even though he admitted to having mugged several people in his lifetime. Whenever the subject came up, Caesar would ridicule Primo's righteous censure of the practice by relating it with irony to the kinds of deeper sociological tensions that I often steered our conversations toward. He enjoyed contradicting my structural and antiracist analyses by emphasizing instead his own heartless psychopathology and by sarcastically conjuring up a racialized notion of "evil Puerto Rican-ness":

Caesar: When I was about sixteen, fifteen – something like that – I was with my cousin; he had just come back from P.R. We was downtown in a shopping mall in Connecticut, in New Haven by Yale. We were kinda starving, and we needed some money. So my cousin had convinced me into robbing a purse.

We noticed this old lady on a corner next to a hospital, but I was scared to do it. But then I said, "Fuck it. I'm gonna do it."

I thought it was a good spot, because she was waiting for a red light.

So I snatched it; but she didn't want to let it go. So I dragged her for a half a block; but she held on.

So I punched her in the head a couple of times, and she got real hurt, and finally let the purse go.

Primo: Shut the fuck up Caesar.

Caesar: Like I'm saying [thrusting his face into Primo's], I dragged her . . . dragged her for a while. She didn't want to let go, so I punched her on the head. [demonstrating the motions]

Then we ran about half a block into somebody's backyard, and we looked in the purse, and there was only forty dollars, and I gave my cousin half. I shoulda took it all, because he didn't want to do it, and so I said, "Fuck it."

We kil't [figurative] that fuckin' bitch. [contorting his face with an evil gleam that caused us all to laugh]

Primo: [irritably suppressing his laughter] I think mugging sucks.

Caesar: [retorting harshly to Primo] You know why I mugged her? Because I was desperate, and was in Connecticut, and I had been in New York, and I didn't have motherfuckin' shit.

I was going to kill that bitch, because I wanted money; 'cause I had been getting . . . dissed.

Ah' kill that fuckin' white lady — no offense [to me] — I would kill that fuckin' white lady, 'cause I was desperate.

[raising his voice] I was Puerto Rican I was nightmarish. I kil't that fuckin' bitch, because I wanted money to get high, and food. 'Cause I was a crazy motherfucking Puerto Rican that didn't know shit. How about that? [shouting into Primo's face]

Philippe: She was white?

Caesar: [spinning into my face] It would not have made a difference if she was Puerto Rican, Portuguese, or Spaniard.

I was starving. [shouting] I was: "Kill that motherfuckin' bitch!"

If it had been a black woman, I would have fucked her up some more you know. Just because she was black; and I hate black people.

Because I don't give a shit. I'm a racist motherfucker.[4]

Adolescent Gang Rape

Witnessing Caesar's celebration of violence and gratuitous cruelty was disconcerting, to say the least. At the end of the second year of my residence in El Barrio, however, I was exposed to an even more brutal dimension of the school-age, childhood socialization of the members of Ray's crack-dealing network: gang rape. I remember vividly the first night Primo told me that Ray and Luis used to organize gang rapes in the abandoned building where the Social Club crackhouse was located. He approached the subject casually in a conversation near closing time at the Game Room, catching me unprepared. At the time, these childhood stories of violently forced sex spun me into a personal depression and a research crisis. Furthermore, Caesar's voyeuristic bonding and sexual celebration of Primo's brutal account made me even more disgusted with my "friends." Although I might have expected such behavior from Caesar, I felt betrayed by Primo, whom I had grown to like and genuinely respect.

> *Primo:* I'm hanging out by myself; nobody's on the block; I'm wandering down the street; the block is quiet. The club's here; [hand motions] the corner's up here; on the last floor they had an apartment.
>
> Standing in the corner, Luis looks out the window, and yells, "Primo, you wanna eat?" I thought he had like a pie — a pizza — something. I said, "Bet!" When he said that, I got the munchies real quick.
>
> But when he looks out the window, he goes like that, with his cock out the window, and I'm like, "Oh shit! Motherfucker!"
>
> So they threw the keys down; I went upstairs, it was Sapo, Luis, Tootie, Papo, Ray, probably Negro; five or six guys there. And that girl.

She was naked in the room, she was naked there with a beer in her hand, a big forty-ounce, getting boned and laughing. They were holding her down.

Caesar: Yeah! Yeah! The bitch was wit'it, though.

Primo: When I opened the door, she was getting fucked by Papo. He was dogging her, and all of us were there looking.

[to me, nervously noticing my horror] It wasn't really all that critical. I'm telling you Felipe! The bitch was laughing with a quart in her hand.

Caesar: Yeah! Mah' man dicked her with *shtrength and animosity*.

Primo: After he left — since he wasn't used to hanging out with us and he couldn't concentrate — we locked the door; turned on the light; she was there, free meat. It was just the fellows.

Caesar: You niggas was training her!

Primo: [concerned again by my expression] She didn't give a fuck. She just ain't nothin'; everybody was there with their cocks all different sizes and widths and everything. All naked; with their pants halfway down; just waiting. Niggas showing off with their dicks.

Caesar: [turning to me and misunderstanding my negative reaction for incomprehension] They just was training her, Felipe. All six niggas boning her in the same room, at the same time.

Primo: [looking back at me] Not me! They wanted me to do it, but I said, "Fuck that! I don't want you niggas' leftovers. Don't want to catch no fucking gonorrhea, herpes."

Caesar: Training her!

Primo: She was there stark naked, and them niggas was saying, "Go ahead Primo." She was there like a hole. They were holding her there.

Caesar: Training that bitch!

Primo: She had a nice body, man. She was great. But I didn't want someone with . . . shit like that.

I finally grabbed some tits and felt her body. She felt'ed good. I felt with my fingers in her hole and that shit felt nice and tight. But I ain't gonna put my dick in that bitch.

Caesar: They were training that bitch!

Primo: I stuck my thumb in her pussy, and my finger in her ass, while they were sucking her tits. It was crazy. I washed my hands after that, but it felted'ed good though.

Caesar: [trying again to bring me into the conversation] Them niggas used to bone some good-looking girls.

Primo: She was seventeen years old. She was already a woman; she wasn't a virgin. She's a piece of meat — already fucked up.

Despite the almost three years that I had already spent on the street at the time of this particular conversation, I was unprepared to face this dimension of gendered brutality. I kept asking myself how it was possible that I had invested so much energy into taking these "psychopaths" seriously. On a more personal level, I was confused because the rapists had already become my friends. With notable individual exceptions, I had grown to like most of these veteran rapists. I was living with the enemy; it had become my social network. They had engulfed me in the common sense of street culture until their rape accounts forced me to draw the line.

From an analytical and a humanistic perspective, it was too late for me to avoid the issue or to dismiss their sociopathology as aberrant. I had to face the prevalence and normalcy of rape in street culture and adolescent socialization. In any case, Primo and Caesar would not let me escape it, and over the next year, as if peeling off layers from an onion's core, they gave dozens of accounts and versions of their direct participation in sexual violence during their earliest adolescent years. Few people talk about rape — neither the perpetrators nor the victims. In fact, rape is so taboo that I was tempted to omit this discussion, fearing that readers would become too disgusted and angry with the crack dealers and deny them a human face. As a man, I also worry about the politics of representation. Most of the dozens of tape recordings I collected on the subject came from the perspectives of the perpetrators. I tape-recorded several accounts by survivors to obtain alternative perspectives, but I did not have the same kinds of long-term relationships with these individuals to allow for the detail and confidence of a meaningfully contextualized life-history interview or conversation.[5]

From a political perspective, as I noted in the Introduction, I am also worried about creating a forum for a public humiliation of the poor and powerless. Readers in the United States are so unconsciously subjected to the racialized common sense of their society, that many of them are likely to interpret these passages as some kind of a cultural reflection on the Puerto Rican community. Such an airing-of-dirty-laundry interpretation runs counter to the theoretical and political arguments of this book. There is obviously nothing specifically Puerto Rican about rape. Once again, as a white male researcher, to avoid pushing unconscious taboo buttons it would have been easier to eliminate this discussion of gang rape. I feel, however, that a failure to address sexual violence in street culture would be colluding with the sexist status quo. Rape runs rampant around us, and it is as if society maintains a terrifying conspiracy of silence that enforces this painful dimension of the oppression of women in everyday life.

Learning to be a rapist was very definitely part of Primo's coming-of-age. Tagging after the big boys on the street, he was repeatedly excluded for being too young – or for not wanting – to participate.

Primo: Back in those days I was younger. My dick wouldn't stand up. It was like nasty to me; I wasn't down with it. I can't handle that.

So they be goin' upstairs with a girl, and of course they already knew that I'm not going to be down with it, so they ask me, "What cha' gonna do man? Go home or what?"

So fuck it, the best thing I could do is break out. "See you guys tomorrow"; or else, I just wait downstairs in the bar, or something.

The alternative was for Primo to bond with his older peer group by participating actively in this violent male ritual.[6] It was only later that Primo learned to become sexually aroused.

I wasn't really with it, but I used to act wild too, because the bitch is gonna have to pass through the wild thing. And sometimes, it could be me acting stupid with a bat or something, so that she has got to stay in the room with whoever is there.

Sometimes the older guys, they would play the nice role for a while with the girl, but once they get that piece of pussy, she gets dished. It's like PSSHHHT, PSSHT. [making slapping motions] She gets beat down: "I own you now, bitch."

I used to play that shit before man: There is always the good one, and then the bad one. My man, here [grabbing Caesar by the shoulders], be the meanest one, and you and me [putting his arm around my shoulder], be the good sweet ones . . . that we don't, like, wanna bother her. Then Luis over here [putting his arm around Luis, who had just walked in to drop off three freshly bagged bundles of crack and retrieve the midshift's receipts], is like both good and bad; but Ray [pointing to the doorway], is the meanest one.

So this way, the bitch get comforted, and we explain to her, that we just want some pussy. "That's what you have to give up; it's the price for freedom." And the whole posse be there; they are like saying, "Yeah, Yeah!"

That was back in the days. Nobody is with that shit no more. Pussy is too easy to get nowadays.

The rapists were careful to develop a logic for justifying their actions. For example, Primo separated the women his peer group raped into categories of worthy versus unworthy victims. He also projected onto them the sexual depravity of his male companions. Despite his attempt to reconstruct some of the women as voluntarily submitting to the gang rape – or even enjoying it, as in his original account at the beginning of this section – when specifically confronted on the issue, Primo admitted that ultimately violent force and physical terror were the organizing mediums. Ironically, the particular conversation recorded below was interrupted by gunshots, as if to illustrate the extent to which life-threatening violence permeates, in an explicitly less gendered manner, much of day-to-day street interaction:

Primo: I mean the way I remember it, I was so fucking young. I looked at it like, most likely, whoever never came back to hang out at the club, passed through some trauma, and it's gonna be hidden within their life, for the rest of their life, and they're never goin'a' hang again. Instead they go home, and chill the fuck out, and keep a dark secret for the rest of their life. [looking at me defensively] I used to feel sorry, sometimes too, for them.

But some bitches was more suitable, and used to just come back and hang. 'Cause I guess it was like they was on the streets, and they passed through their first shit, and now fuck it: *"Voy a hangear."* [I'm going to hang out.]

Philippe: [interrupting] Come on, man, get real! Nobody likes going through that shit.

Primo: [speaking slowly] Well . . . It was their decision, Felipe. I mean, the first time, maybe they weren't into it. Sometimes there be tears in their eyes. They didn't want to be forced.

Caesar: [laughing at Primo's confusion and my anger] But they were forced; but they liked'ed it; and they come back for more; 'cause they're with it. They just get used to the fact: "We own you now bitch!"

Philippe: You motherfuckers are sick! [loud gunshots followed by the sound of someone running]

Primo: No! You gotta understand Felipe, even when they say no, they're loving it.

Caesar: [interrupting from the doorway of the Game Room, where he was looking out] Yo! Yo! Check this out! Felipe, give me that. [grabbing my tape recorder]. I'm gonna say into the mike, that someone shot someone, and just ran by us.

Primo: [ignoring the interruption] Sometimes the girls would end up staying with like, one guy, and maybe having a kid from him. And this is after the whole fuckin' posse – everybody – had fucked her.

I remember this one bitch, she wanted to stay with Luis because he gave her like a tremendous cock fuck. She was a young bitch; she liked'ed that huge cock of Luis's, boy. She fell in love with Luis's cock.

Luis busted out a lot of virgins. He used to soup up the girls, and bone them instantly. If not today, then the next day. He used to *"Da, da, da, boom, bang them!"*[7]

I used to get my nuts off watching that shit there. Word! It was good. Hell, yeah. It was exciting because after a while a girl gets into it.

Luis's favorite was: He fucks and we watch. And I know, I used to get off on that!

Philippe: [interrupting again] Shut up man! What the hell is the matter with you!

Primo ignored my response and continued with an exceedingly explicit account of how Luis would angle his body to maximize the visibility of his actions for the voyeuristic benefit of his gang-rape companions. The pornographic detail of Primo's description supports the interpretation that there is also a homoerotic dimension to male sexual bonding among gang rapists.

Grappling for a confrontational response that would shock Primo into an awareness of the pain he and his friends inflicted on the girls around them, I tried to jostle his conscience by appealing to the patriarchal logic of family honor.

Philippe: Did you ever worry about this happening to your sisters?
Primo: Hell yeah!

But I knew my sisters were innocent. Me and Luis used to talk about it. We used to be in the streets, and we said, "We got those sisters, man."

Caesar: That's why I wouldn't never want to have a daughter, if I was to get my girl pregnant. I couldn't handle the fact of having a baby, and then I have to see her being a ho'. I would probably kill myself. If I was going to have a baby girl, I don't want nothing to do with it. I don't even want to touch it. Word!

Primo: [trying to reassure me] Put it this way, Felipe, these bitches were young, dumb, and full-a'-cum. If they are hanging out too much, and they start seeing that we are wild, and if they are still hanging out, then we know that we can take them.

Philippe: That is some sick shit you're saying. You motherfuckers were nothin' but a bunch of perverts.

Primo: [frustrated that he could not convince me] I mean look at their attitude; if they hang out too long, believe me, then they know what's happening. If the girl is gonna hang then she's gonna get dicked. I mean these bitches, they would just keep hanging out, and hanging out. They be coming back to the bar every day, so then we know that they really want a dick.

So Ray and them guys, they would take the bitch aside, because we had her *confianza* [trust]; and by then it was easy to force her into doing it with all of us.

Besides the bitch get smacked, or something, if she don't.

In some conversations, especially when Caesar was not present, Primo responded to my open condemnations by claiming repentance. Even when he was responding so as not to offend me, however, he still maintained the profoundly patriarchal logic of his peer group.

Primo: Now, every time that I think about those times it makes me feel weak. Because I used to, like, not be with it. And I used to feel *sorry* when I would go back to my house and see my mom and my sisters.

Those fucking girls used to go through shit, and if they were good girls, then we used to ruin their lives. Now I think about the ages of those girls. They might have been fifteen or thirteen or twelve or fourteen or fifteen or sixteen, and that's some crazy shit. They looked exactly like the little girls we see now.

Philippe: Bothers you now?

Primo: There was never a time that it didn't bother me, Felipe. I never liked that. I hated it. I was like the kinda person that pleads, "Don't! Stop!"

It was happening all the fucking time. All over. But I never said nothing. [morosely] I wished that I had told them to stop raping her.

I used to be a fuckin' psychiatrist for these girls. Word, Felipe. I shoulda got paid, because they used to talk to me, like, I used to give them advices and shit. Like: "Get the fuck out of here before your life really gets more fucked up."

But then again, like you said [nodding at Caesar, who had just walked inside the Game Room from the doorway to listen more carefully], they liked'ed it.

Ultimately, the violence against women orchestrated by Primo's older role models, reflected itself back on their own sense of internalized worthlessness:

Primo: We used to talk between each other, that these women are living fucked up, because they want to hang out with us.

And what the fuck we got to offer? Nothing! We used to wonder.

Caesar: We don't be doing nothing! Bitch be stupid to go with a nigga' like us.

6

REDRAWING THE GENDER LINE ON
THE STREET

I used to take all my husband's shit. I even used to support my husband,
but I woke and smelled the coffee, like they say. And I put a bullet in
my man.

Candy

The gang rapes discussed in the preceding chapter were not the isolated
brutal excesses of a fringe group of pathological sadists. On the contrary,
they provide an insider's perspective on the misogyny of street culture
and the violence of everyday life. A biting reminder of the pervasiveness
of sexual violence in El Barrio was the comment made to my wife and me
by our eleven-year-old neighbor, Angel, in the course of an otherwise
innocuous, random conversation about how he was doing in school, and
about how his mother's pregnancy was progressing. He told us he hoped
his mother would give birth to a boy "because girls are too easy to rape."

Witnessing Patriarchy in Crisis

Focused on in isolation, the crack dealers' accounts of gang rape can
overwhelm readers with anger or despair. Women on the street, however,
are not paralyzed by terror. On the contrary, they are in the midst of
carving greater autonomy and rights for themselves in El Barrio, just as
they are among most social classes and ethnic groups in the United
States, and throughout much of the nonfundamentalist world. In East
Harlem, daughters, sisters, and wives can no longer be beaten submissively and sent upstairs as authoritatively as they were in the past for
socializing on the street, or for pursuing careers in the underground
economy. As has been the case historically for all major power shifts

Girls playing stickball: Carving out new spaces for women. Photo by Philippe Bourgois.

between antagonistic groups, the complicated process whereby women are carving out a new public space for themselves is rife with contradictory outcomes and human pain. This is exacerbated by the fact that the fundamental status quos that enforce male domination have not been altered. As many feminist theorists have long since noted, much of the struggles and achievements of women in the past decades have been framed in terms of individual rights that ultimately largely mirror patriarchal models of "empowerment."[1]

As men on the street lose their former authoritarian power in the household, they lash out against the women and children they can no longer control. Males are not accepting the new rights and roles that women are obtaining; instead, they are desperately attempting to reassert their grandfathers' lost autocratic control over their households and over public space. Of course, this does not in any way imply that women in El Barrio, or anywhere else on earth, have provoked male violence against themselves because of their demands for greater rights. Such a blame-the-victim interpretation not only glorifies the stability of previous patriarchal status quos, but also overly individualizes the long-term macro-structural transformation in gender relations that is occurring across the globe, even if that progressive change is bounded by a liberal, middle-class, and largely Anglo-oriented hegemony.

In the Puerto Rican case, the change in power relations between men and women conflates with a structurally induced wrenching of traditional gender roles as men steeped in jíbaro rural identities confront unemployment and social marginalization in the postindustrial, urban United States. Old-fashioned household economies defined around the productivity of an autocratic male have long been under siege in the Puerto Rican diaspora — especially in the inner city. Men and women whose consciousness harks back to idealized memories of jíbaro sugar cane flatland plantations, highland farming communities, or urban shanty-towns find themselves confined inside the isolated towers of public housing projects surrounded by people they do not know or trust. The high-finance, FIRE sector–dominated economy of New York City does not pay high school dropouts the working-class wages that would allow them to support a nuclear family of four on a single income. The traditional "Spanish ideal" of a large, male-dominated household blessed with numerous children is recognized as an anachronism by even the most reactionary men and women of the new generations born in New York City.

As noted in Chapter 4 on legal employment, the male head of household who, in the worst case scenario, has become an impotent, economic failure experiences these rapid historical structural transformations as a dramatic assault on his sense of masculine dignity. Worse yet, the stabilizing community institutions that might have been able to mediate the trauma do not exist in the U.S. inner city. Instead, men struggle violently in a hostile vacuum to hold on to their grandfathers' atavistic power. The crisis of patriarchy in El Barrio expresses itself concretely in the polarization of domestic violence and sexual abuse.[2]

In attempting to document this long-term transformation in gender relations, I faced the inescapable problem of how — as a male — I could develop the kinds of deep, personal relationships that would allow me to tape-record conversations with women at the same intimate level on which I accessed the worlds of men. The challenge of engaging in frank, open, respectful dialogue across gender lines is exacerbated in the Puerto Rican street scene by the way the former family-based male authoritarianism of past generations has been recast around a concern over sexual fidelity, promiscuity, and public displays of male domination. Although my wife and I had many female friends in the neighborhood, and I tape-recorded at least a dozen life histories of women, only in my relationship with Candy have I felt I was able to tape-record sufficiently frank and contextualized conversations that explore the complex subject of changing gender-power relations. Candy also had the advantage of being one of only two female employees in Ray's network, as well as one of his closest childhood friends. In fact, as I noted in Chapter 3 when discussing how crack operations are managed, Candy was the person who sold Ray the rights to the Game Room when her husband, Felix – the original founder and owner – was incarcerated after she shot him in the stomach.

At the same time, there is nothing "typical" about Candy. On the contrary, she is much too charismatic, and her life has been more ridden with violence than most people's. Nevertheless, her experiences as a woman capable of commanding respect on the street embody the contradictory processes through which gender power relationships are being redefined in street culture.

I still vividly remember the night I first "met" Candy, about a year after I moved to the neighborhood. She skidded her oversized black car with tinted glass lopsidedly to a halt by the fire hydrant in front of the Game Room. Bedecked in skintight orange stretch pants, and perfectly balanced on her black high heels despite being six months pregnant, she barged into the Game Room furiously – not even pausing to notice me. I mistook the viciousness of her snarled curses, and the way she was wildly shaking her dyed blond hair, to be an argument over missing money. Naively, I assumed that being the wife of a crackhouse owner, she must control large quantities of money. I thought her expressive comfort in handling herself aggressively in the street was evidence of how skillful she must be as a crackhouse manager. I also remember feeling like a greenhorn because I could not even figure out whom she was cursing. Her rapid-fire chorus of "muthafucka's" and "son of a bitch cocksuckin' assholes" overlapped with many of the most intimate nicknames – Papito, Papi, Papo, Nene, Pops, Negro, Junior – of virtually everyone hanging out on the stoop that night. I was relieved, however, to note that Primo did not appear to be offended. In fact, he seemed to be agreeing sympathetically with everything she said.

I was still a relative novice on the street and I did not yet know how to recognize the suffering of a local "kingpin" drug dealer's wife. Candy was angry – always angry – during those first months that I knew her. Since my own wife was also pregnant at the time, I was fully conversant in El Barrio's folk theories on the psychological stresses of reproduction. I therefore fell into the sexist trap of assuming that Candy's rage was a culturally mediated case of reproductive hormones battling New York City's summer heat.

In fact, of course, there was nothing biological about Candy's problems. Her husband had failed to deliver a $3,000 payment to his lawyer, spending the money instead on a cocaine binge with one of his girlfriends. A few months before, he had been arrested for selling cocaine to an undercover agent; coincidentally, earlier on that very same day a lenient judge had sentenced him to five years probation for firearms possession. His incarceration, consequently, was imminent, but he was obviously giving no thought to providing any savings for his pregnant wife and their five children. While Felix served his prison sentence, his family was going to have to fend for itself on Candy's welfare check and with the SSI payments of their adopted grandfather, Abraham, who boarded with them.

Domestic Violence in Postindustrial Turmoil

It took me two years to develop the *confianza* and *respeto* I needed to tape-record Candy's painful life story, and to realize how profoundly vulnerable the furious pregnant woman really had been on those nights when she cowed all of us on the stoop of the Game Room with her curses. The night I finally broke the ice and began tape-recording, we carefully maintained ourselves in full view of the Game Room lookout, Caesar, so as not to appear improper. In fact, throughout all the years I knew Candy, she never came to my apartment unchaperoned to talk and tape-record with me. It would have been interpreted as suspicious, improper, or even dangerous behavior on her part. This did not prevent us, however, from feeling safely private in our publicly visible and socially approved street conversations. People usually respected our desire to talk in private and gave Candy a wide berth whenever she waved them away if they came within earshot. On this particular night, for example, sitting on the hood of a parked car with my tape recorder between us, our words were safely drowned out by the bustle of midevening street sounds.[3] My opportunistic invocation of our common condition of being the parents of newborns prompted Candy into a jíbara celebration of motherhood:

Candy: I love kids. I believe kids are the most wonderful things alive; that's what made me live until now.

Because . . . you know how you love a mother? You can never love a mother more until you have a baby. I loved my mother more when I had my first daughter; that's when I loved my mother more.

Because when a baby is born . . . when you see a baby . . . and you see it so small, you say, that baby can't come and smack you, and say, "Mommy, don't do this; don't do that." He's so innocent. And that's pure.

And you see so much child abuse, but that baby doesn't know nothing. It's pure and innocent. That's why I still wanna have twelve.

[laughing at my reaction] That's right Felipe; I'm not shitting you. I always wanted twelve children.

This first private conversation with Candy soon focused on the details of her own abusive childhood.

Candy: I was a child-abused daughter. I mean my father beat'ed me like crazy. There was nine of us and for some reason I was the ugly duckling.

Why? I don't know!

So, at the age of thirteen he gave me such a beating, that I told my father, "I'm gonna get married, and get away from you, if you don't leave me alone. I mean it."

So I slept in the street at the age of thirteen. Eventually I met up with my husband who at that time wasn't my husband – but then became my husband – and I came out pregnant.

I didn't know what pregnant was being all about. I mean I didn't know nothing. I was thirteen.

In the traditional small-town context, the family and perhaps the entire rural community or neighborhood might have intervened in this kind of crisis situation when a patriarch's violence against his daughter or spouse becomes so abusive as to force her out of the household. Romantic elopement in the jíbaro context is a legitimate cultural institution allowing a teenage girl to resist her father's domination and to express her needs as an individual with rights. The runaway girl and her abandoned parents suffer no cultural opprobrium so long as the girl resubmits herself to the control of her lover, and establishes a conjugal household with him as soon as she becomes pregnant. In fact, often the new husband's mother shelters the young eloped couple until they are able to establish themselves as a viable economic unit. Should the new husband treat the young woman badly, she has the further option of falling in love with another person and eloping once again. This possibility of elopement, in the traditional context, consequently accords a certain degree of bargaining power to women in rural community or plantation settings, or even in cohesive urban neighborhoods.[4]

At age thirteen, fleeing an abusive father,[5] Candy was faithfully following this traditional cultural scenario. She even had her mother's full cooperation. The disjunction with the rural past at this point in Candy's life could not have been more marked: Instead of being protected from her abusive father and guided into a new male-dominated household by the villagers living around her, Candy faced the closed corporate inner-city street gang, and she was raped by the adolescent boys that Felix, her future husband, led.

When Primo told me his version of Candy's elopement and her eventual marriage to Felix, he harkened back to a past sense of community morals. He explicitly condemned both Felix and Candy's father for their treatment of Candy. Caesar, on the other hand, translated Candy's childhood trauma into the logic of contemporary inner-city misogyny. In a burst of laughter that caused him to spit up his beer onto the Game Room floor, he marveled, "Felix got that pussy brand new, boy!" Caesar and Primo immediately began arguing over whether thirteen was too young an age for a girl to become sexually active. The subject of rape was not alluded to, except indirectly as having to do with rumors about Candy's promiscuity, and the fact that she was "definitely not a virgin" when she married Felix.

Candy interprets these same events in a more traditional framework, but from an assertive women's perspective. She remembers her flight from her father as a love affair with Felix, and she reminisces over the excitement of becoming a first-time mother. The formal state institutions designed to help Candy in her new urban setting, however, interpreted her situation in a completely different manner.

> *Candy:* I had my daughter. The courts was gonna take her away 'cause I was a minor. So my husband at the age of fourteen tried to

marry me, but the judge said, "No, You're too young. You're two kids. You don't know what you want."

Okay, so we didn't get married. But we hide'ed from the family court.

I can't deny that. The cops came to our house and we hide'ed with the baby on the roof.

But I wanted the baby so much that I cried for the baby, so I told my mommy, "The courts can't take the baby away from me."

I remember I slept in the hallway with my daughter next to my mother's doorway. I had nowhere to go with my baby.

So they told my mother, "Since you're having a daughter so young having a baby, we have to take all your kids away too."

My mother sold her furniture, hiding everything, and went to Puerto Rico, but gave me my daughter and told my husband, "Be responsible for my daughter, because she's a baby."

We lived together on 110th Street between Lexington and Third Avenue.

Twenty years later, at the age of thirty-four, Candy has a psychoanalytic understanding of herself as a battered woman. She blends a resigned folk Catholicism with the New York City therapeutic jargon that she learned during her sporadic, mandated referrals to the mental health clinic at Metropolitan Hospital. Felix's beatings and Candy's numerous suicide attempts frequently forced her into the emergency room of East Harlem's public municipal hospital. Consequently, she has had extensive contact with mainstream social service bureaucracies and knows how to manipulate them.

Candy: My husband was like my father: I was a child-abused daughter, and I became a child-abused wife. I escaped my mother's house, because I'm a battered daughter; but then I'm going to be a battered wife. I thought it was love.

I'm not gonna lie. I loved'ed to get beat 'cause I was used to it as a baby to thirteen, and then my husband was doing it from thirteen to thirty-two. So I thought life was that: Getting beat up. I used to look for fights for him to beat my ass.

You see when you're a child-abused daughter from the age of eight months to thirteen then you find an abused husband. You

think that the way a man shows you love is by beating you because
Coño [expletive], I says, "My father loves me, that's why he's
beating me."

I was foolish, because I never got therapy. I never got psychiatry.
And I tried to kill myself since I was eleven. The last time I
succeeded was the time I was thirty-three. I almost made it that
time.

But you know – I've been through a trauma life – but you
know, life goes on. And God is with me.

And the doctors knew that I was an abused woman, but because
I did not want them to know – because I was a battered woman –
they used to cover up for me.

So my husband beat me up.

The psychotherapeutic literature on the battered woman syndrome and
on the intergenerational transmission of violence and substance abuse
could certainly be applied to Candy. No matter how psychoanalytically
appropriate this kind of individualistic, medicalized explanation for
Candy's suffering may appear, however, it misses the key structural
components to her life experiences. It ignores the systematic dislocation
in family structure caused by the massive rural–urban migration of
Puerto Ricans to New York City in the post–World War II period.[6]
Felix's extreme brutality against Candy, especially during her pregnancies, emerges as an almost caricatural expression of this structural maladjustment, rather than being merely the isolated excesses of a psycho-
path.

Candy: Felix broke my arm. He did everything to me – once he
cracked my head.

I used to get three beatings a night, every day, from when I was
thirteen till twenty-one. He made me lose five stomachs [pregnan-
cies]. That's five miscarriages because of him.

I'm talking about five and a half months, five months, four
months. Nothing under four months. He used to give me beatings,
and I would lose them.

Believe me, you don't even want to know.

Perhaps Felix's sadism was the last agonized gasps of the anachronistic
traditional ideal of the large jíbaro family that both he and Candy still

maintained, despite being stranded in high-rise housing projects. A generation earlier, Felix's domineering and bullying would have been understood, within limits, as the "legitimate" role of a father coordinating his household laborers for the urgent agricultural tasks of the small family farm. The material basis for the *respeto* that men commanded on the jíbaro hillsides of Puerto Rico, however, is obsolete – and even contraindicated – in Felix and Candy's new postindustrial world. Grotesque as this may seem, perhaps Felix was unconsciously killing the children he and Candy kept producing but could not possibly raise with dignity on their declining access to factory work. Through all of this, however, Candy still desperately holds on to the primacy of males.

Candy: I wanted twelve kids; I only got five – but I wanted twelve. My husband took out five of them with his punches and beatings.

He made me lose five babies. [holding up all the fingers on her right hand]

And the one that I hold against him more, is the one after my daughter – Tabatha – the one that is twenty-one. Because I was six months pregnant, and that baby died due to the reason that he would beat me up.

When I saw that baby, I knew it was a boy. It was dead when it came out, and the only thing that came out was blood clot, because the beatings that he gave were forming a blood clot, instead of performing a baby.

One day, when I came out pregnant with my son, I told Felix, I said, "Maybe, if you won't hit me I will have this baby." He made a promise to God. And look what happened. I had Junior, my only son. [pointing to her thirteen-year-old son hanging out on the crackhouse stoop]

Female Liberation Versus Traditional Sexual Jealousy

When Candy finally shot Felix in the stomach about a month after my first tentatively polite conversations with her in front of the Game Room, everyone supported her. At the time, I hailed it as an emancipatory act of resistance. Candy, however, understood her liberating act as the traditional outburst of a jealous woman who was uncontrollably romantically in love with an unfaithful man. She was desperately holding on to the traditional family values of a past where gender confrontations and assertions of individual rights express themselves in the romantic idioms of sexual jealousy. Of course, the inner-city context has polarized the old-fashioned scenarios. Easy access to narcotics and guns has raised the stakes and augmented the levels of human suffering of traditional, gender-based household struggles.

As in the case of elopement, romantic love in a conjugal relationship enables a subordinated woman to assert her individual needs while at the same time binding her to the principle of a male-dominated nuclear household. Candy very distinctly identified Felix's sexual betrayal of their marital relationship as the precipitating factor that caused her to shoot him. She had always been aware that Felix "had outside women out there," but when he violated the rules of kinship solidarity she finally exhausted her battered-woman's dependence on him.

Candy: Womens think that their man fooling around with another woman is the worst trauma you can go through; but it's not.

[grabbing hold of the tape recorder] And I tell every woman in New York City: You think your man playing you dirty with a woman is bad. No! The worst trauma you can go through, is when it's sleeping with your own sister — your own blood.

And I'm thirty-four, and I know, 'cause it was with my sister that he started fooling around — I'm not going to lie.

And when you love a sister so much like me [putting the tape recorder back down, her eyes misting] . . . And that's the pain I will die with until now.

Philippe: [holding her forearm] Hold on, Candy, start from the beginning. Explain all this to me better.

Candy: Okay Felipe, people say you're a wife for a man, and that your husband is your life.

Wife for a man! Yeah, maybe when you're an adult, but I was only thirteen. So he trained me. Because it's like, when you grow up drinking a bottle to the age of four years old, you're used to that bottle.

And he had me from thirteen. So I was trained by him; and I was raised stupid, because I was thirteen and he raised me up his way: [snarling] "Be by yourself; don't have a friend; don't believe in nobody; don't look out the window."

I mean I couldn't even look out the window! That's how bad it was.

I'm not going to lie: I had found him before with another woman; but then, when I found out what he did with my sister, I went crazy. They sent me to Puerto Rico to calm my mind. I came back from Puerto Rico. I still hadn't forgot.

I found my husband twice with my sister in a hotel. I wanted to kill him and I wanted to kill her. But when I got to the hotel, I was too late. I threw a knife at him, and I cut him in the leg.[7]

And I'm not going to deny, even if it affects my records in the future [gesturing at the tape recorder]: I tried to kill myself a lot of times. I've been to a state hospital. I've had a record since I was eleven years old because I've tried to kill myself. He throwed me up a wall.

But look at me now. [opening her arms, pulsing her body to the beat of a loud, nearby radio, and smiling radiantly] I don't know, but God wants me alive, 'cause I'm a good-hearted woman. I have no bad for nobody. And God wants me here for some good reason. Maybe it's for my kids.

Candy's violent and sometimes suicidal rages were directed at holding on faithfully to the sanctity of her hearth. It took her another four months of abuse before she finally pulled the trigger on her husband. She condemns her husband within the confines of the cultural rules of her mother's or her grandmother's generations. She expresses her desperation and anger through jealous hysteria caused by her husband's failure to respect the integrity of their conjugal household. In keeping with how Candy frames her rights as an individual in classical romantic terms, a lipstick stain was the final catalyst.

Candy: One day, I went to his mother's house to see where he was at. When we were talking outside, I saw he had lipstick on his mouth, so I got mad. You see, I had found out he was fooling around with another woman — with me, my sister, and another woman!

I went crazy. And I always carry a gun for my protection — I always had that gun for my protection — it was in my pocket-book.

And that's just what I did. I just took it out, and did it. I just went crazy.

So I shot him. I'm telling you, Felipe, I shot him.

I don't know Felipe; it's my nerves. I didn't feel no pain, or no pity, or nothing. I just took out the gun in my pocketbook, and shot him, and kept walking.

But then, when I was walking away, he said, "Candy, I love you; remember! I still love you. Please, please!"

But I said, "I don't give a fuck."

But then, I have a heart of gold. I have a heart of God. I came back, and told him, "Man, you fucked up on me."

He said, "Candy, please, you don't understand." I said, "No. But I'm gonna get you an ambulance."

I got him a van. They took him to the hospital and then the detectives are there, questioning me.

But I don't know. I don't think I had any feelings. I mean, I'm a good-hearted woman, but at that moment, I didn't care.

He hurt me so much. He destroyed me so much. He took my childhood life away. I mean, from thirteen to thirty-two, I was trained his way – streetwise.

[sipping from a pint-sized Bacardi bottle in which she had a premixed supply of "Sex-on-the-Beach" sold as bootleg by one of the few remaining local Italian delicatessens] And I was a respectable wife for eighteen years. When he messed around with my sister, he destroyed me completely. [handing me the bottle]

Philippe: What happened after you shot him?

Candy: I got rid of the gun. And then I went through everything with him. In the hospital they questioned me, and I said, "No, it was a holdup." And we both lied.

In the hospital he tells me, "Don't say anything, because the detectives are recording us."

The cops went to 110th and Lexington, and people there, they said it was a blond-headed woman that had shot him. We had said it was a black guy [laughing]. But it was a lie.

But they kept questioning me, but I said, "I don't know; it was a black guy." [shrugging innocently and then laughing before swigging from the bootleg Bacardi bottle]

I told them I didn't want to go to jail. I was six months pregnant with his daughter Lillian, my baby. So the cops were so good with me, that they did not pay any attention to anything.

[shrugging, laughing, and drinking again] So I got away with it. I think it's because I believe too much in God.

Candy and her network of friends and family had a traditional Puerto Rican folk explanation to account for her dramatic action. It was "her nerves" – what on the island of Puerto Rico is called an *ataque de nervios*. Puerto Rican psychiatrists identify *ataques* as a "culture-bound Puerto Rican syndrome" most commonly found in women who have been abused since childhood by men.[8] The closest equivalent phenomenon in middle-class Anglo culture might be a panic attack. In rural and working-class Puerto Rican culture, *ataques* are a legitimized forum for a woman to vent her anger against the dominant man in her life when his abuse oversteps accepted boundaries. Straightforward jealousy is the most conventionally cited provocation for these culturally scripted violent outbursts by women. In other words, Candy had followed the traditional, abuse survivor's scenario down to its most minute details when she shot Felix. In fact, she almost reaffirmed rather than violated patriarchal etiquette when she cathartically burst her cyclical shackles of intergenerational abuse by putting a bullet in her husband's stomach.

Recovery: Sex, Drugs, and More Romantic Love

Candy gave birth to her fifth child, Lillian, two months after Felix was incarcerated following his recovery in the hospital. She fell into a deep depression as well as a severe economic crisis. During the same confusing months she misplaced her public assistance papers and two of her four children were excluded from her welfare allotment when "a mixup happened with my social security numbers." She soon exhausted the $3,000 Ray had paid her to take over the rights to sell crack at the Game Room.

Candy pulled herself out of her depression and economic crisis by falling madly in love with Primo and by getting a job selling drugs for Ray. She combined the traditional female strategy for making an assertive life-cycle change – falling romantically in love – with the reality of El Barrio's underground economy – selling drugs. In private retrospective accounts, Candy attributed her recovery to the new man she loved. Despite having proven her effectiveness as an independent single mother, she continued to frame her future life and well-being in a conjugal template.

Candy: Without Primo, who knows where I would have been. And forever . . . I could marry anybody in the future, but I would always have Primo in my mind, because he taught me to be the strong woman I am now.

Primo's retrospective descriptions of his love affair with Candy are less adulatory, but they still reveal a supportive sensitivity, despite the stylized, semipornographic lechery that male-to-male accounts of former romances often adopt. According to Primo, they stumbled into having sex by accident after several months of intimate platonic conversations.

Primo: I used to really feel sorry for Candy. She used to cry a lot. So I used to try hanging out with her more at her crib. I saw her every day in those last four months after Felix was locked up, when she had just had the baby – it came out beautiful, boy! Nice and fat – *se ve bién* [it looks healthy].

I used to, you know, be there as a listener. She was telling me everything about my cousin; how he used to hit her. I used to be her *paño de lágrimas* [shoulder to cry on],[9] because I guess you need somebody to talk to.

I was saying, "You gotta go out and enjoy yourself. Whatever is behind – is behind – that's history. Whatever comes up tomorrow, you gotta do something for yourself that will make your life better."

That night when the shit started happening, it started out cool. We just stood there talking. We wasn't on coke or anything. I didn't even used to sniff at all at that time.

So I took her to the kids' room. And it just had a small bed, and I sat her down there, and I started making out with her.

I don't know where the hell the kids were. They were probably all in another room; or sleeping together in her room. 'Cause her room had a big bed, so they probably all stayed there watching TV, and all fell asleep together in a heap.

We was kissing, and then I just slipped her panties to the side. She liked'ed it.

But then she got up; went to the bathroom; and started crying.

And I was like, saying to myself [burying his face in his palms],

227

"God maybe she didn't want to be doing this," and I was like [burying his head again], "Maybe I was forcing her."

You know, I was feeling like shit. I was thinking, "Maybe we should just forget about all this right then and there. Because we could make sure it would never happen again. Nobody has to know." Because you know how I am Felipe, I wouldn't have never told anybody.

I started to tell her that. But she said [hands on hips, shaking his head sternly] "No! Now that we've started, let's finish it off."

And then, we flew to the bed; [giggling] we got more comfortable; and wheeeee [waving his arms in the air]. And we did it right. It's like we were one. [staring upward at the plaster peeling from the ceiling of the Game Room]

To counteract the latent sensitivity of Primo's account, Caesar, who was standing in the Game Room doorway, cackled with laughter, cheering, "Yeah! Yeah! I like that! Pops stuffed her like a Thanksgiving turkey that night."

The economic independence afforded by the drug economy, as well as her love affair with Primo, enabled Candy to break the paralyzing grip that her abusive husband, Felix, still maintained from his prison cell. Ray hired Candy to work the night shift at the Social Club from midnight to 6:00 a.m. This allowed her to return home just in time to prepare her older children for school and the Head Start program, as well as cuddle her newborn. At this point Abraham, her ex-husband's adopted grandfather, who had been left to baby-sit all night while Candy worked, would have long since passed out from some combination of Thunderbird, vodka, Bacardi, and beer.

Ironically, like her imprisoned husband, Candy could not force herself to minimize her profile at "The Club" as a dealer. She could not even manage to stay inside the Club and let the customers come to her for their twenty-dollar packets of powder cocaine and ten-dollar vials of crack. Instead, she took control of the entire corner outside, cursing freelance competitors, chasing off self-appointed steerers, winking at wellbuilt men, and doing favors for all her friends. Her charisma was instantly visible: dyed blond hair with jet-black roots shining through, full-length scar down the left side of her chin, spiked high heels, black leotard pants, proud full body, and the loudest, most confidently rasping voice on La Farmacia's corner. Luckily for Candy, the police were too incompetent and demoralized to notice her, and the Club was never busted during her six-month tenure.

When I expressed concern to Ray that addicts and stickup artists might assault his new female manager–worker on the midnight shift, his retort made me feel like an ignorant sexist: "Candy knows how to get her respect. Can't you see? Didn't you hear what she did to her husband?" Ray's respect and confidence in Candy reminded me, once again, of the crucial role that public displays of violence play in establishing credibility on the street. Meanwhile, from midnight to 6:00 a.m., Candy dominated La Farmacia's corner, supplying much of the cocaine being injected by addicts in between the jungle gyms of the neighborhood's public school playgrounds that the local newspapers subsequently denounced in an exposé series entitled "Devil's Playgrounds."[10] Business boomed. Candy sniffed more coke, lost more weight, saw less of her children, made more money, and had more sex and power than ever before in her life.

I could support my family and my drugs, because I was a dealer. When you're a dealer, you can support any habit.

I did coke. Pure coke – sniffing it for five months. From coke, I could have gone to crack, but I was just sniffing, that's all. I'm against heavy drugs. Because let me tell you something, drugs ain't shit.

I stopped, and look at my weight now. [opening her arms and swiveling her hips] I'm a hundred and thirty-seven pounds.

Inverting Patriarchy

With her husband safely incarcerated, Candy thrived – at least that is what it looked like from external appearances. She effectively resisted the violent males who had been surrounding her since childhood. She even demonstrated solidarity with fellow abused women in her social network. For example, she advised the wife of Felix's older brother, Luis, to shoot her husband for beating her up every time she moved the curtains to look out the window of their eighth-floor project apartment.

Candy: I went to Wanda's house one day, right? I went to look out the window at the kids playing downstairs, and Wanda almost hit me.

"Candy, what you doing?" I thought I did something wrong.

I said, "What the hell is this?" I mean . . .

She said, "Be careful, that's a booby trap. When Luis closes the curtains, he does it a certain way so that if you open it, he'll know that you looked out through the window. We're not allowed to look out the windows here."

He's got like a heavy-duty blanket over the window, and the sun don't even go in.

You know what I told Wanda? That she should put a bullet in her man. But she hasn't put a bullet in Luis because she's a victim. . . .

I told it to Luis too. That I would have killed him a long time ago, if I was Wanda. I would've got rid of him. You think I'm going to go through all those changes!

Candy's solidarity did not run deep, however, and, ultimately she accepted and participated in the patriarchal logic that blames women for male promiscuity and violence.

Candy: I tell you, Felipe, my husband was a lot like that too. It's because the women in that family like to play their husbands dirty. So maybe Felix thought every woman was like that.

Luis always used to sleep with other people's women. He used to sleep with the sisters of his women. Remember [turning to Primo], how he did it with Lucy, his first wife, and her sister.

Primo: And Luis used to have other bitches in the background too, in those days.

Candy: Yup. And Luis always used to say, "Keep it in the family." But when it happened to him [hugging Primo from behind], he didn't like those things. You see, you don't like your own medicine. [chuckle]

Wanda caught it real bad from Luis. Forget it! Ever since Luis caught my husband up there [chuckle], she can't be lookin' out the window. Luis caught him hiding behind the bed. Luis beat the shit out of Wanda.

But that's what Luis deserved. He always used to say, "Keep it in the family."

And when this happens between me and Primo, Luis made a lot

of controversy about it, saying his brother and Primo was cousins. But being a cousin ain't that close. And now he's telling me I can't be with Primo, when he took the sister of his own wife, and when his brother took his wife. That's worse, you know, being brother-in-laws, because they're the uncles of the kids. That's stronger genes.

He should just mind his own business and worry about his own woman.

On a deeper level, Candy never escaped her abusive husband's control. She was following in his footsteps: selling drugs, neglecting her children, and flaunting her sexual conquests. By becoming Candy's kept lover, Primo became her vehicle for confronting these gender taboos of Puerto Rican street culture. At the time, Primo pretended he was fulfilling the inner-city male's street fantasy, *cacheteando* [freeloading] off a woman. In fact, however, in retrospective private conversations Primo admitted that he had felt as if he were creating a Frankenstein: a formerly battered mother of five children was out-machoing all the men in her life.

Primo: That bitch was crazy. She's madness. Because from there on, bro, it was horror. It was horror. [burying his head in his hands]

Boy! That bitch be trying to kill me; trying to beat down all my women, any girl that got near me.

That was some crazy shit I had to go through. That woman dissed me.

Primo could not accept the reversal in gender roles: Candy was bragging publicly about her sexual exploits, much the same as Felix had done by parading his girlfriends in front of the Game Room crowd before being shot.

Primo: Candy was making so, fucking, much money. That bitch was making even more than I knew about.

Then she started going around . . . umm . . . spreading it, telling how, like giving hints out . . . about me being upstairs at her place.

And then when Felix used to call her, she used to say she had a boyfriend. Like, "Don't worry you find out," type shit.

Then, when she told the people in her family, I used to feel stupid, man, I was like . . . I couldn't believe it. I didn't want to deal with this.

And I used to want to be doing my own shit. That used to make her flip.

Then when I didn't want to bother with her – like sexually – she was always telling me that I "used" her. I was like, "Used you! In what sense? Can't be sexually because you are the one that wants it."

She was saying "I buy you things."

But I was saying, "I don't ask you for nothing. It's you're the one that likes to do favors. You just have to have an excuse to be pissed off."

After about six months, Primo finally rebelled against Candy's inversion of patriarchy. He struggled to recoup his personal sense of male respect by the only means immediately at his disposal: physical violence. Classically, their breakup was precipitated by his unwillingness to meet Candy's demands for sex. Years later, on slow nights at the Game Room, Primo provided Caesar and me with detailed accounts of the fateful night of his breakup with Candy. It was almost as if he used these tape-recording sessions as therapy to resolve the confusion generated by the gender taboos he had broken when he fell in love with Candy. He also needed to bond with us, by celebrating his ability to triumph over the misbehaving woman, and Caesar would inevitably oblige Primo even when I remained neutral or critical.

Primo: You see, like she used to get in a mood, or something, and I didn't wanna *bother*.

One day she put on one of her negligees. And I was like, "leave me alone." And she was like [snarling], "You have to!"

I told her to leave me alone, but she didn't wanta get off me, so I pushed her away. It was fucked up, because she had grabbed a knife. [distant gunshots]

Caesar: Yo! Pops! I didn't know you hadda go through all this shit. She was like the woman in *Fatal Attraction*.[11]

Primo: Shut up Caesar! You used to be so high all the time,

232

that I didn't even want to know you. [handing him a quart of malt liquor]

And she was threatening me, all crazy-like. So I tell her, "Go ahead, come at me with that fuckin' knife, because I'm going to hurt you."

Caesar: [unbearably excited once again] That was *definitely* like *Fatal Attraction,* man.

Primo: Yeah! Because I was watching this bitch, seeing how close she was, because I was planning to kick her in the face. And she was gonna get fucked up, because with my kick, I'm gonna break her jaw.

Caesar: [cheering and then drinking] Yeah!

Primo: [taking back the beer bottle] I tell her, "Don't try it, because I'm gonna get you. You're not going to get me; I'm gonna get you. Because, I'm ready for you."

She put it away, the knife. But she didn't want to leave me alone; so I *grabbed* her to take her to the kids' room; so that I could show them what she's doing. I called out to her children, and I looked into her eyes, and told them to look at what their mother's doing.

But she started pretending in front of the kids, saying to me [dismissively], "What the fuck is this? I don't know what you talking about."

She looks at the kids and she says [in a gentle tone], "No, it's all right, I'm just . . . just playing with him."

But then when we stepped out of the room, she turns to me and whispers [snarling], "You motherfucker." She like turns on me again. And then I went [burying his head in his hands], "Oh, my God."

And I got mad [making exaggerated whole-body wrestling motions], and I grabbed her by the neck, and I threw her to the sofa. [pounding fist to palm] BOOM . . . and I WHAAAAAM, POOOM [pounding again], smacked her in the face with all my might.

But the bitch laughed. I hit her like hard, man! Hard man! Hard!

Caesar: [jumping up] Ooh, she laughed. I like that!

Primo: [fanning Caesar's appreciation] Yeah! She was all wild-looking, with her negligee on, and everything.

So I bugged out, I mean this bitch is crazy. So I hit her again [pounding his fist again]. It was like, it was all okay; like she wanted it.

So I hit her again [pounding], and POWW, she like flew to the other sofa, like that [making hand motions of a body flying], and she laughed.

Caesar: Yeah! Yeah! She had a thing about the hitting shit. She had to get hit.

[turning to me, perhaps worried by the uncomfortable expression on my face] You can imagine someone like Felix with her. 'Cause Pops really ain't all that bad.

Yo Pops, you think she was doing that because she loved you? Was that it? She wanted to keep you?

[turning to me again] Imagine, Felipe, that she come at you screaming [waving his arms], "You son of a bitch!"

And it didn't even look like that, man. I would look at Primo and Candy, and they looked like a couple that was just chilling.

They didn't look like they were doing what he is saying now, with knives and shit. They just looked like they used to get high, and just be . . . normal, like high all the time.

Primo: Yeah, you wouldn't know Caesar. You was always on a mission all the time.

[turning to me and looking down] God! I hate to think about this Felipe, because really all that time, she was crying through all this.

And then the kids were there in the room all nervous. I guess they were crying. She was over the limit, and what could I do?

The kids were watching. Even Lillian was there. She was less than a year old.

Caesar: Yeah! Yeah! They wanted to scratch your eyes out. Because you clocked her.

[passing Primo the beer] Pops, she wanted to keep you? Or, did she just want to be boned or something?

Primo: [drinking] She wanted me to hit her. She made me stay. So I sat on the sofa where she had fallen when I hit her.

I was thinking, "She wants to mess around with me," like lovey dovey, which I really didn't want.

But I was sitting there [handing me the beer bottle], just like

234

you sitting here, right? And all of a sudden, she jumps up, and she started walking back and forth, back and forth, with her *tacos* [high heels] on. Making a noise, like clack, clack, clack.

She was high, you know, so that was bothering me. Because she walked into her room. I didn't know what she's doing over there. Like, I didn't trust her.

Caesar: You scared of her?

Primo: Of course! 'Cause I knew she had her gun, and shit, and all that, in her room.

Caesar: [sniffing] You thought she was going to kill you for real, Pops?

Primo: Of course! But wait a minute, be quiet, I need to continue the story.

[turning to me and taking back the bottle of beer] At this point, I would do anything she wanted. So, she started, like, staying quiet, and looking at me. And for some reason, she started looking at me, trying to get me to start some trouble.

I forgot exactly what she was saying, but I got quiet. I was waiting for the *big* one.

So right there, she started mentioning Jackie [Primo's previous girlfriend]: "I know that you must have been kissing her the day before," and this and that.

And I was like, "No! Come on, you know . . . I haven't kissed her, or nothin' like that, for months."

But no matter what I said, she was trying to get it out of me that I was messing around. She just kept going at it.

And so finally I say, "Hey, all right, I'm . . . I . . . I kissed her before."

Like right there, she flipped. She said, "I knew you were a motherfucker!"

She actually tried to hit me. Boom! I caught her hand, and tell her to, "Chill!"

She screams, "You motherfucker!" – like if I was her husband or something – "I knew you were fucking around." And she started crying.

I told her "That's what you want to hear, so I tell you."

So she was like walking back and forth again, with her *tacos*. It was like a whole scandal, man. It was late at night.

Next thing you know . . . she wanted to get dressed to go to Jackie's house, right then and there, to fuck her up. And I was like [shrugging], "Fuck it!"

She put on her sneakers and clothes, and everything. I was like, "Oh shit! This is bugged."

All of a sudden, she changed her mind. It was like she was looking for me to hit her, to start trouble.

So I said to myself, "No!" And I just stood like this [standing at attention], real calm like.

She went into her room and I saw that she had her shirt all tucked in, but when she came out she had her shirt untucked. She screamed at me, "Hey you bugging? You wanta go home?"

She had her shirt untucked like that. [motioning to where a bulge would be, if one were hiding a gun at one's waist] She was looking for trouble. She was standing towards the door, and I was standing, like, sitting towards the window.

And I was *scared,* man! I was looking at her in the eyes, and I said, "I don't want to go."

She said, "Why not? You motherfucker!" And she was cursing at me real nasty.

Caesar: [bothered by Primo's admission of vulnerability] What did she want? She still wanted to be boned or something?

Primo: [irritated] No, man! She wanted me to *hit* her.

She was standing towards the door [delineating the layout with hand motions], and I was sitting towards the window, and the sofa was there; so I was like, there.

I was saying in my mind, "I know this bitch. God, like, now I'm done with. She wants me to do something stupid. She wants me to hit her so she could shoot."

So what I did was, I tell her [in a soothing tone], "Why don't you sit next to me; put your gun away; and then, get bad with me if you need to. First, show the gun to me; take the bullets out of the clip; and get to where I can see both your hands."

She said, "I ain't got my gun with me."

So I told her, "Let me frisk you."

She said, "No!"

So I say, "Forget it [in a soothing voice once again], I'm sorry man, if I ever did anything wrong to you, I'm sorry . . . dah . . .

dah . . . dah . . . let's talk. I don't even know why you're doing this to me; you shouldn't be doing this to me."

So finally she went [sigh], "Okay!" And took the gun out, because she had it on her, all the time, under her shirt.

As soon as she put it down – I don't remember exactly where she put it, but I saw her take out the clip – I went, "Fucking Bitch!" [swinging both fists] And I mushed her.

I was pissed man. I shouted, "Come on, Bitch! I'm not playing with you anymore."

But that bitch was bugging, boy; she still didn't want me to leave. She had like that evil look in her.

Lucky thing, at this point, Tabatha came, and I told her, "Your mother's fucking with me. She don't want to let me go."

It was like a big thing; it lasted a long time. I don't know exactly how long, but I think Tabatha went out to get Luis or something, because then Luis came over. And I told him, "Candy don't want to let me leave."

You see, Candy was chasing me around the house. Man! She was throwing shit; fighting with me; shit was breaking; the clock fell. She was flipping, boy. And this, like, lasted until the afternoon of the next day.

Finally by this time, we was all crying. And I felt like Tabatha was on my side, and that she was going to end up hurt that day too. Because she started arguing some shit over there with her mother, and they got into a scuffle, and Tabatha took a hard swing at Candy.

Caesar: [furiously] Tabatha be fucking everybody up. I think that bitch got a bad attitude. [12]

Primo: No, man! Candy was over the limit, and Tabatha had come to help. She was chilling. What could she do? She was trying to calm her mother down. But [grimly], she had taken a hard swing at Candy.

So Candy started screaming and acting stupid, "My daughter hit me, aaaaaahhhhhh!" And then everybody was saying all kinds of stupid shit, and the kids were all crying.

Philippe: Why didn't you just leave?

Primo: You see, she had one of those inside locks, and I couldn't get out the door. So when she was fighting with Tabatha, I was trying to unscrew the lock to get out. But she saw me and caught me.

Finally Tabatha and Luis held her, and pulled her back, so I kicked her hard in the chest.

Caesar: Yeah!

Primo: But she still had me like this [grabbing my lapels]; and she ripped my shirt; and she bit my hand, so that I couldn't even get my own grip on her, like, to get her off of me.

Caesar: Like the grip of death, man.

Primo: Yeah. So anyway, I just played it off. I just backed off a little and then . . . WHAAAM, POOSH! [making the motions of a karate kick to someone's face]

Caesar: Hit her hard enough to hurt her?

Primo: Not real hard to hurt, but hard enough for her to *fly away*. Luis and Tabatha was right there. But they wasn't even helping me anymore. They were like scared, or something . . . I don't know.

They had gone back into the *sala* [living room] next to the front door. Luis looked'ed like he was going to swing at me after I finished kicking Candy.

They all looked like they was going to swing at me, man, even the kids. Put it this way: The children knew their mother was wrong, but I was hitting their mother, and they wanted to jump on me.

Caesar: [cheering again] Yeah! Yeah! They wanted to scratch your eyes out. Because you clocked their moms.

Primo: When I saw their faces, I knew that I had to be prepared for them, too. I was ready to like, block their swings.

But I turned to them, and I tell them, "She gotta let me go; I wanta get outta here. Hold her, or something. Help me! I wanta get outta here."

And they did; and I ran.

But when I was outside, she still managed to throw a gallon of liquor out the window at me.

In keeping with her new, macho street-dealer identity, rather than flying into an *ataque de nervios* when confronted by Primo in public, Candy pursued the male scenario for revenge against a disrespectful ex-lover. She would loudly proclaim how much she had enjoyed having sex with Primo: "Best sex I ever had!" This inevitably escalated to blows when she chanced upon Primo while he was accompanied by his new girlfriend, Jaycee, whom he had gone back to after breaking up with Candy.

Primo: So Jaycee and me were just walking through Candy's project, and she comes down, all wild. And she's bitchin' at me, "You motherfucker, come to my block with your shit" – she meant Jaycee – "that you be fucking. Why don't you tell her that you fuck me? Why don't you tell her that you fuck me!"

It was wild. And everybody was saying, "Whahh?"

And it was in front of her kids. [passing a ten-dollar packet of cocaine to Caesar for him to crush into powder]

She had me nervous because I see her coming back again the same way at us, walking wildly. I thought she might have her gun. I started shaking inside myself.

She said, "Why don't you tell her the truth, you fuckin' faggot? You're not a man."

And this is in front of the housing [maintenance] men, and everybody else, so they could hear her loud. "Why don't you tell her . . . [waving his arms wildly] He fucked me! And I liked'ed it! [stepping back, arms still waving] And tell her how many times I used to make you do it." [grabbing his crotch with both hands and gyrating his pelvis]

I couldn't believe it, right? And everybody was lookin' out the window. I didn't want to hear that shit. [reaching for the cocaine, and washing down a matchbook sniff of powder with several gulps of beer]

And I told her, "*Vete para el carajo* [Go to hell]. *Tu quieres de esto?* [You want some of this?] [grabbing his crotch again] *Pero no te voy a dar más nada* [but I ain't giving you nothin' no more]. *Vete a cagar en la crica de tu madre* [Go shit in your mother's cunt]."

I swung at her, but she blocked it. She knows the way I get. If I would've been in her house, she would've not done it. I would've *smacked* her flat. [slamming his fist loudly into his palm]

I should've just gone and kicked her in the face. She's just a fuckin', stupid, crazy old bitch that needs some fuckin' psychiatric help.

Caesar: [looking up from the cocaine he was sniffing] What about her gun?

Primo: [drinking] I thought about it, so once I seen her, I try to just play her close, 'cause I know she has to reach for it. Once I see her reach for it, I just *smack* her on the head. Unless she's faster than me, then she would just shoot me once, and then I'll get her, and report the bitch.

Contradictory Contexts for Women's Struggles

When I went to Puerto Rico several months later, I made a point of visiting the picturesque fishing village of Isabela from whence Candy's parents had emigrated. Candy's public, almost schizophrenic agony of behaving like a macho street dealer, while at the same time still wanting to bear twelve children, made more sense to me as I sat in Isabela's central plaza, watching teenagers flirt coyly under century-old trees. It is obvious that gender relations have undergone a profound transformation in rural, and small-town, Puerto Rico as well.[13] Had Candy's father remained in his grandfather's shack, and continued juggling subsistence farming with artisanal fishing, Candy might have grown up to work for minimum wage at one of the garment or pharmaceutical factories located on the periphery of Isabela. At sunset, framed by immaculately white-washed Spanish colonial architecture, and a spectacular vista of the Caribbean, she would have had to encounter the inevitable contradictions of negotiating new women's rights within the oppressive confines of a changing, formerly jíbaro, community. There is no reason to believe that the complicated process of contesting male domination in public and at home would have proceeded smoothly for Candy in this small-town, patriarchal context. Immigration, rapid capitalist development, and manufacturing-to-service restructuring have obviously not invented sexism, and they cannot explain the existence of domestic violence in a reductionist manner. Nevertheless, in her seventeenth-floor New York City Housing Authority project apartment and, even more intensely while she sells crack in front of Ray's Social Club, Candy's problems are compounded by the hostile migration experience and the polarized violence of the underground economy. In either setting, Candy is probably the kind of charismatic person who would have forged a new space for herself in public. She is determined "to get some of mine's." The problem is that her arena for action, fulfillment, and economic advancement is limited to El Barrio's street world. The objective forces that impinge on her struggle for new public rights are rendering her public autonomy excruciatingly painful. Furthermore, as the heading for this chapter's section "Inverting Patriarchy" underscores, Candy's struggle for autonomy and rights have been defined by patriarchal parameters. When she finally broke away from her husband's abuse, she went on to take pride in making money as a street dealer, in having a kept lover, in bragging about her sexual prowess in public, and in requiring her lover to have sex with her upon demand, and so on.

The issue of what kind of liberation, emancipation, or autonomy is being carved out by women on El Barrio's streets raises a complicated question within larger feminist debates over who defines the meaning of women's rights, and what do women's rights mean in the context of class and racial oppression. The new public autonomy that Puerto Rican women have gained over the past few generations is largely defined around liberal, middle-class standards of individual freedom rather than of group solidarity, collective empowerment, or even a countering of patriarchal domination. This was brought home to me by Primo's mother's dissatisfaction with her accomplishments as a single mother in New York City. Her structural oppression as a resident of El Barrio is undeniable. She is economically exploited as an off-the-books seamstress working at home for a garment subcontractor, and she is socially marginalized in a segregated inner-city housing project. When she leaves her immediate neighborhood, she is often subject to racial hostility, and she always has to struggle with a foreign language that she was never been able to learn.

At the same time, in New York Primo's mother has successfully asserted herself as an independent woman in ways that would have been impossible in her natal community, where she had also been economically exploited but where she had not been as subject to a cultural–ideological assault on her ethnic dignity: (1) She left home to come to New York City alone at the age of seventeen; (2) she chose her own husband; (3) she separated from her husband when he proved to be alcoholic and abusive; (4) she raised three daughters and a son by herself in an autonomous household; (5) she picked her own lovers as an adult; (6) she worked full time most of her life; (7) she had complete personal control of her income; and so forth. Primo's mother, however, is dissatisfied with the autonomy she "gained" by uprooting herself to New York. Part of that dissatisfaction is related to the individual isolation that pervades much of the U.S. urban experience. It also stems from being forced to define rights and accomplishments in individualistic terms. She longs for the women/family/community solidarity of her hometown plantation village in Puerto Rico. Even though her memories are bound to be highly idealized in retrospect, they offer an interesting critique, in the context of her working-class, inner-city social marginalization, of the limits to a middle-class, Anglo definition of empowerment that hinges on individual autonomy and upward mobility. [14]

> *Primo's mother:* [in Spanish] In those days in Puerto Rico when a woman gave birth to a child, your neighbor was right there with you; and the midwife was there too. And they all helped you.
>
> For a whole week they brought you soup; they brought you chicken soup, and other things. But now, nothing! No way! No one will bring you chicken soup.
>
> I have given birth to four children in New York, and I've never even eaten anybody's chicken soup. Right the same day that I came out of the hospital, I had to cook my own food. And who came here to help me? Nobody! I had to put the baby down and cook for myself.
>
> In those days, it wasn't like that. There was a lot of respect in those days.

Confronting the State: Forging Single Motherhood on Welfare

As part of this book's argument about how historical political economy processes are internalized in the lives of vulnerable individuals, this chapter has focused thus far on the individual emotional experience of the larger, long-term gender revolution. It is important also to examine the role of the state and public policy. The violent emotional uproars in Candy's life might be categorized as pathological, but they also need to be understood in the specific institutional and state-imposed context that mediates daily survival among the inner-city poor. In the United States, the government agencies that are supposed to be ameliorating, or at least regulating, the difficulties faced by poor immigrants and their children are, in fact, openly hostile to the plight of their "clients." The hostility is reciprocated. Policymakers and the press bemoan what they call the dependency of the poor. As the historian Michael Katz and many others have noted, U.S. policy toward the poor has always been obsessed with distinguishing the "worthy" from the "unworthy" poor, and of blaming individuals for their failings. More recently, conservatives have blamed the paternalistic welfare state for promoting passivity and dependency among the poor.[15] The perspective afforded to me from the bottom up – that is to say, from the family members of the dealers in Ray's network – was not one of passivity, or even of demobilization. On the contrary, most of the wives, mothers, grandmothers, and lovers of the crack dealers were aggressively struggling with the system.

Once again, Candy offers a good example of how mothers actively have to manipulate hostile government agencies in order to keep their children and themselves sheltered, fed, and out of prison. The Welfare Department and the penal system have been the most salient state institutions affecting the stability of her family. To fulfill what she saw as her obligation to nurture her children, she was forced to walk a tightrope between selling drugs, collecting welfare, and working at legal jobs. She even maintained a second, "clean" social security number to register her legal earnings with the Internal Revenue Service without jeopardizing her welfare and medicaid entitlements.[16]

During all the years I was friends with Candy, she was almost always in open conflict with the New York City Welfare Department. Much of the problem revolved around their policy of routinely "churning the rolls," that is, recertifying the eligibility of their clients every six months and occasionally altering the bureaucratic logistics involved in the process. The local Welfare Department claims this unwieldy mechanism discourages fraud and is needed to satisfy frequently changing federal matching-fund requirements for accurate documentation. The net effect, however, is that some 10 to 15 percent of all New York City welfare recipients are routinely terminated each year for failing to present appropriate documentation such as "proof of address," or social security cards.[17] When an individual client is suspected of fraud, as might have been the case for Candy, the recertification process can be enforced with especially zealous bureaucratic rigor.

The particularly hostile institutional quagmire of state-mandated social services in the United States conjugates with personal emotional crises in the daily life of the poor. This was certainly true for Candy's household.

For example, shortly after the incarceration of her husband Felix and during the period before she sold drugs for Ray and fell in love with Primo, Candy had been negotiating unsuccessfully with the Welfare Department to have her biweekly check augmented to reflect the births of her last two daughters.

> *Candy:* A mix-up happened with my social security numbers, so they penalized me for five months. See, at my face-to-face – that's recertification every three months, when you have to go down to the office and bring proof that your kids are in school; that your kids are on the housing list – you know what I mean – proof that you're still illegible for public assistance. They claimed I didn't give them all the information on my daughter, and my baby.
>
> Can you believe it? They wanted my baby's social security card. I don't know why welfare hassles you so much for the social security card of a two-year-old little girl, when a two-year-old little girl can't even work! I don't understand where social security cards come into any of this, because a kid cannot work.
>
> You know what I mean? And besides you don't go, and take the kid to the Social Security Department, and say, "Here, give him a social security card." You go by yourself. And how do they know if you really got that kid? Because you could show any person's birth certificate, and get a fake card.
>
> But you know, now they changed the rule again. They don't ask you for your kid's social security no more today when you go down to face-to-face for recertification. Because that fucking awful bitch, I took her to court, and I won it. All they said in court was [imitating a bureaucrat's nagging voice], "Oh we don't need social securities no more." She had to give me all my money back; this was from May of last year until January.

The court ruling in Candy's favor, with nine months of back pay, came too late. By that time, she was already selling crack and cocaine full time for Ray, and she was deeply immersed in a "successful" dealer lifestyle, with Primo as her lover. When she missed another recertification and, once again, was partially dropped from the welfare rolls, she barely noticed it as she was receiving a steady income working for Ray. Several months later, after breaking up with Primo, Candy finally came to the realization that she was destroying herself and her family through her drug dealing. She reapplied for welfare in an attempt to quit dealing. Hoping to reestablish a stable household for her children, Candy demanded her rights from the Welfare Department. Her aggressive, streetwise single-mother persona, however, did not inspire credibility at the welfare office. This occurred during the same months when Candy was obscenely confronting Primo and his new girlfriend in her project courtyard. By the time I tape-recorded this conversation, Candy and Primo had reestablished a supportive, platonic friendship:

Candy: Let me tell you something about welfare. The last time I reapplied was when I was working for Ray, I had trouble getting all of us back on welfare.

They told me, "How could you survive so many months without welfare?" That was because I was drug dealing. So I didn't really need welfare.

Now I'm not even drug dealing. I stopped selling because I want a better future for my life and my kids.

I had a disrespectful case worker at Welfare. I was so frustrated, because I had so many problems. I wanted to stop working for Ray, and my nerves were a little messed up; and this bitch in the Welfare Office was telling me, "Oh, umh . . . [feigning a bureaucratic tone] you called in and said to take you, and your daughter off the budget."

I said, [incredulous] "I called in to tell *you!* To take *me!* Off the budget? How the hell am I going to call in, if I'm the mother of my kids?"

So I got mad [calmly], and I took the case records and I broke them. So when I took my case record and broke it, she called the supervisor to come in, and then she had to hold me.

So when she was holding me, I hit her. [smiling abruptly and pausing for effect]

Philippe: Come on; tell us what happened.

Candy: [shrugging her shoulders, expressionless] They closed my case.

Candy's deadpan portrayal of the hostile bureaucratic logic of welfare made Primo and me burst out laughing. I actually fell off the car hood we were leaning on in front of the Game Room, when Candy redoubled our mirth by imitating the motions and matter-of-fact tone of a smug welfare clerk snapping shut a file and declaring, "Case closed! Next!" Just as we were catching our breath to sip from our 16-ounce cans of malt liquor, Candy sent us laughing back over the car hood choking on mouthfuls of beer, by continuing her bureaucratic saga still in a deadpan voice:

Then they reopened it. [finally breaking her deadpan expression and joining our laughter] You see, they had me for . . . a, uh, a . . . what did they call it? Oh yeah, they had me for "assaulting a case worker."

Because I'm not going to lie, this was like around Thanksgiving time, and I called her up on the day before Thanksgiving, and I say, "Thank you for my Thanksgiving dinner, I hope you have a *beeeautiful* one." [bitter chuckle]

Then for Christmas, [agitatedly] I call up again. I say, "I hope you have a lousy Christmas."

Then . . . then I threatened her . . . I'm not going to lie. [laughing alone] I told her, "I'm going to go with a gun, and blow your head off." [nervous chuckles from Primo and me]

You see I was like . . . my nerves . . . just couldn't take it anymore. I don't have a husband who supports me; my kids depend on *my* income alone. Felix was in jail at the time. And I mean even if he wasn't in jail, I can't depend on him [piercingly at Primo]; you know what I mean?

So it was like, Christmas was there, and it was gonna be my first lousy Christmas. So I got mad, and I call my old case worker, and I said, "I'm going to go over to welfare, and I'm going to shoot your head off; so you had better think about it."

So the supervisor called me, and asked, "Is that what you said, that you're going to shoot her?"

I say, "Yeah, 'cause she got me mad."

Philippe: Were you really gonna shoot her?

Candy: I didn't have a gun yet, but I was looking for one. I was in the range to do it. I was in a very bad way.

I mean, when it comes to your kid . . . If I don't eat, fine, okay, but I'm not going to let my kids starve, and they didn't, because I was supporting my own self, with my own money. Because I was working at the Club at that time. I wasn't even on welfare, but we were eating.[18]

Six Uzi shots burst from the project courtyard behind us. Candy rolled her eyes knowingly and shook her head disapprovingly. "Ohhh, Carlos is getting wild. I have to talk to him." She was referring to the leader of a group of youths that sold crack in her stairwell. They were feuding with another group of drug-dealing teenagers, from another stairwell in the same housing project. Occasionally, for a fee, she allowed Carlos into her kitchen to "cook" the crack that his boys hawked downstairs for three dollars a vial.[19]

The Internalization of Institutional Constraints

Candy's next personal–institutional crisis landed her in jail. It was precipitated by her husband Felix's release from prison on weekends through a work release program. Concretely, this meant that Primo and I had to stop hanging out publicly with Candy in front of the Game Room, out of "respect" for – or, rather, out of fear of – Felix. Candy had filed divorce papers and had even gone to court to obtain a restraining order against her husband – but she could not bring herself to enforce it. Every Friday and Saturday night, carefully avoiding any cocaine, marijuana, or opiates because of the routine urine testing upon his return to prison, Felix would arrive at Candy's project apartment, furiously drunk. Bursting into tears, he would demand the right to see his children. Hugging them, he would then collapse asleep in a pile with them, on Candy's king-size bed where the entire family usually slept.

The emotional crisis generated by Candy's inability to assert her legal right to single motherhood destabilized Candy's fragile household economy. Abraham, the adopted grandfather whose monthly social security check augmented Candy's insufficient biweekly welfare payments, moved to another adopted daughter's house to avoid the *arrevolús* [uproars] of Felix's weekend homecomings. My tape recordings from the period reveal how depressed Candy was at the time. She was willing to accept a job, any job, so long as it was just above minimum wage.

> *Candy:* You know, Felipe, I don't feel too great . . . I feel when it rains, it rains . . . I mean, it pours. But it'll get better. yeah, I

failed the GED by three points last week. I could go again, but I have too many problems to put my mind to it . . . I don't have my mind ready for it.

I got to get a job first . . . that's my main thing . . . find a job . . . anything, any kind of job that pays more than the minimum wage . . . that pays four to five dollars bottom.

I'm supposed to find a job this week, but I just don't know what happened, see, I . . . I . . . I was supposed to buy a job — you see you can just buy a job from these employment places. But they didn't find me one.

Candy's situation was exacerbated by the churning she was, once again, facing at the hands of the welfare bureaucracy.

You see, Abraham was helping me with my financial problem. But they took him away from me.

I don't really get enough welfare. I don't get welfare for me and the baby, because of a mix-up with the social security papers. Welfare was only giving me a hundred and six dollars every two weeks, which comes out to fifty-three dollars a week for *five* people. You see, they were really only giving me for three people, even though there's five of us. They don't give me for me, or the baby.

And I can't get a job in the daytime 'cause of the baby. I'm not gonna lie; let me just say that it is *hard* for me to get a job.

Felipe, I'm not going to lie to you, but do you know what it is to survive with five of us in the household on only a hundred and six dollars? Think about it; that's fifty-three dollars a week. You know what fifty-three dollars a week is? That ain't nothing. Take my son, Junior, he's heavyset, he can eat fifty-three dollars in one day!

But I'm living on that, with only the help of my mother, who only gets some cheap-ass money off of SSI. But she helps me. She collects cans every day, makes twenty dollars a day picking in the garbage; and then she comes to me and says, "Candy, here's five or ten dollars for you."

But my mother is an asthmatic, I don't think she's got that much to live. But that lady goes out at six in the morning till eleven at night, collecting cans to help me out.

But it's hard. I don't have a lover; I don't have a husband; I don't have nobody giving me money. It's like me, myself, and I. And to support four kids, it's hard.

The Department of Social Security makes you go through the worst changes. You can't be honest with them. It doesn't pay to be honest. 'Cause I have the right for my kids.

You gotta realize one thing, Felipe, you gotta look at a parent who's like me, who's not into drugs; love their kids like babies; have them in Catholic school; want the best for them — what we do, sometimes, they [pointing] make us do.

A few days after this conversation Candy was arrested. She had accepted a daytime job at a badly managed cocaine-copping corner.

So I felt, like I was going crazy, and that's when I went back into drug dealing. But I didn't want to, because I don't like ruining my record for nobody.

I went to Ray, and I told him: "Ray, they took Abraham, and I need a better job, at least twice a week. I don't care what you have me do, but I need it at least twice a week. I need to get paid something for my kids, like a hundred fifty dollars."

And Ray said, "I don't mind taking you back; but wait till I open my place again, 'cause we are going to open up the Game Room again. Wait till it's ready, and I'll put you to work there on days [the day shift]. But right now I don't have anything."

But I was in need. I was hurtin' so I got a job instead selling twenty-fives [$25 packets] of coke for Marvin. It's only five hours a day, and he pays seventy-five dollars a week — I mean it's seventy-five dollars a day. I mean that is *money*, you know. And all I had to do, was just stand there, 'cause I was just a lookout.

You see it was Welfare's fault, because Welfare was penalizing me. As a matter of fact, today it's July nineteenth and they're still penalizing me for that social security paper.

Within hours of hitting the streets as part of a two-person team selling cocaine on 105th Street and Lexington Avenue, Candy was arrested for making a hand-to-hand sale to a member of New York City's Tactical Narcotics Team.

Candy: It was stupid hot on 105th, where we were working. It was stupid that I got busted, because Marvin — he's the owner of the spot — had told us not to sell anymore, because it was stupid hot; but there were three customers in front of the building, and so Chino said, "Okay, do me a favor, Candy. Get the money from those last three customers; I'm going to go upstairs and get the shit, and then we'll close down."

So I did it; and the last one I got money from, was the fucking cop. It was a black guy. I knew the two ladies in front of him, but I didn't know him. I couldn't tell that he was a cop. He looked like any old street guy. So after I served the two ladies, that's when the cops grabbed me.

When they put their hands on me, I said, "Get the fuck off me!" [jabbing her elbows backward into an imaginary assailant]. Because I thought it was like a guy getting stupid . . . And that's when the cop grabbed me by my hair. He said, "Where's the bundle" And he said, "Let me see what's in your bag." So I gave him my bag. They even took my own personal money.

I said, oh shit! And that's when they busted this guy [Chino], and they took his keys, and they checked all the mailboxes, and that's where they found the money. Because the money the cop had given to me, it was marked money — twenty-five dollars — and they found it there in the mailbox. He had only bought one bag of coke.

Okay, after they put the cuffs on me, they put me in a van with a whole bunch of other men. Then they drove us to other blocks to pick up all the other people they were busting. They were taking up, like, the addicts. As a matter of fact, the only other female with me in the van, she was pregnant, and she was a junkie. Once the van was full, they took us to the 137th Street police station.

As if to mark Candy's bad luck with poetic symbolism, she had been in the traditional Puerto Rican act of blessing one of Ray's babies when the narcotics agents grabbed her. We learned this from the infant's mother, Gigi, a former girlfriend of Ray's.

Gigi: Candy actually got busted on Ninety-ninth Street. Yeah, I saw it all on Second [Avenue]. She went to say hi to Ray Junior. I had him with me in his stroller.

Look, she was like this [bending over to hug an imaginary infant], *"Ay mi hijo, qué lindo!* God bless him." [Oh my precious boy, how cute!]

Right then, the DT's [detectives] grabbed her by her arms, and handcuffed her, and threw her in the van.

See, I was right here; she got pulled right there [making hand motions]; I bugged the fuck out.

Caesar, who was still smarting from having been pushed onto his rear in the middle of the street in front of the Game Room by Candy's daughter Tabatha, gloated over the fact that, as a lookout, Candy should not have been taking the risk of "serving" customers. He took professional pride in ridiculing her because he held the same position of lookout at the Game Room under Primo's management:

Caesar: She's a convict; she's a convict, the stupid bitch. Any Joe-Doe-hole with a vibrator on high speed could tell you that Ninety-ninth is stupid hot. It's too close to Caucasian land. You could fry an egg on the sidewalk where they was selling.

That's a stupid ho'. I've never seen such a stupid *bruta* [jerk].

And she's *presenta'o* [pushy], because she had to put her fucking nose in the business, and had to know where the stash was. That bitch wasn't supposed to be making no hand-to-hand sales; she was a fucking lookout.

But *no!* Not Candy! She had to get in on the action.

In subsequent weeks, while waiting in the limbo of court hearings and lawyers' negotiations, Candy silenced our predatory gossiping over her arrest with a firm and painful "Fuck you! I did it for my kids. Can't you understand? I got a class B felony for my kids." Indeed, her children's welfare had been Candy's primary concern through the nightmare of her arrest and during her confinement before posting bail:

Candy: When they put handcuffs on me, and put me in their car with the pregnant girl, the junkie, I was worried because I was thinking, "God, my kids won't know I'm in jail. What if somebody knows? What if someone saw me that I went into jail? And what if they say, "This is the chance to rob Candy's house"? And maybe they'll try to kill my kids; rob the house . . . You know what I mean? Abuse my daughters. You know, all these crazy things runs through your head – *tú sabes* [you know], Felipe.

And I couldn't say anything, because I figured if the cops saw that my kids were minors, they would try to take my kids away. Because they even asked me when they had me in the van; they asked me, "You have any kids?" I said, "Yeah." He say, "What are the ages?" So I thought fast, and I say, "My oldest is twenty." And he say, "Your kids are all right."

When in reality, my oldest at home is fifteen, and my youngest is two.

But thanks God that I got a sister-in-law. Once she found out, you know, she, right away, went and took all my kids to her house; and she send them to school, you know what I mean? She took really good care of them.

In contrast to her sister-in-law's solidarity, Candy's employer failed to stand by his workers:

Candy: It's fucked up, because the people that I'm with, the people I'm working for, they didn't bail me out. Word up! That is messed up. I mean, I was actually there, in jail, because of them. And Chino didn't even get bailed out, and he's been with them for over two years . . . I couldn't believe that. And I heard Chino was the best seller on that block. I mean, Chino made them stupid money, good money.

His bail was only two thousand dollars, and they say they can't bail him out! What happens with his wife and his kids?

I mean, I'd be ready to do the time if my people backed me up. If they bailed me out; got me a lawyer; and then the judge sentences me. But if they just leave me there! Hell! I'm not a squealer, but I would start giving up their names.

I mean, if you don't take me out, then we're all going in, 'cause the DA gives you a chance. He tells you, "If you give us a bigger person, we'll make a deal with you." So if the people I work for were to leave me rotting in there . . . like they're doing with Chino right now . . . I swear to God, I'd call them up and say, "This is the way it is, let me tell you something, I see you don't give a shit about me, or my kids, then I don't need to care about you." And the first name I'd give the DA is Marvin's. Then from Marvin I'd go all the way down.

Then I'd turn to the judge, "Okay, now give me the one-to-three [years], judge." The only reason, I didn't do that to them this time, is because I just started working for them. So I didn't give a fuck.

Ray posted Candy's $2,000 bail.

Candy: So when I got busted working for that other guy [Marvin], I didn't even tell nobody to tell Ray to bail me out, because that wasn't his shit I was busted for. I can't tell him to do that favor for me. I didn't get busted when I was working for him.

But then, when I saw my brother in court, he told me, "Ray told me to come every day, 'cause whatever amount it is, he is gonna pay."

Ray did it out of the goodness of his own heart.

The ordeal proved to be a forum for Candy's extended family and friends to express their love and solidarity for her:[20]

Candy: When I came out of jail, they had cooked up beans and pork chops in my house.

But when you come out, you don't come out with an appetite, and I couldn't eat. My friend Gladys came over, and they all went out and brought me these chicken wings, because you see, they know that I used to love eating chicken wings. But I couldn't even eat that.

It took me, like, a couple of days for me to, like, really eat normally again. Because I used to, like, have this feeling in my stomach. The same with washing; even if I took a bath and everything, I used to still have, like, a smell in my nose, like it stuck there; it was the smell of that cell. I used to like, yeah, feel like, I was going to throw up.

Mothers in Jail

In the anxious months before Candy's felony status was finally annulled by a liberal judge, Primo and I spent many evenings listening to her war stories from jail. Her accounts of resistance and aggression among women in the bullpen evoked, on a personal level, the structural tensions expressed in the spiraling female crime statistics in the United States. The crisis of overcrowding in the penal system provides a snapshot of the underside of the gender revolution in street culture. Concretely, the traditional male space of the county jail is being "invaded" by women, who represent the fastest-growing cohort among felons in the United States.[21] I could sense this tension during our tape-recording sessions, by the way Primo repeatedly interrupted Candy in an almost juvenile, obnoxious manner. It was as if he was jealous that a woman could be considered an expert on such a male subject.

Candy: Jail is no place for a woman; it's only for trash and garbage. It's a place where no clean woman belongs; a place nobody wants to be in. Word up!

They treat you like everybody else. Even if you're innocent, they treat you like you're guilty, without even being proven guilty. It's for women that deserve to be there.

I mean the people in there with you, that you have to deal with, they so disgustin'. They have prostitutes in there; they have addicts; they have gay people.

Forget it! Nothing to brush your teeth; no soap to wash yourself all over. And I couldn't eat nothing, because I was upset.

They served baloney and cheese. It was too disgusting.

Primo: Not for me boy! I ate all that shit up — every crumb. I ain't gonna stay hungry.

Candy: Plus the guys was whistling and all that. Because to get to my cell they had to take me through the men's part of the jail first. And when they was taking my pictures, one of the guys come out and say, "What's your husband going to say about all this?"

So I come out and say, "Hey, Fuck you! Shit on your mother!" You know, like I really didn't pay no mind to him . . . "Fuck you!"

So they took us back upstairs, and the men was whistling.

Primo: [echoing jeers with his hands muffling his mouth] What is your husband going to say now? Bitch!

Candy: [ignoring Primo] Then, in the cell, there was this gay girl who came up to me — a lesbian — and says [exaggerating the rasp in her voice], "You wanna massage."

[fiercely] "I don't want shit from *nobody* in this damn place!" And she went back to her woman; she was rubbing herself all over her woman.

Then this other black girl came in and she says, "Move over, I wanna sleep."

I say back to her, "What you want me to do? What in the *fuck* you want from me? I was here first."

Then this other lady, she was like a pig; she had her hair all disgusted and wild. I told her, "Don't even think of sitting next to me. I don't want no bugs in my hair."

Primo: [grinning] You was bummed, hunh?

Candy: And all we had to cope with the people that was throwing up, was one garbage can.

There's the prostitutes who don't even wear panties, and they be with their feet up and open. The gay people there, they be hugging and kissing to their woman like they were in a private room and nobody's looking at them. They don't care. It stinks.

Primo: [hissing in the background] Felt like a square cement block that's been pissed on — that's been vomited on.

Candy: It's a place where . . . let me tell you something, an honest decent person wants to commit suicide, because that's what I did. You see, I use underwire bras, right? So I think, if its metal, I could cut my veins, right? But after I break into the bra [making the motions], I see that it was plastic, awww . . .

Primo: You got jerked; you couldn't kill yourself.

Candy: I figure if I bleedin' or something, they take me outta here, and put me in a hospital that's cleaner; you know, more decent place; better food, that type of thing.

Primo: Couldn't handle it, hunh?

Candy: Then by the last day I was there, the guards still wasn't calling my name, and I mean people was coming in and out, and I was like, "What about me? Am I gonna stay here forever?" [gunshots]

Philippe: Was that firecrackers?

Candy: Sounds like an Uzi to me.

Primo: Nahh, that's a nine-millimeter.

Candy: So, I thought they had lost my records, or something like that.

I was going to take that cell bar and start screaming, "Let me out of here!" I was like going crazy.

Primo: I'm tellin' you Felipe, people bug out in there.

Candy: Jail is crazy. The bullpen is wild. A place I wouldn't recommend to anybody.

But you know Felipe, that would be a beautiful place for you to interview people. Because there was girls there, who they would actually say, what they used to do. And they used to say it so foul.

Like this one con artist lady . . .

Just as Candy began describing con artist techniques, Primo interrupted with his own accounts of stories he had also heard in jail. My tape recording became an inaudible muddle of competing voices telling different horrific street-crime stories. Surprised by Primo's unwillingness to let Candy continue her account of jail in peace, I tried to shut him out of the conversation by changing the subject completely and asking Candy how her baby was doing. This sent her sprinting towards her project building, as she suddenly remembered that her two-and-a-half-year-old was all alone, in her seventeenth-floor apartment.

Over the next few months, Primo's irritation with Candy became even more pronounced as the charisma with which she was able to manipulate the lawyers and judges assigned to her case began to bear fruit. She had her mental health files from Metropolitan Hospital subpoenaed to document her twenty-year history of battery, attempted suicide, and motherhood. The judge who finally presided over the resolution of her case not only dismissed all felony charges, but even arranged for the state to pay for Candy's enrollment in a job training program for nurse's aides.

Candy's triumph in court suffered several false starts, however. At her first hearing, the judge almost ruled Candy to be in contempt of court because of her clothing. It was a clash over their different class and cultural interpretations of how a contrite mother should dress in a formal public setting. Candy had thought she was faithfully following her lawyer's advice of wearing "a good, new suit" on her first court date, and she had arrived in a skintight, blood-red jumpsuit. In fact, she had borrowed the money to buy the suit especially for the occasion. The judge, a conservative, elderly white woman nearing the end of her career, thought that the thirty-four-year-old Puerto Rican woman, with badly dyed blond hair, dressed for court in a bright red teenager's outfit, was purposefully provoking her. Worse yet, this obviously streetwise defendant with a rasping voice, and a scar down her cheek, was demanding clemency, claiming to be the traumatized battered mother of five vulnerable children.

Candy, of course, had thought she was showing respect to the judge by "dressing sharp," and her feelings were hurt. She immediately sexualized the judge's remonstrations, interpreting them to be the jealous expression of an older, less attractive woman.

Candy: So my first judge, she didn't consider me with respect, because of the way I was dressed.

Well, fuck her! I didn't consider her, because of the way she was dressed. If she doesn't like my clothes, well, why doesn't she give me some money to buy some clothes.

No matter what she gives me, I'll look good in it. I'll look better than her, 'cause no matter what I wear I look good.

I got five kids to think about; I can't think about buying special outfits for the judge.

I tell you, that judge, she gots problems; she's an old bag. Her husband must be miserable with that bitch. If I had a woman like that, every day . . . oouf [feigning a nasal Anglo accent] "I don't like your underwears . . . you can't go to bed with me . . . I don't like your pajamas . . . I don't like your sex."

The whole system itself, it stinks. I tell you something, you're not going to see me in that court system again. If I kill somebody, I'm going to cut out – disappear. Word up! I'll dye my hair. Let me tell you, this is the last time.

I gotta get myself a better lawyer. I gotta talk to Ray about this. He's got a great lawyer who don't give up. He keeps your case out for years. Look at Luis and Ray, they prior felonies like crazy, and they still walking.

Primo: Yeah, but if you do the crime, you gotta be ready to do the time.

Look, Candy, I pleaded guilty. [referring to his first arrest a year earlier]. Check this out . . . I did the fucking *venta* [sale]. I fucked up. Right? A felony, five years probation.

If I fuck up, and do the same thing one more time, I get the maximum.

Candy: Primo, don't you understand? I can't afford a felony, I'm not going to plead a felony. I want a misdemeanor. I don't want to have a class C felony on my records. I have to get me a class A lawyer, and have my case dismissed.

Primo: When I got busted, I didn't fight the fucking case; I was ready to do the time.

Candy: If I plead a felony, I can't sue this guy [Felix] for harassing me. And I got the papers all ready. I just gotta get someone to serve them.

Primo: I didn't have a fuckin' lawyer. [aggressively] Remember? I was working for your husband, but nobody got me no money for a lawyer, and I didn't spoke to nobody; nobody got no money.

Plus I'm guilty; I did the fucking thing.

Candy: You people get attitudes. I don't like that. Break the fuck out.

We had been escorting Candy home to her project apartment and we were in her seventeenth-floor hallway. She grabbed Primo by the shoulders and pushed him into the open elevator. I quickly jumped in after him but, just as the elevator was closing, Candy jammed a leg through the almost shut doors. Grabbing Primo's waist in an affectionate hug she whispered:

Primo, you never believe me when I tell you, you're the only true love I have. Give me a hug. If you want to come back at five in the morning, it's fine with me.

I tried to look away politely, but all I could find to stare at were three spent crack vials floating in the puddle of urine that almost inevitably adorns the corners of New York City Housing Authority elevators in El Barrio at 2:00 a.m. on Saturday nights. Instead, I closed my eyes in denial and imagined that the sound of their kiss was really the distant rumblings from out of a jíbaro time warp announcing a future struggle for the emancipation of women.

7

FAMILIES AND CHILDREN IN PAIN

You know what's wrong with these girls nowadays? They only think of themselves. They only think of their sexual pleasures, their fun and their happiness. But they don't think of their kids first.

Candy

Developmental psychologists and psychiatrists are generally considered to be the "experts" on early childhood socialization and family violence. Most of their large-scale, multimillion-dollar, cross-generational epidemiological surveys of "children at risk" conclude that the bulk of an adult's character is determined in infancy. Their statistical studies demonstrate that most battered children are virtually irremediable by the ages of six to eight. Furthermore, they assure us that a child does not have to be the object of physical violence to be emotionally scarred for life. Simply witnessing violence can induce long-term trauma.[1]

In other words, according to the standard psychological theories of early childhood socialization, most people living in El Barrio, and certainly everyone in Ray's network and the crackhouses I frequented, might be dismissed as antisocial sociopaths because of their early childhood socialization experiences. Certainly, the gun-and-knife-wielding, knockdown fights between Candy and Primo that unfolded in front of twenty-year-old Tabatha, fourteen-year-old Junior, ten-year-old Jackie, four-year-old Mina, and one-year-old Lillian must have inflicted profound emotional scars. But once again, an individualistic, psychological-determinist approach misses the larger political economic and cultural context. It ignores historical processes and the effects of unequal power relations around class, ethnic, or gender and sexual categories. Developmental psychologists tend to focus only on the epiphenomenon of individual neuroses. Their data and analytic tools are also limited by the cultural and class biases of their survey methods. White middle-class families are overrepresented in their epidemiological samples because of the very logistics of collecting reliable statistics.

The restructuring of New York City's economy and the history of Puerto Rican immigration have profoundly changed the ways East Harlem families are organized. For many of the poorer households these changes have been disruptive, and children, of course, are the ultimate casualties when households disintegrate. The problem is integrally related to the contradictory shifts in gender power relations discussed in Chapter 6. Motherhood roles have remained fixed, while women's rights and the structure of the traditional family have undergone profound, long-term transformations. Mothers, especially heading single-parent households, are still saddled with the exclusive responsibility for nurturing their children, even though they may no longer be willing to sacrifice unconditionally their individual freedom for their progeny. This results in a parenting vacuum when mothers take to the streets. It expresses itself statistically in the dramatic increase in child neglect and abuse, and in poisoned fetuses over the past generation.[2] By default, street culture becomes a more important socializing force when fragmented families force children to take refuge in the streets.

Politicians, the press, and the general public in the United States interpret the visible problems faced by poor urban children as evidence of "a crisis in family values." Structural problems of persistent poverty and segregation, as well as the more complex issues of changing gender power relations are rarely addressed in public discussion. The most immediately self-evident policy interventions, such as offering affordable, developmentally appropriate day care for the children of overwhelmed or addicted mothers, are not even part of most policy debates. Similarly, effective drug treatment facilities, or meaningful job training and employment referral services, remain off-limits to women who live in poverty.

Street Culture's Children

Children have always faced difficult lives in East Harlem. The neighborhood has always been a poor, segregated home for first- and second-generation immigrants. As the historical chapter documents, academic

260

and social service denunciations of the "worsening" plight of youth and the exacerbation of violence on the street merge over the past century into a pastiche of clichés portending imminent doom. In the late 1920s, for example, the Italian priest of the Catholic Church two blocks down from the Game Room told a graduate student that "the reckless destructive spirit of youth is getting worse and there is less and less consideration of property rights. This is due to the want of religion and the lack of respect for authority."[3]

Similarly, in the mid-1950s, a Community Service Society report on the conditions of the blocks opposite the Game Room complains of children "feeling unsafe in a fermenting neighborhood." The authors conclude:

> From parents, teachers, Bureau of Attendance and Youth board workers came the same response: "These children don't have much of a chance!"
>   . . . Living constantly in an environment filled with disorder and destruction . . . provoke[s] these youngsters to acts of aggression. . . . they strike out in anti-social behavior.[4]

On a personal level, the most stressful dimension of living in El Barrio's street scene was witnessing the wholesale destruction of the children of my friends and neighbors. I lived in the neighborhood long enough to witness dozens of little girls and boys fall apart as they passed from childhood to adolescence. I watched energetic, bright-eyed children get ground up into what the United States calls its underclass. Within five short years, my little neighbor Gigi metamorphosed from being an outgoing, cute, eager-to-please eight-year-old who gave me a construction paper Valentine's card every year, into becoming a homeless, pregnant, crack-using thirteen-year-old "teenager." Meanwhile, her older brother Hector was transformed from a shy, giggling undersized twelve-year-old into a juvenile inmate, guilty of "assault with a dangerous weapon."[5]

Upon first moving onto the block, I found it heartwarming to see gleeful children running, jumping, shouting, and laughing in front of my apartment window at all hours of the day and night. Once again, ethnographic description of these same blocks from the 1920s applies almost verbatim to the 1990s:

261

The cross streets . . . become the chief playgrounds of children. Hordes of them are seen . . . playing ball, craps, and cards. They become expert in dodging traffic. . . . During 1927, fifteen children were killed by traffic accidents principally on Second and Third Avenues.[6]

My early fieldwork notes revel in the warmth of the dozens of pre-teenage friendships I was able to make within my first few months on the block:

[May 1985]
I love the way the kids run up to me with excited smiles whenever I come home. They shower me with hugs, stories, and questions at any hour of the day or night. Whenever a mother walks by with a newborn it's considered normal for me to bend over it and bless it tenderly, "Que Diós lo bendiga," even if the mother doesn't know me. I hope someday soon I'll be comfortable enough to pick up these newborns and hug them like most other people do.[7]

In dissonance with my public celebration of street culture's relationship to children was the omnipresent underlying wail of crying babies that competed with the salsa and rap music pulsing from my neighbors' windows.

Two years later, with my own newborn, Emiliano, in my arms generating countless blessings and constant cooing, I remained convinced that El Barrio has special energy and love for children. I even learned to appreciate my local supermarket's inefficiency and decrepitude, when every time I walked by on the sidewalk in front, at least three of the four teenage cashiers ran from their machines to tap on the display window and to throw kisses and grimaces at my appreciatively giggling baby. Downtown society's industrialized Taylorist logic would have long since obliged the manager to fire those affectionate wannabe mothers. When I took Emiliano to Anglo-dominated parties downtown, I noticed that he was disappointed with the adults. He expected a more appreciatively physical reaction from them. Very few of my white friends and acquaintances even knew how to hold my baby comfortably; none of them grabbed him spontaneously out of my arms for a cuddle and a blessing the way my acquaintances regularly did on the street uptown. In fact, some of my downtown friends even requested I leave my son at home with a baby-sitter when they invited me to their homes.

My love affair with street life's intergenerational affection and integration began to sour when my son's first words at sixteen months of age turned out to be "tops, tops, tops." I had been trying to penetrate a new and particularly active crack-copping corner, and had been taking him along with me to allay the suspicions of the sellers that I might be an undercover cop. That corner had four competing "spots," each selling three-dollar vials. The sellers on duty shouted or hissed at their prospective clients to advertise their particular brands, delineated by the color of the plastic stoppers on their vials: "Graytop, graytop, graytop! Pinktop, pinktop, pinktop! Blacktop," and so on. A few weeks later, I found myself in the midst of an angry crowd surrounding two white police officers who had just killed an African-American man high on angel dust. It was only when the crowd had begun chanting "Open season on the black man! Murderers! Murderers!" that I noticed that the only other whites present were the two "killer cops" frantically shouting into their walkie-talkies for help.[8] Emiliano, perched on my shoulders, caused the tense crowd to burst into laughter by clapping his hands gleefully in time with the angry chanting.

As a parent, I was learning the lesson faced by all the working mothers and fathers on my block. Either I had to abandon public space and double-lock my child inside my cramped tenement apartment and assume a hostile attitude toward street culture, or I would have to accept the fact that my child would witness drugs and violence on a daily basis. My perspective on the future of the children living around me further soured when Iris, the mother of ten-year-old Angel and eight-year-old Manny, my two favorite shiny-eyed street friends, fell apart on crack and became pregnant. My wife and I stopped dropping by their apartment unannounced after finding them one evening sitting in the dark (because the electricity bill had not been paid), scraping the last corners of peanut butter out of an empty jar. Their mother was passed out on the bed, recovering from last night's "mission."

I began organizing biweekly trips for them, and whoever else happened to be hanging out on the block, to cross New York's invisible apartheid barriers to visit museums and other world-renowned bourgeois havens like the FAO Schwartz toy store and Trump Tower. They loved the Andy

Warhol exhibit at the Museum of Modern Art, and Angel even assured me that the Frick Museum's collection of Dutch masters was "not boring at all." In contrast, they were not impressed by the Whitney Museum's "alternative" multimedia rap/break-dance/graffiti/skateboard extravaganza.

The full force of the racial and class boundaries confining the children of El Barrio became glaringly clear on these outings. In the museums, for example, we were usually flanked by guards with hissing walkie-talkies. Often I was eyed quizzically, as if I might be some kind of pedophile, parading my prey. Angel was particularly upset at the Joan Miró exhibit at the Guggenheim when he asked one of the guards – who himself was Puerto Rican – why he was being followed so closely, and was told, "to make sure you don't lift your leg."

On our way home from the Miró exhibit, I brought Angel and his friends to my mother's apartment in the Upper East Side's Silk Stocking district, located less than twenty blocks from our tenements.[9] I was sobered by Angel's simple but naive wish, "I'm planning on moving my mother into a building like this when I grow up too. I wish my mom lived here." When he added that "the schools probably be better down here too," I pounced on the opportunity to engage him in a discussion of the structural inadequacies of the education system. His response, however, focused on the destructive behavior of the victims themselves:

> *Philippe:* What's the matter? You got mean teachers?
> *Angel:* No, It's the kids I'm afraid of. They be mugging people in the hallways.

Later that evening Angel complained to me that his mother's boyfriend had broken open his piggy bank and taken the twenty dollars' worth of tips he had saved from working as a delivery boy at the supermarket on our block. He blamed his mother for having provoked her boyfriend into beating her and robbing the apartment when she invited another man to visit her in her bedroom. "I keep telling my mother to only have one boyfriend at a time, but she won't listen to me." I was forced to recognize in these guileless expressions of vulnerability on the part of the children surrounding me, the brutal dynamic whereby tender victims internalize the social structures that dominate them, to the point that they eventually take charge of administering their own mutual self-destruction. This was even more forcefully portrayed in the hauntingly sad and violent pictures that they drew, when I provided them with paper and crayons on the car hoods in front of my tenement after dark.

As my youthful friends grew older, places like the Game Room or the Social Club gradually emerged as central institutions in their lives. They were socialized into the "normalcy" of drug dealing. In El Barrio, the crackhouse is virtually the only adolescent space that is heated in the winter and air-conditioned in the summer. There are simply no other healthy social scenes to frequent if one has limited resources and wants to be where the action is. Many – if not most – East Harlem apartments are overcrowded, plagued with vermin, poorly heated in the winter, and stiflingly hot in the summer. The street or the crackhouse consequently offers a more comfortable alternative living room.

Candy's son, Junior, was the first boy I watched graduate into crack dealer status. When I first asked him at age thirteen what he wanted to be when he grew up, he answered that he wanted to have "cars, girls, and gold chains – but no drugs; a big roll [of money], and rings on all my fingers." In one of these conversations, Junior had even dreamed out loud of wanting to be a "cop." It was midnight and we were sitting on the hood of Ray's Lincoln Continental parked in front of the Game Room.

Primo: [with a drunken slur] Naah! You're going to be an idiot like me and Caesar. A no-good, good-for-nothing *desperdicia'o en-vicia'o* [vice-ridden, life-wasting man].

Junior: [earnestly] Unh, uhh! I could be a cop if I wanted to be.

Primo: Yeah, yeah! A cop sexaholic – rape women, too – because you got authority with your badge. [howling laughter in the background from Caesar]

Angelo: [an eleven-year-old friend of Junior's enthusiastically giggling] Right, right!

Junior: [still earnest] Naah, just be a cop and that's it. Bust people.

Primo: [seriously] Yeah, bustin' people like me.

Junior: Naah, only like, if they rob somebody. If they do crime and stuff.

Philippe: [turning to Angelo] What do you want to be when you grow up?

Primo: [interrupting] A pimp or a drug dealer, right?

Angelo: No, a rapper.

As the years progressed, Junior became increasingly involved in Game Room activities. Literally before he knew it, he became a bona fide drug courier. He thought of it as simply "running errands." Junior was more than eager to be helpful, and Primo would send him to pick up ten-dollar packets of powder cocaine from around the corner, or to fetch cans of beer from the bodega two doors down. Junior was not using drugs; he was merely behaving like any eager teenager flattered by the possibility of hanging out with grown-ups. Before his sixteenth birthday, Junior began filling in for Caesar as lookout, when Caesar's crack binges kept him from coming to work on time. Soon Ray promoted him to working at the Social Club as permanent lookout on weekends, replacing Luis, whose crack use was making him an unacceptably erratic employee. Although Junior had dropped out of school by this time, and already had a juvenile record for hot-wiring a car, he was a strict teetotaler, and an obedient worker. He was only available to run errands and work lookout at night, however, because Candy often made him baby-sit his little sister during the day.

When I tried to make Junior realize that he was being sucked into a life of drug dealing, the conversation merely degenerated into a display of how crackhouse logic maintains its hegemony in the daily lives of even those children who want to be good:

Philippe: So Junior, if you don't wanna be a drug dealer what are you doing working here for Primo tonight?

Junior: Nah, I'm only lookin' out. I ain't touching no product. My moms knows about it; she said it was okay.

Besides, I know drugs is wack. They just put you in the hospital.

Philippe: [smiling at Primo] Junior, what's gonna happen to you? Are you just gonna turn into another scum-of-the-earth drug dealer like Primo? [in a serious tone] And keep on selling drugs, and get yourself arrested?

Junior: No, not no more, 'cause if I get busted again, I get in a lot of trouble.

Primo: [interrupting] No, not the first time Junior.

Junior: But I could get sent to a home, 'cause of that shit with the car.

Primo: [condescendingly] If you get busted selling drugs now, you'll be all right. It's the second time that you'll get fucked.

[turning to me reassuringly] He'll have someone lookin' out for him; someone who will send him bail — [giggling] most likely.

Punishing Girls in the Street

By the time I left New York, Junior had begun dabbling in substance abuse, primarily smoking marijuana. He had not, however, been arrested yet for selling drugs. His twelve-year-old sister, Jackie, on the other hand, was more fully incorporated into the rites of passage of street culture at a younger age — but in the brutal manner reserved for girls. It happened during the difficult months when her father, Felix, was on work release from prison and was demanding to be allowed back into Candy's household. Jackie followed her mother's script to evade her father's turmoil, and ran away with a boyfriend. Her would-be prince savior, however, invited two of his best friends to join him in gang-raping her in his car. She was gone for a total of seventy-two hours, and although Caesar subsequently accused Jackie of "being a hole out there," and Primo dismissed her rape with the terse comment "her pussy itched and it got scratched," both of them participated in the wellspring of solidarity that mobilized around Candy and Felix during Jackie's abduction. The event actually became the catalyst for Felix's reintegration on a permanent basis into Candy's household as husband and father.

Caesar and Primo's description of the first night of Jackie's "elopement" became an unusually honest forum for expressing mutual pain and vulnerability.

Primo: We had just bought some ski [powder cocaine] to get lifted, and we went to Candy's house, and see what's up.

There was Felix there, crying. He was getting coked up; crying with coke in his nose. "I just want my daughter back, *ahhhhh.*"

[pretending to lift a folded matchbook with cocaine to his nose with dry, efficient sniffs] Sniff, sniff, this-and-that.

It was like, four-something in the fucking morning.

Caesar: I had flashbacks to my sister.

Primo: [cutting him off] So while we were there, they gave me a picture, so that we could go look for Jackie.

We went downstairs, and we started walking around, asking questions, all through the projects.

The cops already knew about it, the whole shit.

We went back upstairs to see if there had been a phone call or anything. And we started talking so much, that this guy [pointing to Caesar], started tearing. He got flashbacks.

Caesar: [eagerly] Yeah, Yeah, I started tearing.

Primo: Flashbacks from his sister who was stabbed in the projects.

Caesar: I was on *siiiick* [rolling his eyes wildly]. 'Cause I was thinking about stupidities.

And I told Candy – 'cause I was in the room all sad – "Damn, I feel sick."

So she told me, "You should go to the hospital."

And that's when everyone really got, like, serious. Felix was like . . . [raising his eyebrows and shifting his eyeballs back and forth] Word! [shaking both wrists for emphasis] Bugging!

And we were all there.

Primo: [gently to Caesar] I didn't know you was crying until Felix started saying, "Don't cry Caesar; don't cry." And I looked at you, and I looked all around, and I said, "Oh shit."

Caesar: Yeah, 'cause I had thoughts already; you know, like how they killed my sister when she was missing. Motherfuckers stabbed her seventeen times! Why they have to do that?

Primo: [putting his hand on Caesar's shoulder] Tabatha [Candy's oldest daughter] came over. And started crying loud. She got hysterical.

But then afterwards, everybody was cooling, and shit; and we went to the precinct.

The police made some phone calls, and Candy checked every fuckin' facility there could be, even in Queens and New Jersey, to see if Jackie was in jail.

When she came back to the house, she was really fucked up. You could tell from her eyes. She was crying. She hadn't slept.

And that was Friday, and then Saturday came. Jackie was still missing. Candy was out there with posters. She had put a coupla' posters around the neighborhood.

Candy was looking for you, Felipe. She needed to talk to you; I mean for you to help her talk more correctly on the phone, 'cause she was getting dissed at the Twenty-third Precinct.

You know, they were just saying, "Awww, just another runaway, Porta' rrican bitch."

Now, Candy wants to see you. So she could tell you the story her way, for the book.

Candy suffered a great deal through her daughter's ordeal and extended her full solidarity, as only a mother who has shared a similar agony can. She was explicit in making all of us publicly accept the fact that Jackie was raped – despite street culture's double-standard denial of this form of violence.

Candy: Felipe, you don't know how crazy I went. I couldn't eat; I couldn't sleep; it was like . . . I mean like, when you don't know where your daughter is; and you don't know if she's being tortured – killed. All you know is that she needs you.

Your child is screaming for you; and you can't reach out and help her, because you don't know where she's at.

During the three nights she was gone, I even slept in her bed to see if some sign came to me.

When they brought her back, one of the guys that were involved, told me that it was a little scheme they had. Jackie was supposed to be going to a party with them, but there was no party.

They weren't violent to her. But she was scared, and she was way far away from home – Jamaica, Queens. Imagine!

There were three guys and just one other girl.

She says she was too scared; she couldn't think right. She didn't have her thinking cap on – she gave in. She's only twelve years old.

I took my daughter to the hospital. She needs to have counseling, but I didn't take her back, because they put her through so much pain when they were examining her, that she didn't want to go back.

I want her to feel like it's not her fault, even if she let it happen.

She was in a position where she felt her life was going to be in danger, so she did it.

At least she didn't get pregnant, thanks God for that.

Primo and Caesar resisted Candy's solidary interpretation of her daughter's rape. Most of their conversations on the event over the next few weeks centered on exonerating the rapists and excoriating Jackie. They completely convinced themselves that Jackie had not been raped; they unequivocally blamed the twelve-year-old child for her tribulations. As a matter of fact, the very first time they told me the story, Caesar had called out to me from across the street with a cackle of laughter, "Yo Felipe, did ya' hear? Jackie's a little streetwalker now." When I argued with them that Jackie had been raped, Primo countered by comparing Jackie to "one of those girls Luis, Ray, and the posse used to train back in the days above the club." He referred to this as "getting influenced into screwing" rather than being raped. Caesar was marginally more sympathetic, acknowledging that Jackie "got conned into doing shit." Although he recognized that she had been forced to have sex with two or more boys against her will, he nevertheless insisted, "I don't think it was rape, though. It don't seem to me like she was held . . . forced to do it."

To condemn Jackie for sexual wantonness, Primo invoked the guilty symbol of a woman looking out of a window at men — never mind that the window might be seventeen stories high.

It looked'ed like she knew what she was doing, 'cause the way I see it, she's always in the window, calling guys from the block.

Jackie wants to be hanging out; she want to be in the street.

The ultimate exoneration of the rapists hinged on Jackie's lack of remorse and her failure to follow the traditional solution of establishing a nuclear household with her rapist abductor.

Primo: [sniffing cocaine] Jackie's cooling out. She's not like, acting like a victim.

Besides, she still talks to the guy. I asked her if he is good-looking. She said, "Yeah." [making shrugging motions] She wasn't sad.

270

Caesar: What can you do if she got fucked out there, and she liked'ed it?

Primo: Yeah, she probably have a baby, because she got a big itch.

Philippe: That's some sick shit you're saying Primo!

Caesar: She's gonna just be a statistic out there; babies havin' babies.

Primo: [drinking from his 16-ounce can of malt liquor, and then sniffing from a packet of cocaine] You don't understand Felipe? Jackie went, because she wanted to go, and it happened, because she wanted it. She asked for it. Now, Jackie's acting too cool for it to be a tragic thing.

Caesar: [sniffing cocaine] I don't think its such a big thing. It's just a mistake. I mean, if she's just going to have a boyfriend, maybe she should just stay with this guy and do all right.

[sniffing again] I think it's a thing that like could be put in the past, if she could just settle down with her man.

They ultimately blamed Candy for violating gender roles, and for spawning a second generation of flawed females.

Caesar: Besides, if she had sex by accident, by . . . getting raped, then there's no reason why her mother have to tell her, "Well, now you have to use birff controls." 'Cause that's like telling her, "You can keep on fucking, but just avoid having kids." Candy thinks the girl's a saint.

Primo: [drinking and sniffing] Her mother is always acting like a *beyaca*. You know, a horny bitch.

Caesar: You know what the problem is? Nobody showing her no example: Her mother's wild; her sister's wild.

Caesar concluded this particular discussion by turning the ongoing crisis over changing gender roles on the street into the basis for misogyny:

Caesar: That's why I don't really want a daughter.

I can't stand the feeling of another man touching my daughter. I got like a prejudice against women because of that shit.

In a classic example of how the vulnerable prey on one another and internalize their structural marginality, the only "positive" action taken by Candy on behalf of her twelve-year-old daughter — with the exception perhaps of offering her birth control pills — was to mobilize the men in her life to lash out violently against the mother of the girl who was raped alongside Jackie:

> *Primo:* Candy got to bash the moms in the mouth, 'cause she said, "Your daughter's a ho'." And the woman said, "What! My daughter?" and Candy busted her in the lip.
>
> The mother said, "I'm going to go bring my daughter down, so you can fight me and fight my daughter." But that's when Candy's friends, Carlos, and all the other guys rolled up with guns, and some other family members, and some cousins from Tabatha's husband's family. It was a big posse.

In Search of Meaning: Having Babies in El Barrio

Witnessing the maelstrom consuming children on the street in their most vulnerable years, one cannot help wondering why mothers continue to bear so many babies into so much suffering. During my five years of residence, virtually all my friends and acquaintances in El Barrio had at least one baby. This was the case with Primo's girlfriend Maria, who refused to have an abortion when she became pregnant, even though Primo was in the midst of a felony trial for his second arrest for selling crack to an undercover officer. Only two months earlier, Maria and Primo had been thrown out of the project apartment belonging to Maria's sister, who had fled to Bridgeport, Connecticut, when her husband's drug-dealing partner was found murdered in their car. At the time Maria became pregnant she was living with her deeply depressed, alcoholic, 250-pound mother. I described it in my fieldwork notes:

[March 1990]
Primo took me over to Maria's house: strewn with garbage, broken furniture, and empty quarts of Bacardi. It smells of vomited alcohol, and is crawling with cockroaches. Plates full of boiled cabbage, and boiled meat, from Maria's stepfather's unfinished meals lie spilled around the living room, where Maria has to sleep on a broken couch that hurts her back.

Primo assures me that this is nothing compared to the howls, wails, shouts, and sobbings of Maria's bruised mother after she finishes her evening bottle of Bacardi. Apparently, she fights with her husband, accusing him of infidelities. According to Primo, on some nights she actually stabs him, "but she just jigs him a little bit."

Today she has a swollen face, because last night her husband – an equally alcoholic janitor at a public school – retaliated and "clocked her."

Maria was overjoyed to be pregnant. It was the happiest I had ever seen her, and it took me a long time to realize that it was precisely her wretched living conditions that made motherhood so appealing. It offered a romantic escape from her objectively difficult surroundings. The pregnancy also cemented her deep love for Primo, who we all expected would receive a four- to six-year prison sentence. Having Primo's baby was going to be her way of demonstrating her solidarity with him during his incarceration. Maria began writing poetry to celebrate her relationship with Primo and their future progeny. Maria's high self-esteem during this period in her life literally springs from the pages of her diary, which she showed me. In the following excerpt, for example, her appreciation for the beauty of her body both internalizes and overcomes racist and sexist stereotypes:

> I have light brown eyes, sexy cat eyes, and a nice big butt and big juicy balangas . . . and I have big bubble lips that cover my face just right; and I have hair, curly, and I could put it anywhere I want to.

She was also filled with appreciation for her *javao'*[10] boyfriend.

> I'm eighteen years old; he's twenty-six. He has light brown eyes, big eyes. He has beautiful lips too, nice teeth; and he has juicy buns . . . and he has nice curly hair.[11]

Primo, in contrast, was anxious and angry at Maria. He was overwhelmed with anxiety over his court case, and he was at the height of his personal disillusionment at not being able to find a legal job. He begged Maria to have an abortion, and even went out of his way to abuse her verbally when she showed him her love poems, calling her a "fucking crazy bitch that looks like a negro Michelin man; like Black-a-Claus . . . like Blackula."

Maria also had a concrete material interest in bearing a child. It represented her most realistic chance of establishing an independent household given the extraordinary scarcity of affordable, subsidized public housing in New York City. During the years I lived in El Barrio, the waiting list for New York City Housing Authority apartments was eighteen years long.[12] Homeless pregnant teenagers, however, were given priority in obtaining apartments under a special outreach program designed to relieve crowding in emergency homeless shelters and welfare hotels. The "only" negative in Maria's strategy to forge an independent household was that she had to survive for three long months in a homeless shelter before being placed in a "youth action" renovated tenement for homeless teenage mothers. As a matter of fact, Primo Jr. was born while she was still in the shelter.

During this same period, Maria's sister Carmen also became pregnant with her boyfriend, Caesar. Caesar's abusive tendencies did not dampen her joy and love. At the time, Caesar had obliged Carmen to make her oldest sister the foster mother of her six-year-old daughter, Pearl. He also frequently beat her two-year-old son, Papo, claiming that he lacked discipline and was "slow in the head."[13] Just before Carmen's pregnancy, Caesar gave her an ultimatum, "choose between Papo or me." She was negotiating with her older sister to adopt Papo as well.

Carmen's pregnancy solved her immediate crisis. Not only did Caesar agree to become Papo's stepfather, but his grandmother invited Carmen to move into their apartment and live in Caesar's bedroom. Caesar's grandmother even formalized Carmen's status by registering her officially on the Housing Authority lease. Caesar himself had never been legally registered as living in the apartment, to avoid having his SSI payments included in the rent calculation.

Carmen and Maria were following the traditional path of escaping from a troubled home by falling romantically in love with an idealized man, and embracing motherhood wholeheartedly. Carmen showed me her journal entries shortly after becoming pregnant. She was even more infatuated with Caesar than Maria was with Primo, describing her relationship with Caesar as "paradise on an island":

> The years that I've seen Caesar, I've always had a crush on him. But when we first got together, it was like love at first sight. And still to this day I

feel the same. I guess you could say I fell in love with him. But when I see him, my heart skips a beat, and when he gets near, I just want to faint.

I really love him and care for him always, no matter. And as for my son, Benito Jr., [Papo], he loves Caesar, as far as I know.

Both Maria and Carmen were young, but their enthusiastic embrace of motherhood should not be dismissed as the fleeting romantic whims of immature women. The dearth of alternative scenarios for female adulthood on the street not only normalizes motherhood at an early age but also makes it attractive.

In Candy's case, for example, when her love affair with Primo ended violently, it was her love for her children that stabilized her and restored meaning to her life. By wholeheartedly reassuming the traditional "jíbara role" of being a self-abnegating mother at age thirty-four, Candy saved herself and her household from terminal self-destruction in Ray's street-dealing scene.

Candy: I used coke for five months to kill myself. Then I woke up and said, "I love my kids too much to kill myself." Because if you love your kids that makes you do nothing wrong.

I was real skinny, and I was like neglecting my kids, in the way of not paying mind to them. I didn't hit them, but I didn't want to be bothered with them. Like, I was [gruffly], "I don't want to hear no noise."

They used to tell me, "Mommy, what's wrong with you? Mommy, please! People are going to think you are on crack." And yes God is with me, because I had a dream back then. I was dying. I saw my son Junior, my only boy, crying that I was dead. And I saw my other two daughters looking very different. [stopping abruptly] I wish to God I wouldn't even think about it, 'cause I'm against drugs. I think my children would've gone into drugs.

But don't get me wrong. I'm a strict mother where I believe in the best education. I believe in being a strict, strong, good, loving parent.

You know, Felipe, what it is? When you see your kids everyday telling you, "I love you." And you know I've been through a lot —

a beating every day, three times a day, from the age of thirteen. Why you gonna make that baby pay for your mistakes? No!

That's why I'm crazy about my kids. And I still want twelve. Because a baby means purity to me – innocence. And a baby can't come and smack you, and say, "Mommy, don't abuse me." But you do it. And I'm against child abuse.

But I'm thirty-four now, and I still wish I could have five more now. Because my kids come to me, kissing me, saying, "Mommy, love you, love you."

You hardly see that in kids now. You see kids streetwise, like my sister's kids – Angelo, for example – where they don't have a lovable parent.

But I did my best. My children all went to Catholic school from first grade to now. And I have paid for it all.

The Demonization of Mothers and Crack

Candy went back to defining her life around the needs of her children. The irony of the institution of the single, female-headed household is that, like the former conjugal rural family, it is predicated on submission to patriarchy. Street culture takes for granted a father's right to abandon his children while he searches for ecstasy and meaning in the underground economy. There is little that is triumphantly matriarchal or matrifocal about this arrangement. It simply represents greater exploitation of women, who are obliged to devote themselves unconditionally to the children for whom their men refuse to share responsibility.

When abandoned mothers do not sacrifice their individual needs for the sake of their children, chaos wrecks their precarious households. No one remains to feed, hug, and watch them. Street children in El Barrio are caught in a historical limbo: The old-fashioned patriarchal forces that created female-headed households are breaking down, and there is nothing to cushion the fragmentation of the family unit when mothers follow the paths of fathers in seeking independent lives in the underground economy or in substance abuse.

Street culture's double standard on gender became clearly visible to me during the months when Candy sold cocaine for Ray, and maintained Primo as a kept lover. The men in Ray's network roundly decried her failings as a single mother and head-of-household. They completely ignored any obligations for family sustenance on the part of her incarcerated husband, Felix, and none offered to help provide Candy's children with food, shelter, and love. One of their recurrent criticisms was that Candy needed a strong male figure to discipline her.

> *Primo:* That bitch was no good. It was like the kids were all living without their mother. The kids were taking care of themselves, because their mother was just going from the club to sleeping, back and forth, just like that [making a yo-yo motion with his hand].
> Lillian was less than a year old. Hell! Junior was the mother. He was changing the diapers.
> And sometimes I felt sorry and shit, so I would do it. I was there, changing the diapers and she wasn't around!
> *Caesar:* That lady just fell apart after that idiot Felix got locked up.
> *Primo:* And then there was Abraham [the adopted grandfather]; he used to, like, try to change the diapers, but he said, *"No lo aguanto"* [I can't bear it].
> *Caesar:* Fucked up! She just went AWOL once her man left.
> *Primo:* I mean, I couldn't eat her food, because if you go to her house, and look at her kitchen, the way the mess is she's cooking. You don't want to eat that food. I'm talking roaches!

The same dynamic of women increasingly refusing to submit to old-fashioned patriarchal definitions of family roles was also clearly visible in Ray's crackhouses, where women and girls were carving out a new public space for themselves. At the same time, street culture strives to maintain women in subordinated roles as mothers or as dependant girlfriends. Hence, my fieldwork notes from a hot summer night:

> [July 1990]
> I was greeted at the entrance to the Social Club by three, shiny-new, baby carriages parked symmetrically alongside the Pac-Man machine, out of the way of the pool tables. Each one had a tiny newborn in it, sound asleep, clenching tiny fists.
> Their teenage mothers were competing for Little Pete's attention. He just broke up with his old girlfriend after she became pregnant.

277

Fifteen-year-old moms in minimal tank tops peck the necks of the pool players, in between crack sales, while their babies sleep peacefully. One mother danced outrageous salsa steps to the rap.

How many will get addicted to crack this summer? How many more will get pregnant?

When I asked Maria why there were so many teenage mothers and newborn babies in the club, she answered, " 'cause it's air-conditioned." I can't really argue with that. We're having a terrible heatwave, and I am sure none of the girls have air-conditioning at home — if they even have a private room to share with their babies.

As I noted in the opening pages of this chapter, New York City's official statistics demonstrate an explosion of child abuse and neglect. Children have been ordered into foster care in record-breaking numbers since the crack–cocaine epidemic began in the mid-1980s.[14] Politicians, the press, and popular culture have reacted to this phenomenon by sexualizing the antidrug hysteria that gripped the United States through the late 1980s and early 1990s. Drug scares are nothing new to the United States, especially during periods of economic and social strain. Whatever illicit substance happens to be in fashion is invariably portrayed as the "worst ever," harbinging imminent social breakdown.[15] Often, journalists and even medical doctors assign a peculiar pharmacological vulnerability to whatever social class or ethnic group is especially vulnerable in the contemporary social structure. This was the case, for example, with the Chinese opium scares in California in the late 1880s. The same applied to African-Americans during the cocaine hysteria of the early 1900s, when sheriffs in the deep South justified raising "the caliber of their guns" on the grounds that "the cocaine nigger is sure hard to kill." Mexicans in the Southwest were not treated much more humanely during the marijuana scares of the 1930s.[16]

The distinctive feature of the crack epidemic of the late 1980s and early 1990s, however, was that instead of an ethnic group or a social class being demonized for their proclivity for substance abuse, women, the family, and motherhood itself were assaulted. Inner-city women who smoked crack were accused of having lost the "mother-nurture instinct." Quite simply, this was because for the first time in U.S. history women represented almost half of the addicts on the street and, once again, because of the patriarchal gender responsibilities imposed on the female-

Graffiti art of a local crack dealer who marked his sales site with the antidrug slogan of the 1980s. Photo by Charo Chacón-Méndez.

headed households, they were often accompanied by their toddlers and newborns when they went to crackhouses.

The spectacle of publicly addicted women is exacerbated by the misogyny of street culture. The male-dominated ranks of the underground economy exclude females from the more profitable, autonomous entrepreneurial niches such as dealing, mugging, and burglarizing.[17] While this is changing, as women increasingly penetrate violent male preserves in the street economy, women are still forced disproportionately to rely on prostitution to finance their habits and to support what remains of their families. The flooding of women into the sex market has deteriorated working conditions for prostitutes, causing an epidemic of venereal disease among young women and newborn babies in the inner city.[18] Crack addicts are also particularly vulnerable to public sexual humiliation, as they tolerate extreme levels of verbal and physical abuse in their pursuit of the initial sixty- to ninety-second ecstatic rush provided by smoking the drug.

The press, academics, mainstream America, and inner-city residents themselves enjoy speculating over the "mystery" of the feminization of crack use. Explanations range from moralistic denunciations of the breakdown in family values, to arbitrary theorizations around female-specific phobias of hypodermic needles. The most prevalent popular explanation hinges on the allegedly "aphrodisiacal" powers of crack—cocaine, despite all the evidence indicating that most people become sexually dysfunctional when they ingest large quantities of cocaine. The fantasy of crack-gorged women being propelled by insatiable sexual cravings is shared by journalists, social scientists, dealers, and addicts themselves. The sexualized imagery effectively hides the deeper power confrontation over gender roles and family organization occurring throughout the larger U.S. society.[19]

The mothers who elbow their way into crackhouses, thereby violating male taboos, are condemned as animals who have lost their maternal, loving instinct. Hence, the *New York Times* ran editorials with subtitles like "Mothers Turned into Monsters," and published articles with headlines like "The Instincts of Parenthood Become Part of Crack's Toll". The *Wall Street Journal* quoted doctors and nurses as saying, "The most remarkable and hideous aspect of crack use seems to be the undermining of the maternal instinct."[20]

During the height of the public concern over crack's pharmacological subversion of the mother-nurture instinct, I realized that I, too, could be condemned as a deficient parent in my pursuit of street culture because of what I was exposing my son to. I became aware of this while sitting at a conference on drug use listening to an outraged ethnographer: "They'll risk their own flesh-and-blood babies, bringing them to the crackhouse to camouflage their activities." The gasps and judgmental head-wagging of the audience reconfirmed to me the gulf between the inner city and middle-class society. Mainstream society simply has no concept of how "normalized" drug selling has become on inner-city streets. It is virtually impossible not to bring one's baby to the crackhouse if one spends any time on the street. For example, even if I had not been solicitous of the friendship of drug dealers, had I simply been one of the dozens of sociable neighbors on my block who enjoyed public space, I could not have avoided "irresponsibly" exposing my little boy to the violence of drug dealing on a daily basis. On the block where I lived, it was impossible to watch a sunset, to take a walk, or to buy an ice-cream sandwich at the local bodega delicatessen without passing a handful of street-level crack or heroin sellers. When I walked down the block with my son in my arms, one of the local drug dealers would usually politely mumble the traditional Puerto Rican blessing for newborns, or maybe even compliment me effusively on the beauty of my baby. Strolling relaxedly through these settings, mothers and fathers who are steadfastly opposed to substance abuse sometimes find themselves stopping or dawdling for a few moments with their babies on a copping corner, or at the entrance to one of the crackhouses, before they move along to finish their evening errands.[21]

My deconstruction of mainstream society's moralistic condemnation of families in crisis did not withstand the horror of seeing mothers inside crackhouses dragging their infants through the agony of their desperate searches for ecstasy. On several occasions inside the Game Room, I begged crack-craving pregnant women to think through the potential consequences of their urge to get high. I repeatedly argued with Ray and Primo, accusing them of having a personal responsibility for the traumatized lives of the neonates whose mothers they regularly sold crack to.

At first, unaware of my righteousness on this issue, the Game Room dealers openly joked about the surprisingly high number of expectant customers regularly frequenting the crackhouse. Primo and his lookout and partner Benzie, relaxing over beer and heroin in a project stairwell, described one such customer:

> *Benzie:* [passing a 40-ounce bottle of Olde English malt liquor, and opening a packet of cocaine] All of a sudden Rose started screaming out my name: "Benzie, Benzie I'm giving birff! Come help me, come help me! Benzie, please!"
>
> Then she said, "Oh, it's coming out! It's coming out! Look! Help me!"

I looked at her pussy and I saw a head. Felipe, I was shocked! As soon as I saw that little head with blood coming out of her cunt. My whole head went WASHHHHHT. I was like, "No! I can't!" 'Cause I was on crack, and I was *petro*, and I was like shocked out of my fuckin' ass. I saw how that head, that blood, was coming out of her pussy — out of her vagina. And I was shocked.

And she was asking me, "Benzie, Benzie, help me, help me, Benzie. It's coming out; spread my legs; help me."

So I ran out to the hallway, screaming to call an ambulance. [sniffing cocaine]

Philippe: Aww man! Whatsa' matter with you Benzie! Why didn't you help! Why didn't you just pull the baby's head? Whatsa' matter with you anyway, man?

Benzie: [grinning and grabbing the beer bottle back] Give me a fuckin' break, man! Save that shit, Felipe!

I mean let me tell you, if that was you there, and she would be askin' you for help, and that was your first time seeing the baby's head in her vagina, with blood that you never saw before in your life, you'd be in shock too. You wouldn't know what to do.

You act like you'd know what you'd want to do. I mean [imitating a white, upper-middle-class accent and cocking his head back and forth stiffly] "Oh yeah, sure. I'll help you, and pull the baby's head out."

Later for that shit, Felipe. You wouldn't know what the fuck to do either. I mean it was tremendous, and I was cracked up!

[pausing to dip the tip of his house key into the packet of heroin Primo was holding out to him, sniffing stiffly, and then speaking slowly and seriously] In a way, I wanted to help her, but then when I saw the top layer of the baby's head — like the skull or whatever — with blood coming out, I fffflipped man! And her hole was split. She was in pain, like screaming and begging me for help.

[perhaps noting my expression] It's sad, but it happened in my face.

When the ambulance people came they was talking about getting hot water and everything. There was hot water, but there was, like, no towels; no rags; you know, none'a' the shit they need to perform babies.

Primo: [laughing, and dipping into the heroin packet] You know what the baby probably first swallowed when he came out? A couple of capsules, because that was what was all around the fuckin' floor. The baby would have come out, like this [breathing with a gulp and blinking his eyes]. And a little crack capsule would'a' gone in his mouth.

Benzie: [continuing in a serious tone after taking another quick sniff of heroin] So Rose gave birff right there, and she named the kid after the EMS driver; you know, the lady who had taken the baby out for her; she named it after her.

But you know what bugged me out? It was like nothing, like she didn't give birth. Like she was ready for another blast.

They took her to the hospital and everything. But she was like, out the next day, I think, or the next two days – on a mission. Because I was selling at the Game Room, and she came and told me, "Benzie," like, "What's up? Why didn't you help me?"

I told her, "Man! Listen, I was in shock. I was crying and I was lifted up; and I was snift'ed up; and I just didn't know what to do."

Rose was cool though; she didn't even ask for a short [a price reduction on a vial of crack]. She isn't the schemish type. She was a nice crack head.

She was smoking the whole time she was pregnant, and she never asked us for shorts. Matter of fact, after she gave birth she was smoking again right there. Baby was still in the hospital.

It was a crack baby, so it stayed in the hospital.

I remember this particular conversation vividly, because at the time I had recently been told by a doctor that my own eleven-month-old son had cerebral palsy. The first clinical studies on the effects of in utero exposure to crack were just beginning to show that "crack babies" sometimes display symptoms of cerebral palsy–like neuromuscular involvement.[22] Consequently, it was especially distressing to me to think mothers might be "willingly" imposing cerebral palsy on their progeny, and I discussed it with everyone in the crackhouses I visited. Primo and most of the other dealers eventually stopped selling to expectant mothers – at least in front of me. Ray, on the other hand, never agreed formally to forbid his employees from selling to pregnant women, despite our countless vehement arguments. Somehow, the profoundly conservative Catholicism that convinced him that abortion is "murder" did not inhibit his profit motive at the expense of neonatal welfare:

> *Ray:* I don't care Felipe! I'm just gettin' some a' mines. I don't think about none a' that shit you talkin' about. Besides if they don't buy it from me, they'll just go around the corner, and get it from someone else.[23]

Similarly, Candy proved just as internally inconsistent in her righteousness when I condemned her for selling to pregnant women during the months she worked for Ray at his Social Club:

> When you become pregnant, the body doesn't belong to you. It belongs to the baby. So, if the mother don't give a shit, if they don't care, why should I?

I asked an African-American sociologist colleague, Eloise Dunlap, to help me discuss these issues directly with pregnant addicts. She had access to a broader range of crack-using women on the street because of her gender and ethnicity. Our conversations with expectant mothers on the street revealed that the expectant crack addicts were profoundly ambivalent toward their future babies and about their roles as mothers. Some were convinced they were "taking care of themselves" and their fetuses by simultaneously eating snacks when they smoked crack. One woman assured us that she was careful to smoke only during the day so as to allow the fetus to sleep at night. Another claimed the crack was good for her fetus because it had a tendency "to sleep a lot." Smoking made her "lazy baby" finally wake up and start kicking like a healthy fetus should. Several women criticized the hypocrisy of the street culture that condemned them while eagerly making money off them.[24] None of them, however, criticized the society that refused to fund treatment centers and support services for them. As a matter of fact, we were unable to refer any of the desperate women we befriended to drug treatment centers, because only two of the twenty-four state-funded programs located in New York City at that time (1990) accepted pregnant crack users.[25]

It was not until I moved out of El Barrio that it occurred to me that mothers on crack could be reinterpreted as women desperately seeking meaning in their lives and refusing to sacrifice themselves to the impossible task of raising healthy children in the inner city. Pregnant crack addicts can be de-essentialized from the monstrous image of the cruel, unfeeling mother, and be reconstructed as self-destructive rebels. In ethnographic work among starving mothers in a Brazilian shantytown, the medical anthropologist Nancy Scheper-Hughes critiques the industrialized world's bourgeois idealization of maternal bonding. She shows how mothers struggling to survive in abject poverty, where almost half of all children die before the age of three, learn to "let go" of their weakest, most sickly babies in early infancy. They withhold affection and sometimes even facilitate their infants' deaths from dehydration. When mothers fight these inevitable deaths and invest too much personal anguish in each vulnerable infant, they risk destroying their own spirit. If mothers were to dwell on the cumulative tragedies of their sickly children, they would become consumed by grief and anxiety. They would cease to be able to function as coherent parents and as feeling human beings.[26]

In postindustrial El Barrio, a lack of calories and potable water are not killing infants. Instead, the causes are substance abuse, racism, public sector institutional breakdown, and a restructuring of the economy away from factory jobs. In the United States, the death and destruction of inner-city children occurs primarily during adolescence rather than in infancy. The statistics speak for themselves: In the mid-1990s, young males in Harlem aged eighteen through twenty-four had a better chance of dying violently than soldiers on active duty during World War II.[27] Perhaps the addicted mothers I met in crackhouses were simply those who had given up fighting the odds that history has structured against them. Abandoning their children, or poisoning their fetuses in a frantic search for personal ecstasy, accelerates the destruction of already doomed progeny.[28] By destroying the so-called mother-nurture instinct, and by disabling their children during their tenderest ages, vulnerable mothers escape the long-term agony of having to watch their children grow up into healthy, energetic adolescents, only to become victims and protagonists of violence and substance abuse.

Once again, it is obviously not "feminism" or the "empowerment of women" that is causing mothers to abandon their children or to poison their fetuses. On the contrary, the blame lies squarely on a patriarchal definition of "family," and on a dysfunctional public sector that relegates the responsibility for nurturing and supporting children virtually exclusively to individuals – specifically to women. Not only fathers, consequently, but also the larger society that structures social marginalization ultimately have to share the burden and responsibility of reproduction. Gender power relations and family structures have been profoundly transformed over the past few generations throughout the world. As noted at the beginning of this chapter, contradictory processes inevitably accompany all rapid, historical power shifts. Within the worldwide context of accelerated change as mothers struggle for their rights, and especially for their individual selves, on inner-city streets, children are bound to suffer in the short term.

8

VULNERABLE FATHERS

When I think of my son, I wish I was with him. It's hard to think about this. It makes me wish — no, not wish, 'cause it's not gonna be there — but if I was gonna wish, the wish would be that I was never broken up with my wife, so that I could always be there, like a family thing, like old-fashioned. Like just her, him, and me. That's the way it was when I was working. I didn't want nobody else, but Sandra. I was like, "I want to be right here, where I'm at, with my kid."

Primo

The moralistic debates that condemn deficient child-rearing practices in the inner city bemoan the absence of fathers in families. It is assumed that fatherlessness destroys a child's moral fiber, even though the single most overwhelming problem faced by female-headed households is poverty.[1] Based on my relationship to the fathers who worked for Ray, public policy efforts to coax poor men back into nuclear households are misguided. The problem is just the reverse: Too many abusive fathers are present in nuclear households terrorizing children and mothers. If anything, women take too long to become single mothers once they have babies. They often tolerate inordinate amounts of abuse.[2]

There is a clear material basis for the failure of fathers to support their progeny in stable, loving families: High school dropouts can no longer find secure jobs in New York City that would allow them to maintain conjugal households on a single income in traditional, patriarchal style. This is clearly revealed at the national level with a 50 percent rise in the percentage of working poor families between 1979 and 1982, from 12 percent to 18 percent.[3] This economic "logic," however, is not a simple reflection of material exigencies. There is a powerful historico-cultural weight bearing down on sexual inequalities that shapes the specific patterns of paternal neglect and abuse. The historical and contemporary experience of migration and rapid political economic change is different across genders. Specifically, the legacy of the rural household where the omnipotent pater familias defines his worth around the "respect" accorded to him by his wife, abundant children, and neighbors weighs heavily on second-generation male Nuyoricans, who find themselves flitting home-less from one sexual relationship to another, without the protection of a family or an economically viable community.

As noted in Chapter 2, the extended kin-based communities of turn-of-the-century rural Puerto Rico were only minimally under the control of the central state in San Juán. The ruggedly independent settlers in the interior highlands turned their backs on urban elites.[4] Instead they constructed their own hierarchies and definitions of social order and prestige around gender, age, and kinship categories that persist in contra-dictory ways on the streets of East Harlem. An idealized jíbaro identity continues to permeate, or at least to resonate with, bits and pieces of a street culture that rejects its marginalization by the centers of power in U.S. society. It offers an oppositionally based sense of dignity and respect. The patriarchal, formerly order-producing categories of this leg-acy, however, which revolve around gender, age, and kin, are in flux given the disruptive experiences of prolonged colonial dependency, mi-gration, urbanization, and ghettoization. This is exacerbated by the problematic material base of street culture, namely, the entry-level labor market and the underground economy that condemn its participants to poverty, economic insecurity, and high levels of institutional and personal violence.

Celebrating Paternal Powerlessness

Almost all of the men in Ray's network were fathers, but none of them regularly provided money and love to all their progeny. On the contrary, many were consistently violent against their loved ones, as if lashing out against the families they were unable to support. Street culture and the underground economy provided them with an alternative forum for redefining their sense of masculine dignity around promiscuity, conspicu-ous violence, and ecstatic substance abuse. Caesar was most adamant in celebrating his inability to maintain a family. Unable to reproduce the patriarchal aspirations of his grandfather's generation within the context of a repressive nuclear family and an extended kin-based community, he concentrated his male energies into macho one-upmanship and sexual belt-notching. He worked hard at exaggerating his sexual promiscuity and hardheartedness:[5]

> *Caesar:* It's the same thing with us as in nature. You just go for yours, out on your own.
> We's just like those green sea turtles that be in the Galapagos. Those turtles get out of the shell, and they run to the sea, and they never know who their parents was.
> They go through their whole life. Then they bone somebody or they get bone't. They have kids and they never see them.
> I don't feel guilty about the kids I got thrown around out there, because I have no heart Felipe. I'll fuck anybody, anytime. Besides these bitches is crazy nowadays.

Primo was more functional in his sexualization of male power, focusing on discretely controlling the women in his life emotionally and economically. Following street culture's celebration of the gigolo image, he converted the shame of his inability to maintain a household into a celebration of the street art of being an economic parasite, *cacheteando* [freeloading] off his girlfriends. Unable to support his children faithfully – but repressively – as his grandfathers had done before him, he furthered his waning sense of old-fashioned masculinity by becoming a superstud instead. One night late at the Social Club pool hall where we were relaxing and watching Little Pete serve his emaciated crack clients until six o'clock in the morning, Primo pointed to three women playing pool together – Flora, Jaycee, and Maria. Giggling, he waved at them, and feigning an old-fashioned Puerto Rican rural accent, he said in Spanish, "Look how well my women get along with each other [*Mira como mis mujeres se llevan bién*]." The rap music was too loud for them to hear us, even though we were only six feet away. I knew Primo was having a simultaneous relationship with both Maria and Jaycee. I had no idea, however, that he was also seeing Flora "on the sneak tip."

> *Philippe:* Hey, you're not with Flora too, are you?
> *Primo:* [nodding grimly] Last month. She works at Key Food

[supermarket] packing meat so she only hangs late on weekends. She was hanging with Rosie on a Friday — you know Rosie; she used to work at the Game Room; and now Caesar be seeing her.[6]

But tonight I'm going to be with Jaycee. This girl [pointing his thumb at Maria] went to my house today. She called, and I told her not to come, because I already had a weekend of screwing with this bitch Jaycee, but she wanted to come around anyway.

I took a shower, and when I came out, she was there; and I said, "Come on! Then Jaycee and now you?" I left it at that, and said "Nah, maybe tomorrow."

She's going to call me up early tomorrow, and like [raising his eyebrows and grinning], 'ah'm'a' be fucking!

Philippe: What about that phone call you're supposed to make tomorrow to the employment office? Remember what your probation officer said?

Primo: Oh shit, Felipe, you're right! But you know what? What would be good about it, is that once I see her face [jerking his head toward Maria], I know I got to get up.

[shrugging his shoulders] Out of all these bitches hanging around, I take that one [pointing to Maria].

This has happened to me before. One day in front of the Game Room, I saw a legion of girls on the corner. Like a herd of girls talking to each other. And when I looked, I said, "God damn! I had all of them." It was my ex-wife Sandra, Candy, Maria, Jaycee, and I think some other girl that I don't remember.

Philippe: How'd that make you feel — good?

Primo: No. It felted'ed weird. [noticing Caesar eavesdropping eagerly through the blasting music] No, it felted'ed good, then weird.

I'm telling you Felipe, I got a golden dick. All my cousins be that way [slapping Caesar five]. We all got golden dicks.

I began steering conversations onto the ethics of sexual relationships with as many people as possible within Ray's network. Luis's position could be summarized by the tone of his voice when he stood in front of the Social Club entrance and shouted across the street at the crack-addicted women who serviced him with oral sex in exchange for puffs on his crack pipe, "Yo, mouf! Yo, m'ah mouf! Come here!"[7] Others in the crackhouse scene, especially the younger men, acknowledged the right of women to celebrate promiscuity the way men did. This was the perspective, for example, of eighteen-year-old Pedro, who worked as a nurse's aide at Mt. Sinai Hospital, and who subsequently died when some angel dust dealers he was attempting to hold up "put ten shots in him." Although tempted by Pedro's sexually egalitarian logic, Caesar took refuge back in sexual violence to reestablish his more traditional conception of appropriate sex roles.

Pedro: If I was a girl, I'd be a freak [nymphomaniac]; but I'd make the niggas pay.

I'd be a ho', but I try to jerk men though, for money, and not just to get dicked by dirty niggas without getting paid. I want money. I want money.

Caesar: Yeah, I would get my rocks off and live well. I would try to get ahold of some niggas on my block who are really souped up. And if they look like they got something, then I'll let them . . .

Until I get jerked, and then I'll learn my lesson. Because I'll finally get boned by somebody, and not get any money.[8]

Only Eddie, Caesar's half-African-American cousin, formulated an analysis of sexuality that integrated notions of class and racial oppression — even if he did not act constructively on his insights:

Maybe it's thyroids, or an ego thing partially or to prove to friends how many girls I could get; but for me, it's an escape from reality, to make me think I'm not tied down, that I don't got a kid, and that I didn't do it too early.

I mean we don't have no money so we make up for it with women. I mean if you going to come into a a hundred thousand dollars, you going to make it. Your friends be envying you. Now, if you don't got nothing, but you going to have five women, you going to be self-satisfied. It's just a thing we do.

But if you have money, you don't have to be defined through women. Or, if you're a millionaire, maybe you just do it more discreet.

Plus, there's more black and Puerto Rican women than men. It's like three to every one man. Especially now, black men are being killed off like this — [pointing to Primo who was making a hand-to-hand sale to a black customer at that very moment] — with all this drug problem.

Masculinity in Historical Crisis

Ray was older than all his employees with the exception of Candy and Luis. Their generation has a more traditional relationship to rural — perhaps jíbaro — notions of family and masculinity. In their grandparents' traditional agricultural economy, children contribute to economic security: By the age of six or seven they are useful laborers on the family farm, and in the long term they guarantee the social security and retirement pension of their parents. Since there are no expenses for formal education in the rural economy, and since food is produced on the household plot, the benefits of raising numerous children greatly outweigh their costs. Masculine respect centers on having large families and taking full responsibility for supporting them economically. Ray, Luis, and even Candy — who is convinced she really wanted to have twelve children — are all in their late thirties, and are embroiled in a historico-cultural time warp that propels them to maximize their progeny, even though it is impossible for them to maintain their large households economically.

In Ray's and Luis's cases this was illustrated by their multiple sexual relationships with different women: They had as many children as possible with as diverse an array of mothers as feasible. The inconsistency of their failures to support these children was covered by denial and hypocrisy, which usually involved condemning the mothers of their abandoned children for transgressions that made them unworthy to receive their economic support. Luis, for example, enjoyed bragging about how many teenage women he had managed to impregnate during the same nine-month period during his adolescence. He referred to them as "holes out there." Two decades later, in his mid-thirties, he has no problem with the fact that he does not support emotionally or financially seven of the twelve children he has engendered by four different women.

Luis: Fuck it! I ain't got nothing to give my kids, so why should I see them?

In the beginning their mothers get angry, but like I said, you gotta learn to handle things in life.

Ray, on the other hand, presented himself as being well-off economically. He could not take refuge in being broke or addicted to crack. When he was in the process of negotiating the purchase of the Game Room from Candy following Felix's incarceration, I had a series of moralistic conversations with him about fatherhood. I was never confident enough to tape record Ray, but I remember vividly his insistence that it was possible for children to "grow up healthy" if they "had the proper role model as a father." At the time that he told me this, he was still fresh out of prison and was working legally as a security guard in a supermarket. He claimed that the only way for him to "do good by" his half-dozen children scattered between New York, Pennsylvania, and Puerto Rico was to switch to selling crack full time. It was impossible for him to be a responsible father to so many far-flung children on his $150-a-week security guard salary. He claimed that his dream was to make enough money selling drugs to gather together all his children under one roof in El Barrio.

Four years later, after passing through three more girlfriends and having three new babies, Ray proved to be just as irresponsible toward his children as the perennially broke street dealers that he employed. The men in his network, however, saw no contradiction between his economic success and the abject, isolated poverty of his children and their abandoned mothers. In fact, in the same breath that they enjoyed enumerating how many cars Ray owned, they marveled at how many babies he had sired. A man with such diversely scattered progeny and such obvious business acumen commanded respect. His penniless, childbearing women, on the other hand, were consistently denigrated.

> *Primo:* He got a Mercedes, and the green Continental that he bought a while back. He sold the Camaro, but still has the Corvette. And his new van only cost him six hundred dollars. I think he bought something else new too, like a four-door Mark IV.
>
> *Philippe:* He takes better care of his cars than his kids. How many does he have?
>
> *Primo:* He's got something like nine of them now. I don't even think he knows how the kids look like.

I mean, maybe he would look them out if their mothers asked, like buy them clothes and shit. He looks-out a little bit.

He just doesn't want to be hawked. So he just forgets about them, I guess — even if they need something.

I know he doesn't take care of Natalie's kid. [sniffing from a ten-dollar heroin packet]

Caesar: Once his women fuck up, Ray just erases them off his list completely.

Primo: I mean, take Nancy, she's a nasty bitch. She fucked up, so he left her. Nancy's with a new man now. Ray told me she went into a drug program. She's my *comai* [mother of my godchild], actually.

After he had that baby from Nancy, it was like, "Fuck you!"

Now, Natalie was one of Luis's bitches out there before. When Luis got locked up, she ended up being Ray's woman.

Caesar: They used to rack in them days.

Primo: But they broke up because of fights. Ray used to leave her stuck in the house, and disappear to have his meat chewed by some dirty crackhead out there on the street. But Natalie was doing wrong too — dirty bitch.

He got a daughter by some other woman in the Bronx, but he never even saw her. It was just a thing that the girl said she was pregnant, but Ray said, "Fuck it!" And then there's some Cuban woman in Pennsylvania that got a kid by him too.

But the other kids got his name. Their mothers just don't demand support, so why should he give it?

Ray's girls are bugged. They don't even ask him for shit. Some of them might even have robbed him. Ray would probably look them out, but they would have to come around, and ask for it the right way, and these girls don't even have no fucking brains to do it right.

He told me one night that he has all kinds of babies by other women.

The only woman that is lucky, and that is cool, is Gloria, his current girl; but they fight a lot, because she hawks him. She's jealous of that man, boy!

But she's cool, though, and he lives with her and her four-year-old son, Bennie.

Philippe: So how many children does Ray have out there?

Primo: Let me see . . . Ray's got two daughters; then Nancy's son and then the one by the crackhead. That makes eight other ones if you count the kids from before he was locked up.

Caesar: How about that other bitch . . . What's her name?

Primo: You mean, Natalie?

Caesar: Yeah, but how do you count eight, if he had four, and then five, and then one more coming up?

Primo: Oh yeah, I forgot, Gloria is pregnant — that little squirrel with her new baby — that'll make nine. And she be hawking him, 'cause he doesn't leave her stuck in the house, like he did with Nancy, or he did with Natalie. He listens to her.

Although younger-generation men still have a certain amount of respect or fascination for men like Ray and Luis who have sired many children, masculine identity no longer hinges as intensively on having children. The weight of cultural history in defining masculinity's relationship to changing gender–family arrangements is clearly visible in the difference between the reproduction-centered imperatives of Ray, Luis, and Candy's generation versus the sexual belt-notching of Primo, Caesar, and the other younger crack dealers. Primo, for example, consistently urged his girlfriends to have abortions when they became pregnant. Ray, on the other hand, was convinced that abortion was a capital sin. Primo was perplexed by Ray's old-fashioned attitudes toward the value of children.

> *Primo:* Ray was telling me I should have all the kids that I can have now, because I'm going to get old. But that doesn't make any sense. Why should I have kids now? To have an army?

Youths in their early twenties, like Caesar and Primo, are one more generation removed from the large families of their rural grandparents. My tape recordings of their casual conversations on the household compositions of their kin, encapsulate the historical-structural transformations around family demographics that they are living.

> *Caesar:* My immediate family is pretty small. My grandmother had eight kids, but a lot of families was bigger back in the days.

Primo: That's exactly what my grandmother has. My grandmother had eighteen kids, and ten passed away.

Caesar: I can't have eight kids. I'd go crazy.

Primo: That's a lot of kids. My cousins, they all had a lot of children. It must have been easier to support kids in those days.

Transformations in the relationship between masculine identity and household composition also involve the loss of the kin-based, age-graded, and gender-hierarchized community that formerly acted almost as an extended family that socialized and controlled women and children. The traditional definitions of masculinity with their ideal of the large, stable household involved a slew of cultural institutions and values buttressing the power of the patriarch. Male heads of households, however, were obliged to provide economically for their families despite the bitter poverty of the rural and the plantation economies of Puerto Rico in the nineteenth through mid-twentieth centuries. This is richly documented in Primo's mother's idealized childhood reminiscences.

In those days in Puerto Rico, when we were in poverty, everyone will tell you, life was better. Life was healthier, and you could trust people, and now you can't trust anybody. And now, even with money in your hand, you can't even trust people to do a favor for you.

And what I liked best about life in Puerto Rico was that we kept all our traditions. And in my village, everyone was either an Uncle, or an Aunt. And when you walked by someone older, you had to ask for their blessing. It was respect.

In those days children were respectful. There was a lot of respect in those days. My father was very strict. When a visitor came, my father only spoke to us with his eyes, because children were not supposed to be in the room. He would just look at us.

So when the visitor entered, my father only had to look at us, and when he looked at us, that meant we had to disappear; we had to go to our room. We weren't allowed to be in the same room as the older folks.

He just spoke to us with his eyes, and so we disappeared. And we couldn't come out of our room until the visitor left. Sometimes we would try to make the person leave with a broom. You know, it's a Santería thing, where you try to make contact with the person to make them leave.

I tried to teach my children a little of what my father had taught me.

Some people have done better by coming here; but many people haven't. Even people from my barrio, they came trying to find a good atmosphere [*buén ambiente*]. There were couples, married couples, who came here looking for a good atmosphere, and instead, they just found disaster. The husband ends up running off with another woman.

A man in El Barrio can no longer "speak" to his children "with his eyes" and expect to have his commands immediately obeyed.[9] The former modalities of male respect are no longer achievable within the conjugal household or the extended kin-based community. Several generations of men caught in different phases of this fundamental cultural transformation in family forms and gender hierarchies have been crushed. Primo brought this issue to my attention. In his concern over the fate of the men in his kin network, one can discern the gender-specific form of the experience of social marginalization in the Puerto Rican diaspora:

I tell you I gotta check myself out. 'Cause like I was telling my mother, in my family, it goes like this: all the men are bugged.

My mother's oldest brother is bugged. He stands in the window talking to himself.

My mother's oldest brother – another uncle of mine – he just walks along like a zombie, and he don't look at nobody. I'm his nephew and his godson. He writes some script, it look like shorthand, but it is absolutely no fucking shorthand. He writes in his notebook and scribble scrabble on the notebook. But the guy has his job. He keeps his job. He keeps his place, but he is out of his mind.

If you look at him walking down the street, he look like a bum. He just walks straight, looking down. He's bugged.

I remember when he wasn't bugged. He and my mother went to Puerto Rico, when he wasn't bugged.

You know, I tell my mother I got a feeling that all the people in my family, I mean all the guys, are gonna snap one day in the future. I think about myself in the future and I'm gonna be bugged.

She said, "You're not bugged, and your father is just a sick man."

But for some reason, somehow, my grandfather wasn't bugged. My grandfather passed away, he wasn't bugged, he just died.

I ask my mother, "What kind of day I'm looking forward to? 'Cause I'm a good candidate to get high blood pressure and diabetes like my father?"

She said, "You're beautiful when you're sober."

You see, Felipe, I'm a nervous person, I'm a tense person. I get upset easily. If I'm working and it doesn't work, I just wanna break what I'm working on. I don't want to get into nothing crazy.

When Primo's father died toward the end of my residence in El Barrio, I was provided with further insight into the traumatic weight of the failed international rural–urban migration in his particular, personal experience of masculinity in crisis. One of Primo's sisters visited their father on his deathbed in the small town in western Puerto Rico where he grew up before seeking his fortune in East Harlem.

My sister said the part where my father's from, Cabo Rojo, is like real poor and it's a little community . . . and, terrible, like . . . fucked up.

She says she saw the house where he was born at. He was raised there as a kid. It was a real old house and . . . and uh . . . it was terrible. Like it's poor there. It's squalor. She didn't like it.

She told me that it looks like those people . . . the people there, were just placed on that spot and left there to just . . .

She said it looked like they probably wake up in the morning, come out of their little shack or house, and they only travel like probably two blocks.

I asked her this question: "Comparing Cabo Rojo to Arroyo – where our family from our mother's side comes from and where I lived when I was fourteen – which is worse?" She says, "Oh yeah, Arroyo is better. It's more exciting."

I perked up at this comparison, having gone myself the previous year to Arroyo to visit Primo's grandmother and to see his roots on his mother's side of the family. The village where his grandmother, cousins, and surviving uncles and aunts were from was a little slip of narrow land covered by a low-rise, concrete, zinc-roofed, public housing project painted drab gray and surrounded claustrophobically by a waving sea of sugar cane. It was hard for me to imagine a community much more depressing than the corner of Arroyo that Primo's grandmother inhabited. Nevertheless, through the shacks and squalor of Cabo Rojo, Primo's sister caught a glimpse of the reservoir of extended family solidarity that somehow endures in marginal corners of rural Puerto Rico.

> She told me that I got people that look like me in Cabo Rojo. She was saying, "Primo, these guys want to meet you. They were expecting you. Primo, they look *just* like you."
>
> They cousins, I guess. They got the same mustache, beard, face. The only thing is that my father got dead hair, so they got long hair, the kind I like, not kinky like mine.
>
> My sister be braiding on one of my cousin's heads so they could look like me. They reminded her of me and my older sister. She was jiving me, saying that if I had hair like them people, I would look like Jesus.
>
> She said they drink; they act cool. They really nice people; they really nice. They just like me. How they joke around, they goof, and the same shit.
>
> But there's not too many jobs around Cabo Rojo. It's kinda hard.

By all accounts Primo's father was a broken man. In the months before his father's death, Primo discussed his memories of him. After the Game Room closed, he would buy a fifteen-dollar vial of powder cocaine and a ten-dollar packet of heroin to sniff speedballs on the back stairs of the Manhattan Center for Science and Mathematics, the magnet high school on 115th Street and the East River Drive.[10] It was as if he were trying to resolve his painful memories of how his father had broken the traditional Puerto Rican taboo of being a disrespected father. For several evenings, we were accompanied by Little Pete because the Social Club had been sealed temporarily by New York City fire marshals for not having a rear emergency exit door. Little Pete's stories of his father's destruction were even sadder than Primo's. Like Primo, he had never had the option of respecting his father either. At the time, both Primo and Little Pete were living as bachelors with their mothers, and neither of them was contributing toward the upkeep of his children.

> *Primo:* My father's a sick man now. He's got diabetes. He's a chronic drinker; he smokes Winstons. One time I dreamt that he was dead.
>
> I mean, he's a *borrachón sucio* [dirty ol' drunkard]. And when he gets drunk he gets violent. So its like he's no fucking good, so why be with him? That's why my mother had to say, "Hike!" [grinning abruptly and jerking his thumb over his shoulder like a baseball umpire calling him out]
>
> And every time I would see my father, once they were separated – 'cause they were never divorced – it was every other week. And he was just like not correct. Always with a beer in his hand. Always drunk and crying.
>
> He didn't get violent with us, but he used to curse all the time. And we used to be by ourselves, and he used to be drinking with old friends, talking shit.
>
> We were kids. We were thinking "Fuck you. I don't care."
>
> He used to buy us candy. And we used to be chillin' with our candy. And then he used to come to me, and ask questions about my mother. And I never wanted to tell on my mother's life, because when I answered his questions, I used to make him cry.
>
> I wasn't stupid. When he used to ask me something, I would just tell him.
>
> Like he would say, "Is your mother with anybody?" I don't remember my answers but I probably used to say "yes," or whatever. He was drunk and stupid.
>
> Maybe he regretted the things that he did. And he could have been better off. I don't remember really too hard. And then he collapses, shakes. I used to hate that.

This particular detail of Primo's father collapsing in a shaking fit of jealousy when his son tells him about his estranged wife's boyfriends is probably a depiction of the same classically Puerto Rican psychosomatic medical condition, *ataque de nervios,* that overcame Candy when she shot Felix. Significantly, these kinds of *ataques,* provoked by jealousy, abuse, or failure in love, are usually confined to women. That Primo's father might engage in such a feminine expression of despair and helplessness in front of his children and close friends illustrates the sense of male impotence he must have felt as a failed migrant in the United States. As if by clockwork in the style of a failed macho, he would recover himself by beating up the nearest vulnerable female whose respect he no longer commanded.

Primo: Then he used to start off fighting with my sister, the oldest one. Later, she would hit me.

Little Pete: [interrupting] I was always scared of my father because he was on hair-ron [heroin]. And he was always high, and I was a little kid, you know. And they told me bad things about him. And they just drew a bad picture about him, and I was scared. And deep down inside, my father was a good man, you know.

When I would see him, he was all high. And then when I grew up, we used to see him on the street, and I'd say, "Hi" to him and I'd say, "Dad, take care of yourself; stop doing this; stop doing that."

And he was good, man. When he was a baby, he was good. I mean, when I was a baby, my father was a merchant marine. He was always on the boat after I was born. It's like, he started using that shit, from the boats. So I was raised by another man, ever since I was six months.

After I grew up and they started telling me, "This is your father," he was already all fucked up. I realized that was my father, regardless. It's sad, though.

My father overdosed. Yeah, he died of dope, you know, heroin.

Primo: [staring out at the East River Drive] All of a sudden, my father stopped coming around. Like I don't even know why. I think he was too sick. He felt ashamed to let us see him like that.

The Material Basis for the Polarization of Intimate Violence

As earlier chapters discussing Candy's life history and the adolescent experiences of Primo and Caesar have demonstrated, the contemporary crisis of patriarchy manifests itself not only in individual self-destruction but also in a polarization of domestic violence and sexual abuse. This painful, seemingly personal pathological phenomenon also needs to be

understood within a historical, political economy context. On the level
of an individual psyche, it might appear to be simply the result of
intergenerationally transmitted patterns of family violence. Such an individualistic psychological reductionist understanding of pathology and
failure, however, does not explain much, and it does not offer realistic
paths for breaking out of these kinds of family "cycles." Primo's earliest
memories of his "nasty, alcoholic [*borrachón sucio*] father" are of him
beating up his mother. Worse yet, all the subsequent men in his mother's
life offered Primo similarly brutal masculine role models.

Primo: When I was a kid I never really liked'ed nobody to be
with my mother. I didn't like any of her men, because I didn't like
it when they would have fits, and hit her; get wild and beat
her down.

I just used to lower my head, and wanna kill them. The only
one of us kids that used to jump in between them, was my older
sister. I never used to get involved. I'm a nervous person, I
can't . . .

When her boyfriends would beat her up, I never used to jump
in. I used to think: The kitchen! The knife! I'm goin' a' kill you."

I used to put my hands up. I remember that a coupla' times.
[slowing his speech pensively] Because sometimes they would go
over the limit, with like, blood.

Philippe: What!

Primo: [reassuringly] But there was never no killing, or nothing
like that involved.

Like maybe, they would give her a black eye, or something like
that. I didn't like it.

[picking up again] What I used to do, was just lock my head
under the pillow, or something, and go, "Ahhhhh, I hate my
mother."

But my sisters, they would jump on the guy, and say, "Fuck
you!" Like that [waving his arms].

And he would chill out. I think if he would have touched my
sisters, then that's like, the end. 'Cause it's like, my mother first;
then my sister; then that's just the end. I think that's what I
woulda done.

[looking up at me in surprise] Matter of fact – this is getting personal; Felipe, your mom's always been with the same pops, right?

Philippe: Not really; you've heard my mother's story. [pausing] It's all right man.

Primo: But it doesn't bother me, speaking to you about this though.

There was another guy when I was still a little kid in the '70s, named Luis, who was dating my mother. He would hurt her, just to hurt her.

She wouldn't leave him alone, even my grandmother was saying, "*Deja ese sinvergüenza* [Leave that shameless good for nothing]."

I found out afterwards, through the years, that on the sneak tip, he used to use drugs. As a matter of fact, he was a junkie.

I still see him on the street, because he works on Third Avenue, in one of those Ay-Rab stores that sells children's toys and other bullshit. But I always pretend I don't know him.

One time he got wild on my mom. The son of a bitch was arguing with my mother, and it escalated.

My mother wanted to call the police to get him out, but he didn't want to leave. I was sleeping, and woke'd up.

That was the only time I got up, and came through for my mother. My mother called the cops, and the motherfucker grabbed a knife. My heart stopped, but I stood in between, after he had made a coupla' swings at my mother.

He had a big knife in his hand, and I thought he was gonna kill me, my mother, everybody. It seemed like he was gonna do it.

But then like, he thought about it, and he just went to the other room. We were all there screaming, and he left.

Primo reproduced this same cycle of brutality when he beat up Candy in front of her children. As I have already noted several times, it is not enough to understand intimate violence in psychological or individualistic terms. For example, many of the crack dealers not only admitted to aspiring to the ideal-type nuclear family but had actually lived in such households for significant periods of time. This usually occurred during their bouts of stable, legal employment. The complex interrelationship between joblessness, personal pathology, family instability, and structural vulnerability in the labor market, came up frequently in the schoolyard conversations about fatherhood that I held with Primo and Little Pete while they sniffed speedballs and drank beer in the troubled months before Primo's father's death.

Primo: I was nineteen when I had my kid. He was born in '83, on May twenty-something. We were teenagers going steady – me and Sandra. I had found a job and stayed steady with her. We got a crib, and I was making good money.

I was a good nigga', boy. Every penny that I used to get was for my hobby, which was radio C.B.-ing. She got pregnant. We didn't really want it. But then I told her, "I'm just as responsible as you are, so if you keep it, I'll take the consequences." So she kept it. It's too bad. But that's all right.

We weren't married. Her parents wanted us to get married. But I knew we were too young, and there's a future: and I wanted more out of life – school and work. Between us two, it was like a struggle. Let's suffer now, and maybe in ten years it will be all right. But it was just about sitting back, and bullshitting. And now she knows.

The only thing I used to complain about, was work, and money, and stuff. And I didn't want to live in that neighborhood in the Bronx for the rest of my life. That apartment was too small.

I'm a perfectionist. I want everything perfect. I used to tell her, "I want you to work too, and get welfare too maybe, while I'm working. Let's pay a baby-sitter so we can save up money to get the hell out of this place here.

And I wasn't selling drugs or doing nothing. I was a goodie, goodie. I had money in the bank, I had money in the house. Sandra never suffered. She was big, and pregnant, and fat.

When Papito was born I was working at U.S. Litho. I was a good nigga'. I had good hours. I was working from four to twelve at nights.

I had stopped sniffing. You know, maybe I would have an occasional beer, but it wasn't like now. I was a hard worker, I was into that overtime. Whatever they give me, I gonna work. I want to bring money to the house.

I noticed my son was growing up. This is how I stopped sniffing: One day, my son wanted to play with me. I was in the rocking chair, and I didn't want to play with him. It was like, "Leave-me-alone" type shit. And I was thinking about it, and I realized it. Plus I bled one time.

One day, I even went down, and bought a dime, and threw it in the toilet bowl. I said, "Nah, this can't be." This ain't me, 'cause I'm always lovable with my kids, singing songs, little school songs that I learned when I was a kid in school. . . .

I used to sit in a rocking chair, reading him his ABC's and numbers, just to keep his mind busy. You got to read to your kids when they're little, like even when they're only months old, so that they always got things in their brain.

Little Pete: [sniffing from the cocaine pile] Yeah, I used to read my son the ABC's even before he had a year.

Yeah, I was good with my family. I was a good nigga'. And I used to say, "My family comes first," and I wouldn't hang and stuff. I was good with my kid. You remember Primo, how I used to dress my kid?"

Primo: Then they changed my hours to two a.m. to ten a.m. I said, "I can't handle them hours; I have a family."

I used to fall asleep on the job; 'cause I had my son. And this girl, Sandra, my son's mother, had found work off the books. And as she was leaving, I was coming in, and my son was on top of me. He wanted to play. He already slept, you know, so I couldn't sleep.

And that's when I started fucking up. That's when I started smoking "woolas" [marijuana cigarettes laced with crack], and I was drinking a little. I was staying up all day, and then I didn't want to go to work.

I was getting high, recovering, and then going to work. Imagine, I was working from two a.m. to ten a.m. They fucked me up, those people at U.S. Litho. If they would have left me at my shift from four to midnight, I would be working there to this day. I was doing good. They fucked up my social life, man, from two a.m. to ten a.m.

Man, it's like, oh, God! I used to come from work; I didn't know whether to go to sleep, or hang out and sleep later. And my son, was there, wide awake; he was two, and wanted to play with me.

So they fired me because I was falling asleep on the job. They said, "We have to let you go because you have a family, and I know you want to be with your family, because you have these hours, and we can't switch you back to the daylight hours. We need somebody for these hours, where you don't seem to fit in."

They were firing everybody; just looking for reasons. It was like business was bad.

After that I went AWOL smoking crack.

You know, Felipe? Now my son is six years old. It gets me sad when I think about shit like that . . . It's like, I'm not there for 'im. Just like my father was never there for me.

And my son loved being with me. Sometimes I was always fixing something in the apartment. So this kid, he used to grab the tools, and just start hammering things, like, look at me, and start trying to do the same thing. I love that shit.

That's why I used to cry a lot when I first left my son. It was only a couple months after they fired me at U.S. Litho.

I used to go to the bathroom and cry like a bitch. 'Cause I knew I was leaving soon and that meant: no more kid.

My wife told me to stay and be her roommate. But, hell no! We were sleeping separate; there was no more love.

I guess we started too young. We got tired of each other. She used to be a bitch. She probably got tired of my dick. That's what I figured.

I told her, "No, I don't want to stay here." And finally she cried. I had to tell her, "We're going to kill each other, so I'm going to go." It was hard for me, you know, but I took my *maleta* [suitcase], and I went.

I moved back to my mother. My mother accepted me with open hands, you know, like, "You're my son."

My son Papito was small at the time, but he noticed it. I had to tell her not to call me, or keep in touch with me for several months, because I couldn't handle it. " 'Cause if you call me, I'm going to feel the same way. And I can't handle it. Let me call you."

Finally, after two, three months, I called. She had a new telephone, because I had cut off the one in my name, and she put in another one. I didn't want anyone else – like some other man – putting bills under my name.

Little Pete: I was twenty when we had the kid. You know why I broke up, 'cause she was rushing me into marriage. I was trying to get it together, so we could move out on our own, and get married, but she was like, desperate.

To my surprise, Primo cut short Little Pete's whining over his previous rocky relationship, with a class analysis of family pathology.

> *Primo:* Basically, when a woman who is poor dedicates herself with a man who's poor too, then something will always go wrong. When you're poor, things just don't work. And when there's a kid involved, then everything just totally fucks up.
> But there's nothing else you can do if you're poor. You try, but it still fucks up. It just doesn't work when you're poor.

In contrast, all of Primo's sisters — he had no brothers — were succeeding by street culture's standards. They all either worked full time at stable entry-level jobs (i.e., managing a McDonald's, managing a clothes boutique, and working as a nurse's aide) or were married in long-term relationships with young children. Primo's pride in their success illustrates not only how rigidly women's roles are defined, but also, once again, how differently they are affected by the experience of growing up poor in El Barrio.

> You know my mom's good! She raised up three beautiful daughters that didn't fuck up.
> Maybe they got married early and bullshit, but there's nothing about drugs in the streets. They know what's good and wrong. My sisters ain't violent. They not in the street — none a' that.
> The only one that got pregnant when she was a teenager was the middle one, but she's doing well. My mother threw her out when she got pregnant, and she had to go to her boyfriend's mother's house until the baby was born.
> And then after the baby was born, my mother was like, "Owwww [raising his arms in celebration]!" That was her first grandchild, and she took it back, and my sister moved back home.
> She left her guy, 'cause he was a fuckin' asshole. And from there, until this day, my mother and her, they're like this [intertwining his index fingers]; they're like buddies.

She's good. She got married now with her other kid's father. And my other sister, she wants to be a nurse.

I'm telling you Felipe, my home life was good. My mother raised me pretty well. She did a great job, even though she doesn't have an education.

Yearning for Fatherhood

On several occasions our conversations focused specifically on how Primo's objectively difficult economic situation was hurting his son at that very moment. The subject catalyzed a wellspring of paternal emotional turmoil for both Little Pete and Primo.

Philippe: Thinking about your father, how does that make you feel about your son right now?

Little Pete: It's a hard question, you askin' us, Felipe, about how we feel about our sons.

Primo: When I think of my son, I wish I was with him. Because right now, he and I are in the same predicament. Because I came from a broken home already.

It's like, I'm not there for him. It's sad and that's why I didn't want my son to go through that. I wanted to grow up with my son. With me and the family.

That's the way it was when I was working. I've told you about it; I was a goodie-goodie. I was sitting back at home. I wasn't into street life then.

Little Pete: Now that you ask this question, Felipe, I hate to answer it. I lived with my wife for five years, and my son is growing up. Now if I was drunk out of my mind [pausing to sniff from one of the envelopes of heroin], and you asked me that question, I'd probably start tearing. Gets me sad.

I mean look, I have a kid right now, and I have nothing! Nothing to offer him for the future. It's like, I'm still growing up. Still trying to get ahead, and yet I want to give a better life to him, but I'm not doing too well; you know, my life is hard.

I have a clear mind and a good heart but, like I said, I fell into drugs. In this environment, it's hard to stay awake. It's hard; it's hard. You know. I know you know it. You've been around us for a while.

Primo: [dipping into the cocaine] My son loves me. He's crazy about me.

Little Pete: [also sniffing cocaine] He wants to live with me, but he's not old enough to choose. But as soon as he's old enough, I'll take it up with the court.

Primo: [switching to heroin] No, I wouldn't take it to court, because I have this understanding with my wife. I can go visit. It took her husband a while for him to understand me and her.

I've sat him down, and I've talked to him. I've told him: "Look I don't want your woman; I wouldn't diss you; I wouldn't disrespect you; I wouldn't do nothing stupid. I'm only here for my son."

But there's still that feeling of, "Fuck you, Primo, don't come around."

Sandra, my ex-wife, told me that when I'm there, he just covers up, but that afterwards, they fight.

[energized by a cocaine rush] But you know what, man! I believe in . . . I believe that when you're with someone, and you have a child, you should make the fucking best of it, whether you're doing good or not. You gotta make a commitment.

It always seems like I'm full of shit when I say things like that, 'cause I don't support my kid, but that's because, I . . . right now, I'm not supporting my son, but . . .

[mellowing on a heroin ebb] Matter of fact, you know last weekend, when we were talking one time about the last time we had cried, that's the last time I teared, was last weekend. I was thinking about my little nigga'. I was supposed to keep him for the weekend, but I called too late. I fucked up. It was a hassle.

[perking up again] Matter of fact, I remember my father once saying to my mother that he used to cry, because he misses me, because I'm his only son.

But I want to get Papito to come here, so he can see what I'm all about. But I think the best thing is for him . . .

[mumbling confusedly] I don't know, man. I don't know . . .

Little Pete: [morosely on a heroin lull] I got two credit cards, MasterCard, Visa, I got Citicard. I'm applying for Macy's, but I'm not a success. Yeah, I am, and I'm not. I mean, I got laid off at work.

But don't you understand that I'm not together with my woman; I'm not together with my child; and I'm not settled like I was before.

[sniffing cocaine] When I was with my woman and my kid, I had no time to think about drugs; no time to think about hanging out. You know I just wanted to be there with my people.

[energized] They say a woman makes a man, and a man makes a woman. My wife helped me out a lot. She was very good to me. Very good when I was with her. Then, when we broke up, I went through a lot of mishaps, you know. Like I became lazy.

Primo: [still in a lull] My father was an alcoholic, and he beat down my mom every time he got drunk. So they just got separated, you know.

[energized] But it's like it's okay. That didn't really affect my growing up.

[calm again] The only thing I could say, that could affect the family, is the lack of true parents for a child, when there's only one parent there's something missing. I really think so.

I mean, we always wondered why he wasn't around. And I felt bad too.

Philippe: And what about what you're doing to your son Papito now? Do you think that you're repeating the relationship of your father between you and your son?

Primo: No, no, because I don't even remember being with my father anyway.

Philippe: Doesn't your son miss you?

Primo: [swigging from a pint of Bacardi] Of course! My son wants to be near me.

Like I was talking to him last Sunday and I spoke to him and I said, "Look, I'm going to give you my phone number, get a paper and pencil. I want you to call me Friday, when you get out of school, so you can spend some time with me."

He said, "Hold on, Daddy," and he told his moms immediately after I had told him. He said, "Hold on. Hold on." Then he called out [covering an invisible phone receiver, and imitating a child's voice], "Mom, my daddy said, that on Friday, when I get out of school, that I gotta call him, and he's going to come pick me up, so I can be with him in Manhattan."

He was happy, boy! Right now he must be thinking about it, because I wasn't at home to get his call, and I didn't pick him up. I didn't want to disappoint him, and now I can't call, because I don't got carfare, and his mother's not going to come bring him to me. She's going to say, "You come pick him up." And he's going to be, "Oh, Daddy, you told me . . . HHHHHHUUU" [makes crying sound].

I cry too, when I think back to the days when I was living with my kid. Now I feel bad, 'cause a few days away from today, it's Papito's birthday, and I'm not gonna give him anything. I don't got the money.

Philippe: You wouldn't rather have those twenty-five dollars you just paid for the dope [heroin] and the *perico* [cocaine], to spend on your son's birthday present instead?

Primo: Well, if I was to have the money, if it was there, well then I would do it. But once I'm out here on the streets, and that's just, like . . . what I have . . . I'll spend it; I'll fuck it up.

Little Pete: [interrupting] Like right now, I'm not working. But when I was working I used to mail my wife a money order every month. My wife gave my social security number to the court, but they didn't have to take the money out of my check. I used to mail it to them.

Primo: I'm not good with money, anyway. I won't see him this weekend, because I'm broke. I could have him every weekend if I wanted it. But I don't want it like that. 'Cause once I see him one weekend, I like to have the next one for me.

Naah, I'll definitely get him a present. I love that nigga'.

Primo never bought Papito his seven-year-old birthday present. In fact, he did not even go visit him that week. Coincidentally, during these same days in front of my tenement stoop, my pre-teenage neighbors, Manny and Angel, provided me with glimpses of the flip side of the father–son generation gap. Eyes sparkling, Angel told me proudly, "I'm going to see my father this weekend." His little brother Manny immediately responded with his eyes dark and sad, "I'm not gonna see my father." As if by script, just moments later on the sidewalk in front of our stoop, we saw another little boy nicknamed Papito, who was my neighbor's three-year-old son, shrieking with delight. A twenty-year-old man swaggered up almost embarrassedly to hug the little boy, mumbling affectionately "*Ay mi hijo* [Oh, my son]," while the mother watched expressionlessly. Papito's father had just been allowed out of prison for the afternoon on a drug rehabilitation–work release arrangement. An hour or so later, little Papito was screeching again, but this time in pain. His father had to leave in a rush in order to report back to prison before dusk. The superintendent of our tenement later explained to me that Papito's father was the person who had burglarized Papito's mother's apartment two and a half years ago when Papito was only six months old. Papito's father had known the apartment was empty because he was supposed to be meeting his son, Papito, in the park at the time. His new girlfriend served as lookout while he stole the VCR and television from his son's apartment.

Meanwhile, a few hours past midnight, back on the steps overlooking the East River Drive, Little Pete waxed emotional on a cocaine rush within the roller-coaster ecstasy of the contradictory ebbs and flows of his speedball high. He jumped up to celebrate what appeared to me, at the time, to be a historical vestige of his parents' idealized jíbaro past:

> *Little Pete:* If I was sixty years old right now, you know what really make me, wanna be alive, is that I would wanna be there for my kids.
>
> You know what really make me be there, and hang in strong? *My kids.* I would want to be there for my kids. I would want to love my kids. I would want to teach my kids. That's the only thing. And I swear to God. And it's coming from my heart. That's the only thing that would make me stay alive, and have *ánimo* [spirit]; to stay around; to survive; is my kids.

When Primo's father finally died, Caesar and I took him, once again, behind the local high school to help him grieve. He lifted several scoopfuls of cocaine into his nose, using the edge of a folded matchbook cover, and spoke to us in a sober, halting tone:

Primo: I act like nothing, but I feel sad inside. You know, I started thinking about it, my father didn't see none of his grandchildren. I just felt like . . . like a little part of me just went away.

But my mother took it like nothing, because my father wasn't good to my mother, he was a nasty motherfucker; used to hit her; get drunk; and diss the shit out of her.

Caesar: Yeah, when my grandpa died too, my grandmother didn't care. She said, "If he dies, fuck it! 'Cause he wasn't really good."

Primo: Maria was there too, when my sister called, to tell us he died.

Maria told me like this, "You, and your mother are taking it like it was nothing."

I told her, "What you want me to do? If I start crying right now, that's not going to bring him back. The only way I could keep him alive, is by thinking about him, in my mind, you know. That's it. And I haven't seen him for so long."

If he would've been part of my life for all these years, I would've been hysterical, but it's been so long, you know. It's just that I feel sad in my heart, but not . . .

Caesar: Yeah, if my father was to die. It be like nothing to me, "Hey, bury him." I mean, I didn't ever know him, or nothing; so I don't have no feelings towards him. I ain't angry at my father. He was just an impossible pops. And that was a long time ago, and that's it.

Now if my step-pops passed away, I would feel for him, because he's my Pops to me. I grew up with him; he was around me.

I don't see him, as much now, as I used to, but . . . he was a part of my life when I was little, so I would feel for him. Because to me, he's always going to be my Poppy.

I call him, "Poppy," right now, as big as I am. To me, I always say, "Yo, there's my Poppy." That was my Pop, I loved that man.[11]

But he's wild too. I mean he never treated me bad, man. I never remember him hitting me all that much. He only got stingy with me when I got big.

Primo: Yeah, my pa was a stingy motherfucker, but I never had nothing against him.

Caesar: Yeah, now my Pops is like, "Get a job, already" and shit.

Primo: [morosely again] I told my sister to take pictures of our father, like in the coffin, but she told me that she don't want to, because it's sad. I told her I'd develop the roll.

Caesar: It must have been a superstition thing. That runs in my family too.

Primo: Yeah, she flipped on me. It must have been my father's sister that scooped her with all her *"espiritismo"* [Santería beliefs], because she took pictures of my mother's side of the family, when my great-grandmother passed away; and she took pictures of my grandfather when he passed away; and she took pictures of my cousin . . .

I mean she didn't have to take pictures in the hospital, when my father was going to have tubes and stuff; but in the coffin, so I could see him when they buried him, like if I was there.

I was jolted out of Primo's mourning by a wave of panic when I saw a half-dozen young men walking across the East River Drive coming toward us, and I realized it was at least 3:00 a.m. and there were more of them than us. A year earlier, a thirty-five-year-old homeless man had been killed with baseball bats, knives, and a meat cleaver along this same East River esplanade, and a few months later the body of a thirteen-year-old new immigrant from Colombia was found raped, strangled, and stabbed to death at the same spot.[12] Looking at Primo tearing in the darkness, and Caesar hunched over glumly under a sweatshirt hood, I realized I was probably safe. My companions automatically inspired a reciprocal fear in anyone who might think of mugging us at this hour of the night, in an isolated setting such as this one. Nevertheless, I could not stop myself from muttering nervously, "Yo, static [motioning at the oncoming youths with my chin]. You think it's dangerous here?" Primo simply responded gently and calmly, "No." He and Caesar could be completely secure in their hoodlum-like demeanor.

Accommodating Patriarchy

Most of the wives and girlfriends of Ray's employees eventually broke their abusive relationships and expelled their men from their households. They usually went on, however, to fall in love with a new man who was equally insolvent and irresponsible toward their children. This process of serial household formation has spawned a street culture logic that partially exonerates fathers from the responsibility of maintaining progeny. Candy used to argue with me when I "dissed" the men around us for failing to support their children.

> *Candy:* You don't understand, Felipe. Some men are just like that. It doesn't mean they are very bad fathers. Maybe they don't got a job and they don't support their kid right now. But maybe they will support him some other day.
>
> And suppose the mother's got another man. I mean, I'll be damned, if I'm a man, and if I'll be giving a woman money to support another nigga'. Just because she wants — excuse my language — sex pleasure; or just because she wants to be with another guy.
>
> Because let me tell you something, if your woman got kids, and you got the woman, then you gotta take the whole package completely.
>
> [smiling at Primo over the slang term "package," meaning vagina] It's a whole package deal. Whoever wants me, gotta take my whole package deal. All five of us. Me and my four kids.
>
> My man better not come to me and say, "I'm not going to give you no twenty dollars for your little girl's shoes . . . That's not my kid." No, no, no, you want the package [grabbing her crotch with both hands and making us roar with laughter], you pay for the whole package deal [pointing at two of her children, Junior who was pushing Lillian in a baby carriage by the Game Room stoop].
>
> I mean I haven't gotten involved with another man lately, because people wants everything for nothing. I don't go like that. Meat is too expensive. [knocking Primo's arm into his crotch] Do you hear me? Meat is too expensive. [giggles]

I frequently heard this kind of refrain legitimizing the formation of serial households by both men and women. Luis, for example, righteously berated the mothers of his children whenever they asked him for money.

> I tell them, "Whoever be with you; they have better look out for my kids. Because they ain't going to get your pussy for free."

Because you know, if you going out with a lady, it's just common sense: If she got other kids, you look out for them. Just because they ain't yours, doesn't mean you got to dish [diss] them.

I went out with this lady on 104th Street for three years; she got five kids; none of them are mine; and I used to look out for them, bro. On school days, I used to buy them their first day of school clothes, and all that shit. You shoulda seen me, how I was stealing car radios, like a madman. Breaking into cars – getting three, four, five radios in one night – just to buy them new sneakers.

Now there are some women that say, "Fuck it. As long as he loves me, he doesn't have to love my kids." No way, man. I say, "Boy . . . if you don't love my kids you don't love me. Fuck you!"

There some men that'll hit a woman's kids, and they ain't even their father!

Although many of the dealers often claimed publicly to be merely parasites on their girlfriends' resources – *catcheteando* – they in fact often contributed significant resources during moments of crisis or celebration. Indeed, there might be a material basis, as well as emotional and cultural ones, for Candy's accommodation to machismo. Given the available men in her life, her only other alternative would be to live in isolation as a single mother with her children. Her interpretation is even more militant, a female-essentialist celebration of mother love. Ultimately, her interpretation provides her with greater autonomy over her sex life and household resources.

Candy: You don't understand Felipe. Those are our kids, we carry them in our stomach. Sure, I feel a father's responsibility is to support his kids when he's together with his wife. But when he leaves, the mother has to support her kids, because kids feel more towards us – their mothers – because we are the ones having them. We get the pain; the feeling is inside our stomach.

All the man does is – excuse my way of saying this – is just give us sperm and that's it. But we're the ones really risking our *lives* to have kids, because it's not easy to have a baby. Okay? It's painful; it's hard; it's a matter of life and death.

So do you think I'm going to go through that, and just, leave the responsibility to the father?

No! It's *my* kid. I had him in there [pointing to her stomach]. It's like a part of my own body. You know, just taking a piece of your own body, and putting it out there.

Candy's celebration of motherhood is paralleled by her celebration of a father's patriarchal rights, even when he does not support or love his children.

> *Candy:* If the father leaves the kids, you know, it's bad enough that the kid is neglected by a father. So why do you want to teach a kid to hate a father? It's enough for a kid, not to have a parent, not to have a father, right? I ain't gonna say, "Your father's a bastard, he's no good."
>
> You know what happens? They wind up turning against the mother. It's going to make them hate me, for reminding them, how bad their father is. Let them learn on their own.

Perhaps Candy was simply realistic about the embeddedness of the male prerogative in everyday life. Confronting patriarchy from a position of powerlessness wreaks havoc on the psyches of children when they are conditioned culturally to respect male authority unconditionally. Candy's efforts to include men in her life by accommodating male prerogatives over children were not reciprocated, however. After Felix was jailed, for example, Caesar cited the absence of a man in her household as proof that her qualities as a mother were flawed. It was a Catch-22 triumph of of old-fashioned patriarchal logic.

> *Caesar:* Candy ain't no fuckin' fine example. She ain't no Leave-it-to-Beaver mom. She don't know shit about raising kids. Just 'cause she got five kids don't mean she know how to raise them.
>
> If Candy's such a good parent, she'll have a husband right? Because if you're really a good parent, you're supposed to be two parents.
>
> Why doesn't she have a husband?

9

CONCLUSION

Ooh, Felipe! You make us sound like such sensitive crack dealers.

Caesar [commenting on the manuscript]

There is no panacea for the suffering and self-destruction of the protagonists in these pages. Solutions to inner-city poverty and substance abuse
framed in terms of public policy often appear naive or hopelessly idealis-
tic. Given the dimensions of structural oppression in the United States,
it is atheoretical to expect isolated policy initiatives, or even short-term
political reforms, to remedy the plight of the poor in U.S. urban centers
in the short or medium term. Racism and class segregation in the United
States are shaped in too complex a mesh of political-economic structural
forces, historical legacies, cultural imperatives, and individual actions to
be susceptible to simple solutions.

There are also the inevitable limits of political feasibility. For a number
of complicated historical and ideological reasons the United States simply
lacks the political will to address poverty in any concerted manner.
Nevertheless, I hope my presentation of the experience of social marginalization in El Barrio, as seen through the struggles for dignity and
survival of Ray's crack dealers and their families, contributes on a concrete practical level to calling attention to the tragedy of persistent
poverty and racial segregation in the urban United States. I cannot resign
myself to the terrible irony that the richest industrialized nation on earth,
and the greatest world power in history, confines so many of its citizens
to poverty and to prison. In these final pages, consequently, I address
some of the short-term public policy debates, even if ultimately they

prove to be nothing but sideshows for confronting long-term structural problems.[1]

Confronting Racial and Class Inequality – Instead of Drugs

Substance abuse is perhaps the dimension of inner-city poverty most susceptible to short-term policy intervention. In part, this is because drugs are not the root of the problems presented in these pages; they are the epiphenomenonal expression of deeper, structural dilemmas. Self-destructive addiction is merely the medium for desperate people to internalize their frustration, resistance, and powerlessness. In other words, we can safely ignore the drug hysterias that periodically sweep through the United States. Instead we should focus our ethical concerns and political energies on the contradictions posed by the persistence of inner-city poverty in the midst of extraordinary opulence. In the same vein, we need to recognize and dismantle the class- and ethnic-based apartheids that riddle the U.S. landscape.

The crack–cocaine–heroin epidemics of the late-1980s through mid-1990s, however, have been qualitatively worse than the narcotics and alcohol scourges of most previous generations. The contemporary exacerbation of substance abuse within concentrated pockets of the U.S. population has little or nothing to do with the pharmacological properties of the particular drugs involved. Indeed, history teaches us that the effect, or at least the meanings, of drug use are largely culturally constructed. Most important, in the United States they articulate with class inequalities and racial–ideological hierarchies. To reiterate: The problem of substance abuse in the United States is worse in the 1990s than in the recent past because of a polarization of the structural roots that generate self-destructive behavior and criminal activity. The economic base of the traditional working class has eroded throughout the country. Greater proportions of the population are being socially marginalized. The restructuring of the world economy by multinational corporations, finance capital, and digital electronic technology, as well as the exhaustion of social democratic models for public sector intervention on behalf of the poor, have escalated inequalities around class, ethnicity, and gender.[2]

The 1990 U.S. Census reveals sharp bifurcations in socioeconomic status at the margins of society. This is part of a longer-term trend between 1968 and 1992, when poverty rose by one-third in the United States. More specifically, the poorest sectors of the population during these years experienced the greatest increment in poverty levels at the same time that the rich increased their relative numbers by 40 percent. Children suffered the most, with an almost 100 percent increase in the number of children living below the official poverty line between 1968 and 1992.[3] Polarization occurred at all levels, both across class and within ethnic groups. For example, while the aggregate socioeconomic statistics for many ethnic groups, including Puerto Ricans, improved during the 1980s, this masked internal class, gender, and regional increases in inequality and social suffering. The class stratification of African-Americans has already been well documented. The same phenomenon is emerging among Puerto Ricans living in the United States.[4] This assumes a regional dynamic as well. Puerto Ricans residing in New York City are considerably poorer than Puerto Ricans in most other parts of the mainland United States.[5] Even within New York City there has been an increasing polarization of social inequality among Puerto Ricans along class, gender, and generational lines. For example, during the 1980s, at the same time that Puerto Rican household incomes rose by 28.5 percent in New York City, Puerto Rican female-headed households with children lost 6.1 percent of their incomes, and elderly household incomes decreased by 7.6 percent. Married Puerto Ricans in New York dramatically increased their incomes by 40.6 percent to a figure that is almost 70 percent higher than the median Puerto Rican family income. Perhaps most significantly, more than half of New York City's Puerto Rican children remained below the official poverty line, as did 38 percent of all Puerto Rican New Yorkers as a whole.[6]

These secular trends in the polarization of U.S. poverty as well as the longer-term transformations in the structure of the world economy need to be related back to the public policy debates I promised to broach in the opening paragraphs of this conclusion – specifically, substance abuse. Any realistic attempt to address the "drug problem" has to alter the economic imbalance between the rewards of the legal economy versus those of the underground economy. In the case of narcotics retail sales – the biggest equal opportunity employer for males in the street economy – this requires a two-pronged attack: (1) The economic dynamism of the drug economy must be reduced; and (2) the fragility and hostility of the entry-level legal labor market needs to be transformed.

In terms of concrete, short-term public policy, the single cheapest and simplest way to wipe out the material basis for the most violent and criminal dimensions of street culture is to destroy the profitability of narcotic trafficking by decriminalizing drugs. Experts estimate it costs approximately $8 to $10 to produce an ounce of pure powder cocaine.[7] This same ounce in East Harlem is worth more than $2,000, once it is adulterated and packaged into $10 quarter-gram vials. This extraordinary $1,990 profit represents the economic incentive for participation in the most violent and destructive facet of the underground economy. Ironically, therefore, decriminalization would make drugs less accessible to youths on inner-city streets because it would no longer be worthwhile for dealers to hawk their wares in small quantities on street corners. Street dealers would be forced out of business by the laws of neoclassical economics. If illicit drugs were decriminalized, youths walking to school every day in East Harlem would no longer be bombarded with offers of psychotropic stimulants because the retail sale of drugs would no longer be so extraordinarily profitable. The government would also not have to waste billions of dollars prosecuting and confining drug users in ridiculously inefficient and expensive prisons. Violent crime, property theft, and medical costs would be dramatically reduced once addicts no longer had to pay exorbitant sums for their daily doses. Dealers would also no longer have such high profits to fight over. The alternative, of course, is to lock everyone up. Incarceration is not only prohibitively expensive, but it cannot be accomplished without violating individual human rights. In the 1990s, the United States already bore the shame of having the highest per capita incarceration rate in the world. The U.S. prison population increased threefold from 1980 through 1994.[8]

Decriminalization of drugs in a vacuum would not significantly reduce violence and self-destruction in the inner city so long as it remains so difficult in the United States for high school and college dropouts to earn a dignified subsistence income by legal means. The private sector and the free market over the past several generations have proven themselves incapable of generating materially and emotionally rewarding entry-level jobs. Aggressive political intervention is necessary to promote economic opportunities for the marginal working class. Another simpler and shorter-term solution would be to dismantle the hostile bureaucratic maze that punishes the poor for working legally. This means that transfer payments for obvious human needs – which are taken for granted in almost all other industrialized nations in the world – such as health, shelter, education, and nutrition – should not be rigidly penalized when an impoverished household reports supplemental legal income. Once again, dozens of concrete policy initiatives come to mind that would help to rebalance the incentives for pursuing legal careers instead of illegal ones – from allowing the unemployed workers to be enrolled in educational programs while they receive their unemployment stipends, to continuing food stamp payments, income subsidies, and Medicaid eligibility to individuals and households that leave public assistance and enter the labor market. In the long term this would allow mainstream society to benefit from the immense brain drain and crushed human potential within the cohorts of energetic, entrepreneurial inner-city youths who choose to bank on drugs rather than on minimum-wage jobs. The "American Dream" of upward mobility has to be reinvented by boosting the credibility of the legal economy as an alternative to crime. On a theoretical level, it is clear that no society is propelled by "values" alone. From a practical perspective, it is simply unrealistic, in the highly materialistic context of the larger U.S. culture, to deny the straightforward economic logic of criminal enterprise. Concrete, material alternatives have to be available to motivated youths who live in poverty if anything is to change.

The increasing material and political powerlessness of the working poor in the United States needs to become a central concern. The concentration of poverty, substance abuse, and criminality within inner-city enclaves such as East Harlem is the product of state policy and free market forces that have inscribed spatially the rising levels of social inequality discussed earlier. More subtly, this urban decay expresses itself in the growing polarization around street culture in North America, giving rise to what some observers call a "crisis in U.S. race relations." Middle-class society and its elites increasingly have been able to disassociate themselves from the ethnically distinct, urban-based working poor and unemployed who inhabit the inner city. Budget cuts and fiscal austerity have accelerated the trend toward public sector breakdown in impoverished urban neighborhoods, while services improve, or at least stay the same, in Anglo-dominated, wealthy suburban communities.

Public sector breakdown in El Barrio. Photo by Philippe Bourgois.

The psychological-reductionist and cultural-essentialist analyses of social marginalization that pass for common sense in the United States
frame solutions to racism and poverty around short-term interventions
that target the "bad attitude" of individuals. The biggest sociological
unit for most poverty policy intervention, for example, is the nuclear
family. Job training programs emphasize attitude and personal empowerment. Seminars designed to promote multicultural sensitivity are fashionable in both public and private sector institutions. While these initiatives are not harmful, and might even help superficially on the margins,
it is the institutionalized expression of racism – America's de facto
apartheid and inner-city public sector breakdown – that government
policy and private sector philanthropy need to address if anything is ever
to change significantly in the long run.

In other words, to draw on a classic metaphor from sports, the United States needs to level its playing field. Concretely, this means that the garbage needs to be picked up, schools have to teach, and laws must be enforced, as effectively in Latino/a, African-American, Asian, and Native American communities as they are in white, middle-class suburbs. There is nothing particularly complicated or subtle about remedying the unequal provision of public funds and services across class and ethnic lines. Hundreds of short-term policy and legal reforms immediately jump to mind: from tax reform – namely, taxing the home mortgages of the upper middle class, and exempting the federal and state transfer benefits of the poor – to streamlining access to social welfare benefits and democratizing educational institutions – namely, universal affordable health care coverage, free day care, equalizing per capita funding for schools and universities, and so on.

Hip Hop Jíbaro: Toward a Politics of Mutual Respect

One message the crack dealers communicated clearly to me is that they are not driven solely by simple economic exigency. Like most humans on earth, in addition to material subsistence, they are also searching for dignity and fulfillment. In the Puerto Rican context this incorporates cultural definitions of *respeto* built around a personal concern for autonomy, self-assertion, and community within constantly changing social hierarchies of statuses based on kinship, age, and gender. Complex cultural and social dimensions that extend far beyond material and logistical requirements have to be addressed by poverty policies if the socially marginal in the United States are ever going to be able to demand, and earn, the respect that mainstream society needs to share with them for its own good. Specifically, this means evaluating how public policy initiatives and the more impersonal political economy forces of the larger society interact with rapidly changing cultural definitions of gender and family. Women, children, and the elderly constitute most of the poor in the United States. Public policy intervention consequently should prioritize the needs of women and children instead of marginalizing them. Most important, poor women should not be forced to seek desperate alliances with men in order to stay sheltered, fed, clothed, and healthy. Current welfare policy explicitly encourages mothers to seek men with unreported illegal income. In this vein, the lack of safe, affordable child care in the United States contradictorily encourages mothers to stay at home and have more babies rather than seek careers in the legal economy, because anything they might earn goes to pay for private baby-sitters.

Almost none of the policy recommendations I have made so far are politically feasible in the United States in the short or medium term. I only attempt to raise them for discussion in the hope that in the inevitable ebbs, flows, and ruptures around popular support for new political approaches to confronting poverty, ethnic discrimination, and gender inequality in the coming years, some of these ideas could be dragged into the mainstream of public debates, and that maybe bits and pieces of them could be instituted over the coming decades in one form or another. Once again, on a deeper level, the U.S. common sense, which blames victims for their failures and offers only individualistic psychologically rooted solutions to structural contradictions has to be confronted and changed. We have to break out of the dead-end political debates between liberal politicians, who want to flood the inner city with psychiatric social workers or family therapists, and conservatives, who simply want to build bigger prisons, cut social welfare spending, and decrease taxes for big business and the wealthy. The fact that Head Start is widely considered to be the most successful poverty intervention program indicates the banality of policy debates in the United States. Essentially, Head Start seeks to take inner-city preschoolers who live in lead-painted, rat-infested tenements without steady heat or hot water, and metamorphose them into bright-eyed, upper-middle-class overachievers. It illustrates well the long-term inadequacy of policy initiatives that focus on individual symptoms of social misery, such as low self-esteem, violent persona, or deficient academic skills, instead of addressing the material and political forces that generate the neglect, battery, or hunger of children in economically fragile families. The painful symptoms of inner-city apartheid will continue to produce record numbers of substance abusers, violent criminals, and emotionally disabled and angry youths if nothing is done to reverse the trends in the United States since the late 1960s around rising relative poverty rates and escalating ethnic and class segregation.

Given the bleak perspectives for policy reform at the federal level, on the one hand, or for political mobilization in the U.S. inner city, on the other, my most immediate goal in this book is to humanize the public enemies of the United States without sanitizing or glamorizing them. In documenting the depths of personal pain that are inherent to the experience of persistent poverty and institutional racism, I hope to contribute to our understanding of the fundamental processes and dynamics of oppression in the United States. More subtly, I also want to place drug dealers and street-level criminals into their rightful position within the mainstream of U.S. society. They are not "exotic others" operating in an irrational netherworld. On the contrary, they are "made in America." Highly motivated, ambitious inner-city youths have been attracted to the rapidly expanding, multibillion-dollar drug economy during the 1980s and 1990s precisely because they believe in Horatio Alger's version of the American Dream.[9]

Like most other people in the United States, drug dealers and street criminals are scrambling to obtain their piece of the pie as fast as possible. In fact, in their pursuit of success they are even following the minute details of the classical Yankee model for upward mobility. They are aggressively pursuing careers as private entrepreneurs; they take risks, work hard, and pray for good luck. They are the ultimate rugged individualists braving an unpredictable frontier where fortune, fame, and destruction are all just around the corner, and where the enemy is ruthlessly hunted down and shot. In the specifically Puerto Rican context, resistance to mainstream society's domination and pride in street culture identity resonates with a reinvented vision of the defiant jíbaro who refused to succumb to elite society's denigration under Spanish and U.S. colonialism. The hyper-urban reconstruction of a hip-hop version of the rural jíbaro represents the triumph of a newly constituted Puerto Rican cultural assertion among the most marginalized members of the Puerto Rican diaspora. The tragedy is that the material base for this determined search for cultural respect is confined to the street economy.

At the same time, there is nothing exotically Puerto Rican about the triumphs and failures of the protagonists of this book. On the contrary, "mainstream America" should be able to see itself in the characters presented on these pages and recognize the linkages. The inner city represents the United States' greatest domestic failing, hanging like a Damocles sword over the larger society. Ironically, the only force preventing this suspended sword from falling is that drug dealers, addicts, and street criminals internalize their rage and desperation. They direct their brutality against themselves and their immediate community rather than against their structural oppressors. From a comparative perspective, and in a historical context, the painful and prolonged self-destruction of people like Primo, Caesar, Candy, and their children is cruel and unnecessary. There is no technocratic solution. Any long-term paths out of the quagmire will have to address the structural and political economic roots, as well as the ideological and cultural roots of social marginalization. The first step out of the impasse, however, requires a fundamental ethical and political reevaluation of basic socioeconomic models and human values.

EPILOGUE

Sometimes at night I stand in front of my son. I just look at him, and I cry. I be thinking: "I don't deserve such a good little nigga'. And besides Felipe, what's gonna happen to him? I'm twenty-six years old already. I mean, I don't know what the fuck I'm doing in life. I don't got no direction. You gotta help me Felipe – please!

Caesar

I returned to New York City during the spring and part of the summer and fall of 1994 to make the final revisions on this manuscript and prepare this epilogue. As it goes to press:

Primo has not sold drugs for more than three years and has cut his ties to Ray. He no longer sniffs cocaine or even drinks alcohol. As a matter of fact, on one occasion when an acquaintance from the Game Room insisted on buying him a beer, he discreetly poured it into the gutter.

For the third summer in a row, Primo has found a temporary job, earning $500 a week before taxes, as a night porter in a luxury high-rise condominium building on the Upper East Side. He is replacing the full-time, unionized night porters who go on vacation during the summer months. Primo missed several days of work when he was hospitalized for a week because of an asthma attack precipitated by an allergic reaction to debris he cleaned up in the condominium building's maintenance–repair facility. Primo persuaded his doctors not to "write him up for asthma," because he fears that management will not hire him on a full-time basis, due to his medical condition.

Primo's only outstanding legal problem is caused by a collection agency attempting to recover the money he borrowed to pay for the tuition of the maintenance-engineer vocational training institute that went bankrupt and never issued him a graduation certificate. The interest on his original $2,400 loan has raised his debt to more than $4,000. The collection agency seized $1,700, the full amount of his 1994 income tax refund.

Maria asked Primo to move out of her household because of his sexual involvement with another woman. Primo now lives in his mother's high-rise housing project apartment along with his oldest sister. Despite breaking up with Maria, Primo visits her regularly and has a close, warm relationship with his youngest son, three-year-old *Primo Jr.,* whom he frequently takes out for walks.

Primo's fifty-nine-year-old mother has AIDS and is suffering from dementia. He wonders if the fact that her brain has been affected is related to a battering she received several years ago from a boyfriend who beat her unconscious with a New York City police lock, "you know those long metal bars that come up from the floor and lean against the middle of a door to keep it from getting bashed in – that's what he hit her with." She suffered a serious concussion and the doctors warned her at that time of possible long-term neurological complications.

New York City Housing Authority inspectors took advantage of Primo's mother's mental vulnerability and arranged to interview her in private in order to document the amount of her son's income and his dates of residence in her apartment. They are threatening to institute collection procedures for several thousand dollars in recalculated back rent to reflect Primo's undeclared legal income.

Primo also worries about the safety and welfare of his eleven-year-old son, *Papito,* who failed fifth grade in a parochial school in the South Bronx, where he lives with his mother and his three half brothers and sisters. For four months, Papito's mother, *Sandra,* forbade Primo from seeing Papito after Primo's mother reported her to the Bureau for Child Welfare (BCW) when Papito took shelter in her apartment following a beating by Sandra's newest boyfriend, the father of her fourth child. This tension, however, defused sufficiently for Papito to spend six weeks at Primo's mother's apartment during the summer.

Maria lost her subsidized apartment and was forced to move back with her young son into her alcoholic mother's project apartment. She is determinedly looking for her own, independent place, but has not been able to save enough money to pay for the security deposit for an apartment in a private tenement building. After several attempts at working at fast-food restaurants – including at a McDonald's managed by Primo's oldest sister – Maria continues to receive welfare and food stamps. Primo voluntarily provides her with child support payments when he is working legally, but this does not change her economic situation significantly as his cash contributions are monitored by New York City's Family Court and are deducted from the payments Maria receives for food stamps and from Aid to Families with Dependent Children. Although Maria hopes eventually to be reunited with Primo in a conjugal household, she refuses to let him live with her until he commits himself to long-term sexual fidelity.

Caesar no longer sells drugs. He continues to receive a monthly SSI check and lives with *Carmen,* their three-and-a-half-year-old son, *Caesar Jr.,* Carmen's seven-year-old son, *Papo,* and her nine-year-old daughter, *Ruby,* in his grandmother's former project apartment opposite the Game Room. *Caesar's grandmother,* who is now in the advanced stages of Alzheimer's disease, left the old-age home where she had been interned and moved into her younger sister's nearby tenement apartment.

Caesar continues to smoke most of his SSI checks during once-a-month crack binges. He also sniffs heroin regularly. Carmen supplements her welfare check by selling Avon products. The household was recently visited by an inspector from the BCW when a public school teacher reported Carmen's eldest daughter, Ruby, for exhibiting signs of psychological and physical abuse. Apparently Ruby is deeply depressed and never talks in class. Carmen periodically takes refuge at her sister Maria's house with her children to escape Caesar's beatings.

When my wife and I visited Caesar and Carmen, their youngest son, Caesar Jr., joined us in the living room and exhibited the vitality of a healthy, happy three-year-old. His older brother and sister, however, were "visiting their father's grandmother in Florida." This was in early June when school was still in session, so they may be shifting their permanent household to their father's kin because of their stepfather's abuse.

Caesar came to a Father's Day party at Maria's project apartment. He arrived with Carmen and their son, Caesar Jr., who had a fresh bruise on his right cheekbone that Caesar and Carmen say comes from falling off of a bed. Caesar left the party early when he became angry at Primo for refusing to lend him money to buy heroin. In May, Carmen placed Caesar on a waiting list for admittance to a drug treatment program run by Phoenix House. Caesar agreed to intern himself in the facility, but when treatment spaces had still not been made available by August, Carmen finally threw Caesar out of the household after he sold their television set. His aunt paid for his train ticket to visit another aunt in Ocala, Florida, hoping this will keep him away from crack.

Candy no longer sells drugs or works. She suffered a grave disappointment upon graduating from her court-ordered nurse's aide training course when the downtown podiatry office where she found a job proved to be "a bunch of scandalous, conniving schemers." They specialized in diagnosing fictitious ailments and operating needlessly on people's feet. This enabled them to submit padded bills to Medicaid and other, private, insurance companies. Candy lasted almost a year before becoming too disgusted to continue with her employer's illegal antics. She did not, however, miss any welfare payments as she had been working under her false social security number.

Candy continues to live with her husband, *Felix,* and four of their five children in the same high-rise project apartment. Both Candy and Felix drink and use cocaine on weekends, but Felix supposedly no longer beats Candy. According to Primo, "No way! Felix don't hit Candy. That nigga' learned his lesson, boy." Candy also became the foster parent for two of *Luis* and *Wanda's* four children when they were seized by BCW following Luis's incarceration and Wanda's full-time addiction to crack three years earlier.

Felix continues to work in demolition and window renovation. His $200-per-week salary is off the books, however, and does not jeopardize his family's welfare payments or its Medicaid eligibility. He recently renovated the windows of the apartment of the television star Joan Rivers. He claims she gave him a gold-plated pin and served lunch to the entire construction crew.

Felix and Candy's twenty-year-old son, *Junior,* has fathered two children by two different teenage girls. According to Primo, "Junior is an idiot out there." He dropped out of high school at fifteen when his mother was hired at the podiatry center, so that he could baby-sit his little sister, Lillian, during the day. Candy helped him evade New York's truancy by promising the authorities that he would join the Conservation Corps upon turning sixteen. He subsequently dropped out of the Conservation Corps after only two months because "them niggas was too wild."

In the years since then, he has been smoking marijuana every day. He passed through a period of robbing from everyone around him until he was finally arrested for his second felony offense, selling crack to an undercover police officer. He spent a year and a half in prison, where by coincidence he served time on Riker's Island with his Uncle Luis. Primo told me that Luis tried to give Junior a weapon, "you know, like, a pencil or something sharp so he could stab somebody in the eye. You know, like, just to defend himself, in case somebody tries to mess with him." Junior refused his uncle's weapon, and according to Primo, "He started tearing instead." Junior consequently had to be placed in "P.C., that's protective custody, where they lock up the feeble niggas, in solitary confinement."

After his release from prison, Junior worked briefly as a cable television installer. According to Primo, he is now "in-and-out of selling drugs — but he's scared of prison boy!" He continues to live with his mother, father, and younger sisters in their project apartment. I ran into Junior at the entrance to his mother's building at 1:00 a.m. I would not have recognized him had he not called out to me. He was sporting a scruffy beard, had a blue bandanna wrapped, gang-style, around his head, and had lost all his baby fat. In fact, he appeared almost emaciated. I invited him to come to a baptism party that Tony was hosting for his six-month-old baby, but he declined with embarrassment. I politely left the scene when a crack addict approached him, as I had suddenly realized he did not want to have to admit to me that he was working the late-night shift for Carlos, the same stairwell crack dealer who sometimes pays Candy to let him use her kitchen to prepare his product.

Junior keeps in touch with his younger cousin, *Angelo,* who also dropped out of school to become a pothead. Angelo lives with his grandmother, as both his parents are heavy drug users, and are constantly "in-and-out of jail."

Candy's oldest daughter, *Tabatha,* still lives in her own separate project apartment in Brooklyn and just gave birth to her second child. She broke up with the child's father, but according to Primo she is doing well. The new boyfriend she lives with has adopted the baby, treating it as his own. She works legally, but off the books in a boutique in Brooklyn. *Jackie* is now seventeen years old and has successfully completed tenth grade at an alternative public school downtown. Her boyfriend was recently incarcerated in a federal prison.

Candy's brother has full-blown AIDS and receives welfare. I saw him walking fast down the street, well past midnight, toward an active crack-copping corner.

Benzie continued to work in food preparation at a downtown health club until June 1994. He kept his job for more than five years and was earning $320 a week before taxes. I visited him with Primo in Metropolitan Hospital where he was having seven screws and a metal plate removed from his calcaneus bone (heel), which he shattered into five pieces last year in a drunken midnight car accident in El Barrio with Caesar and Primo. He continues to live in a tenement in Brooklyn with his girlfriend from four years ago. She works as a radio dispatcher for a taxi service in El Barrio. Upon his release from the hospital, Benzie "invested" the $1,500 he won in a lawsuit over the car accident by hiring two friends to open a new marijuana sales spot, three blocks uptown from the Game Room.

Willie married an African-American woman and lives in Virginia, where his older brother found him "a paperwork job in the military." On his last visit to El Barrio he went on a crack binge, but apparently managed to return to his job and family in Virginia once his money ran out.

Tony manages a heroin-copping corner in the neighborhood. Before that, he had quit working for Ray to manage a crack sales point in his mother's building. He continues to live with his three-year-old daughter and his twenty-one-year-old wife, *Clara,* who recently had a new baby. The size of the baptism party he organized for his newborn in a local housing project community center rivaled any of the parties Ray sponsored when the Game Room and the Social Club were still in business.

Ray is occasionally seen in the neighborhood, "driving around in an Excalibur – always with a different woman." According to Caesar, "looks to me like he's a retired drug kingpin," but Primo says "he's scrambling somewhere up in the Bronx," where he lives with his wife, Gloria, and their two children in one of the buildings he bought at a police auction. When Primo asked Ray why he never visited, Ray answered aggressively that he had his own friends in the Bronx and did not have the time or the need to come to El Barrio anymore.

Little Pete is in prison on a felony count of crack sales to an undercover officer. Six months before his incarceration he was shot six times in a phone booth in the Bronx, where he was trying to open up an independent crack sales point with an African-American partner. At the time he was living with his mother, whose heroin-addicted husband (Little Pete's stepfather) had just died of AIDS.

Nestor is serving an extended prison sentence for shooting a Mexican immigrant he was trying to mug. New-immigrant Mexicans continue to move into El Barrio despite the violence against them. In the mid-1990s, half of all the foreign-born children in the school district came from Mexico. Their proportion of the officially censused population of El Barrio grew by 332.9 percent in the 1980s – more than twice the rate for Mexicans in the rest of New York City, who increased by 159.8 percent.[1] Tensions are palpable, as Primo explained to me while pointing to a young Mexican man crossing the street ahead of us. "Makes me feel like shit when I see them, 'cause I know they work for cheaper than me."

Luis was given a two-and-a-half-year prison sentence for selling crack. He enrolled in a drug treatment program while incarcerated and was promoted to peer counselor. This granted him an early release from prison on a four-month probationary drug treatment furlough. He lives with a sister in his former housing project and has been looking – so far unsuccessfully – for space in a residential treatment facility. Instead, he receives acupuncture as an outpatient from a downtown hospital. He admits to intense cravings for crack whenever "I got money in my pocket," but he anticipates being able to remain clean until his early-release probationary period formally ends and he will no longer be subject to weekly urine tests. Currently, if he "gives a dirty urine," he will be returned to prison to finish the remainder of his sentence.

According to Primo, "Luis even said he was willing to work." Luis's wife, *Wanda,* is living with a lover in her same project apartment after recovering from being a sex-for-crack prostitute on upper Park Avenue. She has filed for divorce papers and has placed a legal order of protection on Luis. Luis claims she enjoys taunting him by affectionately embracing her new lover when she passes him on the street. Luis is obsessed by Wanda's new boyfriend and promises to beat both of them up once he completes his probation and parole. All four of Luis and Wanda's children have been split up among three different foster parents. Their oldest boy is thirteen but has already dropped out of school. Their oldest daughter, who became HIV positive after receiving a tainted blood transfusion at Metropolitan Hospital, was placed in foster care with Candy. She died in February 1995 at the age of twelve. Primo commends Luis for seeking out all of his other children, "those he had by outside women," to "take them out on walks" and express his affection.

Primo's former girlfriend, *Jaycee,* still drinks and sniffs cocaine. She moves back and forth with her twelve-year-old son between her mother's project apartment in El Barrio and the West Side home of a new Colombian boyfriend, who sells drugs and frequently beats her up.

Angel and *Manny* still live with *their mother, Iris,* in her tenement apartment, which is also used by her new boyfriend as a base for storing the crack that he sells downstairs on the stoop of their building. Their mother continues to work as bartender at an after-hours club, and Manny serves as a runner in her boyfriend's crack operation. Angel used to sell crack for one of the companies operating in the housing projects opposite their tenement: "I worked for a *moreno* [African-American] company even though I used to hang out with the *boricuas* [Puerto Ricans] – and that was a problem." He and a lookout used to each earn ten dollars for every bundle (fifty vials at three dollars each) they sold. He claims they could sell fifty vials in approximately forty-five minutes on a good night, earning about a hundred dollars during a typical eight-hour shift. He recently quit selling drugs, however, when a judge sentenced him to five years probation on a felony plea bargain for "reckless endangerment." The police had arrested Angel after he shot at a cabdriver in a bungled holdup. He managed to convince the police that he was merely drunk and had been shooting aimlessly in the air. In fact, as he explained to me, "I was mad, and aimed right into the back of the cab, but the driver just drove away." His best friend, *Lestor,* who also used to visit museums with us and drew crayon pictures in my apartment, is currently serving a ten-year sentence for shooting a member of a rival project stairway youth crew–gang. Angel currently works off the books cleaning a restaurant downtown and his little brother, Manny, sometimes helps him. His girlfriend moved in with him following the birth of their son in April 1994. She receives SSI.

Caesar's cousin *Eddie* (who spent time in reform school with Caesar as a youth) continues to work as a New York City Transit Authority bus driver and he has fathered several new children by different women.

Abraham, Primo's adopted grandfather, passed away in 1994 from old age and alcoholism. He was living in a housing project for the elderly with one of Candy's sisters and her three daughters. Candy's sister's family was evicted by the Housing Authority following Abraham's death.

Epilogue

A substitute apartment was eventually found for Candy's sister's family in a nearby set of projects a few blocks from the Game Room. In the process, however, Candy's sister had a nervous breakdown and had to be hospitalized for her depression. Her boyfriend was allowed to keep custody of her three teenage daughters during the interim and they were not placed in foster care. Nevertheless, two of her daughters became pregnant during the transitional months.

Primo's oldest sister no longer manages a McDonald's downtown; she reduced her hours to half time so she could look for a better job. She is one of the 120 individuals who buy the Sunday *New York Times* on La Farmacia's corner. Primo says, "She buys it for the want ads, and sends out hundreds of resumés every week." I helped her rewrite her standardized cover letter and resumé, and learned that she had no other work experience besides McDonald's, despite being almost thirty years old. She refused my suggestion of constructing an "exaggerated" work history, and hopes nevertheless to find an "office job" through the want ads. She recently bought a new Jeep Cherokee on credit. She parks it in front of their housing project but it has never been vandalized or burglarized because, as Primo explains, "people know her, and respect her, I guess."

Primo's middle sister recently moved out of her project apartment in El Barrio to a private apartment complex in New Jersey. She has separated from her husband because of his "verbal abuse." He continues to work as a porter in an office building on Wall Street and pays child support. Primo's sister is looking for an affordable day-care arrangement for her three young children so she can return to work as a nurse's aide at Beth Israel Hospital in downtown Manhattan.

Primo's youngest sister just moved from the South Bronx to Poughkeepsie, New York, where she bought a $170,000 house with her husband, who qualified for a "veteran's loan." Her husband continues to drive a United Parcel Service delivery truck, but she had to leave her job at a small department store in El Barrio. She is pregnant with their second child.

The block where I lived has not changed appreciably, despite the closing of the Game Room in 1992. The Game Room's premises were renovated and it is currently occupied by a legal video movie–rental outlet. There are two new crack sales spots on the block: One operates out of a formerly legal hairdressing salon; the other is on the stoop of Angel and Manny's building. Both of the teenage-run, discount crack-selling spots, located

336

in separate project stairways, are still in business. The bogus *botanica* that sells powder cocaine on the block is also still in operation. A new and apparently well-run and completely legal bodega opened on the block. One of the abandoned tenements opposite the housing projects was renovated with public funds and it houses formerly homeless families. The tenement where Manny and Angel live, however, has fallen into grave disrepair since the death of its elderly Italian landlord, and is on the verge of becoming uninhabitable.

La Farmacia's corner has also not changed significantly despite the permanent closing of Ray's social club. The Palestinian-run grocery store that subsequently occupied the social club's former premises is closed, following a major fire that also damaged the abandoned building above it. The other Palestinian–Yemeni-owned corner grocery store still sells 120 copies of the *New York Times* every Sunday, and has even begun stocking 65 copies of the newspaper for sale each weekday. Emaciated addicts and dealers continue to congregate at La Farmacia's corner, twenty-four hours a day, hawking a wide array of illicit drugs.

I saw one of the formerly pregnant women who used to frequent the Game Room, hanging out on the curb in front of the new hairdressing salon crackhouse. She is pregnant once again. Caesar claims she has had a total of four babies since she started smoking crack, and that none of her children live with her. Witnessing her situation, and seeing several other incidents with parents abusing their children during the few weeks that I spent back in El Barrio in the spring and early summer of 1994 made me realize I had lost the defense mechanisms that allow people on the street to "normalize" personal suffering and violence. For example, I still cannot forget the expression in the terrified, helpless eyes of the five-year-old boy who was watching his mother argue with a cocaine dealer at 2:00 a.m. in the stairway of a tenement where Primo and I had taken shelter from a thunder shower on my second night back in the neighborhood. Primo shrugged when I tried to discuss the plight of the child with him, "Yeah, Felipe, I know, I hate seeing that shit too. It's wack."

EPILOGUE 2003

I have maintained a warm friendship with Primo since publishing the first edition of this book. I visit him at least once a year, usually over a period of several weeks each summer. He tells me how everyone who used to sell crack for Ray is doing, and we try to visit as many of our old friends and acquaintances from the block as possible. As of my last visit during the summer of 2002:

Primo's mother died and Primo was evicted from her housing project apartment on the one-strike-you're-out ruling for an outstanding charge of heroin possession (not sale!). For five years he lived in the project apartment of *Candy's sister, Esperanza*. He has maintained a stable relationship with her daughter, *Jasmine*, who worked as a cashier in a discount store for three years and then switched to becoming a teller with full benefits at a neighborhood bank in the South Bronx. Primo continues to refrain from drug dealing and from consuming alcohol or cocaine. An undocumented Senegalese street vendor of bootleg videotapes converted him to the Muslim religion and he no longer eats pork. He does, however, occasionally sniff heroin and claims to still enjoy the high despite being on a new semiexperimental heroin treatment medicine derived from a longer-acting version of methadone, levo-alpha-acetyl-methadol (LAAM). He developed a full-blown addiction to heroin when he was working during the summers as a night porter in a luxury high-rise building (Bourgois, 2000). Primo now works off the books in construction for a small-time, unlicensed contractor who specializes in renovating kitchens and bathrooms for a gay clientele. His boss smokes marijuana chronically all day long and is disorganized: He owns few tools, often runs out of money, and forgets to order materials and equipment on time. Consequently, Primo is trying to break away to become an independent contractor on his own. The last time I saw

339

Primo, he was taking a call on his new cell phone to negotiate the price of a sub-subcontract for retiling thirteen bathrooms in a publicly owned tenement that was under renovation.

A few days later he called me in California, disappointed. He had been awarded the subcontract but was unable to accept the project because he could not find experienced workers whom he could trust to help him. Primo's fifteen-year-old son, Papo, who dropped out of high school in ninth grade and has run away from his mother's home in Florida, is especially disappointed by this because Primo had promised to move him back up to New York and hire him to help on this large renovation contract. Papo's mother is moving with a new boyfriend back to New York, and she has told Primo that she is not going to make any effort to bring his son Papo back up with her: "He's good for nothing, running wild on the streets." Primo confided to me that he feels deeply ashamed over not being able to help his son who is "living wrong" in Florida.

In January, 2001, I invited Primo to my grandmother's funeral. She used to visit the Game Room, and most of the dealers took pride in having a respectful conversation with an elderly grandmother. After extending condolences to me, bursting with pride and anticipation Primo asks me to guess his good news. I guessed correctly on the first try: "Jasmine's pregnant?"

"Yeah! Finally! Isn't that great? And, you know, it's like her body was just waiting for her to get that good job at the bank with health benefits and everything. Yeah! She's feeling great."

Primo's youngest son, *Primo Jr.*, is now seven years old and living with his mother *Maria* and a stepfather in Connecticut who was recently released from prison. They were evicted from their New York City Housing Authority apartment because of the stepfather's felony record. Her sister *Carmen* was also evicted by the same law when she allowed *Caesar* to remain in her household following his release from jail for beating Carmen's twelve-year-old daughter *Diamond*. Carmen did not press charges against Caesar at the time, but the neighbors called the police because of the girl's screams, and a new mandatory domestic violence enforcement law caused him to serve a three-month jail sentence. Following his release, Caesar went to Florida to live with relatives and attempt drug rehabilitation. Carmen followed him to Florida with her children to try to rebuild the relationship together. They are now all staying in Maria's living room in Connecticut. On his last crack binge, Caesar sold the Gameboy and bicycle that Primo had given Primo Jr. for his birthday. Primo has vowed to stop giving Maria any money to help with Primo Jr. until she evicts Caesar.

Candy, who was working as a home-care attendant for the elderly, slipped a disk in her spinal column lifting a patient. She is now homebound in chronic pain. She cannot "even lift the phonebook" and has grown physically addicted to her pain medication. Primo reports that she is severely depressed and angry at the world. Her husband *Felix* continues to work legally in demolition and window renovation. He sniffs cocaine only on Fridays because he does not work on Saturdays. He cleans out his body and mind by Sunday, ready for work on Monday morning. Everyone insists that Felix has never again beaten Candy since the day she shot him during her *ataqué de nervios*. Their son *Junior* is back in prison for selling crack. For several years Candy's household increased its income by taking in several foster care children. There was a rumor that two of the older boys (actually Luis's sons who had been entrusted to her as foster children by the courts when their mother fell into crack addiction during Luis's imprisonment) were sexually molesting little girl twins that the Bureau of Child Welfare (BCW) had entrusted to the family. The foster care system investigated and ceased making further placements in Candy's household.

To everyone's surprise, *Luis* has remained drug free since his release and has settled down to live with an African American girlfriend. He did not regain custody of his five children, who had been placed in three different foster care families, but he has two new babies with his new companion. They both receive SSI disability checks, but he supplements their income by working off the books for Primo's contractor. In fact, Luis is the one who is urging Primo to attempt more aggressively to establish himself independently so that they can make more money together more stably. He is also "into computers now. He is always opening his computer apart: constantly souping it up. You know, adding memory chips and shit like that."

Tony no longer sells drugs. He is working as a unionized doorman and has moved back into his mother's house following a difficult breakup with his girlfriend *Clara,* who graduated from community college. She evicted Tony so as not to be subject to the loss of her subsidized apartment because of his pending felony case for sale of heroin to an undercover officer. He has not forgiven her and refuses to provide child support.

Little Pete and his brother *Nestor* are still in prison.

Angel and *Manny* moved with their mother to a new project apartment on the West Side and are reported to be "up to no good, but still friendly."

All of *Primo's sisters* have moved to the suburbs of New York City and are employed, the eldest as a secretary for a trade newspaper. The two younger sisters are hospital workers, and one goes to night school part time to become a registered nurse.

Benzie still works as a cook's aide in a downtown health club and continues to live in Brooklyn with his girlfriend, who also continues to be stably employed as a taxi dispatcher.

Ray no longer visits East Harlem. Primo thinks that he has completely retired from drug selling and instead supports himself and his family by collecting rents in formerly semiabandoned buildings that he renovated with his drug profits. He bought the buildings for almost nothing at a police auction of property confiscated from drug dealers.

Each time I revisit El Barrio, I am forced to confront the everyday violence against children that is routinized into the fabric of U.S. inner-city social suffering. Hence my second-to-last set of fieldwork notes:

[July, 2000]
Esperanza's grandson, Briancito, is now five years old and his learning disability has become much more noticeable. Esperanza tells me that he did not talk until he was three and that he flies into rages. Last month, he hit one of his special education teachers with a chair. She is worried that he has his father's anger. Photographs of his father, Brian Sr. (Esperanza's only son), who is in federal prison cover the walls of the apartment. He was condemned to life without parole for multiple drug-and-gang-related murders. In the photos he is dressed incongruously in white tennis clothes, looking like a harmless chubby nerd. Only the solid cement gray wall backdrop in the photograph suggests anything out of the ordinary. Esperanza avoids the subject, but apparently, he killed his victims with automatic weapons over drug debts. Esperanza has legal custody of Briancito and dotes on him. Her eyes well up with tears when she says, "I have to bless God – when they took away my baby [Brian Senior] they gave me a new one [hugging Briancito]."

Esperanza is worried over the welfare of the three other grandchildren who live with her. She says she can no longer do much for their mothers – her two youngest daughters. When I ask Esperanza what she thinks of this book, she abruptly shifts the conversation to talk about the way her neighbors treat their children badly. One mother on the floor below has a fourteen-year-old son, a five-year-old son, and a nine-year-old daughter whom she hits publicly. The mother screams especially viciously at her daughter while they wait for the elevator, telling her she has a big head, that she's ugly, stupid, etc. Primo interrupts, "Oh, man, but that little girl is cute." He shakes his head slowly from side to side: "I know that little girl. That's wrong; that's just wrong." Then he smashes his fist into his palm. Esperanza replies that the little girl drops her head and stares at the ground ashamedly while they are waiting for the elevator, peeking up every now and then to see who might have heard her mother berating her. The five-year-old boy in that same family had a tumor on his head that was operated on last year. The mother is angry at her fourteen-year-old son who is telling everyone in the building that she caused the tumor by hitting the five-year-old too hard in the head too often in the exact same spot. Esperanza claims the mother continues to hit the child on the head even since the operation. Someone finally called the Bureau of Child Welfare, but the social workers did not confiscate any of the children because there were "no signs of abuse." Esperanza throws her arms up in the air: "What can you do?" She says the mother now brags that she is not afraid of "BCW" because she doesn't even care if they take away her children. Almost as a non sequitur, Esperanza sighs that she thinks mothers should only do coke when their kids are asleep and when "their head is good, you know, in the right place. . . . Otherwise, they should just have abortions. Do you believe in abortion, Felipe?"

Esperanza also complains about the violence of her immediate neighbors in the apartment next door. Recently, their ten-year-old daughter screamed so loudly for help when they beat her that Esperanza called the Bureau of Child Welfare. She says, "I don't like turning parents in, but I would have felt bad if that child had been killed with me hearing her HELP! calls coming right through the wall. They were loud. I'm telling you." She condemns child abuse — using that word — and says she is trying to break the cycle of violence in her grandson, Briancito. Every time he does anything wrong, however, she can't refrain from shouting, "Stop that! You want me to hit you?" And I have to keep myself from startling noticeably because when Esperanza screams she is LOUD.

Esperanza is sad that she had to throw her twenty-one-year-old daughter out of the apartment, but she has a one-strike-you're-out felony for aggravated assault and drug possession, and the Housing Authority began inspecting Esperanza's apartment to ensure that her daughter is no longer living on the premises. The evicted daughter's cute eighteen-month-old little girl still lives with Esperanza and appears to be everyone's favorite. The tiny girl gets a lot of love and attention and bosses everyone about – even me – as only a confident toddler can.

An angry-faced, 6'5" young man walks in with a message for Esperanza's middle nineteen-year-old daughter Sandra who is unemployed and still lives here in Esperanza's apartment with her six-year-old daughter. I am worried about the child because I have never seen her smile or even interact with anyone and she is the only person in the family who is seriously overweight. Sandra's new boyfriend works at the post office sorting mail at night and he gives her money for partying.

The angry young man is on his way to collect money owed to him by someone on the floor below. He has a bunch of gold chains on his chest and impressive biceps covered in tattoos, one of which is a scorpion decorated with the Puerto Rican flag. He is carrying a baseball bat in his left hand as if it were a toothpick and stands with his feet apart even more toughly than I ever remembered being possible. He makes me feel old and square . . . not to mention thankful that we are meeting safely inside Esperanza's apartment and not out on the street in the middle of the night. Primo asks the guy who he was going to play baseball with. He giggles, "Nigga's heads," and fakes a swing at Briancito's head who also giggles from in front of the television where he spends most of his time. Once again I fail to contain my startle reflex, which makes everyone else think that the simulated baseball bat beating to five-year-old Briancito's head is even funnier. The big guy, who by now no longer looks angry to me, starts bragging about how well his boxing training is going and how, on his trainer's orders, he has quit smoking pot and drinking anything artificial with sugar in it. Primo discusses some technical boxing stuff with him that I cannot follow, but we all watch as he demonstrates new positions and punches that he has just learned at the gym using Primo as an imaginary opponent. With a mischievous wink, he tells us not to tell his trainer, but that he is trying to build up his strength and punch with enough force and precision to break someone's neck with one punch. He shows us with a slow-motion swing where the would-be magic disabling spot is located on Primo's neck.

Primo finally introduces me to the marijuana-selling, wannabe boxer who no longer looks angry at all, and it turns out that he is Luis's oldest son. He is now nineteen, and I tell him that I have a fading Polaroid family portrait of him as a ten-year-old child in a blue windbreaker with his father and three of his little brothers and sisters when they were at a New Year's Eve party at Primo's mother's apartment. They were clutching their father, whom they did not want to leave and go "on a mission [smoke crack]," I do not tell him that my last fieldwork note referring to him six years back describes him at 2:00 in the morning standing on top of a bus shelter: "June 1994. What is going to happen to him? His father Luis has just been jailed and his mother is exchanging sex for crack under the elevated railroad tracks on Park Avenue." He now has three young children of his own. Primo assures me that he is a "good homebody . . . gives his money to the mother – at least some of it." Luis's son mumbles politely that he remembers me and, turning into the awkward little kid I remember from the past, he shakes my hand with touching formality.

Heading home just before midnight, I share the elevator going down from Esperanza's eighteenth-floor apartment with a harried mother of three children, pushing a baby carriage. The biggest of her kids, less than three years old, drops his jacket across a puddle of urine in the corner of the elevator by mistake. His mother explodes, choking her voice into a hiss as if losing total control over herself and raising her arms to pummel him. The child cowers, but his mother lowers her fists at the last moment. I suddenly realize that she had only feigned her fury in order to make her little boy cower appropriately. Instead, she shouts at him, chopping him up into a million pieces with the tone of her voice. He hangs his head, staring at the puddle of urine on the elevator floor.

The subway breaks down at the 116th Street stop on the way home. I have a chance to study my fellow passengers closely. Nobody in the subway car seems to find it unusual that there are so many underweight children out at midnight, tagging along after distracted and emaciated mothers who are obviously on crack missions. Several of the skinniest mothers are pushing baby carriages. Two well-dressed women sitting next to me do not appear to be involved with drugs. They are heading downtown to go dancing at a new club, chitchatting relaxedly about their boyfriends, one of whom "just got outta jail."

My last extended set of fieldwork notes spanning visits and telephone conversations in 2001–02 focuses more on the institutional violence of the new panopticon that enforces "quality-of-life crimes" on El Barrio's streets. The notes begin with a description of me leaving my grandmother's memorial service to visit my old block. I proceed uneventfully to walk around the neighborhood looking up old friends and acquaintances. I find out my former landlord recently died and the superintendent of a neighboring building tells me what has happened to the children I used to take to the museum in the old days. The notes describe appreciatively the increased working class visibility and energy along my old block. Toward the end of the afternoon, however, I commit the quality-of-life crime of buying a fifty-cent sixteen-ounce can of El Coqui malt liquor – named after the frog on the endangered species list that lives only in Puerto Rico. The notes end abruptly with undercover police officers issuing me a citation for a misdemeanor offense for drinking in public and warning me to leave the neighborhood right away in yet another example of the micropractices that enforce U.S. apartheid:

Who the fuck do y'a think you're bullshitin'! We know what you're up here for. We've been following you; watchin' every move you've been making. We seen you lookin' all over the place; talkin' to people; waving. So who you lookin' for – huh? Who? Huh!

Awright, awright, go ahead play dumb. Don't tell us nothin'. But don't think you can get away with shit up here. You're just lucky we're not rookies or we'd be searchin' you more strictly – not just giving you a ticket. It don't bother us 'cause you're just gonna get picked up a half block further down by some other undercovers right down there on the next corner – this neighborhood is hot now buddy.

And don't think you can just skip the court date on this ticket just 'cause you're from California. They'll issue a bench warrant and the next time you get stopped for anything, you'll come right up on the computer and bingo! They'll haul your ass right in – I don't care if you're in California or Hawaii [laughing].

Two months later, heeding the police officer's warning, I returned to New York to appear in court:

My fine is only $10, but it takes four hours to be processed through the misdemeanor court system, which is much less organized than I expect. The courts seem to be run more by the charisma of the guards and police officers, who shuttle scared, confused, and sometimes angry quality-of-life criminals from one courtroom doorway to another. They call out to passing clerks and colleagues – sometimes even whistling to get their attention from all the way down the hallway – "Yo! Do me a favor? Put this guy on your waiting list." Or "How many ya' got left to go? Can you take one more?"

We spend most of our time waiting in hallways while the guards try to figure out which courtroom is not too crowded to take us. A friendly African American police officer waiting for his turn outside one of the courtrooms advises me in a loud voice so that the woman waiting next to me also hears him: "Just deny it. Just deny it. The officer who ticketed you won't be there and the judge will have to let you go." I thank him and he succeeds in shifting the conversation onto the situation of the woman next to me.

I finally make it into one of the courtrooms, but only after telling the clerk who is doing me the favor of squeezing me onto his docket before lunch that I am "just gonna plead guilty – I promise." He squints at me, waves me to a bench and hisses, "OK...But remember just say you're guilty." I nod my head several times, eagerly and ironically thankful, and take my seat. The first five cases before me are all for marijuana possession, and each one is immediately dismissed with no discussion whatsoever. The de facto decriminalization of marijuana in New York City is one of the many unintended consequences of Mayor Guiliani's campaign against quality-of-life crimes. I learn this from the bored guard in the back of the courtroom who is preventing us from reading the newspaper or from falling asleep. He notices my surprised expression at each rapid marijuana dismissal and whispers, "The judges hafta' dismiss all the marijuana cases. It's too expensive to have marijuana tested. So all's a defendant's gotta do is say it ain't marijuana and then he walks."

In contrast, a young African American man who is called up right before me is issued a $35 fine for spitting. Out in the hallway he had explained to me that the police caught him on a Saturday night with an empty paper cup in his hand: "They wanted to ticket me. But I had already finished my Hennessey and I know my rights. They can't do nothin' to you for no empty cup. So I cursed the motherfucker when he hassled me and I spit on the ground. He told me there was a law against spitting on the street. So, I spit again, but this time on the side of his van. I'm telling you, I'm moving to Florida. You can't even walk sideways anymore in New York City without getting arrested."

When I am finally called up before the judge, they make me sign a semilegible photocopied waiver expressing my willingness to be heard by a retiree who has been recalled to service in an effort to ease the crowding caused by the increase in misdemeanor arrests. The two-minute interaction ends with me pleading "guilty with an explanation" and with the judge issuing me a $10 fine, but also expressing his condolences for my grandmother's death.

After another forty-five minute wait outside in the hallway, a police officer finally takes us to the cashier line to pay our fines. I make friends with a young Puerto Rican man in front of me in the line who has been issued the exact same public drinking fine. We commiserate about how strict the cops have become. When it is his turn to pay, he has to plead with the cashier to give him a special temporary voucher in order to be let out of the courthouse: "I'm broke. I'm tellin' you I'm broke. I don't got the money. I'm fuckin' broke." He looks embarrassed and depressed. It feels natural for me to offer to pay his $10 fine after his second "I'm broke," but I do not dare because he might think I will demand a sexual favor in repayment.

After court, I go uptown and see Esperanza in her housing project courtyard waiting alongside a half dozen other mothers for the special education school bus to bring their children home. Esperanza's daughter, Sandra, who is very pregnant, is also waiting for her six-year-old. She tells me "you're going to live long, Felipe, because I was just talking about the dream I had about you earlier today."

Esperanza is feeling much better. Her son, Brian Sr., was finally moved to a prison in Pennsylvania that is closer and easier to visit. The children pour off the bus with that overflowing energy unique to kids who have just been released from school on a sunny afternoon. Several of the mothers threaten violence to their children as they climb into the fenced-off grassy areas that are sandwiched between the housing project's cement walkways. The kids do not seem to be very worried about their mothers' threats and romp in the tiny patches of forbidden green grass.

I called Primo shortly after the September 11, 2001, World Trade Center disaster in New York City to tell him I am going to be visiting:

Primo advises me against traveling by airplane and tells me that he does not dare take the subway downtown anymore to his methadone maintenance program out of fear of terrorism. He is trying to persuade the nurse to ask the doctor to give him take-home doses so that he does not have to face the risk of public transportation. I hear his baby, Primo Jr., fussing in the background, and Primo tells me he has to put down the phone to fix his bottle: "I'm the one who takes care of him because Jasmine went back to work." When she tried to take her maternity leave, the bank told her they would promote her to supervisor if she kept coming to work. She complied, but now, five months later they still have not promoted her. Primo's oldest son, Papito, is doing better. He moved out to the suburbs to live with one of Primo's sisters and works at a Subway Sandwich Shop.

Primo's contractor is trying to persuade Primo to come back to work, but there is no one to take care of the new baby: "At least that motherfucker finally paid me most of the money he owes me and he has offered to raise my pay. He's respecting me a little more now, but I'm still gonna just make him wait a little more. I might be broke, but I'm not a slave. And I want to be there for my kid. He's four months old now and he needs me." Primo is most excited by the fact that he is down to only 30 milligrams of LAAM per day. Apparently, they have discovered that LAAM cause "serious cardiac arrhythmia" and they are taking everyone off that drug. He is hoping to be completely clean soon. When he occasionally sniffs a little heroin, he always makes sure to carry a vial of clean urine from Jasmine or his son Papito in case they do a random drug test. He has not come up dirty in over a year.

Several months later Primo leaves an urgent message on my answering machine. Esperanza sent a copy of my book to Brian in prison and the prison officials "confiscated your book. They told him they wanna investigate the author, and like figure out who's who." They think the book will reveal the identities of the other individuals who committed the multiple murders with Brian. They are threatening Brian that he should now give up all the names because it is all going to come out anyhow now that they got your book. I immediately called Esperanza to reassure her that there is nothing about Brian or his fellow murderers in the book. He was less than six years old at the time of the fieldwork. I also remind her that a Federal Certificate of Confidentiality legally prevents my research data from being used in a court of law.

Just to be safe, however, I sent a copy of this epilogue to a lawyer friend who specializes in federal drug and murder cases. She confirmed that there was nothing particularly incriminating in this epilogue, but advised me to delete all references to drug dealing inside the housing projects: "The Feds are just so crazy now. All they care about is drugs."

When I visited Esperanza on my last trip to New York, she is in a great mood:

Esperanza's son Brian filed a lawsuit claiming the interrogation they subjected him to when they confiscated my book was harassment. They threatened to transfer him back to Texas if he did not drop the suit. He dropped the suit and now they are transferring him to an even closer prison on the Hudson River. Jasmine was promoted to head teller at the bank: "She's marching straight A!" They even offered another promotion but she turned it down because she does not want to supervise people. The county hospital assigned Esperanza a new Latina psychiatrist, who has told her that her mental health treatment for the past dozen years was botched: "She is going to fix me up with better meds and more intensive therapy." Esperanza is hopeful. She says she was even able to handle the death of her mother three months ago:

We were all there. All her kids and even my daughters. Everyone was there except my brother Felix. It was a Friday and that's the nights that Felix gets lifted – you know, sniffs his little bit of coke.
I had called my son Brian in prison and left a message for him to try to get permission to come visit his grandmother in the hospital. Instead they gave him an extra phone call. He called, but her eyes

were already closed and she wasn't talking no more. Just breathing real slowly.

The phone line couldn't reach her so he asked me over the phone to ask his grandmother to bless him. And when I called out across the room, "Mama, Brian *pide bendición,*" it was like that was all she was waiting for. She opened her eyes, made a little noise, and died right then.

We went back to Candy's and Felix was there. He could tell something was wrong, but we didn't want to tell him because he was lifted. He kept asking all night how our mother was. He could tell something was wrong, but we just played it off and cooked some food.

The next day I told him and he thanked me for not telling him when he was lifted. He couldn't have handled it. Felix used to visit our mother every day. But now he comes over and visits me instead – every day.

I ask Esperanza about the little girl in the apartment next door who calls for help when her parents beat her. She stops smiling. "I don't know, Felipe, the City finally came and took her away." I promise to include the little girl in this epilogue.

San Francisco, April 2002

NOTES

Introduction

1. In New York the term "barrio" is not used generically to delineate a working-class Latino neighborhood as it does in the West or Southwest of the United States. El Barrio in New York City refers specifically to East Harlem.

2. Crack is processed from powder cocaine (cocaine hydrochloride) by dissolving the cocaine in hot water, adding baking soda, and letting the concoction cool into a hard, smokeble pellet that burns evenly, making a "crackling" sound when a flame is applied to it. In New York City, crack is smoked in 5-inch-long glass cylinders, with a circumference of about 1 inch, known as "stems." These distinctive pipes are sold surreptitiously at corner grocery stores for one dollar. The crack is placed on a crumpled wire mesh screen that is pushed about an inch inside one end of the stem, which is tilted upward. Immediately upon inhalation, crack provides an intense, minute-and-a-half "rush" comparable – but allegedly superior – to the one obtained by injecting a powder cocaine solution directly into a main vein. Hardcore users are capable of binging nonstop on crack with no food or sleep for "missions" that can last several days and nights (Williams 1992). Similarly, cocaine injectors are capable of "shooting up" dozens of times in a single session, converting their bodies into needle-pricked, bloody, and bruised messes.

3. Violent crime (murder, rape, and assault-and-robbery) increased 41 percent between 1984 and 1988 in my neighborhood's police precinct (#25). In Manhattan, only Hell's Kitchen (around Times Square on 42nd Street), and occasionally Washington Heights, had higher violent crime rates than East Harlem (*New York Daily News,* January 23, 1989, 18).

4. See *New York Times,* August 8, 1993:A1, A18. In 1991, shortly before I left New York City, two of the crack spots I studied were converted into heroin-copping corners. The standard street price for heroin was $10 for a

1.5-by-.75-inch glassine, postage-stamp-style envelope containing a pinch of white powder resembling confectioner's sugar. In 1994, one heroin company in El Barrio discounted their product to $5 per packet and virtually all of them increased the purity of their heroin. The shift in the mid-1990s from selling crack cocaine to heroin had few organizational implications for the underground economy. It merely represented a shift from selling one profitable illegal substance to selling another.

5. I calculated the poverty figures for my microneighborhood by combining two census tracts in the 1990 Census of Population and Housing. I also used figures from New York City Department of City Planning, 1993 (March).

6. In 1989 in El Barrio, approximately 37 percent of all residents received some combination of public assistance, Supplemental Social Security income, and Medicaid benefits (New York City Department of City Planning, 1990 [September]: 221, and New York City Department of City Planning 1993 [March]).

7. The dramatic booms in the late 1980s and 1990s of coca production in South America and of opium in Asia testify to the explosive expansion of the international drug economy (cf. Rensselaer W. Lee III 1991; *New York Times,* August 8, 1993:A1, A18).

8. Angel dust, known as PCP or "zootie," is an animal tranquilizer that is sprinkled on mint leaves, which are then smoked. Angel dust was the drug scourge of the mid-1970s, and it continues to have a limited popularity in El Barrio.

9. The official unemployment rate in New York City was 10 percent for males and 5.7 percent for women (Department of City Planning, March 1993). According to the *New York Times,* of all major cities in the United States, only Detroit had a lower labor force participation rate than New York City. Of New York City's working-age population, 55 percent was employed in 1994, compared to 66 percent at the national level (*New York Times,* February 18, 1994:A1, A12).

10. Many of the women who were outside the labor force, of course, were taking care of young children, and some were in school.

   Statistics calculated from: 1990 Census of Population and Housing disaggregated by tract; 1990 Census of Economic Development Indicators disaggregated by tract; and New York City Department of City Planning, March 1993.

11. Cf. Bourgois 1990, and Robinson and Passel 1987.

12. Personal communication, Kevin Kearny, Assistant Director of Research, NYCHA; see also New York City Housing Authority, Department of Research and Policy Development 1988.

13. Starobin 1994.

14. Economic Development Indicators, 1990 Census, disagregated by census tract. See Edin 1991 for a discussion of household strategies for supplementing public assistance income in Chicago.

15. Jazz is a good example of a cultural form created by segregated street culture but subsequently appropriated by highbrow culture.

16. A symbolic marker of the presence of a "mainstream-oriented" population on even the most active drug-copping corners of East Harlem is that all through the height of the crack epidemic, the Palestinian-owned grocery store on 110th Street and Lexington sold 120 copies of the Sunday edition of the *New York Times*.

17. Rodriguez 1995.

18. Benmayor, Torruelas, and Juarbe 1992; Katz 1986; Rainwater 1994; Stansell 1987; and Ward 1989.

19. As the anthropologist Nancy Scheper-Hughes (1992: 172) notes in her ethnography of a Brazilian shantytown:

> For anthropologists to deny, because it implies a privileged position (i.e., the power of the outsider to name an ill or a wrong) and because it is not pretty, the extent to which dominated people come to play the role . . . of their own executioners is to collaborate with the relations of power and silence that allow the destruction to continue.

20. See Behar 1993; Portelli 1991; Rosaldo 1980. Tape recordings are always difficult to edit, especially when they are in street idiom whose grammar and vocabulary differ from that of the academic mainstream. One of my biggest problems in editing, however, is the impossibility of rendering into print the performance dimension of street speech. Without the complex, stylized punctuation provided by body language, facial expression, and intonation, many of the transcribed narratives of crack dealers appear flat, and sometimes even inarticulate, on the written page. Consequently, I often deleted redundancies, dangling phrases, incomplete thoughts, and sometimes even entire passages in order to recover the articulate – often poetic – effect the same passage conveyed in its original oral performance. To clarify meanings, I sometimes added additional words, and even subjects and verbs, to sentence fragments. I also occasionally combined conversations of the same events, or on the same themes, to make them appear to have occurred during a single session within the text, even though they sometimes took place over a period of several months or several years. In a few rare instances of minor characters in the book, I conflated more than one person for brevity's sake.

Having said all this, I tried as much as I could to maintain the grammatical form, the expressive vocabulary, and the transliterated Spanish forms that compose the rich language of New York–born Puerto Ricans who participate in El Barrio's street culture. Most important, I hope I have respected their message. Our conversations where usually in English with occasional Spanish words interspersed as a way of affirming Puerto Rican identity. Whenever a conversation, or a portion of a sentence was in Spanish, I have noted that fact in the text.

21. Rodriguez 1995, citing G. Lewis 1963.

22. Harvey 1993; Katz 1986; O. Lewis 1966; Moynihan 1965; Rainwater and Yancey 1967; Wilson 1987.

23. To name just a few examples of cultural production theorists and critical ethnographers of education, see Bourdieu 1980; Devine 1996; Foley 1990; Fordham 1988; Gibson and Ogbu 1991; MacLeod 1987; Willis 1977.

24. In fact, I did exclude a number of conversations and observations I thought projected an overly negative portrayal of the crack dealers and their families out of context. Much of my "censoring" occurred around descriptions of sexual activities. In several cases, I felt the passages might be considered straightforward pornography. I also wanted to avoid excessively invading the privacy of the major characters in the book, and I discussed these issues at length with all of them. Only one person actually asked me to delete some material from the epilogue, which, of course, I did. The problems of selection, editing, and censorship have tremendous political, ethical, and personal ramifications that ethnographers must continually confront, without ever being confident of resolving them.

25. Scheper-Hughes 1992:25; Wolf 1990.

26. Nader 1972.

1. Violating Apartheid in the United States

1. The corner of 110th Street and Lexington is featured periodically in the national and local press as "A Devil's Playground" or as "the worst and druggiest corner" in the city. In 1990 alone, it boasted photo spreads in *National Geographic* (Van Dyk, May 1990), *The American Lawyer* (Frankel and Freeland, March 1990), and the *New York Daily News* (October 19, 1990:1). When I looked up the legal real estate records for Ray's Social Club, I found that the City of New York had seized it from its original Italian owner for tax default and donated it to Operation Open City, a nonprofit affordable housing coalition. Budget cuts prevented the nonprofit organization from developing the site. Instead, Ray continued paying rent for the space to the elderly Italian landlord who no longer legally owned the property.

2. May 4, 1989:4.

3. Ironically, the only real survivors of the holocaust on La Farmacia's corner

are the two Palestinian refugee families that own the bodegas catty-corner to Ray's social club–crackhouse. These Middle Eastern exiles have even expanded into local real estate, buying the few still standing tenements along the avenue. They do a brisk business in beer, candy, and drug paraphernalia – including glass crack-pipe stems, and plastic crack and cocaine vials.

4. "Cheeba" is a New York term for marijuana.

5. *La Mafia Boba* is difficult to translate. Literally, *boba* or *bobo* means "slow-witted," but Primo's gang used the term ironically to convey their ability to prey on people unawares:

> Like they think we're *bobos* but we're *guapos* [aggressive, streetwise]. We know what we're doing. Ray used to start shouting *"la Mafia boba a botellazo* [to the bottles]!" And we start grabbing bottles and throwing them at whoever – like if we used to see a faggot, or a punk, or whatever – someone we just didn't like.

6. In New York City, a "bundle" refers to an established quantity of prepackaged drugs ready for individual retail sale. The number of packets in a bundle changes depending on the drug and its cost, i.e., a bundle of heroin is ten $10 glassine envelopes, whereas a bundle of crack is twenty-five vials when they cost $5 each and fifty-five vials when they are worth $3 each. Payments to street sellers are usually made as a percentage of the profit on each bundle sold. For example, in the housing projects opposite the Game Room the lookout and the server who sold crack at $3 a vial shared $20 for every bundle of fifty-five vials they sold.

7. See Bourgois 1989b. When the Jamaican owner of a gold pawnshop that sold powder cocaine around the corner from the Game Room shot one of his employees in the kneecaps for skimming from a night's receipts, Primo told me, "Jamaicans don't fuck around – they're not like Puerto Ricans." Indeed, on the street Jamaican drug dealers enjoyed a reputation for extreme brutality (cf. Gunst 1995).

8. It is part of an immense swath of uninterrupted housing projects that covers a thirty-two-square-block perimeter, extending from East Harlem through Central Harlem, with an approximate population of 17,800.

9. It was not until two years later that I finally gained full access to that particular crack corner by befriending the owner, Tito, a twenty-one-year-old who shot his older brother in the spine and paralyzed him for life in a struggle over control of the block. Tito was an extraordinarily talented graffiti artist. He covered the six bricked-up abandoned tenements on his block with huge spray-painted murals depicting his glory in the drug-dealing world – including comic character self-portraits of himself covered in gold chains (see photos on pages 10, 157, and 279). He lived in one of the abandoned buildings with his grandmother. His father had been killed and Tito introduced me to his cocaine-addicted mother, who happened to

be visiting on one occasion. She nervously tried to hide the needle-mark scabs covering the top of her hands. With the warm encouragement of Tito's grandmother I tried to connect Tito to downtown art galleries. We encountered only a cold reception in the New York City art world, and halfway through the process Tito lost control of his block and disappeared in a cloud of angel dust.

10. I moved to El Barrio in March 1985, and we moved out in September 1990. Economic constraints forced us to spend several academic semesters outside New York City, so our actual length of physical residence in the neighborhood was a total of 3.5 years – two of which (1988–90) were uninterrupted. During the first year after moving out of El Barrio, from September 1990 to August 1991, we lived nearby in West Harlem (along Morningside Park) and I continued to spend at least two nights a week with Ray's crack dealers. Since moving to San Francisco in late 1991, I have maintained telephone contact with several of the dealers, and I never visit New York City without seeing Primo. During the spring and part of the summer of 1994, I spent almost two months in New York City, visiting Primo and other East Harlem friends regularly.

11. Bensonhurst is a working-class Italian-American neighborhood in Brooklyn. On August 23, 1989, a group of young white men in the neighborhood killed Yusuf Hawkins, a sixteen-year-old African-American who had come to Bensonhurst to buy a used car advertised in the local newspapers. They thought he was dating an Italian-American woman who lived on the block (*New York Times,* August 25, 1989:A1, B2).

12. The Puerto Rican faction of the Mafia eventually wrested control of East Harlem's numbers racket from the Genovese crime family. The new Puerto Rican director of this $30 million gambling empire was eventually arrested in 1994 (*New York Times,* April 21, 1994:A13).

13. In one case, a stray bullet ricocheted off the curb next to us while we lounged in front of the Game Room. I hesitated including this particular incident for fear of oversensationalizing my experience of neighborhood violence in a self-celebratory macho manner. In fact, we did not feel as if we were in imminent danger of getting shot. At the same time, the transcriptions of my tape recordings are frequently punctuated by gunshots. In my original round of editing, I was so close to the material that I did not transcribe the sound of gunshots, treating them instead like static interference or traffic noises.

14. Taussig 1987.

15. Based on his research on Chicago's Southside, the French sociologist Loïc Wacquant (1993a) calls this "the depacification of everyday life." He links it to structural economic as well as political factors, such as the breakdown

of state-provided infrastructure and social services in the wake of deindustrialization.

See also John Devine's (1996) discussion of the culture of violence in New York's "lower tier," inner-city high schools.

16. My childhood census tract was listed as the richest in all of New York City in the 1990 census. Its average household income ($249,556) was more than eleven times higher than the average household income (just over $21,000) of my census tracts in El Barrio and its median household income was more than thirteen times higher (*New York Times*, March 20, 1994:A6; *1990 Census of Population and Housing Block Statistics*).

17. Al Sharpton is an African-American inner-city reverend in New York City who caught the attention of the media for his flamboyant denunciations of racism and his community-level mobilizations in the early 1990s.

18. See, for example, *New York Times*, March 23, 1990:A1, B4.

19. *New York Times*, November 16, 1988:A1, B5. The TNT strategy was declared a failure and discontinued in early 1994.

20. Caesar was acutely aware of the hype and hypocrisy driving the anti-drug hysteria that swept the United States in the late 1980s and early 1990s along with the "family values" and abortion debates.

I could be some dumb scumbag ho' that have a lot of money to push my campaign. And all I gotta say is "Drugs!" and they'll elect me immediately.

Abortion and drugs is the best thing for politicians in America, man.

Why you think they gettin' elected? Look at Idaho with all them bureaucrat delegates making all these promises about stopping abortion and all that.

Over here in New York they got a drug problem, and all you gotta say is "I'm gonna stop the flow of drugs. Hire more police!" and you got the job, man.

In the mid-1990s, the words "violent crime," "unwed welfare mothers," or "illegal immigrants" could be substituted verbatim for "drugs" in Caesar's harangue.

21. That particular year, the neighboring housing projects where Maria lived had the highest murder rates of all the Housing Authority projects in Manhattan.

22. See Rodríguez 1989:chap. 3 for a discussion of race relations among Puerto Ricans.

2. A Street History of El Barrio

1. Marsh 1932:362.

2. Meléndez 1993:43–44. Only 40 percent of the population actually received food assistance because the eligibility requirements in Puerto Rico are stricter (General Accounting Office 1992; personal communication, Ann Gariazzo, Food and Nutrition Service, U.S. Government).

3. Quintero-Rivera 1984:5–12.
4. I am grateful to Eric Wolf for his conversations with me about changing jíbaro images and categories.
5. Cf. Bonilla and Campos. 1986; Dietz 1986; Centro de Estudios Puertorriqueños, History Task Force, 1979.
6. *New York Times* 1995:A4.
7. Robinson and Passel 1987.
8. Rodríguez 1989.
9. Romo and Schwartz 1993.
10. *Caribbean Business,* November 29, 1990, cited in Caban 1993:note 21. Vertically integrated multinational companies are able to shift profits from production plants located in other countries with higher tax rates to their Puerto Rican subsidiaries through a practice known as "transfer pricing." They accomplish this legally by having their non–Puerto Rican subsidiaries purchase the inputs produced at their Puerto Rican subsidiary at artificially inflated prices (see Meléndez and Meléndez 1993:8, and Dietz and Pantojas-García 1993:114).
    "In 1988, U.S. firms in Puerto Rico realized profits of $8.9 billion, or about 19.7 percent of their declared global profits attributable to direct foreign investment activity" (Cabán 1993:29).
11. Rodríguez 1995. The use of Spanish above the fifth-grade level in Puerto Rican schools was forbidden by the U.S. government until 1934.
12. Rosenberg 1990. See also Institute for Puerto Rican Policy 1992; Lemann 1991; Moore and Pinderhughes 1993:xix; New York City Department of City Planning, December 6, 1993; Rivera-Batiz 1994; Rivera-Batiz and Santiago 1994.
    The family income figures from the housing project across the street from the Game Room confirmed the national statistics on Puerto Rican poverty. According to the 1989 Housing Authority census – which, of course, is grossly inaccurate because rents are calculated as a percentage of income – African-American households earned, on average, over $3,000 more per year than Puerto Rican households ($12,557 versus $9,301) (New York City Housing Authority, Department of Research and Policy Development, January 1, 1989). This official income gap was reduced to approximately $2,000 ($13,803 versus $11,489) in 1993 (New York City Housing Authority, Department of Research and Policy Development, January 1993).
13. Giachello 1991; Institute for Puerto Rican Policy 1994; Rosenwaike 1983.
14. Hell Gate Bay's inauspicious name comes from the whirlpools and sinkholes in the East River at this point in its course (Bolton 1922).
15. Bolton 1922:68–74; Janvier 1903:79–81.
16. Rubinson 1989; see also *New York Times,* May 3, 1931:14.

17. Fischler 1976; Rubinson 1989; Tilley 1935.
18. Cf. Concistre 1943:16; Corsi 1925:90–92; Marsh 1932:50; and Tilley 1935;32.
19. Tilley 1935:32, citing Corsi 1925:90. According to the 1920 Census there were a total of 276,641 residents in East Harlem. This included 43,642 Russians, 41,879 Italians, 8,791 African-Americans, 8,088 Austrians, 6,769 Irish, 6,117 Poles, 4,367 Germans, 3,706 Hungarians, and 1,382 Finns. (Statistics facilitated by Frank Vardi of the New York City Department of City Planning.)
20. Tilley 1935:199.
21. Cordasco and Galatioto 1970:31:309–10, citing Mayor's Committee 1937:16; Meyer 1989:7.
22. Orsi 1985:14.
23. Marsh 1932:186.
24. Orsi 1985:54. The Italians got revenge on the racist Irish and German parishioners by importing from southern Italy a Renaissance-era jewel-encrusted statue of the Virgin Mary that had been personally blessed by the pope. This ancient, sacred statue converted their church into an official holy sanctuary with healing powers. Once a year a pilgrimage, attracting hundreds of believers from all over New York, arrives at the church to accompany the ancient statue on a parade through East Harlem's streets.

    I witnessed the latest phase in the cycle of ethnic conflict at the church when I brought my one-year-old son to be baptized by the resident Italian-American priest. Puerto Ricans were glaringly absent from any of the baptism training sessions. A coterie of elderly Italian-American women complained loudly to one another about the crude manners of the Puerto Rican parishioners. They were especially furious over the most recent "invasion" of Haitian pilgrims, who had arrived from Brooklyn to adore their Renaissance-era southern Italian statue. They claimed to be worried for the statue's safety, and discussed restricting Haitian access to the nave area of the church.
25. Kisseloff 1989:343. In 1990 the final two blocks of Pleasant Avenue, just upwind from my tenement, were sealed off due to the discovery of toxic waste that had been dumped illegally in an abandoned wire factory following a protracted racketeering redevelopment scandal that involved a lawsuit between Proctor and Gamble and a local Italian-American Mafia contractor (*New York Daily News,* October 18, 1989:37; *New York Daily News,* July 10, 1990:22; New York City Department of Environmental Protection 1990; *New York Times,* June 15, 1986:8:6). A group of homeless crack addicts took over the immense factory site, converting it into their personal crack parlor. Not unlike the original 1900 inhabitants who had "collected

all this garbage and junk and would sell it all bundled up in newspaper" (Kisseloff 1989:343), the contemporary crack addicts were ripping the decayed factory's plumbing system out of its asbestos-lined walls to sell as scrap metal.

26. Orsi 1985:160.

27. *New York Times,* May 16, 1893:9.

28. Marsh 1932:65, 64, 49.

29. Thrasher 1936:74

30. Orsi 1985:161, citing Covello 1958:43.

31. Cordasco and Galatioto 1970:307. Ironically, the parents of these racist, class-conscious Jews had not only been socialists but had also precipitated white flight because of their own "racial impurity" less than one generation earlier. "The Germans . . . have all moved away, all but twelve. They have moved to the Bronx . . . and elsewhere. The reason given for this was the undesirable conditions created in the neighborhood, due to the moving in of Jews and Italians" (Marsh 1932:356).

32. Archives of the New York City Department of City Planning, facilitated by Frank Vardi.

33. Marsh 1932:49, 62.

34. *Time* Magazine November 4, 1946:24–25. For accounts of race riots see Meyer 1989:123–24; Covello 1958:237–43.

35. Schepses 1949:56, citing Chenault 1938:123.

36. After the 1898 invasion, the United States formally changed the spelling of Puerto Rico to Porto Rico to reflect an anglicized pronunciation.

37. Marsh 1932:55.

38. Cimilluca 1931:30.

39. Tilley 1935:38, citing Leonard 1930:9.

40. Schepses 1949:57, citing Armstrong, Achilles, and Sacks 1935:57.

41. Lait and Mortimer 1958:126–27.

42. Tilley 1935:34, 48–49.

43. Marsh 1932:49.

44. *New York Herald Tribune,* December 15, 1946:36.

45. Marsh 1932:421–22.

46. Thrasher 1927, 1932, 1936. See also the extensive bibliography on Italian Harlem provided by Meyer 1989:292–94.

47. King 1961; Levitt 1965; Levitt, Loeb, and Agee 1952.

48. Cf. Rivera 1983; Rodriguez 1992; Thomas 1967. See also the discussions by Acosta-Belén 1992; Flores 1993; and Rodriguez 1995.

49. Tilley 1935:192, 32.

50. *New York Times,* March 18, 1957:A1, 29, 30.

51. Camilo Vergara (1991a; 1991b) has documented how New York's poverty

programs deliberately reconcentrated poor households in the South Bronx during the late 1980s. See also Wacquant 1995.

52. Community Service Society 1956.
53. Community Service Society 1956:11–12.
54. Concistre 1943:74.
55. Marsh 1932:61.
56. Reed 1932:18.
57. Marsh 1932:61–62.
58. Tilley 1935:32–33, citing Cimilluca 1931: n.p.; Durk 1976.
59. Reinarman and Levine 1989.
60. Frankel and Freeland 1990; Van Dyck 1990. See Chapter 1, note 1.
61. Dumpson 1951:42, 43.
62. *New York Daily News,* October 19, 1990:A1.
63. Ibid.
64. Dumpson 1951:40.
65. Concistre 1943:66, citing Thrasher 1936.
66. Reed 1932:32.
67. *New York Times,* May 16, 1893:9.
68. *New York Times,* January 29, 1947:A4.
69. Reed 1932:32.
70. *New York Herald Tribune,* December 15, 1946:36.
71. Marsh 1932:354–55; see also Kisseloff 1989:367.
72. A Puerto Rican eventually wrested control of numbers rackets in the neighborhood from Fat Tony. See note 12 on page 344, and the *New York Times,* April 21, 1994:A13.
73. *New York Daily News,* October 18, 1989:A1. The ease with which "Fat Tony" paid his $2 million bail prompted the U.S. Supreme Court to change the federal bail statute to allow for the preventive detention of dangerous criminals without bail (*New York Times,* May 28, 1987:A22).
74. Vince Rao made front-page headlines in the *New York Times* in the 1950s for his half-dozen homicide and grand larceny arrests, for which he was never convicted (*New York Times,* November 18, 1952:A1).
75. O'Brien and Kurins 1991; *New York Times,* March 21, 1987:A31; *New York Times,* April 30, 1988:34; *New York Times,* October 14, 1988:B3; *New York Times,* January 23, 1990:B3; *New York Times,* March 5, 1990:B1; *New York Times,* January 21, 1991:B3.
76. O'Brien and Kurins 1991:335.
77. Drug Enforcement Administration 1988. Francis Hall, the founder of the Tactical Narcotics Team (TNT) and a thirty-five-year veteran in the New York City Police Force's Narcotics Division, told students at a forum on drugs at the State University of New York, Westbury, in May 1990:

Despite these press conferences that you've seen – and I've participated in a number of them – there's more cocaine in the streets of New York today than ever before in its history; no question about it.

Last August, 5,000 pounds of cocaine seized in an apartment house in Forest Hills in Queens, an absolutely mind boggling amount of cocaine. Did that seizure of 5,000 pounds have any effect, any impact at all on the availability of cocaine on the street? None, whatsoever. Not at all. And as we're standing at the press conference in police headquarters, within walking distance of the building, people were selling cocaine on the street.

There is even reason to believe that the South Florida Task Force that was established by President Reagan in 1981 under the direction of then vice-president Bush, that task force actually resulted in more cocaine coming into the United States rather than less. And I say that because the marijuana dealers got out of the marijuana business because of the incredible bulk of transporting marijuana into south Florida. They got out of the marijuana business and they got into the cocaine business. A kilo of cocaine, that's 2.2 pounds – about half the size of a five pound bag of sugar.

3. Crackhouse Management

1. "007" is the brand name of a large folding knife with a wooden handle.
2. Later, Candy explained to me that the woman "Felix was fooling around with" was her sister, and that his ankle was not damaged by his jump but, rather, was cut by the knife she threw at him.
3. See discussion of *compadrazgo* and rural labor relations in Wolf 1956.
4. *Moreno* literally means dark-skinned, but it is used to denote black skin or, in this case, to differentiate African-Americans from black Puerto Ricans.
5. In private, Caesar admitted to being intimidated by violence on the streets. In fact, he even showed some evidence of post-traumatic stress disorder:

   Caesar: People gets wilder when the temperature gets hotter and I'm scared to go out in the street sometimes.

   Word! I was thinking of not coming down today because it's wild out there. I don't want to get hit by a stray bullet when I'm on my way to buy a bag of potato chips.

   Word up! I threw myself on the floor the other day when I just heard an ash can [firecracker] go off. I was just strolling along with my girl Carmen and BOOM! And I went, "Oh shit!" I was *petro;* that shit had my nerves wrecked and I jumped to the floor.

   And I seen them niggas get shot in front of me. It don't look correct. It don't look like you could defend yourself no way!

   And I know because I seen it one time when I was walking with my girl in Jefferson Park. We was crossing this little bridge to get to the other side of the FDR

Drive so we could walk along the water and cross over to Ward's Island. You know that bridge where they chopped that homeless dude up with a meat cleaver last Halloween. [*New York Times* November 4, 1990:A39]

Philippe: Oh yeah, where they found that little Colombian girl strangled, stabbed, and raped last month? [*New York Times* January 26, 1991:A27]

Caesar: Yeah. We were crossing that bridge 'cause I was going to make sex to her, right?

So there were these three guys walking in front of us, like about fifteen feet.

And they talking; and I'm talking at my girl; and all of a sudden, the tallest of the three dudes pulled out a gun and handed it to the shortest guy – 'cause there was two short guys and one taller guy. And the little guy just shot the third dude in the head.

And me and my girl, we was scared. We was so scared that we didn't run or nothing. We was petrified.

So then when the middle dude fell on the floor, he shot him twice in the head again.

And me and my girl were like, "Oh, shit!" You know, I was like, "Oh, shit!" My girl started crying and I told her to, "Shut up, man. Don't say nothing."

So they started walking my way; so I was figuring that this was the end of my life and shit. You know what I'm saying? And I was hugging my girl. I was scared.

But they walked by me – just walked away. They didn't run or nothing; just kept going.

And I be seeing the nigga' every day now. He's a real crackhead! He's just walking around like nothing happened.

6. Before being able to return to El Barrio, Benzie had to negotiate with Ray, through an intermediary, a payment plan for his "debts."

7. Unfortunately, Abraham dropped the replacement glass eye that the hospital had made for him into a vat of soup he was preparing in the hospital cafeteria. Medicaid subsequently refused to pay for a second replacement glass eye.

8. This arson occurred in January 1990 at the Happy Land social club–dance hall, which was frequented primarily by Honduran immigrants. A heroin company operating around my block renamed its brand "Happy Land" shortly after the fire.

9. The intermittent pattern of arrests of corrupt New York City police officers in inner-city precincts in the late 1980s through the mid-1990s illustrates the prevalent, but fundamentally haphazard, nature of police corruption around narcotics at the street-dealer level. Officers are so alienated from the communities they patrol that rather than take payoffs, they specialize in orchestrating fake raids and pocketing the drugs and money they confiscate (cf. *New York Times,* May 8, 1990:A1, B10; *New York Times,* July 7, 1994:B2). Until mid-1994, New York City police officers were specifically

discouraged from arresting drug dealers because of the inherent tempta-
tions for petty corruption (*New York Times,* July 7, 1994:B2). Narcotics
arrests were supposed to be handled exclusively by specially trained elite
units.

10. To illustrate the incompetence of the local police force: When I went to the
precinct to report the burglary of my apartment in midwinter, I noticed
graffiti scrawled on the blackboard in the main office, saying "No more
arrests till we get heat."

11. For accounts of how overwhelmed the New York City courts became in
1989 at the height of the "War on Drugs," see *New York Times,* May
31, 1989:B1.

4. "Goin' Legit"

1. New York City Department of City Planning 1993 (January): 37, Table 6.
In 1950, factory work provided 30 percent of New York City's jobs; by the
early 1990s it provided only 10 percent. In contrast, in 1950 service jobs
accounted for 15 percent of employment; by 1992 service work represented
well over 30 percent of all city jobs. Just in the 1980s alone, manufacturing
decreased 31 percent, whereas "producer services" increased 61 percent and
"all services" rose by 16 percent (Romo and Schwartz 1993:358–59; New
York City Department of City Planning Population Division 1993.)

2. *New York Times,* February 13, 1991:D1; *New York Times,* September 6,
1990:D17.

3. In contrast to that of men, the labor force participation rates of Puerto Rican
women rose from 34 percent in 1980 to 42 percent in 1990 (New York City
Department of City Planning 1993 [December]: Table 6-1).

4. *New York Daily News,* October 30, 1990:1.

5. "Fight the Power" was a best-selling rap song in 1990 by the African-
American group Public Enemy.

6. *Salal* would be spelled *salar* – literally "to salt" – in standard Spanish.
Puerto Rican Spanish, however, converts certain "r's" into "l's."

7. Romo and Schwartz 1993.

8. cf. Colburn 1989; Scott 1985.

9. Becker 1963; Hebdige 1979.

10. According to the 1990 Census of New York City, 22.6 percent of all Latinos
were employed in construction compared to 13.5 percent for whites and 8.8
percent for African-Americans. Between the 1980 Census and the 1990
Census, construction jobs in New York City increased as a proportion of
total employment from 2.3 percent to 3.2 percent (New York City Department of City Planning 1993 [January]: Table 6).

11. *New York Daily News*, August 13, 1991; *New York Times*, July 28, 1991:A29; *New York Times*, March 5 1990:B1; *New York Times*, April 30, 1988:A34.

12. Exceptionally, the head orchestrator of this particular multimillion-dollar round of window bid-rigging contracts was indicted (cf. *New York Daily News*, August 13, 1991:20; *New York Times*, July 28, 1991:29). He was none other than Fat Tony Salerno, the don of the Genovese crime family traditionally headquartered in East Harlem. Little Pete's union subcontractor, however, was much too far down in the chain of corruption to be affected by the indictments.

13. Bourgois 1989a.

14. Covello 1958:223.

15. Berlin 1991:10.

16. See Smith 1992. Sassen-Koob 1986. Undocumented new-immigrants are so crucial to New York City's economy that its politicians, both Republican and Democrat, publicly embraced the right of the undocumented to live and work in the city during the same years (mid-1990s) when the rest of the United States, especially California, was in the throes of an anti-immigrant hysteria (*New York Times*, June 10, 1994:A1, B4).

17. Smith 1992.

5. School Days

1. Abdelmalek Sayad (1991) developed this idea of "the first delinquency" in his analysis of the cultural limbo of second-generation Algerians in France.

2. The Nuyorican poet Tato Laviera (1985:53) expresses this poignantly in his poem "Nuyorican."

3. I visited Caesar on one of the occasions he was interned in the violent wing of the psychiatric ward at Metropolitan Hospital. He told me he wanted to "stay locked up" at the end of the mandatory four-week observation period established for suicide attempts. He also complained that the psychiatrists would not listen to his pleas for stronger medication.

   Upon his subsequent release, however, Caesar made light of his vulnerable mental condition.

   Yeah. I was in a high-security mental ward. It was like a Freddy Krueger scene. I was in there for a while. And it was wild man. I was scared there. I thought that somebody was going to murder me at night, one of those nuts. I became a *nut*. [hunching his shoulder] I started going around everywhere, around the other people that was crazy from drugs.

   And there was one man there that he was Jewish, and I used to call him Woody Allen. And he was there, like for two years, boy. You know Woody Allen? He's a famous Jewish guy. This guy talked just like Woody Allen – a fuckin corny ass Jew. I wanted to kill him. When I came out of the warehouse, I was into killing, boy!

4. Caesar enjoyed infusing his social critiques with irony when I was tape-recording. He understood fully my theoretical orientation, which strives to uncover the linkages between individual pathology and social-structural oppression. Perhaps he was taunting me for being so concerned with the issues of social marginalization and racism.

5. Cf. Bourgois and Dunlap 1992.

6. See discussion of gang rape in the college fraternity context by Sanday 1990.

7. By the time I knew him, Luis was in his mid-thirties and was the father of several daughters. He used to complain righteously of the sexual irresponsibility of young men, even though he himself still reveled in promiscuity and publicly flaunted his addiction to crack.

Luis: I told my daughter, "I don't want some guy to take you, and do what he gotta do, and then throw you out. I don't want him to be calling you a hole, and shit like that, man."

Things are more wild today. There's a whole new generation of assholes out there. Back in the days, there wasn't no crack, or nothing like that.

But now! Now, forget it man. Nowadays, these guys on the streets, just want to destroy a girl's life, you know. And these girls got a future in front of them, but these guys will come, and fuck her up. These young guys, that's what they're all about now. They take a girl; they screw her, and then when they come downstairs, they be saying, "Ah . . . I fucked that bitch. I had that bitch."

6. Redrawing the Gender Line on the Street

1. Jaggar 1983; Hooks 1994.

2. For a cinematographic representation of many of the themes around masculinity, family structure, women's rights, and inner city street culture, see the Nuyorican film *I Like It Like That*. In a more caricatural and tragic manner the polarization of domestic violence was illustrated in a nearby housing project with the brutal serial murder of a six-person family by the jealous former boyfriend of the mother who headed the household. The killer was an unemployed factory worker who hacked everyone to death with a butcher knife following several months of feuding with his ex-girlfriend and her children over whom he could no longer impose his former autocratic control (*New York Times,* May 4, 1993:B1, B3).

Conversely, as one anthropological study of machismo and family life in rural Mexico from the 1960s claims, the successful patriarch, secure in his machismo and omnipotent at home, does not need to engage in overt physical violence against the members of his household (Hunt 1971:116).

3. The hood of the maroon Renault Alliance that we were sitting on was pocked with shotgun bullet holes from a blast that had killed the mother of a three-year-old child earlier that summer. It had occurred directly in front of my apartment window, only moments after I had parked my car and carried my sleeping baby to my second-floor walkup. Candy had dismissed the murdered mother as deserving her fate for having smoked the consignment of crack she was supposed to sell.

4. In her historical analysis of the Cuban family, Verena Martinez-Alier (1974:135) treats elopement as an assertion of individual freedom of choice. She demonstrates how romantic elopement can be understood as a form of individualistic resistance to the institutional racism of Cuban society.

5. One night I actually saw Candy's father at a corner grocery store near La Farmacia's corner. Primo nonchalantly pointed out a shabbily dressed, fragile old man who was rolling humbly on the balls of his feet drinking a Budweiser by the beer cooler that we were reaching into. He was standing bleary-eyed in the background, careful to keep himself out of the way of customers. Primo whispered to me, "That's Candy's father." I could hardly believe that this broken-down, humble alcoholic was the violent patriarch who had traumatized Candy's childhood. He was so lonely and decrepit-looking – like a fish out of water blinking and gasping for breath – that it would not have surprised me had he started drooling or babbling incoherently. Primo giggled at my shocked expression, adding a somewhat sad "Yeah, can you fucking believe it?" Had this dislocated, failed immigrant remained in his natal fishing village of Isabela instead of coming to New York in search of factory work, he might still have been an alcoholic, and he probably would have beaten Candy as a child. The consequences, however, would most certainly not have been so devastating.

6. For examples of how individuals internalize wider social structural contradictions see the literature in the field of critical medical anthropology (Davila 1987; Scheper-Hughes 1992; Singer 1986; Singer et al. 1992).

7. This was the incident that forced Felix to hire Primo as temporary manager of the Game Room. To minimize the humiliation of having been stabbed by his wife for being caught in bed with her sister, Felix had pretended he had sprained his ankle jumping off the motel balcony – at least that is the way Primo originally told me the story. (See Chapter 3, note 2.)

8. Guarnaccia, De la Cancela, and Carrillo 1989; Lewis-Fernandez 1992.

9. Literally, a "towel for tears."

10. Cf. *New York Daily News*, October 19, 1990:1.

11. *Fatal Attraction* was an Academy Award–winning Hollywood movie in 1987 about a woman who terrorizes her ex-lover and his family.

12. Caesar vehemently disliked Tabatha because they had been lovers several years earlier. Tabatha made a point of periodically demonstrating in public her enduring distaste for Caesar. Some three weeks before this conversation — as Primo enjoyed reminding all of us in Caesar's presence — Tabatha "knocked Caesar flat on his ass, in the middle of the street, right in front of the Game Room." Worse yet, she did this on the night Ray had rented the social club two doors down from the Game Room in order to celebrate the simultaneous two-year-old and four-year-old birthdays of two of his sons by different mothers. I missed witnessing Tabatha's legendary diss of Caesar, as I was inside the club at the time supervising my own one-and-a-half-year-old son, who was mesmerized on the dance floor by the rap/disco/salsa music combinations, and the multigenerational potpourri of celebrators, ranging from newborns to great-grandparents.

13. See the discussion on changing motherhood gender roles in a small plantation community by Seda Bonilla 1964.

14. See the discussion by researchers at the Centro de Estudios Puertorriqueños of the struggle for what the authors call "cultural citizenship" on the part of poor Puerto Rican women (Benmayor, Torruellas, and Juarbe 1992). See also the critique of "white, middle class feminism" by Hooks (1994), and of "liberal feminism" by Jaggar (1983). See also discussions by Acosta-Bélen (1993), and Mohanty (1984).

15. Katz 1986. See also Rainwater 1984.

16. Even Caesar was forced to express grudging admiration for Candy's resourcefulness at hustling welfare:

Primo: Candy used to clock when she worked in the bus for retarded children, because she had two social security cards. She worked with one social security card, and at the same time she's collecting welfare on another social security card, and then she has Abraham's money — his SSI — every month.

She was getting paid well, boy!

Caesar: Yeah, then she used to do those tax things.

Primo: Oh yeah, and then at the same time she used to work right there [motioning next door to the Game Room], where the beauty salon is at. It used to be an insurance place that filled out tax forms.

Caesar: That lady is an animal.

Primo: It was like, for just a few hours, because she had just enough time to go back to her bus job before the kids get out, and then later, after dropping off the kids, she'd go back to the tax place.

Caesar: Hey, that lady was scam, a Jew scam, boy!

Primo: Hell yeah! That lady always had a bank. She had her money in a bank account. I remember when a few years ago I had some income tax money that came in, and I told her to hold it for me in her bank.

She's good, man, she never took out money.

Caesar: I remember she did my income tax one year, and she got me *a thousand five hundred,* man. I didn't even think I was going to get five dollars.

It was the first time I did income tax, and I got paid, boy. She didn't charge me nothing, either.

Primo: She did my taxes for me too.

Caesar: She's stupid. She shoulda stood working in that retarded bus thing. That's a good job; it's with the City; that's a good pension, and it's union.

17. Surveys reveal that routine termination from welfare rolls owing to the failure of heads of households to fulfill the bureaucratic requirements of recertification is the single most frequent cause of family homelessness in New York City. The cost of emergency housing and social services for homeless, terminated families far exceeds the amount of money the city would have been penalized by the federal government's matching fund program for maintaining inaccurate files (Berlin 1991; Dehavenon 1989–90).

   A survey of welfare recipients in Chicago in 1988 revealed that none of a snowball sample of twenty-five welfare-receiving families complied fully with the Department of Social Services' income requirements. Every single household had an outside source of income. They simply could not have stayed sheltered, fed, and clothed on the amount of money they officially received from welfare (Edin 1991). In New York City the real dollar value of welfare benefits dropped 30 percent between 1970 and 1992 (*New York Times,* August 30, 1994:A14).

18. Disrespect from welfare social workers and clerks was a frequent theme of conversation on the street, especially among women. Confrontations with welfare investigators over supplementary sources of income constitute some of Primo's earliest childhood memories. His mother's resistance to the bureaucracy was not as aggressive as Candy's, although the final outcome was not significantly different. She successfully supplemented her below-subsistence-level family allotment with outside income from the underground economy.

   Primo: After my father left we had to go on public support. She had a hard time with four kids by herself. My little sister who is twenty-five now, used to still be in a crib.

   My mother used to have perfumes that she was selling, and when the welfare investigators would come, she used to have to hide the little bullshit perfumes' models, in my sister's crib.

   I was a little kid, and I used to wonder who these people were? I hated them. They used to knock and my mother used to say, "Wait a minute." Then she'd be running all over the house [waving his arms in mock frenzy] hiding the perfumes in the baby's crib.

   I used to wonder why, because I was a kid, and I didn't know what the hell it was. But my mother used to always say, *"Investigadores!"* She used to say [waving his arms again, knotting his brow, and shrieking in a high pitch], *"Los investigadores! Los investigadores!"*

It was wack because the house was poor. We didn't used to have too much things in the house, but they used to come, and investigate. But still she used to have to hide her little bullshit things.

That was like in '69 or 1970, or '68, when they used to come and investigate.

Nowadays they don't. When I lived with Sandra no one used to come and investigate her house. No one. I was living with her from day one and I always had her on welfare. [chuckle]

I think they don't got the funds no more to be sending investigators out.

19. Candy's talk with Carlos proved ineffective because a half-dozen teenagers in her projects were struck by automatic gunfire over the following three-month period. Luckily, no one was killed, and the feud eventually ended. Before it was over, however, on three separate occasions I stumbled right onto the edge of the shoot-outs. The first time I was with my wife on our way to have dinner at a local restaurant. The shots stopped us from being able to take a shortcut through the project courtyard, forcing us to walk around the block to reach our final destination.

20. The ultimate fragility of Candy's support system is illustrated by Ray's having to send her two siblings, together, to pay her bail. He could not trust either one individually to deliver the cash safely. Candy's younger brother was an HIV-positive crack-cum-heroin speedballer, and her youngest sister was a welfare-dependent single mother with a compulsive taste for powder cocaine and alcohol.

21. *New York Post*, April 11, 1989:5, 30–31; *New York Times*, April 17, 1989:A1, A16; *New York Times*, July 3, 1994:E3.

7. Families and Children in Pain

1. Farrington 1991

2. During the 1980s, child abuse statistics in New York City escalated almost 700 percent. From 1985 to 1994 they increased 232 percent (cf. *New York Daily News*, November 19, 1990:5, 10; *New York Times*, December 28, 1988:B3; *New York Times*, December 19, 1989:B1). It is impossible to know how much of this increase reflects a real increase or is the result of improved reporting procedures and changing social definitions of child abuse.

3. Marsh 1932:361.

4. Community Service Society 1956:25.

5. For more examples of the destruction of children, see the life scenarios of Manny, Angel, Lestor, Junior, and Angelo in the epilogue.

6. Marsh 1932:48.

7. Coincidentally, a few years later, I noticed a photograph of this same corner in the *New York Times* depicting a shrine of flowers commemorating the murder of a fifty-two-year-old woman caught in crossfire while accompanying her five-year-old grandson home from school (December 1, 1993:A20).

8. I found out the next day in the *New York Times* that the victim was forty-four years old (*New York Times*, November 16, 1989:B2).

9. I grew up seven blocks from the border between Manhattan's Upper East Side and El Barrio. As noted in Chapter 1, note 16, the median household income of my childhood neighborhood was more than thirteen times higher than that of the two census tracts surrounding my apartment on the Game Room's block. Less than 1 percent of the residents in my childhood neighborhood lived below the poverty line in 1990, compared to approximately 47 percent in the two census tracts surrounding my tenement in El Barrio. Only three Puerto Ricans lived in my childhood census tract in 1989 despite its being a five-minute walk from the neighborhood with one of the highest densities of Puerto Rican residents in the entire United States (*1990 Census of Population and Housing Block Statistics*).

10. In Puerto Rican Spanish, *javao'* refers pejoratively to someone with African features and "white" skin.

11. I significantly edited or, rather, censored these excerpts of Maria's poetry for fear of portraying decontextualized racist and sexist material as well as excessively private perspectives.

12. In 1991, there were as many people waiting for public housing (189,000 families) in New York City, as there were living in public housing (approximately 600,000 individuals) (*The Christian Science Monitor*, August 19, 1991:14).

13. Caesar confided to Primo that he sometimes grabbed the toddler by his feet as he lay sleeping and spun him in the air over his head. When Carmen would come running to the bedroom, Caesar pretended he was comforting Papo, who had just woken up, shrieking, from a nightmare. On another occasion, Papo had to be taken to the municipal hospital's emergency room when Caesar ripped his foreskin while bathing him.

I began fretting over whether or not I should file a child abuse report against Caesar, but simultaneously the *New York Times* began running exposés on how overwhelmed the foster child system had become with 45,000 children flooding into its care in 1990 alone. According to one reporter, children were sleeping on the desks of the intake officers at the Bureau of Child Welfare headquarters. Brothers and sisters seized by the foster care program were routinely split apart (cf. *New York Times*, July 3,

1989:B21–22; *New York Times,* October 23, 1989:A1, B4; *New York Times,* December 19, 1989:B1, B4; *New York Times,* March 29, 1992:A1, A20; *New York Times,* February 9, 1989:A1, B9; *New York Times,* October 19, 1990:B3).

I also wondered how to interpret the shrieks of crying children that regularly rose through the heating pipes in my tenement. Was I ethnocentrically misreading the expressively aggressive child-rearing practices of inner-city families, or should I go downstairs and intervene?

Someone else eventually reported Caesar for child abuse, but the investigator took no action; on the contrary, she provided Caesar with enough information to be able to figure out who had reported him, leading to a long-lasting enmity.

14. See again, *New York Daily News,* November 19, 1990:5, 10; *New York Times,* December 28, 1988:B3; *New York Times,* February 9, 1989:A1, B9; *New York Times,* October 23, 1989:A1, B4; *New York Times,* December 19, 1989:B1; *New York Times,* March 17, 1990:A8; *New York Times,* October 19, 1990:B3; *New York Times,* March 29, 1992:A1, A20.

15. See the critique of the sexualization of crack by Bourgois and Dunlap 1992. For a prime example of an editorial in a major newspaper that fully succumbed to the drug hysteria, see *New York Times,* May 28, 1989:A14. See also the critique by Reinarman and Levine 1989.

16. Morgan 1981:89–101, 139–140. In this century's first decade, a U.S. doctor assured the general public in a footnote in a respected medical journal that the violent transformation of African-Americans under the influence of cocaine had been "verify[ed] clinically [through] experimental observations made in 1897 . . . in a series of experiments on cocaine administered hypodermically." This same doctor told his readers that after ingesting cocaine,

    sexual desires are increased and perverted, peaceful negroes become quarrelsome, and timid negroes develop a degree of "Dutch courage" that is sometimes almost incredible. A large proportion of the wholesale killings in the South during recent years have been the direct result of cocaine, and frequently the perpetrators of these crimes have been hitherto inoffensive, law-abiding negroes. Moreover, the negro who has once formed the habit, seems absolutely beyond redemption.

    . . . A very few experimental sniffs of the drug make him an habitué – he is a constant menace to his community until he is eliminated (Williams 1914:247).

17. For example, only two of the more than thirty dealers who worked for Ray while I lived in El Barrio were women.

18. Althaus 1991; Bourgois and Dunlap 1992.

19. *Wall Street Journal,* July 18, 1989:A1, A6; Bowser 1988.

20. *New York Times,* May 28, 1989:A14; *New York Times,* March 17, 1990:A8; *Wall Street Journal,* July 18, 1989:A6.

21. To illustrate the "normalcy" of hanging out at crackhouses, I have several photographs of my wife posing with my son in front of the Game Room, despite the fact that she disapproved of drug use and drug dealing.

22. *New York Times,* May 25, 1990:A1, B5. In fact, the medical literature on the effects of intrauterine alcohol and narcotics use is very confusing. Studies show uneven results, and doctors do not have a coherent explanation for why some babies are severely damaged and others are born completely healthy (cf. Koren et al. 1989). Follow-up studies in the mid-1990s suggested that most crack-exposed infants recover fully if they are provided with adequate social support and treatment during childhood (Day and Richardson 1993).

23. Ceasar defused a heated argument I was having with Ray over the hypocrisy of his Catholic dogmatism on abortion versus his greediness for selling to pregnant addicts by supporting Ray, and attacking the larger hypocritical logic of the U.S. military-industrial complex:

    Caesar: I ain't into abortion neither, Felipe. Abortion is whack, it ain't right. Besides it's a cardinal sin.

    It's better that you just put all these scum to war when they get older. That's why you have a war, once in a while – every four years. That's better than killing it before the child has a chance. Just have a war every four years and get rid of some of the population.

    War is a big business, man. It's the most powerful business. These fuckin' [aircraft] carriers be costing billions and billions. Drug dealers [pointing at Ray] don't have billions, yet [general laughter] – maybe millions and millions, but not billions. Drug dealers don't have more than the military. They don't make more than the military.

24. We befriended a pregnant crack addict who we saw in midwinter opening her coat widely to display her distended belly on a well-known prostitute stroll a dozen blocks from the Game Room. She explained that her pregnancy increased her business: "They [her customers] like pregnant pussy. They say pregnant pussy the best for them" (Bourgois and Dunlap 1993).

25. *New York Times* February 9, 1987; *Newsday,* October 29, 1990:8, 30; *Village Voice,* April 3, 1990:11–12.

26. Scheper-Hughes 1992.

27. Majors and Billson 1992.

28. In his moving personal account of adopting a Sioux baby, the Native American anthropologist Michael Dorris (1989) notes that fetal alcohol syndrome has increased among Native American children as traditional gender relations on reservations have changed, and as women increasingly have the right, or at least the option, to drink publicly. See also the critical review by Pollitt (1990:416), which argues that Dorris failed to contextualize adequately the structural oppression of Native Americans. She accuses him of falling unaware into a reactionary "fetal rights" trap. Cook-

Lynn (1989), herself a member of the Sioux Nation, attacks Dorris for imposing a middle-class, Anglo distortion on his child's tragedy. She also notes long-term Sioux struggles to address the problem of alcoholism holistically through cultural revitalization and healing.

8. Vulnerable Fathers

1. In the two census tracts surrounding my tenement, slightly more than 70 percent of the female headed households with young children were below the poverty line, compared to approximately 47 percent of all families in the same micro-neighborhood (*1990 Census of Population and Housing Block Statistics*).
2. In a book of essays, the sociologist Herbert Gans (1991:291) notes, "A family headed by a capable if unmarried mother may thus be healthier than a two parent family in which the father is a marginal appendage."
3. *New York Times,* March 31, 1994:A18. Family poverty rates rose even faster for young workers. The proportion of workers between the ages of eighteen and twenty-four who had wages that were too low to keep a family of four over the poverty line (defined as $6.50 per hour) increased from 23 percent in 1979 to 47 percent in 1992.
4. Quintero-Rivera 1984.
5. See De la Cancela's analysis of the relationship between machismo and capitalism in the Puerto Rican experience (1986). See also the critique of Anglo stereotypes of machismo by Paredes (1971). Ramirez (1993) offers a detailed analysis of Puerto Rican masculinity.
6. Rosie worked for Ray for about six months until she saved enough money for the down payment on a Section-8 subsidized rental apartment. She had just had a baby and was desperate to move out of her mother's crowded project apartment. At the Game Room she spent most of her time knitting a pink security blanket for her newborn, whom she had left at home with her mother.
7. Luis insisted on using his own "stem" when he shared a five-dollar pipeful of crack with sex-for-crack prostitutes, so as to benefit from the additional buildup of resin. (See Bourgois and Dunlap 1992.)
8. A Puerto Rican friend who grew up on the Game Room's block and who works as a secretary in a local job-training program, complained to me that some of her childhood friends tell her to "stop acting white" when she criticizes them for being promiscuous.
9. In his discussion of machismo in a Mexican village, Hunt (1971) notes that contrary to the stereotype of macho men being driven to violent promiscuity and substance abuse by deep inferiority complexes, the "real machos" are

375

completely confident in their total domination and can be "highly puritani-
cal, and often deeply committed to what they call progress, honesty, and
justice. They are the pluperfect example of what by their cultural norms the
perfect father ought to be: tolerant, wise, just, honest" (p. 116). See also
note 2 on page 354.

10. Some six months later a man was apprehended for raping his three year-old
niece in broad daylight at this exact same spot (*New York Times,* July
17, 1991:B1).

11. I had witnessed Caesar's uncharacteristic submission to his stepfather a few
months earlier, on a hot Saturday night when we ran into his "Poppy"
drinking with a few friends. They were sitting on a bench around a cooler
full of beer in the courtyard of a neighboring housing project. A short,
overweight man in his mid-forties, Caesar's stepfather grabbed him by the
crotch and, with a big grin, called over his friends slumped on the playground bench. "Yo, look at the size of my boy. This is my son and he's got
a big one." Caesar cracked a serious smile, but, to my surprise, remained
subdued. Normally he would not have tolerated such physical disrespect. It
struck me that maybe he was grateful that a male figure would publicly take
genetic responsibility for his existence and lay patriarchal claim to it. In
contrast, Primo never had a stable stepfather figure in his life. Perhaps this
explains the gentleness of his relationship to his "adopted grandfather,"
Abraham, who sometimes collected the quarters from the video machines in
the Game Room. Primo watched over Abraham "like a hawk," making sure
he did not have more than three 16-ounce cans of malt liquor on the nights
that he visited. Primo also always escorted Abraham back to his high-rise
project apartment. On the nights when Abraham managed to drink extra
beers "on the sneak tip," Primo would have to support him in a stumbling
bear hug all the way through the project courtyards to keep him from falling
down.

Primo respected Abraham despite his decrepitude.

Primo: Abraham was cool. When he use to live with Luís' mother, he didn't use
to beat the kids. If anything, he got beat down. Word! Eva used to beat Abraham
down, and play him dirty to his fucking face. She used to beat the shit out of
Abraham because of his severe alcohol problem.

12. *New York Times,* November 4, 1990:A39; *New York Times,* January 26,
1991:A27.

9. Conclusion

1. See Devine's (in press) call – despite his postmodernism – for policy engagement in the field of critical, inner-city education.

2. Cf. Phillips 1990; Sassen 1991; Wacquant 1993; Wilson 1987.

3. Rainwater 1994; *Business Week*, August 15, 1994:78–83. See also note 3 on page 362.
4. Cf. Collins 1983; Wilson 1987; New York City Department of City Planning 1993 (March).
5. Rivera-Batiz 1994.
6. New York City Department of City Planning 1993 (March).
7. Blachman and Sharpe 1989–90:154.
8. Smolowe 1994:58; *New York Times*, July 9, 1994:A19. In 1993, Russia surpassed the United States, which had surpassed South Africa in 1992, to have the highest per capita incarceration rate in the world (*New York Times*, September 13, 1994:A8).
9. Robert Merton (1994) made this point in the 1930s with respect to Chicago street criminals when he developed his analysis of "social structure and anomie."

Epilogue

1. New York City Department of City Planning 1993 (March). School district statistic courtesy of Robert Smith.

BIBLIOGRAPHY

Acosta-Belén, Edna. 1992. "Beyond Island Boundaries: Ethnicity, Gender, and Cultural Revitalization in Nuyorican Literature." *Callaloo* 15(4): 979–98.

Acosta-Belén, Edna. 1993. "Defining a Common Ground: The Theoretical Meeting of Women's, Ethnic, and Area Studies." In Edna Acosta-Belén and Christine E. Bose, eds., *Researching Women in Latin America and the Caribbean,* pp. 175–86. Boulder, Colo.: Westview Press.

Althaus, F. 1991. "As Incidence of Syphilis Rises Sharply in the U.S., Racial Differentials Grow." *Family Planning Perspectives* 23(1): 43–44.

Armstrong, C. P., E. M. Achilles, and M. J. Sacks. 1935. "A Study on Reactions of Puerto Rican Children in New York City to Psychological Tests." Chamber of Commerce of the State of New York.

Becker, Howard S. 1963. *Outsiders: Studies in the Sociology of Deviance.* New York: Free Press.

Behar, Ruth. 1993. *Translated Woman: Crossing the Border with Esperanza's Story.* Boston: Beacon Press.

Benmayor, Rina, Rosa Torruellas, and Anna Juarbe. 1992. "Responses to Poverty Among Puerto Rican Women: Identity, Community, and Cultural Citizenship." New York: Centro de Estudios Puertorriqueños, Hunter College. Report to the Joint Committee for Public Policy Research on Contemporary Hispanic Issues of the Inter-University Program for Latino Research and the Social Science Research Council.

Berlin, Gordon. 1991. "The Poverty Among Families: A Service Decategorization Response." New York: Manpower Demonstration Research Corporation. Photocopied report.

Blachman, Morris J., and Kenneth E. Sharpe. 1989–90 (Winter). "The War on Drugs: American Democracy under Assault." *World Policy Journal* 7(1): 135–63.

Blumstein, Alfred, and Joel Wallman. 2000. "The Recent Rise and Fall of American Violence." In Alfred Blumstein and Joel Wallman, eds., *The*

Bibliography

Crime Drop in America, pp. 1–12. New York: Cambridge University Press.

Bolton, Reginald P. 1922. *Indian Paths of the Great Metropolis*. New York: Museum of the American Indian Heye Foundation.

Bonilla, Frank, and Ricardo Campos. 1986. *Industry and Idleness*. New York: Centro de Estudios Puertorriqueños, Hunter College.

Bourdieu, Pierre. 1980. *The Logic of Practice*. Stanford, Calif.: Stanford University Press.

Bourgois, Philippe. 1989a. "In Search of Horatio Alger: Culture and Ideology in the Crack Economy." *Contemporary Drug Problems* 16(4): 619–49.

Bourgois, Philippe. 1989b. *Ethnicity at Work: Divided Labor on a Central American Banana Plantation*. Studies in Atlantic History and Culture Series. Baltimore: Johns Hopkins University Press.

Bourgois, Philippe. 1990. "Hypotheses and Ethnographic Analysis of Concealment in the Underground Economy: The Economic and Ideological Dynamics of the Census Undercount." *Ethnographic Exploratory Research Report #6*. Washington D.C.: Bureau of the Census, Center for Survey Methods Research.

Bourgois, Philippe. 2000. "Disciplining Addictions: The Bio-politics of Methadone and Heroin in the United States." *Culture, Medicine, and Psychiatry* 24(2): 165–95.

Bourgois, Philippe, and Eloise Dunlap. 1993. "Exorcising Sex-for-Crack Prostitution: An Ethnographic Perspective from Harlem." In Mitchell Ratner, ed., *Crack Pipe as Pimp: An Eight-City Ethnographic Study of the Sex-for-Crack Phenomenon*, pp. 97–132. Lexington Mass.: Lexington Books.

Bowser, Benjamin. 1988. "Crack and AIDS: An Ethnographic Impression." *MIRA, Multicultural Inquiry and Research on AIDS* (Spring), 2(2): 1–2.

Business Week. 1994 (August 15). "Inequality: How the Gap Between Rich and Poor Hurts the Economy," pp. 78–83, by Aaron Bernstein.

Cabán, Pedro. 1993. "Redefining Puerto Rico's Political Status." In Edwin Meléndez and Edgardo Meléndez, eds., *Colonial Dilemma: Critical Perspectives on Contemporary Puerto Rico*, pp. 19–40. Boston: South End Press.

Camp, Camille Graham, and George M. Camp. 1998. *The Corrections Yearbook 1998*, pp. 246, 248. Middletown,: Criminal Justice Institute.

Centro de Estudios Puertorriqueños, History Task Force, Hunter College. 1979. *Labor Migration Under Capitalism: The Puerto Rican Experience*. New York: Monthly Review Press.

CESAR FAX. 2001. "Current Cocaine-Positive Rates Among Male Arrestees Remain Dramatically Lower than Historic Peaks," no. 10: 39.

Chenault, Lawrence. 1938. *The Puerto Rican Migrant in New York City*. New York: Columbia University Press.

Christian Science Monitor. 1991 (August 19). "New York City's Oases of Safety," p. 14, by Lucia Mount.

Cimilluca, Salvatore. 1931. "The Natural History of East Harlem from 1880 to the Present." Master's thesis, New York University.

Colburn, Forrest, ed. 1989. *Everyday Forms of Resistance.* Armonk, N.Y.: M. E. Sharpe.

Collins, Sharon M. 1983. "The Making of the Black Middle Class." *Social Problems* 30(4): 369–82.

Community Service Society. 1956 (September 20). "Interim Report on Jefferson Site Service Pilot Project." Manuscript. File in Box 347 of the Community Service Society Archives, Butler Library, Columbia University.

Concistre, Marie J. 1943. "A Study of a Decade in the Life and Education of the Adult Immigrant Community in East Harlem." Ph.D. dissertation, New York University.

Cook-Lynn, Elizabeth. 1989. "(Review) *The Broken Cord.*" *Wicazo Sa* 5(2): 42–45.

Cordasco, Francesco, and Rocco G. Galatioto. 1970. "Ethnic Displacement in the Interstitial Community: The East Harlem Experience." *Phylon: The Atlanta Review of Race and Culture* 31: 302–12.

Corsi, Edward. 1925 (September 16). "My Neighborhood." *The Outlook,* pp. 90–92.

Covello, Leonard, with Guido D'Agostino. 1958. *The Heart Is the Teacher.* New York: McGraw-Hill.

Davila, Richard D. 1987. "The History of Puerto Rican Drinking Patterns." In Merrill Singer, Lani Davison, and Fuat Yalin, eds., *Conference Proceedings: Alcohol Use and Abuse Among Hispanic Adolescents.* Hartford, Conn.: Hispanic Health Council.

Day, N. L., and G. A. Richarson. 1993 (September 1). "Cocaine Use and Crack Babies: Science, Media, and Miscommunication." *Neurotoxicology and Teratology* 15(5): 293–334.

Dehavenon, Anna Lou. 1989–90. "Charles Dickens Meets Franz Kafka: The Maladministration of New York City's Public Assistance Programs." *New York University Review of Law and Social Change* 17(2): 231–54.

De la Cancela, Víctor. 1986. "A Critical Analysis of Puerto Rican Machismo: Implications for Clinical Practice." *Psychotherapy* 23(2): 291–96.

Devine, John. *The New Panopticon: The Construction of Violence in Inner City High Schools.* Chicago: University of Chicago Press.

Díaz Valcarcel, Emilio. 1978. *Harlem todos los dias: Novela.* First edition. San Juán: Ediciones Huracán.

Dietz, James L. 1986. *Economic History of Puerto Rico: Institutional Change and Capitalist Development.* Princeton, N.J.: Princeton University Press.

Dietz, James L., and Emilio Pantojas-García. 1993. "Puerto Rico's New Role in the Caribbean: The High-Finance/Maquiladora Strategy." In Edwin Meléndez and

Edgardo Meléndez, eds., *Colonial Dilemma: Critical Perspectives on Contemporary Puerto Rico*. pp. 103–18. Boston: South End Press.

Dorris, Michael. 1989. *The Broken Cord: A Family's Ongoing Struggle with Fetal Alcohol Syndrome*. New York: Harper & Row.

Drug Enforcement Administration (DEA). 1988. "Crack Cocaine Availability and Trafficking in the United States." Washington, D.C.: U.S. Department of Justice, Drug Enforcement Administration, Cocaine Investigations Section.

Dumpson, James. 1951. "The Menace of Narcotics to the Children of New York: A Plan to Eradicate the Evil." New York: Welfare Council of New York. (Manuscript report, in Narcotics file, Box 370, Community Service Society Archives, Columbia Rare Books, p. 43.)

Durk, David, with Arlene Durk and Ira Silverman. 1976. *The Pleasant Avenue Connection*. New York: Harper & Row.

Edin, Kathryn. 1991. "Surviving the Welfare System: How AFDC Recipients Make Ends Meet in Chicago." *Social Problems* 38(4): 462–74.

Farrington, David. 1991. "Childhood Aggression and Adult Violence: Early Precursors and Later-Life Outcomes." In Debra Pepler and Kenneth Rubin, eds., *The Development and Treatment of Childhood Aggression,* pp. 5–29. Hillsdale, N.J.: Lawrence Erlbaum.

Fischler, Stan. 1976. *Uptown Downtown: A Trip Through Time on New York's Subways*. New York: Hawthorn/Dutton.

Flores, Juán. 1993. *Divided Borders: Essays on Puerto Rican Identity*. Houston, Tex.: Arte Publico Press.

Foley, Douglas. 1990. *Learning Capitalist Culture: Deep in the Heart of Tejas*. Philadelphia: University of Pennsylvania Press.

Fordham, Signithia. 1988. "Racelessness as a Factor in Black Students' School Success: Pragmatic Strategy or Pyrrhic Victory?" *Harvard Educational Review* 53(257): 293.

Frankel, Alison, and Lisa Freeland. 1990 (March). "Is Street-Level Enforcement a Bust?" *The American Lawyer*, pp. 100–9.

Gans, Herbert J. 1991. *People, Plans, and Policies: Essays on Poverty, Racism, and Other National Urban Problems*. New York: Columbia University Press and Russell Sage Foundation.

General Accounting Office. 1992 (July). "Food Assistance Nutritional Conditions and Program Alternatives in Puerto Rico." Washington D.C.: United States General Accounting Office Report to Congressional Committees, GAO/RCED-92-114.

Giachello, Aida L. 1991 (March). "Selected Health Characteristics of Hispanic Children and Adults in the United States." Fact sheet presented to the Inter-University Program for Latino Research and the Social Science Research Council Grantee meetings, Miami.

Gibson, Margaret, and John Ogbu, eds. 1991. *Minority Status and Schooling: A Comparative Study of Immigrant and Involuntary Minorities*. New York and London: Garland Publishing.

Golub, Andrew, and Bruce Johnson. 1999. "Cohort Changes in Illegal Drug Use among Arrestees in Manhattan: From the Heroin Injection Generation to the Blunts Generation." *Substance Use and Misuse* 34(13): 1733–63.

Guarnaccia, Peter J., Víctor De la Cancela, and Emilio Carrillo. 1989. "The Multiple Meaning of Ataques de Nervios in the Latino Community." *Medical Anthropology* 11: 47–62.

Gunst, Laurie. 1995. *Born Fi' Dead: A Journey Through the Jamaican Posse Underworld*. New York: Holt.

Harvey, David L. 1993. *Potter Addition: Poverty, Family, and Kinship in a Heartland Community*. New York: Aldine de Gruyter.

Hebdige, Dick. 1979. *Subculture: The Meaning of Style*. London: Methuen.

Hooks, Bell. 1984. *Feminist Theory from Margin to Center*. Boston: South End Press.

Hunt, Robert C. 1971. "Components of Relationships in the Family: A Mexican Village." In Francis L. K. Hsu, ed., *Kinship and Culture*, pp. 106–43. Chicago: Aldine.

I Like It Like That. 1994. Directed by Darnell Martin. 35 mm, 105 minutes. New York: Columbia Tristar.

Institute for Puerto Rican Policy. 1992. "Puerto Ricans and Other Latinos in New York City Today: A Statistical Profile." Pamphlet.

Institute for Puerto Rican Policy. 1994 (June). "Puerto Ricans and Other Latinos in the United States: March 1993." *IPR Datanote* 16: 1–2.

Jaggar, Alison. 1983. *Feminist Politics and Human Nature*. Totowa, N.J.: Rowman & Allanheld.

Janvier, Thomas A. 1903. *The Dutch Founding of New York*. New York: Harper & Brothers.

Katz, Michael. 1986. *In the Shadow of the Poorhouse: A Social History of Welfare in America*. New York: Basic Books.

Kelling, George, and Catherine Coles. 1996. *Fixing Broken Windows: Restoring Order and Reducing Crime in Our Communities*. New York: Free Press.

King, Ben E. 1961. *Ben E. King's Greatest Hits*. New York: Atco.

Kisseloff, Jeff. 1989. *You Must Remember This*. New York: Schocken Books.

Koren, Gideon, Karen Graham, Heather Shear, and Tom Einarson. 1989 (December 16). "Bias Against the Null Hypothesis: The Reproductive Hazards of Cocaine." *Lancet* 2(8677): 1440–42.

Lait, Jack, and Lee Mortimer. 1948. *New York: Confidential*. New York: Crown.

Laviera, Tato. 1985. *AmeRican*. Houston, Tex.: Arte Publico Press.

Lee III, Rensselaer W. 1991. *The White Labyrinth: Cocaine and Political Power*. New Brunswick, N.J.: Transaction Publishers.

Bibliography

Lemann, Nicholas. 1991. "The Other Underclass." *The Atlantic* 268(6): 96–110.

Leonard, Caroline. 1930. "A Descriptive Study of Social Settlements of East Harlem." Unpublished manuscript, New York University.

Levitt, Helen. 1965. *A Way of Seeing: Photographs of New York,* with an essay by James Agee. New York: Viking Press.

Levitt, Helen, Janice Loeb, and James Agee. 1952. *In the Street* (motion picture). New York: Museum of Modern Art.

Lewis, Gordon K. 1963. *Puerto Rico: Freedom and Power in the Caribbean.* New York: Monthly Review Press.

Lewis, Oscar. 1966. *La Vida: A Puerto Rican Family in the Culture of Poverty – San Juan and New York.* New York: Random House.

Lewis-Fernández, Robert. 1992 (December 2). "Ataques de Nervios or Panic Attacks: An Embodied Contestation of Puerto Rican Ethnicity." Paper prepared for AAA session on "Healing, Bodily Practices, and Caribbean Ethnicity," San Francisco.

Macallair, Dan, and Khaled Taqi-Eddin. 1999. "Shattering 'Broken Windows': An Analysis of San Francisco's Alternative Crime Policies." San Francisco: The Justice Policy Institute.

MacLeod, Jay. 1987. *Ain't No Makin' It: Leveled Aspirations in a Low-Income Neighborhood.* Boulder, Colo.: Westview Press.

Majors, Richard, and Janet M. Billson. 1992. *Cool Pose: The Dilemmas of Black Manhood in America.* New York: Lexington Books.

Marsh, May Case. 1932. "The Life and Work of the Churches in an Interstitial Area." Ph.D. dissertation, New York University.

Martinez-Alier, Verena. 1974. *Marriage, Class, and Color in Nineteenth Century Cuba: A Study of Racial Attitudes and Sexual Values in a Slave Society.* Ann Arbor: University of Michigan Press.

Mayor's Committee on City Planning. 1937. "East Harlem Community Study." New York: East Harlem Council of Social Agencies.

Meléndez, Edgardo. 1993. "Colonialism, Citizenship, and Contemporary Statehood." In Edwin Meléndez and Edgardo Meléndez, eds., *Colonial Dilemma: Critical Perspectives on Contemporary Puerto Rico,* pp. 41–52. Boston: South End Press.

Meléndez, Edwin, and Edgardo Meléndez, eds. 1993. "Introduction." In *Colonial Dilemma: Critical Perspectives on Contemporary Puerto Rico,* pp. 1–18. Boston: South End Press.

Merton, Robert K. 1994. "Opportunity Structure: The Emergence, Diffusion, and Differentiation of a Sociological Concept, 1930s–1950s." In Fred Adler and William S. Laufer, eds., *The Legacy of Anomie Theory;* vol. 6 of *Advances in Criminological Theory,* pp. 3–78. New Brunswick, N.J.: Transaction Books.

Bibliography

Meyer, Gerald. 1989. *Vito Marcantonio: Radical Politician 1902–1954*. Albany: State University of New York Press.

Mohanty, Chandra Talpade. 1984 (Spring/Fall). "Under Western Eyes: Feminist Scholarship and Colonial Discourses." *Boundary* 2, 12(3)/13(1): 333–58.

Moore, Joan, and Raquel Pinderhughes. 1993. "Introduction." In Joan Moore and Raquel Pinderhughes, eds., *In the Barrios: Latinos and the Underclass Debate*, pp. xi–xxxix. New York: Russell Sage Foundation.

Morgan, H. Wayne. 1981. *Drugs in America: A Social History, 1800–1980*. New York: Syracuse University Press.

Moynihan, Daniel P. 1965. "The Negro Family: The Case for National Action." Washington D.C.: Office of Policy Planning and Research, U.S. Department of Labor.

Nader, Laura. 1972. "Up the Anthropologist – Perspectives Gained from Studying Up." In Dell Hymes, ed., *Reinventing Anthropology*, pp. 284–311. New York: Pantheon.

Newsday. 1990 (October 29). "Pregnant Addicts, Aborted Funds," pp. 8, 30.

New York City Department of City Planning. 1985 (December). "The Puerto Rican New Yorkers: Part II – Socioeconomic Characteristics and Trends 1970–1980." New York: Department of City Planning.

New York City Department of City Planning. 1990 (September). "Community District Needs." New York: Department of City Planning.

New York City Department of City Planning. 1993 (January). "Citywide Industry Study: Labor Force Technical Report." New York: Department of City Planning.

New York City Department of City Planning. 1993 (March). "Socioeconomic Profiles: A Portrait of New York City's Community Districts from the 1980 & 1990 Censuses of Population and Housing." New York: Department of City Planning.

New York City Department of City Planning. 1993 (December). "Puerto Rican New Yorkers in 1990." New York: Department of City Planning.

New York City Department of City Planning, Population Division. 1992 (August 26). "1990 Census: Economic Development Indicators (Poverty Status, Unemployment Rate and Per Capita Income). New York City, Boroughs and Census Tracts. (Summary Tape File 3A)." New York: Department of City Planning. Photocopied Report.

New York City Department of City Planning, Population Division. 1993 (February). "1990 Census: Industry Classifications of Employed Persons 16 Years and Over. New York City, Boroughs and Census Tracts. (Summary Tape File 3A)." New York: Department of City Planning. Photocopied Report.

New York City Department of Environmental Protection. Files obtained through the Freedom of Information Act on October 15, 1990, concerning the former Washburn Wire Company factory site.

New York City Housing Authority, Department of Research and Policy Development. 1988 (December 28). "Summary of Overcrowding in Authority Apartments." Photocopied manuscript.

New York City Housing Authority, Department of Research and Policy Development. 1989 (January 1). "Special Tabulation of Tenant Characteristics." Photocopied pages.

New York City Housing Authority, Department of Research and Policy Development. 1993 (January 1). "Special Tabulation of Tenant Characteristics." Photocopied pages.

New York Daily News. 1989 (January 23). "Violent Crime in the City: 1984–1988," p. 18.

New York Daily News. 1989 (September 8). "Mob Boss Up to 175 Years," p. 1.

New York Daily News. 1989 (October 18). "TV Center Finds Life Taxing," p. 37.

New York Daily News. 1990 (July 10). "Toxic Cleanup Will Have to Wait," p. 22.

New York Daily News. 1990 (October 19). "Devil's Playgrounds," p. 1.

New York Daily News. 1990 (October 30). "Child's View of Hell Devil's Playgrounds," pp. 1, 3.

New York Daily News. 1990 (November 19). "'She Had Sad Eyes': Abused, and Dead at 5," pp. 5, 10.

New York Daily News. 1991 (August 13). "N.J. Corpse is 'Windows' Witness," pp. 1–5.

New York Herald Tribune. 1946 (December 15). "Inquiry Focuses Spotlight on Ills of East Harlem," p. 36.

New York Post. 1989 (April 11). "Babies Who Spend Their First Year in Jail," pp. 5, 30–31.

New York Post. 1989 (May 4). "Calm After the Storm," p. 4.

New York Times. 1893 (May 16). "Mafia's Code in New York: Italians Who Avenge Their Own Grievance in Blood," p. 9.

New York Times. 1931 (May 3). "The East Side is Awakening to Its Glory of Olden Days," p. 14, by R. L. Duffus.

New York Times. 1947 (January 29). "Marcantonio May Sue Wallander to Bar 'Harassing' Harlem Clubs, " A4.

New York Times. 1957 (March 18). "Housing Projects Make Bitter D.P.'s," A1, by Charles Grutzner.

New York Times. 1957 (November 18). "Rao, Lanza Knew Public Officials," A1, by Emanuel Perlmutter.

New York Times. 1986 (June 15). "East Harlem TV Deal Unraveling," sec. 8, p. 6, by Anthony De Palma.

New York Times. 1987 (February 9). "Crack Addiction: The Tragic Toll on Women and Their Children," B1, B2.

New York Times. 1987 (March 21). "Major Mafia Leader Turns Informer," A31, by Arnold Lubasch.

New York Times. 1987 (May 28). "Dangerous Until Proved Innocent," A22, editorial.

New York Times. 1988 (April 30). "Mob Role in New York Construction Depicted," A34.

New York Times. 1988 (October 14). "Salerno, Now 100 Years, Gets 70 More in Bid-Rigging Case," B3.

New York Times. 1988 (November 16). "Crackdown on Drug Sellers Is Expanded to East Harlem," A1, B5, by George James.

New York Times. 1988 (December 28). "Domestic Violence Arrests Quadruple in New York City," B3, by Celestine Bohlen.

New York Times. 1989 (February 9). "Destroyer of Families, Crack Besieges a Court," A1, B9, by Felicia R. Lee.

New York Times. 1989 (April 17). "Number of Mothers in Jail Surges with Drug Arrests," A1, A16, by Celestine Bohlen.

New York Times. 1989 (May 28). "Crack: A Disaster of Historical Dimension, Still Growing," A14, editorial.

New York Times. 1989 (May 31). "Attack on Crack: More Arrests, Fewer Long Sentences," B1, B3, by Felicia R. Lee.

New York Times. 1989 (July 3). "For Child Welfare Agency, Small Gains and Big Flaws," L21, L22, by Suzanne Daley.

New York Times. 1989 (August 11). "Link to Mafia Is Investigated in Union Deaths," B2.

New York Times. 1989 (August 25). "Black Youth Is Killed by Whites; Brooklyn Attack Is Called Racial," A1, B2.

New York Times. 1989 (September 29). "For Pregnant Addicts, A Clinic of Hope," B1, B2, by Howard W. French.

New York Times. 1989 (October 23). "Treating Kin Like Foster Parents Strains a New York Child Agency," A1, B4, by Suzanne Daley.

New York Times. 1989 (November 1). "Bush and Congress Reach Accord Raising Minimum Wage to $4.25," A1.

New York Times. 1989 (November 16). "Police Kill Harlem Gunman; Drug Suspect Shot in Bronx," B2, by John T. McQuiston.

New York Times. 1989 (December 19). "New York's Sinking Child-Care System Awaits Help," B1, B4, by Suzanne Daley.

New York Times. 1990 (January 23). "Organized-Crime Turncoat Testifies in Gotti Prosecution," B3.

New York Times. 1990 (March 5). "New York City's Biggest Concrete Supplier Facing U.S. Inquiry," B1, by Selwyn Raab.

New York Times. 1990 (March 17). "The Instincts of Parenthood Become Part of Crack's Toll," A8, by Michael deCourcy Hinds.

New York Times. 1990 (March 23). "Trapped in the Terror of New York's Holding Pens," A1, B4, by William Glaberson.

New York Times. 1990 (May 8). "He Wore a Badge, Then He Sold It for Crack," A1, B10.

New York Times. 1990 (May 25). "Crack Babies Turn 5, and Schools Brace," A1, B5, by Susan Chira.

New York Times. 1990 (June 15). "AIDS Travels New York–Puerto Rico 'Air Bridge,' B1, B4, by Bruce Lambert.

New York Times. 1990 (September 6). "Dollar Off in Heavy Selling on Talk of Fed Rate Move," D17.

New York Times. 1990 (October 19). "Addicted Parents' Children Pose Foster Care Challenge," B3, by Thomas Morgan.

New York Times. 1990 (November 4). "Youths Are Sought in Killing of a Homeless Man," A39, by James C. McKinley, Jr.

New York Times. 1991 (January 21). "Unions at Javits Center Are Accused of Abuses," B3, by Selwyn Raab.

New York Times. 1991 (January 26). "Girl, 13, Is Raped and Killed on Way Home from School," A27, by James C. McKinley, Jr.

New York Times. 1991 (February 13). "Bush View Upbeat on Economy: Recovery Expected to Begin in Summer in Economic Report," D1, by David E. Rosenbaum.

New York Times. 1991 (July 17). "Man Seized in Rape of 3-Year-Old in Public," B1, B4, by Lee A. Daniels.

New York Times. 1991 (July 28). "Informer Insists Bid-Rigging Testimony Was Truth," A29, by Arnold H. Lubasch.

New York Times. 1992 (March 29). "Collapse of Inner-City Families Creates America's New Orphans," A1, A20, by Linda Gross.

New York Times. 1993 (May 4). "6 Are Found Slain in a Harlem Home That Was Set Afire," B1, B3, by Ian Fisher.

New York Times. 1993 (August 8). "With Supply and Purity Up, Heroin Use Expands," A1, A18, by Joseph Treaster.

New York Times. 1993 (December 1). "Woman Lives, and Dies, for Her Family in East Harlem," A20.

New York Times. 1994 (February 18). "An Evolution in an Economy: Jobs in Thinking, Not Making," A1, A12, by Tom Redburn.

New York Times. 1994 (March 20). "Two Census Tracts, at the Extremes," A6, by Sam Roberts.

New York Times. 1994 (March 31). "Sharp Increase Along the Borders of Poverty," A8, by Jason DeParle.

New York Times. 1994 (April 21). "Using Fax Spells Arrest for Numbers Ring," A13, by Selwyn Raab.

New York Times. 1994 (June 10). "New York Officials Welcome Immigrants, Legal or Illegal," A1, B4, by Deborah Sontag.

New York Times. 1994 (July 3). "Women Doing Crime, Women Doing Time," E3, by Clifford Crauss.

New York Times. 1994 (July 7). "Excerpts of What the Commission Found: Loyalty over Integrity," B2.

New York Times. 1994 (July 7). "Giuliani Announces Assault on Quality-of-Life Crimes," B3.

New York Times. 1994 (July 9). "Billions for New Prisons? Wait a Minute," A19, by Philip B. Heymann.

New York Times. 1994 (August 30). "Researchers Find a Diverse Face on New York's Poverty," A14, by Celia W. Dugger.

New York Times. 1994 (September 13). "More Inmates in the U.S. Than Ever Before," A8, Associated Press item.

New York Times. 1995 (February 20). "The Irish Revisit the Terrible 1840's," A4, by James F. Clarity.

New York Times. 2000 (January 19). "Widest Income Gap is Found in New York," B5, by Nina Bernstein.

New York Times. 2000 (September 28). "Effect of Prison Building on Crime Is Weighed," A16, by Fox Butterfield.

New York Times. 2001 (September 26). "Poverty Rates Fell in 2000, But Income Was Stagnant," A12, by Katharine Q. Seelye.

New York Times. 2002 (March 27). "Justices Rule Drug-Eviction Law Is Fair," A20, by Linda Greenhouse.

O'Brien, Joseph, and Andris Kurins. 1991. *Boss of Bosses: The FBI and Paul Castellano.* New York: Island Books.

Orsi, Robert A. 1985. *The Madonna of 115th St: Faith and Community in Italian Harlem, 1880–1950.* New Haven, Conn.: Yale University Press.

Paredes, Américo. 1971. "The United States, Mexico, and Machismo." *Journal of the Folklore Institute* 8(1): 17–37.

Phillips, Kevin. 1990. *Wealth and the American Electorate in the Reagan Aftermath.* New York: Random House.

Pollitt, Katha. 1990 (March 26). "A New Assault on Feminism." *The Nation,* pp. 408–17.

Portelli, Alessandro. 1991. "Introduction." In *The Death of Luigi Trastulli and Other Stories,* pp. vii–xvi. New York: State University of New York Press.

Quintero-Rivera, Angel. 1984 (August 28–September 1). "Stratification and Social Class in the Hispanic Caribbean with Special Emphasis on Puerto Rico." Paper presented at the Conference "New Perspectives on Caribbean Studies: Towards the 21st Century," New York, Research Institute for the Study of Man and the City University of New York.

Rainwater, Lee. 1994. "A Primer on U.S. Poverty: 1945–1992." New York: Russell Sage Foundation Working Paper #53.

Rainwater, Lee, and William L. Yancey, eds. 1967. *The Moynihan Report and the Politics of Controversy*. Cambridge, Mass.: MIT Press.

Ramírez, Rafael. 1993. *Dime Capitán: Reflexiones sobre la masculinidad*. San Juán: Ediciones Huracán.

Reed, Dorothy. 1932. "Leisure Time of Girls in a 'Little Italy,'" Portland, Ore.: Published by author. (Copy available in the library of the University of Arkansas, Fayetteville.)

Reinarman, Craig, and Harry L. Levine. 1989. "Crack in Context: Politics and Media in the Making of a Drug Scene. *Contemporary Drug Problems* 14(4): 535–77.

Rivera, Edward. 1983. *Family Installments: Memories of Growing Up Hispanic*. New York: Penguin Books.

Rivera-Batiz, Francisco L. 1994 (April 22). "Education and the Economic Status of Women in Puerto Rico, 1980–1990." Paper presented at a conference held at the Consejo General de Educacion, Hato Rey, Puerto Rico.

Rivera-Batiz, Francisco L., and Carlos Santiago. 1994 (April). "The Labor Market and Socioeconomic Performance of the Puerto Rican Population in the United States 1980–1990." Monograph prepared for the National Puerto Rican Coalition, Washington, D.C.

Robinson, Gregory J., and Jeffrey S. Passel. 1987 (April 30–May 2). "Evaluation of Coverage of the 1980 Census of Puerto Rico Based on Demographic Analysis." Paper presented at the annual meetings of the Population Association of America, Chicago. (Available from the Population Division of the U. S. Bureau of the Census.)

Rodríguez, Clara E. 1989. *Puerto Ricans: Born in the U.S.A.* Winchester, Mass.: Unwin Hyman.

Rodríguez, Clara E. 1995. "Puerto Ricans in Historical and Social Science Research." In James A. Banks and Cherry A. McGee Banks, eds., *Handbook of Research on Multicultural Education*, pp. 223–44. New York: Simon & Schuster and Macmillan.

Rodríguez, Victor. 1992. *Eldorado in East Harlem*. Houston, Tex.: Arte Publico Press.

Romo, Frank, and Michael Schwartz. 1993. "The Coming of Post-Industrial Society Revisited: Manufacturing and the Prospects for a Service-Based Economy."

In Richard Swedberg, ed., *Explorations in Economic Sociology*, pp. 335–73. New York: Russell Sage Foundation.

Rosaldo, Renato. 1980. "Doing Oral History." *Social Analysis* 4: 89–99.

Rosenberg, Terry J. 1987. "Poverty in New York City: 1980–1985." New York: Community Service Society, Department of Research, Policy and Program Development.

Rosenberg, Terry J. 1990. "Changes in Household Composition and Income Strategies of Poor Women in New York City." Madison: Institute for Research on Poverty Discussion Paper #924–90, University of Wisconsin.

Rosenwaike, Ira. 1983 (March). "Morality Among the Puerto Rican Born in New York City." *Social Science Quarterly* 64(7): 375–85.

Rubinson, Karen. 1989. "Stage IA Documentary Study for the New York City Landmarks Preservation Committee, CEQR #89-048M, Police Service Area #5 of the New York City Housing Authority." New York: Key Perspectives. Manuscript.

S., Tina, and Jamie Pastor Bolnick. 2000. *Living at the Edge of the World: A Teenager's Survival in the Tunnels of Grand Central Station*. New York: St. Martin's Press.

Sanday, Peggy R. 1990. *Fraternity Gang Rape: Sex, Brotherhood, and Privilege on Campus*. New York: New York University Press.

Sassen, Saskia. 1991. *The Global City: New York, London, Tokyo*. Princeton, N.J.: Princeton University Press.

Sassen-Koob, Saskia. 1986. "New York City: Economic Restructuring and Immigration." *Development and Change* 17: 85–119.

Sayad, Abdelmalek. 1991. *L'immigration ou les paradoxes de l'altérité*. Paris: Editions Universitaires and De Boeck Université.

Scheper-Hughes, Nancy. 1992. *Death Without Weeping: The Violence of Everyday Life in Brazil*. Berkeley: University of California Press.

Schepses, Erwin. 1949. "Puerto Rican Delinquent Boys in New York City." *Social Service Review* 23(1): 51–61.

Scott, James C. 1985. *Weapons of the Weak: Everyday Forms of Peasant Resistance*. New Haven, Conn.: Yale University Press.

Seda Bonilla, Edwin. 1964. *Interacción social y personalidad en una comunidad de Puerto Rico*. San Juán: Ediciones Juán Ponce de León.

Singer, Merrill. 1986. "Toward a Political-Economy of Alcoholism: The Missing Link in the Anthropology of Drinking." *Social Science Medicine* 73(2): 113–30.

Singer, Merrill, Freddie Valentin, Hans Baer, and Zhongke Jia. 1992. "Why Does Juán Garcia Have a Drinking Problem? The Perspective of Critical Medical Anthropology." *Medical Anthropology* 14: 77–108.

Smolowe, Jill. 1994 (February 7). ". . . And Throw Away the Key." *Time*, pp. 55–59.

Smith, Robert. 1992 (April). "Mexican Immigrant Women in New York City's Informal Economy." Conference Paper #69. New York: Columbia–New

York University Consortium, Center for Latin American and Caribbean Studies.

Stansell, Christine. 1987 [1982]. *City of Women: Sex and Class in New York 1789–1860*. Urbana and Chicago: University of Illinois Press.

Starobin, Paul. 1994 (June 18). "The Economy You Can't See." *National Journal*, pp. 1407–10.

Stringer, Lee. 1998. *Grand Central Winter: Stories from the Street*. Berkeley, Calif.: Seven Stories Press.

Substance Abuse and Mental Health Services Administration. 2000. *Summary of Findings from the 1999 National Household Survey on Drug Abuse*. Rockville, Md.: Department of Health and Human Services.

Taussig, Michael. 1987. *Shamanism, Colonialism, and the Wild Man: A Study in Terror and Healing*. Chicago: University of Chicago Press.

Thomas, Piri. 1967. *Down These Mean Streets*. New York: Knopf.

Thrasher, Frederic M. 1927. *The Gang*. Chicago: University of Chicago Press.

Thrasher, Frederic M. 1932 (December). "Ecological Aspects of the Boys' Club Study." *Journal of Educational Sociology* 6(1): 52–58.

Thrasher, Frederic M. 1936. "The Boys' Club and Juvenile Delinquency." *American Journal of Sociology* 42(1): 66–80.

Tilley, Margaret Campbell. 1935. "The Boy Scout Movement in East Harlem." Ph.D. dissertation, New York University.

Tilton, Edgar. 1910. *The Reformed Low Dutch Church of Harlem, Organized 1660: Historical Sketch*. New York: The Consistory.

Time. 1946 (November 4). "Veto Vito?," pp. 24–25.

U.S. Census Bureau. (1990). *1990 Census of Population and Housing Block Statistics (Summary Tape File 1B)*. CD-Rom. Washington D.C.: U.S. Department of Commerce, Bureau of the Census, Data User Services Division.

U.S. Census Bureau. (2001). *Money Income in the United States, 2000 Current Population Reports, P60-213*, by Carmen DeNavas-Walt, Robert Cleveland, and Mark Roemer. Washington, D.C.: U.S. Government Printing Office.

Van Dyk, Jere. 1990 (May). "Across the Line in East Harlem. *National Geographic* 177(5): 52–75.

Vergara, Camilo. 1991 (March). "Lessons Learned, Lessons Forgotten: Rebuilding New York City's Poor Communities." *The Livable City* 15(1): 3–9.

Vergara, Camilo. 1991 (June 17). "The View from the Shelters: New York's New Ghettos." *The Nation* 252(23): 804–10.

Village Voice. 1990 (April 3). "Pregnant Addicts Turned Away," pp. 11–12, by Jan Hoffman.

Wacquant, Loïc. 1993a. "Décivilisation et démonisation: La mutation du ghetto noir americain." In Christine Faure and Tom Bishop, eds., *L'Amerique des français*, pp. 103–25. Paris: Editions François Bourin.

Bibliography

Wacquant, Loïc. 1993b. "Urban Outcasts: Stigma and Division in the Black American Ghetto and the French Urban Periphery." *International Journal of Urban and Regional Research* 17(3): 366–83.

Wacquant, Loïc. 1994. "The New Urban Color Line: "The State and Fate of the Ghetto in Postfordist America." In Craig J. Calhoun, ed., *Social Theory and the Politics of Identity*, pp. 231–76. New York: Basil Blackwell.

Wacquant, Loïc. 1999. *Les Prisons de la misère*. Paris: Èditions Raisons d'Agir.

Wacquant, Loïc. 2000. "The New 'Peculiar Institution': On the Prison as Surrogate Ghetto." In *Theoretical Criminology* 4(3): 377–89.

Wall Street Journal. 1989 (July 18). "Born to Lose: Babies of Crack Users Crowd Hospitals, Break Everybody's Heart," A1, A6, by Cathy Trost.

Ward, David. 1989. *Poverty, Ethnicity, and the American City 1840–1925: Changing Conceptions of the Slum and the Ghetto*. New York: Cambridge University Press.

Williams, Edward Huntington, M.D. 1914 (February 7). "The Drug-Habit Menace in the South." *Medical Record* 85: 247–49.

Williams, Terry. 1992. *Crackhouse: Notes from the End of the Line*. New York: Addison-Wesley.

Willis, Paul. 1977. *Learning to Labor: How Working Class Kids Get Working Class Jobs*. Aldershot, U.K.: Gower.

Wilson, Julius. 1987. *The Truly Disadvantaged: The Inner City, the Underclass, and Public Policy*. Chicago: University of Chicago Press.

Wolf, Eric. 1956. "San José: Subcultures of a 'Traditional' Coffee Municipality." In Julian Steward, ed., *The People of Puerto Rico*, pp. 171–264. Chicago: University of Illinois Press.

Wolf, Eric. 1990. "Distinguished Lecture: Facing Power – Old Insights, New Questions." *American Anthropologist* 92(3): 586–96.

INDEX

abortion, 272, 273, 284, 295, 345n20, 361n23

academics, 11–12, 14–18, 61–2
Anglo/middle-class biases, 11–12, 14, 15, 44, 145, 176, 215, 241–2, 280, 285, 325, 356n14, 360n13, 362n28, n5
and inner-city/poverty research, 12, 14–15, 16, 17, 46–7, 56, 58–9, 62, 63–4, 260–1, 280, 284, 341n19, 361n28
sanitizing/editing data, 12, 13, 14–15, 17–18, 207–8, 325, 341n19, n20, 342n24, 344n13, 359n11
see also anthropology; author; ethnography; theoretical approaches; U.S. ideology

Acosta-Belén, Edna, 356n14

African-Americans, 6, 16, 32, 36, 46, 160, 163, 284, 291–2, 320, 324, 345n17, 352n5, n10
among dealers, 37, 44–5, 108, 194, 225, 291–2, 333, 335
in East Harlem, 7, 31, 33, 36, 41, 56, 61, 65, 76, 190, 225, 263, 346n12
in history, 60, 61, 278, 347n19, 360n16
racism against, 1, 26, 37–8, 45, 60, 61, 74, 85, 167, 169, 172, 273, 278, 344n11, 359n10, 360n16
relationship to Puerto Ricans, 26, 37–8, 44–6, 85, 174, 182, 205, 273, 335, 350n4

Africans, 58, 167
slavery, 48, 50

Afro-Caribbean culture, 25–6

Agee, James, 64

agency/social structure, 12, 15, 16–18, 53–4, 55, 115, 118, 120, 121, 123–4, 137, 138, 140, 143, 191, 193, 203, 221, 240, 242, 243–4, 301–2, 323, 325, 354n4, 355n6
personal responsibility, 1, 16, 17, 54, 96, 116, 117, 118, 125–8, 162, 179, 189, 191, 193, 196, 212, 240

AIDS/HIV, 38, 53, 329, 332, 333, 334, 358n20

alcohol, 49, 79, 179, 191, 206, 299
and alcoholism, 40, 106, 125–6, 128, 129, 183, 228, 241, 272, 273, 302, 310, 313, 329, 355n5, 361–2n28, 363n11
bootleg, 19, 29, 49, 66–8, 99, 225
conversations while drinking, 20, 26–7, 40, 41, 42–3, 95, 96, 97, 98, 110, 112, 122, 125–7, 130, 133, 177, 178, 189, 193, 219, 225–6, 233, 234, 239, 246, 265, 271, 281, 304, 310
dealers drinking, 26, 86–7, 90, 94, 97, 100, 103, 105, 124, 125–9, 185, 247, 266, 298, 308, 310, 331, 333, 335

Alger, Horatio, 326

Algerian immigrants, 353n1

Allen, Woody, 353–4n3

Alzheimer's disease, 330

American Dream, 75, 322, 326

American Lawyer, 342n1

American Society for the Prevention of Cruelty to Animals (ASPCA), 98–9

angel dust, 3, 19, 30, 88, 263, 291, 340n8

anthropology, 13–18, 31, 44, 46, 64, 176, 189, 341n19, 355n6
cultural relativism, 15, 189, 360n13
see also academics; ethnography; theoretical approaches

393

Index

Index